Brazilian Cinema and the Aesthetics of Ruins

WORLD CINEMA SERIES

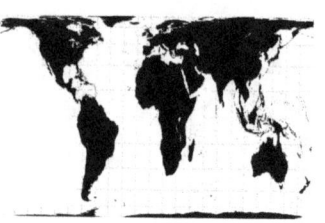

Series Editors:

Lúcia Nagib, Professor of Film at the University of Reading
Julian Ross, Research Fellow at the Leiden University

Advisory Board: Laura Mulvey (UK), Robert Stam (USA), Ismail Xavier (Brazil), Dudley Andrew (USA)

The *World Cinema Series* aims to reveal and celebrate the richness and complexity of film art across the globe, exploring a wide variety of cinemas set within their own cultures and as they interconnect in a global context. The books in the series will represent innovative scholarship, in tune with the multicultural character of contemporary audiences. Drawing upon an international authorship, they will challenge outdated conceptions of world cinema and provide new ways of understanding a field at the centre of film studies in an era of transnational networks.

Published and forthcoming in the World Cinema series:

Allegory in Iranian Cinema: The Aesthetics of Poetry and Resistance
Michelle Langford

Amharic Film Genres and Ethiopian Cinema
Michael W. Thomas

Animation in the Middle East: Practice and Aesthetics from Baghdad to Casablanca
Stefanie Van de Peer

Basque Cinema: A Cultural and Political History
Rob Stone and Maria Pilar Rodriguez

Brazil on Screen: Cinema Novo, New Cinema, Utopia
Lúcia Nagib

Brazilian Cinema and the Aesthetics of Ruins
Guilherme Carréra

Cinema in the Arab World: New Histories, New Approaches
Edited By Philippe Meers, Daniel Biltereyst and Ifdal Elsaket

Contemporary New Zealand Cinema
Edited by Ian Conrich and Stuart Murray

Cosmopolitan Cinema: Cross-cultural Encounters in East Asian Film
Felicia Chan

Documentary Cinema of Chile: Confronting History, Memory, Trauma
Antonio Traverso

East Asian Cinemas: Exploring Transnational Connections on Film
Edited by Leon Hunt and Leung Wing-Fai

East Asian Film Noir: Transnational Encounters and Intercultural Dialogue
Edited by Chi-Yun Shin and Mark Gallagher

Eastern Approaches to Western Film: Asian Reception and Aesthetics in Cinema
Stephen Teo

Impure Cinema: Intermedial and Intercultural Approaches to Film
Edited by Lúcia Nagib and Anne Jerslev

Latin American Women Filmmakers: Production, Politics, Poetics
Edited by Deborah Martin and Deborah Shaw

Lebanese Cinema: Imagining the Civil War and Beyond
Lina Khatib

New Argentine Cinema
Jens Andermann

New Directions in German Cinema
Edited by Paul Cooke and Chris Homewood

New Turkish Cinema: Belonging, Identity and Memory
Asuman Suner

On Cinema
Glauber Rocha, edited by Ismail Xavier

Pablo Trapero and the Politics of Violence
Douglas Mulliken

Palestinian Filmmaking in Israel: Narratives of Place and
Yael Friedman

Performing Authorship: Self-inscription and Corporeality in the Cinema
Cecilia Sayad

Portugal's Global Cinema: Industry, History and Culture
Edited by Mariana Liz

Queer Masculinities in Latin American Cinema: Male Bodies and Narrative Representations
Gustavo Subero

Realism in Greek Cinema: From the Post-War Period to the Present
Vrasidas Karalis

Realism of the Senses in World Cinema: The Experience of Physical Reality
Tiago de Luca

Stars in World Cinema: Screen Icons and Star Systems Across Cultures
Edited by Andrea Bandhauer and Michelle Royer

The Cinema of Jia Zhangke: Realism and Memory in Chinese Film
Cecília Mello

The Cinema of Sri Lanka: South Asian Film in Texts and Contexts
Ian Conrich

The New Generation in Chinese Animation
Shaopeng Chen

The Spanish Fantastic: Contemporary Filmmaking in Horror, Fantasy and Sci-fi
Shelagh-Rowan Legg

Theorizing World Cinema
Edited by Lúcia Nagib, Chris Perriam and Rajinder Dudrah

Queries, ideas and submissions to
Series Editor: Professor Lúcia Nagib –
l.nagib@reading.ac.uk
Series Editor: Dr. Julian Ross –
j.a.ross@hum.leidenuniv.nl
Publisher at Bloomsbury, Rebecca Barden –
Rebecca.Barden@bloomsbury.com

Brazilian Cinema and the Aesthetics of Ruins

Guilherme Carréra

BLOOMSBURY ACADEMIC
LONDON • NEW YORK • OXFORD • NEW DELHI • SYDNEY

BLOOMSBURY ACADEMIC
Bloomsbury Publishing Plc
50 Bedford Square, London, WC1B 3DP, UK
1385 Broadway, New York, NY 10018, USA
29 Earlsfort Terrace, Dublin 2, Ireland

BLOOMSBURY, BLOOMSBURY ACADEMIC and the Diana logo are trademarks of Bloomsbury Publishing Plc

First published in Great Britain 2022
This paperback edition published 2024

Copyright © Guilherme Carréra, 2022

Guilherme Carréra has asserted his right under the Copyright, Designs and Patents Act, 1988, to be identified as Author of this work.

For legal purposes the Acknowledgements on pp. xii–xiii constitute an extension of this copyright page.

Cover design: Ben Anslow
Cover image: Joana Traub Csekö, "HU series - Sugarloaf" (2008)

All rights reserved. No part of this publication may be reproduced or transmitted in any form or by any means, electronic or mechanical, including photocopying, recording, or any information storage or retrieval system, without prior permission in writing from the publishers.

Bloomsbury Publishing Plc does not have any control over, or responsibility for, any third-party websites referred to or in this book. All internet addresses given in this book were correct at the time of going to press. The author and publisher regret any inconvenience caused if addresses have changed or sites have ceased to exist, but can accept no responsibility for any such changes.

A catalogue record for this book is available from the British Library.

Library of Congress Cataloging-in-Publication Data
Names: Carréra, Guilherme, author.
Title: Brazilian cinema and the aesthetics of ruins / Guilherme Carréra.
Description: New York : Bloomsbury Academic, 2021. | Series: World cinema | Includes bibliographical references and index.
Identifiers: LCCN 2021021556 (print) | LCCN 2021021557 (ebook) | ISBN 9781350203020 (hardback) | ISBN 9781350203037 (epub) | ISBN 9781350203044 (pdf)
Subjects: LCSH: Motion pictures–Brazil–History and criticism. | Ruins in motion pictures. | Motion pictures–Aesthetics.
Classification: LCC PN1993.5.B6 C37457 2021 (print) | LCC PN1993.5.B6 (ebook) | DDC 791.430981–dc23
LC record available at https://lccn.loc.gov/2021021556
LC ebook record available at https://lccn.loc.gov/2021021557

ISBN: HB: 978-1-3502-0302-0
PB: 978-1-3504-9619-4
ePDF: 978-1-3502-0304-4
eBook: 978-1-3502-0303-7

Series: World Cinema

Typeset by Newgen KnowledgeWorks Pvt. Ltd., Chennai, India

To find out more about our authors and books visit www.bloomsbury.com and sign up for our newsletters.

Contents

Figures x
Acknowledgements xii

Introduction: In search of Brazilian ruins 1
    Documenting the ruins: The Angel-documentarist 6
    Towards a cartography of ruins 11

Part One Framing the ruins through underdevelopment: From Cinema Novo to contemporary Brazilian documentary

1 A realm for the ruins of Brazil 19
    The Cuban axis 26
    Pessimistic views of progress 29
    Cinematic ruins: Theoretical notes 37

2 Cinema Novo: A country in crisis 43
    Documentary impulse as revolutionary cinema 53
    Branching to Tropicália and Cinema Marginal 57

3 Documentary in the wake of Cinema da Retomada 61
    The contemporary documentary within the *unviable nation* 66

Part Two The other side of progress: Cinematic (re)constructions of Brasília

4 A controversial spatiality: Myth and apartheid 79
    The contentious capital on screen 81

5 *Realism under erasure* or not quite: New imagery and storytelling 85
    The sci-fi way into reality 87

6 *The Age of Stone*: The uchronic mode of a monument 91
    The Earth and the Stone: Brasília is delirium 95
    The science *friction* documentary of Ana Vaz 102

7	*White Out, Black In*: Exploding the Third World from a *laje* point of view	109
	Two cyborgs of the past against one Red Light bandit	115
	The science *non*fiction documentary of Adirley Queirós	120
	The heterotopic Brasília	128

Part Three Constructing ruins in Rio de Janeiro: An intermedial visualization of failing projects

8	Tropicália: An intermedial counterculture	135
	The anthropophagic tropicalist appearance	141
	Beyond anthropophagy: Commodification and neoliberalization	144
9	The rubble as the legacy: A ruin for the World Cup and the Olympics	149
	Imploding the Perimetral in *ExPerimetral*	153
	An alternative anchorage in *The Harbour*	158
10	The Carmen Miranda ruinous spaceship in *Tropical Curse*	163
	Tropicalist intermedial flavour: Flying saucers, ghosts and *gringos*	167
11	A lame-leg architecture: Half-hospital, half-ruin in *HU Enigma*	175
	A fractured building is a fractured ethos	180

Part Four The long-standing ruination: Indigenous territory in dispute

12	Setting the ground: Cinema Novo and indigenous representation	191
	The (absent) figure of the Indian	197
	The Coca-Cola-Indian allegory	199
13	The Vídeo nas Aldeias case: For an indigenous media to emerge	203
	An *integral process* for *a kind of Faustian dilemma*	208
	Un Indien, Tonacci and Cowell	213
14	'Here, in this scenario of destruction …': Territory of ruins in *Corumbiara*	217
	A four-sequence pilgrimage	220

15 Made of stone and ruins: Indigenous filmmaking in *Tava, The House of Stone, Two Villages, One Path* and *Guarani Exile*	231
No fake ruins allowed: Guarani (hi)storytelling	236
Conclusion: A walk amid the cinematic ruins	245
Of ruin-gazers and ruinscapes	254
Expanding the map	261
Notes	267
References	281
Filmography	305
Index	315

Figures

- 6.1 The timid first appearance of a fragment of the monument   92
- 6.2 The sun rising above the Palácio da Alvorada in *The Age of the Earth*   99
- 6.3 The uchronic sunrise in the Central Plateau in *The Age of Stone*   101
- 6.4, 6.5 and 6.6 From Chapada dos Veadeiros to Pirenópolis through the gaze of the *boiadeiro*   104
- 6.7 and 6.8 Ivonete looks at the horizon, and the horizon looks back at Ivonete   106
- 6.9 Ivonete recites Clarice to the camera   107
- 6.10 and 6.11 The monument-Brasília   107
- 7.1 Marquim on the *laje*   115
- 7.2 Sartana in the no-wall house   115
- 7.3 Flying saucers hit Boca do Lixo in the closing sequence of *The Red Light Bandit*   119
- 7.4 and 7.5 Sartana/Shokito speaks to the camera in the documentary, whereas Dimas Cravalanças watches him speaking in the sci-fi film   122
- 7.6 Marquim (right) and Sartana assemble the sonic-atomic bomb   125
- 7.7, 7.8 and 7.9 Brasília under attack   126
- 9.1 Excavation work in *ExPerimetral*   154
- 9.2 and 9.3 The veins and the roots: The first image shows '*nossa senzala*' graffiti at the bottom left   155
- 9.4 Digitally, the Elevado da Perimetral gives way to aseptic trees in *The Harbour*   159
- 9.5 and 9.6 Phantasmagoric carnival parade in the harbour zone   161
- 10.1 and 10.2 Colours, textures and superimpositions in *Tropical Curse*   166

Figures

10.3 and 10.4	Flying saucers: From *The Red Light Bandit* to *Tropical Curse*	169
10.5 and 10.6	A Third World ghost in *Copacabana Mon Amour* and *Tropical Curse*	170
10.7 and 10.8	Montage effect: Carmen Miranda/Darks Miranda escapes the modernist museum	172
11.1	Split-screen interviews in *HU Enigma*	179
11.2	Two square-format screens: Two halves of the HU building	181
11.3, 11.4, 11.5 and 11.6	The human body, the HU body	183
11.7	Nature takes over: A woman wanders amid the ruins	185
11.8	The final collapse of the lame-leg	187
12.1	Macunaíma and the ruined *tapera*	196
12.2	White turned into fake Indian in a devastated Brazil	198
12.3	Iracema and Tião Brasil Grande clamber over logs	200
12.4 and 12.5	Views of destruction from the truck and airplane viewpoints	201
14.1	The damaged indigenous territory as a consequence of so-called progress	221
14.2	In the second sequence, a *tapera* is incorporated into the frame	223
14.3	The Indian-guardians	224
14.4 and 14.5	Two frames, two realities: The white space and the indigenous space	226
14.6	A conversation in the remains of the village	227
14.7 and 14.8	The views from the airplane and the 'window screen'	229
15.1	Tava São Miguel	235
15.2	Ariel Ortega and his camera in action	239
15.3	The glass demarcation: Sellers and buyers, indigenous and non-indigenous	240
15.4 and 15.5	Two different versions of history in dispute through documentary montage	242

Acknowledgements

I am immensely grateful to Bloomsbury Publishing for believing in this book project, and particularly to Visual Arts publisher Rebecca Barden and her assistant Veidehi Hans for leading the team. No words could be enough to thank Professor Lúcia Nagib, editor with Dr Julian Ross of the World Cinema Series, whose enthusiasm for the manuscript was assured from the very beginning. I am also aware that the anonymous readers of the material must remain unknown, but I would like to thank each of them for the comments made in their attentive reading. *Brazilian Cinema and the Aesthetics of Ruins* results from four long years of conducting my doctoral research at the Centre for Research and Education in Arts and Media (CREAM), at the University of Westminster in London, between 2015 and 2019. For that reason, I would like to express my gratitude to Professor May Adadol Ingawanij, whose inspiring supervision guided me throughout; Dr Roshini Kempadoo, second supervisor; and Professor Joram ten Brink, former supervisor and who accepted my doctoral proposal. Refraining from citing specific names to avoid the risk of being unfair, I extend my gratitude to the Graduate School for its institutional assistance, the Westminster School of Arts members of staff for their precious insights and my PhD colleagues for the partnership along the way to completion. The thesis defence took place in 2020, resulting in a deeply rewarding outright pass as an outcome. None of that would have been possible if it was not for the sponsorship of the Coordination for the Improvement of Higher Education Personnel (CAPES, Ministry of Education, Brazil).

The discussion proposed in the following pages was also nurtured in relevant academic events worldwide. Apart from taking part in CREAM symposiums, where feedback from peers was key to the progress of the work, I am highly appreciative of the valuable comments received after paper presentations at the Visible Evidence 2017 (Buenos Aires, Argentina); the Association of Moving Image Researchers Meeting 2018 (Aveiro, Portugal); the NECS – European Network for Cinema and Media Studies Conference 2018 (Amsterdam, Netherlands); the Landscape and Cinema International

Conference 2018 (Lisbon, Portugal); the University of Oxford's Brazil Week 2019 (Oxford, UK); the Society for Latin American Studies Conference 2019 (Leicester, UK); the British Association of Film, Television and Screen Studies Conference 2019 (Birmingham, UK); and the International Screen Studies Conference 2019 (Glasgow, UK).

I am also pleased for having been able to interview filmmakers Ana Vaz, Adirley Queirós, Daniel Santos, Ricardo Pretti, Luisa Marques, Pedro Urano, Joana Traub Csekö, Ariel Ortega and Vincent Carelli, as our conversations made feasible the developing of a theory on the aesthetics of ruins in contemporary Brazilian cinema. The third-party copyrighted material features in this book on the basis of 'fair dealing for the purposes of criticism and review' or 'fair use for the purposes of teaching, criticism, scholarship or research' in accordance with international copyright laws, and it is not intended to infringe upon the ownership rights of the original owners.

Finally, I extend this acknowledgment to family and friends who directly or indirectly contributed to this project. In particular, I thank my parents, Carlos and Márcia, for having taught me the value of hard work, and my brother, Leonardo, whose bond makes me stronger.

To Clarissa, who was by my side during this journey and did not let go of my hand for a second. Thank you for everything.

Introduction: In search of Brazilian ruins

This book aims to define an aesthetics of ruins in contemporary Brazilian cinema. More specifically, it seeks to investigate the strategies used by present-day filmmakers to depict ruins and why these filmmakers have decided to focus their attention on them. That is, it sets out to be an investigation about the visual elaboration of ruins within the national context. In order to do this, I look at three unconventional groups of documentary films focusing on three different, yet complementary, spaces: the Brasília of *The Age of Stone* (A Idade da Pedra, 2013) and *White Out, Black In* (Branco Sai, Preto Fica, 2014); the Rio de Janeiro of *ExPerimetral* (2016), *The Harbour* (O Porto, 2013), *Tropical Curse* (A Maldição Tropical, 2016) and *HU Enigma* (HU, 2011); and the indigenous territories of *Corumbiara: They Shoot Indians, Don't They?* (Corumbiara, 2009), *Tava, The House of Stone* (Tava, A Casa de Pedra, 2012), *Two Villages, One Path* (Duas Aldeias, Uma Caminhada, 2008) and *Guarani Exile* (Desterro Guarani, 2011). I argue that the figure of the ruin in representations of a national condition pertains to a failed modern project, which in Brazil is deeply marked by the notion of underdevelopment. On that note, I draw on the conceptualization of underdevelopment as discussed by Celso Furtado (2009), expanded to the film domain by Paulo Emílio Salles Gomes (1996) and central to the influential film analyses carried out by Ismail Xavier (2012). Furthermore, I focus on Claude Lévi-Strauss's (1973) impressions of Brazil that were echoed in Caetano Veloso's (2017) ideas, as they famously identify a sense of ruination in the country.

Though resorting to distinct cinematic strategies, as will be discussed throughout this book, these films seem to share a similar sensibility in gazing upon the federal capital, the former federal capital and the Native territories, which allows them to turn these emblematic spaces into ruinscapes. My hypothesis is that, in bringing images of ruins to the fore, filmmakers articulate a critique of the controversial notions of progress and (under)development in the context of Brazil. Brazilian cinema first delved into such issues when the Cinema Novo movement emerged in the 1960s, followed by the Tropicália and Cinema Marginal's notable contributions. With this in mind, this study also considers their cultural legacy and discusses to what extent contemporary production relates to it. In methodological terms, each of the analyses reflects on that tradition in a different way. Part One is mainly theoretical, but Part Two engages with the explosive rhetoric of Rogério Sganzerla's debut film, *The Red Light Bandit* (O Bandido da Luz Vermelha, 1968), and Glauber Rocha's last film, *The Age of the Earth* (A Idade da Terra, 1980). Part Three deals with tropicalist-like values, mainly intermediality, through the contributions of Caetano Veloso and Hélio Oiticica, and Part Four analyses the representation of damaged indigenous territory in *Macunaíma* (Joaquim Pedro de Andrade, 1969), *Brazil Year 2000* (Brasil Ano 2000, Walter Lima Jr., 1969) and *Iracema* (Iracema – Uma Transa Amazônica, Jorge Bodanzky and Orlando Senna, 1974–81). In opening a fruitful yet sometimes conflicting dialogue with that past, the selected corpus illustrates how the conventions of documentary-making may be redefined, either by the radical blurring of the boundaries between fiction and nonfiction or by the pioneering assimilation of the indigenous perspective as well. Ultimately, in expanding the limits of traditional filmmaking, the filmmakers in question also expand the viewers' understanding of the country by challenging its official narrative precisely through images of ruins. But, after all, what ruins are these?

In 2014, Tate Britain put on an exhibition entitled *Ruin Lust*. Curated by Brian Dillon, Emma Chambers and Amy Concannon, *Ruin Lust* offered 'a guide to the mournful, thrilling, comic and perverse uses of ruins in art from the seventeenth century to the present day' (Tate website, no date). One of the world's most relevant shows devoted to the subject, it included more than one hundred works by J. M. W. Turner, John Constable, Rachel Whiteread, Tacita Dean and many others. It played with the prolific imagery of ruins in artistic practice throughout history, and how that imagery ended up foregrounding an imaginary of ruins in our world. Most importantly, *Ruin Lust* seemed to enquire into the roles played by ruins, what they mean and why we care about them. Dillon claims that the ruin continuously encapsulates a 'radical potential' (2011: 18), demanding the ruin-gazer to take account of its possibilities. As a fusion of the past, present and future, the ruin encourages one to wonder what was there before the collapse, what to do with the remains and what vision is yet to come. While I was at the Tate Britain exhibition, wandering through the wreckage, I caught myself wondering what would be on those walls if Brazil was depicted there. If ruins are usually associated with the debris of the so-called Old World (the imperial ruins of Greece and Rome, the bombed-out buildings of the First and Second World Wars, the crumbling of the Berlin Wall), how can one associate ruins with such a young Latin American nation? If not the classical, romantic ruins of Europe, what, then, forges an imaginary of ruins in Brazil?

To start with, there are no walls. There are no walls for one to hang still images or project moving images on to. On 2 September 2018, five days prior to the traditional celebration of Brazilian Independence Day, the National Museum was no more. Located in Rio de Janeiro, one of the country's leading museums, Brazil's oldest historical and scientific institution, home of the Portuguese Royal Family in the nineteenth century, the National Museum collapsed due to a huge fire that ruined the buildings over an area of 13,600 m² – 122 rooms in all. It is believed that 90 per cent of the archive of twenty million items was destroyed. The National Museum was two hundred years old but its collapse had nothing to do with the passage of time. Museum Deputy Director, Luiz Fernando Dias Duarte, pointed to neglect by successive governments as the cause of the fire. He argued that many curators had fought with different governments for adequate resources to preserve what has now been completely destroyed (G1 Rio 2018a). Even more tragic, Rio's Fire Chief, Colonel Roberto Robadey, said the firefighters did not have enough water because two hydrants were dry. Water trucks were brought in and water used from a nearby lake (G1 Rio 2018b). Months later, the federal police found that the fire had started from a poorly maintained air conditioning unit (Silveira 2019). The images of the fire, the flames and the smoke over the roofless building went viral. They became a sort of metaphor for the country's chaotic present, to say the least – corruption scandals, a deep recession, a controversial impeachment, increasing unemployment and criminal violence.[1] As Bernardo Mello Franco, one of Brazil's best-known journalists, put it: 'The tragedy this Sunday is a sort of national suicide. A crime against our past and future generations' (2018).[2]

The link between the Tate Britain exhibition in London and the National Museum fire in Brazil is more than a narrative arc – it helps me situate this monograph in time and space. When I embarked on this journey, lured by the ruin's radical potential, I had no means of foreseeing the ruination of Brazil's most important museum. While this theoretical investigation was being conducted between 2015 and 2019, however, there were many hints at the state of a country in collapse. We witnessed not one but two of the world's most dreadful environmental catastrophes in the state of Minas Gerais: the Mariana tailing dam collapse on 5 November 2015 was considered the greatest environmental disaster in Brazilian history resulting in nineteen deaths (Dieguez 2016) until the Brumadinho tailing dam collapse unbelievably caused 240 fatalities and a second river of mud on 25 January 2019 (G1 Minas 2019). If nature was being punished by the Brazilian State and the mining companies, the built environment brought about by the highly anticipated 2014 FIFA World Cup and the 2016 Olympic Games lacked preservation or purpose after each of these events had taken place. Apart from bribery scandals and forced evictions, major venues like the Maracanã stadium and the Olympic golf course were already in a state of disrepair just six months after the Paralympics closing ceremony (Guardian sport and agencies 2017). Those circumstances resulted in rural and urban post-apocalyptic landscapes of a seemingly crumbling country.

Running in parallel with the destruction of the National Museum, the largest Brazilian environmental disasters and the complete obsolescence of a failed architecture was the socio-economic chaos. While Brazil was among the fastest growing economies in the first decade of this century, it then found itself in a deep recession and uncertain times (Carvalho 2018). In 2016, the controversial impeachment of the then president, Dilma Rousseff, was a process that many believed had been orchestrated by the vice president, Michel Temer, who took over the office of president until the end of 2018. The extremely polarized political environment divided the country down in the middle and made way for the election of far-right candidate, Jair Bolsonaro, in that year. Resorting to a nationalist, military, conservative and neoliberal discourse, he defended, for instance, the flexibility of the gun control law and the suspension of public policies aimed at black and LGBTQIA+ communities. He also downplayed the coronavirus pandemic that erupted in 2020, which resulted in thousands of deaths and certainly did not facilitate the replanning of economic measures to handle the financial crisis. Long before that, however, two of the covers of the influential *The Economist* (14 November 2009 and 28 September 2013) magazine had helped one acknowledge the sense of economic ruination taking place – though by no means a novelty in a country historically accustomed to ups and downs. In 2009, the Christ the Redeemer statue was portrayed as a powerful rocket on the cover with 'Brazil takes off' as the headline; in 2013, the magazine featured that same rocket-Christ, but this time out of control, and asked: 'Has Brazil blown it?' More recently, a 5 June 2021 *The Economist* cover showed a montage with the Christ the Redeemer statue breathing with the help of an oxygen cylinder in a reference to the pandemic. The headline was straightforward: 'Brazil's dismal decade'.

Analysts have also been critically addressing the chaos in a variety of news articles, such as the *New York Times*' 'The End of the World? In Brazil, It's Already Here' (Barbara 2017), *Nexo*'s 'The End of Brazil' (Burgierman 2017) and *Folha de S.Paulo*'s 'Descent into Decay' (Conti 2019), to name but a few. In the latter, renowned journalist Mario Sergio Conti sees 'a present of "inadequate things", of decadence, of production not of the future, but of ruins'. Moreover, one wonders if the ongoing reality is being documented accurately, as it seems like the 'real Brazil is in disarray with idyllic self-images, widespread for decades' (ibid.). In an attempt not to disregard a present that produces ruins, not futures, anthropologist Eduardo Viveiros de Castro aims, in fact, to preserve the debris of the National Museum. In an interview with Prado Coelho (2018), he claims that the debris should neither be restored nor turned into something else: 'My will … is to leave that ruin as *memento mori*, as memory of the dead, of dead things, of dead people, of dead archives, destroyed in that fire. … I would like the ashes to remain, the ruins, with only the facade standing, so that everyone could see and remember.' His discourse values the potential significance of those ruins for a country like Brazil, as 'this is the destruction of *ground zero*, the central place that was the symbol of the genesis of the country as an independent nation'. Viveiros de Castro's reasoning is mostly underpinned by the imbrication between neglect and catastrophe, a dynamic that has been shaping the country for a long time. 'Brazil is a country where governing it creates deserts. Natural deserts, in space, with the devastation of the savanna, of the Amazon. Nature is destroyed and now culture is being destroyed, creating deserts in time' (ibid.).

It is within this context that this volume looks at the cinematic presentation of ruins. More specifically, I am interested in how an imaginary of Brazilian ruins is constructed via imagery. That is, how contemporary filmmakers frame the ruinous reality. In this sense, it is important to stress that the ruinous reality not only refers to the present but, perhaps, most significantly, epitomizes the trajectory of a nation constructed through processes of colonization, post-Independence neocolonialization and post-dictatorship neoliberalization. As mentioned above, I argue that the ruins in Brazil are the ruins of a failed modern project marked by the notion of underdevelopment – and that contemporary Brazilian cinematic production renders these ruins visible on screen. They are the marriage of a rotten process of modernization that was never achieved with a savage neoliberal agenda that continues to deepen the socio-economic abyss. The sloppiness and abandonment present in the majority of Brazilian cities are the symptoms of a long-standing colonial mindset: forever devoted to an extractive economy, Brazil has always lacked long-term planning. Here, Latin America shies away from touristic ruins, such as those of Machu Picchu, in Peru, or the Mayan pyramids, in Mexico. The ruins in question are a peripheral, precarious branch of what Julia Hell and Andreas Schönle (2010) refer to as the *ruins of modernity*, also the title of their inspiring edited collection. In it, various authors, including the editors themselves, write about modern ruins, from post-war Germany to ruinscapes in Detroit, and their sociocultural reverberations – some of the essays being cited throughout this study. As Hell and Schönle claim, the ruin can be 'the end of the old, or the beginning of something new' (ibid.: xiii). In exposing Brazilian present-day ruins, the selected film corpus might be envisioning a future that, regrettably, the fire, the flames and the smoke engulfing the National Museum still prevent us from seeing.

Documenting the ruins: The Angel-documentarist

When I started to look at images of ruins framed by contemporary Brazilian filmmakers, it was not rare for me to come across people wondering what

I meant by ruins. It was almost like a ritual: they would double-check to make sure I really had said the word *ruins*, then reassure if I meant physical, concrete ruins and, finally, would seem intrigued by the potential presence of ruins in the South American tropics. Of course, that was a common-sense, general reaction and interaction, but also a reminder of the fact that I was conducting this theoretical investigation while I was based in London. Furthermore, it was a reminder of the tradition of European literature on this topic. Indeed, a particular branch that could range from the Comte de Volney (1853), the eighteenth-century French philosopher whose meditation on ruins projected what he saw as the inevitable fate of all cities, becoming rubble, to Rose Macaulay (1966), the English novelist who wrote about the history of aesthetic appreciation of ruins and wondered if this was still possible in the wake of the Second World War bombings. These are but two of an endless list of authors who have considered the ruin either as an object, a method, a theme or a metaphor within the European context. Possibly no one, however, has left an imprint as meaningful and reverberating as that of Walter Benjamin (1968, 1977, 1979).

Inspired by Paul Klee's painting *Angelus Novus*, Benjamin's famous description of the Angel of History is mentioned in numerous essays and books as an emblem of his idea about history as catastrophe, a thought that will implicitly resurface throughout this book. 'His face is turned toward the past. Where we perceive a chain of events, he sees one single catastrophe which keeps piling wreckage upon wreckage and hurls it in front of his feet' (1968: 257), as Benjamin puts it in his *Theses on the Philosophy of History*, written in early 1940. In the meantime, there is a storm coming from paradise. 'This storm irresistibly propels him into the future to which his back is turned, while the pile of debris before him grows skyward. This storm is what we call progress' (ibid.: 258), he concludes. This antipositivist idea of history being dialectical was encapsulated in his '*modern critique of* (capitalist/industrial) *modernity*' as Michael Löwy (2005: 3) declares. From Löwy's perspective, he feels Benjamin's 'Angel of History would like to halt, to bind the wounds of the victims crushed beneath the pile of ruins, but the storm carries it on inexorably towards the repetition of the past' (ibid.: 16), which Löwy considers to be Benjamin's definition of hell. On the other hand, when Benjamin says 'there is no document of civilization which is not at the same time a document of barbarism' (1968: 256), a whole range of possibilities seem to emerge for one to redeem the past while under the yoke of the present.

That present was to be addressed through allegories rather than symbols. 'Allegories are, in the realm of thoughts, what ruins are in the realm of things' (1977: 178), writes Benjamin, still in the 1920s, interrelating allegories with ruins. In this regard, the allegorical mode became more than an aesthetic device; it allowed 'to make visibly palpable the experience of a world in fragments, in which the passing of time means not progress but disintegration', as Susan Buck-Morss (1989: 18) remarks. In contrast to the symbol (attached to nature in an organic way and leaving no room for alternative meanings), the allegory turns history into a petrified, decayed nature, made of fragments claiming multiple interpretations, as she explains in her monumental research on Benjamin's *Arcades Project*. When scrutinizing both Charles Baudelaire's poetry and *flânerie* instinct, Buck-Morss underlines how Benjamin enhanced his critique of modernity turning the Parisian environment into petrified, decayed nature itself. In exploring this resonance, she wisely questions 'why does the most modern face of Paris remind him of a city already in ruins?' (ibid.: 179), touching on the wreckage upon wreckage that the Angel of History associates with progress. Taken as modern allegories, the commodification of nineteenth-century objects, places and customs played a major role in Benjamin's investigation of the decadence of the present. 'The image of the "ruin," as an emblem not only of the transitoriness and fragility of capitalist culture, but also its destructiveness' (ibid.: 164).

More recently, studies carried out by André Habib (2008) and Johannes von Moltke (2010) continued the theoretical debate, particularly by focusing on the links between ruins and moving images, though to a certain extent tailored to the specificities of the European context. Although I touch on their contributions in Part One, my approach rather sides with and extends Rodrigo Lopes de Barros's (2013) Third World ruins discussion, one that privileges the notion of ruins in the Latin American artistic environment. Barros's view of Glauber Rocha's *Entranced Earth* (Terra em Transe, 1967) and Sganzerla's *The Red Light Bandit* sets the scene for an exploration of Brazilian cinema in light of ruins aesthetics. At the same time, Barros claims that the importance of documentary strategies in cinematic production is that revolutionary cinema 'is nothing but an invasion of the documentary into fictional work' (2013: 29).

His rumination is much inspired by Xavier's (2012) watershed analysis of the allegories of underdevelopment in Brazilian Cinema Novo, Tropicália and Cinema Marginal. It is no coincidence that Xavier finds a link between the strength of the 1960s and 1970s production and the boldness of contemporary documentary films, especially those experimenting with 'new frictions with the real' (ibid.: 27). Inescapably, the relationship between present-day documentaries and Cinema Novo (as well as Tropicália and Cinema Marginal) is a pivotal element to be explored, as they are all devoted to questioning controversial notions of progress and (under)development via their imagery. It is worth mentioning that that relationship indistinctly involves fiction and nonfiction films, as the Cinema Novo outputs incorporated into the discussion are fictional ones, albeit sometimes also informed by nonfiction strategies. In thinking of the present-day documentaries in question, the contamination of fiction is often present in the very premise of the projects. Investing in this sort of dialogue contributes to my discussion about the definition of the documentary film itself, something that runs in parallel in this monograph.

Central to this discussion, Paula Rabinowitz (1993) brought the wreckage upon wreckage of the Angel of History closer to the documentary field. For her, the figure of the Benjaminian *Angelus Novus* 'might also represent the documentary filmmaker who can only make a film within the historical present, even as it evokes the historical past' (ibid.: 119). Avoiding the perception of the documentary as being a true reflection of reality, Rabinowitz is more interested in how far cinematic apparatus can intervene in the historical world – an attempt bravely carried out, for instance, by New Latin American Cinema filmmakers, Fernando Solanas and Octavio Getino. 'The historical documentary not only tells us about the past, but asks us to do something about it as well – to act as the Angel of History and redeem the present through the past,' says Rabinowitz (ibid.: 132). While intervening in reality, documentary films may end up blurring the boundaries between fiction and nonfiction. In this sense, 'the questions documentary films raise about the transparency of the cinematic image and the status of truth imbedded in it seem particularly urgent' (ibid.: 127). Instead of depicting reality in a conventional way, the dialectical approach opens up a multifaceted historical world to the viewer. 'In the deconstructionist documentary …, the object of the film is to produce a new and disturbing knowledge of history and of its rhetoric – of both its content and its form' (ibid.: 136), much like the group of documentaries comprising the corpus of this volume. The assumption that the documentary can lead to the emergence of other (hi)stories and therefore expand our understanding of the world can be prompted by the documentary's boundary with artistic strategies. Rabinowitz suggests that 'this desire to dream, to provoke imagination, seems to lead the documentary away from the realm of history and truth into the realm of art and artifice' (ibid.: 136). In fact, the overlap between documentary and the avant-garde led to the strengthening of the former in the first decades of the twentieth century. 'Without the capacity to disrupt and make new, documentary filmmaking would not have been possible as a discrete rhetorical practice. It is the modernist avant-garde that fulfills Grierson's own call for the "creative treatment of actuality" most relentlessly,' as Bill Nichols (2001: 592) points out. For him, 'modernist experimentation favored an open-ended, ambiguous play with time and space that did less to resolve real issues than to challenge the definition and priority of an issue per se' (ibid.: 594). Furthermore, this formal innovation regularly finds some correspondence in what Nichols (1991) calls 'political reflexivity', bringing different aspects of the historical world to the surface. 'What provides the litmus test for political reflexivity is the specific form of the representation, the extent to which it does not reinforce existing categories of consciousness, structures of feeling, ways of seeing', that is, it is 'the degree to which it rejects a narrative sense of closure and completeness' (ibid.: 68).

When exploring the influence of the avant-garde on documentary-making in her conceptualization of experimental ethnography, Catherine Russell (1999) returns to Benjamin to connect his allegorical thinking to film studies once again. For Russell, his perspective 'suggests that allegory itself is a means of articulating utopian desires for historical transformation within a nonteleological critique of modernist progress' (ibid.: 6). With the advent of the cinema, 'mechanical reproduction broke history down into discrete fragmentary moments, generating a discontinuity that Benjamin saw as having revolutionary dialectical possibilities' (ibid.: 9). In Benjamin's words, 'our taverns and our metropolitan streets, our offices and furnished rooms, our railroad stations and our factories appeared to have us locked up hopelessly'. Nevertheless, 'then came the film and burst this prison-world asunder by the dynamite of the tenth of a second, so that now, in the midst of its far-flung ruins and debris, we calmly and adventurously go traveling' (Benjamin 1968: 236). In travelling amid the debris, documentary-makers – the Angels of History of cinema – indeed do seem to find in the ruins *revolutionary dialectical possibilities*. 'If the ruin contains the trace of original form, it is a model of representation that is in constant flux, bearing a shifting relation to a prior site of authenticity' (Russell 1999: 9–10), as will be discussed.

Towards a cartography of ruins

In a world full of images, the Brazilian case, of course, is integrated into a wider context. Needless to say, the presentation of ruins is also much seen in cinemas coming from elsewhere. From more straightforward ruminations like Portuguese Manoel Mozos's *Ruins* (Ruínas, 2009) and Austrian Nikolaus Geyrhalter's *Homo Sapiens* (2016) to ruinous tales like Argentinian Pablo Trapero's *White Elephant* (Elefante Blanco, 2012) and Chinese Jia Zhangke's *Still Life* (2006), contemporary culture flirts with abandonment and destruction no matter the language. Not to mention Hollywood's dystopic obsession exposed in productions like Roland Emmerich's *The Day After Tomorrow* (2004), *2012* (2009) and *Independence Day: Resurgence* (2016). As already stated, this book draws upon three unconventional groups of documentaries centred on Brasília, Rio de Janeiro and indigenous territories as ruinscapes in Brazil. In mapping the images that mirror these spaces, the geographical axes have engendered a cartography of ruins for the reader to navigate. This division is the direct result of extensive film research focused on finding images of ruins produced by contemporary filmmakers. Of course, other films were found along the way, but the decision to look at these particular films was validated by the quality of their own strategies and their potential to be grouped together. The idea of suggesting a hypothetical map between the current capital, the former capital and the territories of the original peoples was incorporated into this study as an additional way of connecting the films, after they already had been selected.

Conducting in-depth film analysis, this book explores both the mode of production and the cultural context in which the films were made, as well as the narrative structure and the visual elaboration deployed in them. More specifically, I will focus on the formal aspects of portraying ruinscapes on screen through the elaboration of science fiction documentaries in Part Two, the tropicalist intermedial aesthetics in Part Three and the non-governmental organization (NGO) Vídeo nas Aldeias (VNA) pro-indigenous filmmaking in Part Four. In addition, I will relate present-day imagery resulting from these portrayals to the revolutionary artistic contributions of the 1960s and 1970s. Apart from that, it is important to mention that interviews with filmmakers Ana Vaz, Adirley Queirós, Daniel Santos, Ricardo Pretti, Luisa Marques, Pedro Urano, Joana Traub Csekö, Ariel Ortega and Vincent Carelli were crucial to the development of the notion of ruins in Brazilian cinema, as the images created by these filmmakers were the starting point of this theoretical investigation. The film analysis and the interviews together enabled me to carry out the discussion of how present-day directors articulate a critique of progress and (under)development precisely through images of ruins. The monograph's cartography sketched below was conceived as a route to that end.

In Part One, Chapter 1 will lay the groundwork for the theoretical debate, which follows major frameworks providing the basis for the discussion of how contemporary Brazilian filmmakers use images of ruins to articulate their critique. It will survey key writings on ruins in contemporary Latin American/Brazilian culture in order to frame the ruin debate through the lens of underdevelopment by discussing the valuable inputs from Furtado (2009) to Lévi-Strauss (1973), among other theoreticians that contribute to the topic. In addition, it will bring the debate on ruins closer to the cinematic domain, also putting emphasis on Barros's (2013) particular interest in 1960s Brazilian cinema, as an entry into the investigation of ruins within national production. Following that, Chapter 2 will explore the pioneering contribution of Cinema Novo filmmakers in visually articulating discussions on progress and (under)development. Most importantly, the chapter will draw on the sense of catastrophe developed by Xavier (2012) when he famously looked at Cinema Novo, Tropicália and Cinema Marginal. The discussion centred on Cinema Novo will also consider the movement's overlap with documentary strategies as an essential means of depicting the precarious reality of that time. It will also branch to the Tropicália and Cinema Marginal movements as important pieces in this intellectual thread. I will dedicate time to exploring the major influence of Tropicália, in particular, when discussing intermediality in Part Three of this book. With this in mind, Chapter 3 will delve into contemporary

Brazilian documentary in the wake of the rebirth of Brazilian cinema production in 1990s (widely known as Cinema da Retomada) and then consider that specific context through the timely concept of *unviable nation* developed by Fernão Pessoa Ramos (2003). Documentary scholars will also address the debate on the multiple aesthetics and narrative possibilities of this particular mode of (hi)storytelling, which will assist in problematizing the common-sense understanding of the definition of documentary. In this sense, Cezar Migliorin's (2011) concept of *post-industrial cinema* and Dellani Lima and Marcelo Ikeda's (2011) notion of *garage cinema* help to locate the growth and the experimentation of contemporary Brazilian documentary in today's society.

In Part Two, I will focus on the Brasília of Vaz's *The Age of Stone* and Queirós's *White Out, Black In* as the other side – or the underside – of progress. In order to cinematically (re)construct the federal capital, both directors created what they call 'sci-fi documentaries'. These productions question the official narrative by exploring the multifaceted condition of underdevelopment through images of ruins. Brasília as a ruinscape also resonates with the legacy of Cinema Novo and Cinema Marginal, as *The Age of Stone* opens a direct dialogue with Glauber Rocha's *The Age of the Earth*, whereas *White Out, Black In* seems to echo, to a certain degree, Sganzerla's *The Red Light Bandit*. Chapter 4 will discuss the invention of Brasília as a grand yet controversial project led by Lúcio Costa and Oscar Niemeyer, as scrutinized by James Holston (1989) and poetically addressed by writer Clarice Lispector (1999a,b). In parallel, Chapter 5 will examine the current trend in Brazilian cinema that seems sceptical of realism as the most appropriate means of depicting national issues, as suggested by Ângela Prysthon's (2015) notion of *realism under erasure*. Subsequently, discussions of the sci-fi genre developed by Fredric Jameson (2005), Vivian Sobchack (2016) and Alfredo Suppia (2007) will help me relate the documentary impulse to the codes of sci-fi in both films.

Inspired by the rhizomatic thinking of Gilles Deleuze and Félix Guattari (1987), Vaz's film is a sci-fi documentary centred on a CGI monument-ruin that is an allegory for Brasília – whether under construction or about to collapse. In it, the monument is a ruin that comes from the future, shifting our perceptions of time and space. In Chapter 6, I argue that Vaz has constructed a science *friction* documentary, as the film plays with the structure of reality itself. In contrast, Queirós's film looks at Brasília from Ceilândia, a satellite city on the outskirts, through two of its inhabitants, Marquim and Shokito. In Chapter 7, I suggest that the city, the houses where the characters live and the characters' own bodies are marked by a sense of ruination. Here, I argue that *White Out, Black In* is a science *non*fiction documentary, as its plot is derived from an actual violent police episode that harmed both characters during a night out in 1986. In a vengeful yet redemptive move, they both plan to drop a sonic-atomic bomb on Brasília to leave the white and wealthy capital in ruins.

Aimed at exploring an intermedial visualization of failing modern projects in Rio de Janeiro, Part Three will investigate the relationship between contemporary experimental documentaries and the legacy of Tropicália. More specifically, it will explore how present-day filmmakers hint at tropicalist-like values through the execution of intermedial aesthetics in the documentary mode in order to visualize ruins in Rio. In this sense, I believe it is important that Chapter 8 deepens the discussion about the origins and the implications of Tropicália in order to articulate the film analyses adequately. It will discuss the intermedial aspects of Tropicália linked to the modernist anthropophagy, as explored by Stefan Solomon (2017), and it will take into consideration the risk that countercultural motifs become commodified through the neoliberalization of artistic creation, as argued by Suely Rolnik (2006, 2011). I suggest that the films selected seem to react against the loss of the radical power of art precisely by exposing the architectural failures nurtured by the neoliberal regime, what Idelber Avelar (2009) calls the *neoliberal ruin*.

Following that argument, Chapter 9 introduces the 2014 FIFA World Cup and the 2016 Olympic Games (de)construction works as emblematic images of the current dynamic of capitalist extraction. Experimental short documentaries like Daniel Santos's *ExPerimetral* and Clarissa Campolina, Julia de Simone, Luiz Pretti and Ricardo Pretti's *The Harbour* comment on this scenario by creatively elaborating on the debris of the Elevado da Perimetral, a 5.5-km elevated highway located in Rio's harbour zone, using intermedial tactics. By looking at the abandoned Carmen Miranda Museum, Luisa Marques's *Tropical Curse* takes a similar course. In Chapter 10, the film comes to the fore questioning national development through the two Mirandas: the commodified Portuguese-Brazilian artist and the decaying, modernist building where the museum dedicated to her is housed. Visual arts, performance and literature are fused in Marques's meditation on the ruinous spaceship-like museum. Finally, Chapter 11 will examine Joana Traub Csekö and Pedro Urano's *HU Enigma*, a documentary feature about the university hospital of the Federal University of Rio de Janeiro – half of it being a hospital per se, while the other half is in a state of complete disrepair. Apart from drawing on photography, architecture and installation art, the conception of the project lies in the theoretical contributions of Glauber Rocha (2017) and Hélio Oiticica (1999a,b), as explained by Csekö (2008).

After exploring Brasília and Rio de Janeiro, Part Four will look at indigenous territories as damaged territories, the final geographical axis in this investigation. In discussing a territory in constant dispute, I will argue that that dispute is rendered visible through images of ruins present in NGO VNA's documentaries. Before that, however, Chapter 12 will shed light on the Cinema Novo films that framed the indigenous territory as damaged territory – a critique of the so-called progress and (under)development under the military dictatorship. I will briefly discuss the specificities of *Macunaíma, Brazil Year 2000* and *Iracema*, as well as their use of allegorical indigenous figures to address the imminent destruction of the nation itself. Next, Chapter 13 will introduce VNA (within the context of the emergence of indigenous media elsewhere) and its strong link to reclaiming land through documentary-making, drawing on Freya Schiwy (2009), Charlotte Gleghorn (2017) and Faye Ginsburg (1991). Although very different from each other, I will argue that VNA comes closer to Cinema Novo in its willingness to take over the critique of progress in relation to indigenous territory and its understanding of film as a militant tool to change society.

In this respect, Chapter 14 will analyse Carelli's *Corumbiara: They Shoot Indians, Don't They?* as the epitome of the visualization of indigenous territory as damaged territory – an imaginary foregrounded by Cinema Novo in the past. The documentary follows Carelli from 1986 to 2006 in his effort to gather evidence of the existence of the Kanoê and Akuntsu groups in the Corumbiara territory, North of Brazil, after the attacks on them by farmers and agribusinessmen. I will discuss in greater detail four sequences that build a sense of ruination in this documentary. In addition, Chapter 15 will dive into three VNA collaborative documentaries that frame indigenous ruins as evidence of territorial disputes: Ariel Ortega, Jorge Morinico and Germano

Beñites's *Two Villages, One Path*, and Ariel Ortega, Patrícia Ferreira, Ernesto de Carvalho and Vincent Carelli's *Guarani Exile* and *Tava, The House of Stone*. Ruben Caixeta de Queiroz (2008) and Philipi Bandeira (2017) emphasize the role played by these collaborative film projects, with the participation of the Indian at last, as co-author. Most importantly, in telling their own story, the Guarani people contest the way white narratology addresses their history.

In approaching the end of this manuscript, the conclusion will invite the reader to take a walk amid the cinematic ruins. Drawing on Xavier's (2012) concept of *allegories of underdevelopment* and Barros's (2013) notion of *Third World ruins*, I will return to specific points discussed throughout. The conclusion will indicate the differences and similarities between the selected ruin-gazers (i.e. the filmmakers). Furthermore, it will connect the ruinscapes of Brasília, Rio de Janeiro and indigenous territories: the sci-fi documentaries in dialogue with Glauber Rocha and Sganzerla, the tropicalist intermediality in Rio's experimental documentary films, and VNA's pro-indigenous film projects updating Cinema Novo's depiction of damaged indigenous territory. Finally, the conclusion will work towards expanding the map of ruins, suggesting alternative routes and different artistic practices to consider in future research. In looking at the country's recent past and facing its failures, the three unconventional groups of documentaries under analysis have not only created thought-provoking moving images but also appeal to critical thinking to investigate perceptions of the world.

Part One

Framing the ruins through underdevelopment: From Cinema Novo to contemporary Brazilian documentary

Part One of this study is devoted to the three major frameworks underpinning the discussion of how contemporary Brazilian documentaries make use of images of ruins to visually articulate a critique of progress and (under)development. As mentioned in the introduction, Chapter 1 surveys key writings on ruins in contemporary culture and, more importantly, their connection to the notion of underdevelopment in Brazil/Latin America as postulated by Celso Furtado (2009) in his investigation about national development. After that, I shed light on the unique contribution of French anthropologist Claude Lévi-Strauss (1973) to the development of a sense of Brazilianness informed by the idea of decadence. I then dwell on theoretical notes concerning the imbrication between the cinema and ruins, especially the cinematic sense of ruination recently developed by Rodrigo Lopes de Barros (2013).

Chapter 2 examines the pioneering contribution of Cinema Novo in foregrounding progress and (under)development in its discourse, aesthetics and mode of production. The sense of catastrophe (Xavier 2012) present in many films is a pivotal point of departure for defining an aesthetics of ruins in present-day Brazilian documentary films. Paulo Emílio's[1] (Salles Gomes 1996) analysis of Brazilian cinema's trajectory within underdevelopment is also key – it deserves attention as it is intimately attuned with Furtado's (2009) view and in need of being unpacked in light of contemporary times. In addition,

I underline the dialogue that *cinemanovistas* established with documentary strategies as a means of depicting the precarious reality, and with Tropicália and Cinema Marginal.

Finally, Chapter 3 looks at the emergence of Cinema da Retomada to discuss the development of contemporary Brazilian documentary within the *unviable nation*, a term coined by Fernão Pessoa Ramos (2003) that partially underpins my analysis. I investigate the context and the efforts made in order for that production to flourish. In doing so, I attempt to briefly comment on the purpose of the documentary and its ability to make assertions about the historical world as well as pinpoint its conventions and question their use today. In a *post-industrial cinema* context (Migliorin 2011), I aim to pave the way for analysing meaningful images of ruins in the chapters that follow.

1

A realm for the ruins of Brazil

According to Svetlana Boym, 'the early 21st century exhibits a strange ruinophilia' (2011). By acknowledging the paradoxes of modernity, physical (as well as metaphorical) ruins seem to be a means of questioning the so-called progress and development that have profoundly defined the modern project of the twentieth century. It was a decisive historical moment marked by the urbanization and industrialization of the modern nation state in the belief that science and technology were the inevitable path to social progress and economic development. For Boym, ruins have the ability both to recall the initial utopia planned by the project and, at the same time, point out its utter failure. 'The ruins of modernity as viewed from a 21st-century perspective point at possible futures that never came to be. But those futures do not necessarily inspire restorative nostalgia. Instead, they make us aware of the vagaries of progressive vision as such' (ibid.). In this sense, the contemporary obsession with analysing the failures of the past implies a sort of *reflective nostalgia*, to use a term coined by Boym (2001) herself. That is, a nostalgia that prompts not the pursuance of restoring the past but reflecting upon it. Ruins, ruined as they inescapably are, can be a trigger for reflection. Embarking on the same journey, Andreas Huyssen argues that 'we are nostalgic for the ruins of modernity because they still seem to hold a promise that has vanished from our own age: the promise of an alternative future' (2006: 8). For him, the nostalgia for ruins – that took artistic practices and academic studies by storm – concurs with the current emphasis on memory and trauma as key discourses for our times. When highlighting the catastrophic achievements of history, 'our imaginary of ruins can be read as a palimpsest of multiple historical events and representations' (ibid.).

Julia Hell and Andreas Schönle's notion of *ruins of modernity* is key in this matter. They argue that 'the destruction of the world's most famous symbolic icon of capitalist modernity on 9/11 brought to a climax the debate about how modernity, broadly conceived, seems to have invented, framed, and produced ruins' (2010: 5). The collapse of the World Trade Center, followed by the invasions of Iraq and Afghanistan, ushered in the new millennium, bringing the imagery of ruins to the foreground with an unprecedented impact. Most importantly, not only the imagery but also the meaning of ruins was put under scrutiny, considering both their spatial and temporal aspects. For Hell and Schönle, 'the ruin is invoked in a critique of the spatial organization of the modern world and of its single-minded commitment to a progress that throws too many individuals and spaces into the trash' (ibid.: 8). Albeit rooted in the here and now, the ruin has 'a difficult relationship with the present, a disenchantment that encourages a leap into heterogeneous temporalities, often embodied in speculation about the future of the past' (ibid.: 9). For that reason, Brian Dillon, theoretician whose investigation of ruins goes beyond the previously mentioned *Ruin Lust* exhibition, believes that 'the ruin is a site not of melancholy or mourning but of *radical potential* – its fragmentary, unfinished nature is an invitation to fulfil the as yet unexplored temporality that it contains', the ruin being 'freighted with possibility' (2011: 18, emphasis added).

The modernity in ruins pointed out by Hell and Schönle is part of Marc Augé's intellectual effort in *Time in Ruins*. In it, Augé affirms that 'the 20th century has been the century of devastation, destruction and reconstruction' (2003: 99).[1] In this sense, he argues that the world's urbanization (which certainly involves migrations, evictions and economic conflicts) is intimately linked to a social, political and warlike violence – a perception that underpins my interpretation of ruins as well. 'And that because there is no doubt that it is violence that is at the origin of urban remodelling and especially of construction works that, in different parts of the world, at the same time bear witness to the conflicts that produced the ruins and to the voluntarism that defines the reconstructions' (ibid.: 100). Within this scenario, Augé refers to the collapse of the World Trade Center, like Hell and Schönle, as a turning point: the tragic event made the world seem more connected (suggesting that we all belong to the same world) and also rendered visible new forms of violence (the falling of the Twin Towers being the outcome of a global civil war). Augé sees that collapse as a paradox of ruins: 'It is at the time of the most widespread destruction, at the time when there is a greater capacity for annihilation, that the ruins will disappear both as reality and as concept' (ibid.: 101), he writes at the threshold of the new millennium.

When one thinks of Latin American ruins, it may be the case of being the far-away past that comes to mind. In her seminal work about *ruin lust*, Rose Macaulay's[2] few references to the region include the ruins of Machu Picchu, in Peru, and the pyramids of Chichen Itza, in Mexico, precisely because they 'become part of that encroaching green, often to be no more found or seen, sometimes to be discovered by travellers of other races many centuries later' (1966: 266). Today, decay and dereliction have turned into tourist attractions, like the above-mentioned ruins of Machu Picchu and Chichen Itza. In this regard, editors Michael J. Lazzara and Vicky Unruh (2009) invested in the telling of ruins in Latin America to scrutinize those clichéd ruin scenarios in a number of essays. More fundamentally, their groundbreaking contribution seems to problematize the (neo)colonial viewpoint frequently applied to the topic. In her essay, Regina Harrison (2009), for instance, unpacks the Machu Picchu ruin complex from the arrival of the North American explorer Hiram Bingham to the impressions of poet Pablo Neruda, Walter Salles's film *The Motorcycle Diaries* (2004), travel magazines and virtual tourism promotions. In taking account of the multiple layers that shape such an iconic ruin, the author identifies it as an narrative element whose trajectory and meaning are always under analysis.

Following on from that approach, what strikes one the most is the further step taken by the editors in expanding the debate to ruin scenarios engendered by the political environment and socio-economic measures typical of Latin American countries. From the authoritarian modernization led by dictatorial governments to the neoliberal policies implemented in the 1990s, such contexts have propelled, the authors argue, a shift in the way both artists and academics relate to the question of ruination. As Lazzara and Unruh point out, the 'ruin returns with fervent intensity at the turn of the millennium as a measure of the era's own structure of feeling and as a new interpretive path for revisiting earlier manifestations of ruins in Latin American cultural discourse' (2009: 3). In so doing, the authors extrapolate from stereotypical, historical ruins and reach other spheres of present-day society, making the reading of ruins in the subcontinent more complex.

Marked by fiscal austerity and the privatization of public assets, the turn of the millennium did not find in the political and socio-economic dynamics of neoliberalism a way to cope with problems engendered by the utopias of the twentieth century. The rotten modernization process and the savage neoliberal agenda that followed resulted not only in income concentration and high unemployment but also in neglect and, at times, destruction itself, as the films under analysis demonstrate. Although not particularly focusing on the production of images linked to this phenomenon, Lazzara and Unruh shed light on a specific backdrop that enables current narratives of ruins to find common ground in which to emerge.

Interested in examining the effects of neoliberalism in Latin American society, Idelber Avelar (2009) coined the notion of *neoliberal ruin* in that context. Exploring post-dictatorship Argentinian literature, he came up with the term while analysing writer Gustavo Ferreyra's *El Director*, as its protagonist is 'a subject who has also been shaped by the savagely selfish logic of neoliberalism, imposed in Argentina by the Menem government in the 1990s and directly responsible for the 2001 economic collapse'. According to Avelar, 'the reworking of ruins, then, is an apt metaphor to describe not only the subject's relation to his past, ... but also the polis in which he operates' (ibid.: 191). Even though he only dedicates a brief paragraph to the discussion (Avelar's essay reaches that conclusion but centres on the literary strategies employed by Ferreyra), the concept of *neoliberal ruin* is successful in encapsulating the sense of ruination often present in contemporary society. 'The destructive utopia of privatization' (ibid.: 192), in Avelar's own words, not only means the commodification of social life followed by economic and political collapse, but also paves the way for discussing how the polis itself is affected and transfigured. Worth mentioning, insights into the ruination of neoliberalism have recently been taken up by North American political theorist Wendy Brown (2019) in her *In the Ruins of Neoliberalism*, which seems to be the first attempt to investigate the phenomenon as leading to catastrophic right-wing populism.

If neoliberalism as an ideology can be highly controversial in the context of developed nations, the inception of neoliberal policies in so-called developing or underdeveloped countries aggravates the picture even more. The origins of the term *underdevelopment* itself date from the end of the Second World War, when in 1948, the United Nations created the Economic Commission for Latin America and the Caribbean (ECLAC) to encourage economic cooperation among peripheral nations – or Third World nations, bearing in mind the Cold War context. The peripheral nations were defined as those left behind in comparison with Western European nations that had fully completed the industrialization process initiated in the eighteenth century. With Argentine intellectual Raúl Prebisch as one of its foremost members, the *cepalista*[3] school believed that a nation had to accomplish industrialization in order to overcome its structural obstacles. Against the neoclassical and modernization theories in vogue at the time, his centre-periphery paradigm guided Latin American studies throughout the 1950s and 1960s. As Cristóbal Kay (1991) puts it, the school had a structuralist understanding of (under)development from a holistic-historical perspective, as the periphery's issues were part of the capitalist world system, albeit the result of a very particular economic trajectory. 'Underdevelopment and development are thus two faces of the same world historical process, as both processes are historically simultaneous and interlinked' (Kay 2009: 161).

Many have argued, however, that underdevelopment has far more distant roots going back to the European colonization characterized by an extractive economy and lack of long-term planning. According to Rodolfo Stavenhagen, 'underdevelopment is the state of being of Latin American countries in modern times, just as "colonial society" was its state of being during three centuries of Iberian domination' (1974: 125). Nevertheless, Steven Topik (1987) remarks that those colonial societies were not exactly recessive. 'For most of the first three centuries of colonial rule, Latin America was still not considered economically backward. Indeed, the wealth of the silver mines of Potosí in Upper Peru, Guanajuato in Mexico, and Ouro Preto in Brazil was legendary' (ibid.: 548). Topik argues that things started to change when the Industrial Revolution came along in England and nearby countries. Inspired by the legacy of the Enlightenment, 'with the idea of progress came the beginnings of the idea of evolution, the notion that societies went through the same stages as people: infancy, adolescence, adulthood and old age'. Bluntly put, 'the colonies of Latin America', therefore, 'were not just different from Europe, as they had been perceived before; they stood at an earlier stage of development' (ibid.: 550).

In Brazil, the debate about underdevelopment in the work of economist Celso Furtado is a watershed. Initially linked to the *cepalista* school, he also created the Superintendency for the Development of the Northeast in 1959, became the first Minister of Planning in 1962 (interrupted by the 1964 military coup) and, later in his career, was appointed Minister of Culture in 1986 (in the first democratic government following the end of the dictatorship). Focusing on the Brazilian experience, Furtado's main contribution lies in his understanding of underdevelopment as an autonomous historical process directly affected by the industrialization of the Western European nations and the way those nations established a controversial network with peripheral countries. That is, underdevelopment as the underside of the capitalist world system that benefited the advanced economies. According to Furtado, 'underdevelopment is not a necessary stage in the process of the formation of modern capitalist economies'; rather, it is 'a particular process resulting from the penetration of modern capitalist enterprises into archaic structures' (2009: 171). The dualism of relying on a pre-capitalist agrarian-exporting system and yet having to trade with capitalist industrial economies characterizes the phenomenon of underdevelopment in Brazil. 'The relations that exist between these two types of society involve forms of dependence that tend to self-perpetuate' (Furtado 2014: 88). Other thinkers have also referred to this sort of relationship as dependency capitalism (Sampaio Júnior 1999) or the national-dependent society (Bresser-Pereira 2012).

In a theoretical debate dominated by European and North American viewpoints, Furtado contributed to the underdevelopment discussion from a Brazilian perspective. To solve the dualistic problem, he invested in a national-development mindset based on State intervention in the economy that would modernize the country and safeguard its internal market. That mindset was in tune with the country's political mood at that time, the creation of modernist Brasília – the purpose-built new capital city – being its most obvious example, as Chapter 4 will demonstrate. Irrespective of his industrialist-bourgeois viewpoint that never completely broke with the ideology of progress (Borja 2013), Furtado identified with a leftist discourse whereby economic strategies had to be intrinsically attached to social criteria. For him, 'the starting point of the study of development should not be the rate of investment, the capital-output ratio, nor the size of the market, but the horizon of aspirations of the collective in question' (Furtado 1969: 19). In his view, technical progress in underdeveloped countries brings about social conflict that can only be mitigated by political measures and structural reforms. In this sense, Kay (1991) positions Furtado as a contributor to dependency theory,[4] developed from the *cepalista* school framework of the 1950s. As soon as transnational capitalism imposed itself, Kay claims that Furtado would remark that 'the control of technical progress and imposition of consumption patterns from the centre countries are the key factors which explain the perpetuation of underdevelopment and dependence in the periphery' (ibid.: 47). In other words, not only do multinational interventions in the national economy accentuate the concentration of income and the surplus of labour, but they also succeed in seducing the peripheral elite, which remains oblivious to the people's real needs.

Although successful in pointing out the specificities of underdevelopment within Brazil (from the colonial economy and slave labour to incomplete industrialization), Furtado's structural-historical method and praxis did not result in the completion of the modernization process, partly because of a continued dependency status (Borja 2013). The twentieth-century modern project was mainly carried forward by the democratic presidential mandates of Getúlio Vargas (1951–4), Juscelino Kubitschek (1956–61) and João Goulart (1961–4), and the military regime that followed. Apart from the building of Brasília, it could be said that the construction of the Perimetral Elevated Highway in Rio de Janeiro (inaugurated in 1960) and the Trans-Amazonian Highway (1972) stand as concrete translations of that mindset. Even more so, the controversies attached to their construction also expose their failures as modern projects, as I will discuss in Parts Two, Three and Four by looking at films such as *The Age of Stone* (A Idade da Pedra, 2013) and *White Out, Black In* (Branco Sai, Preto Fica, 2014) in relation to Brasília; *ExPerimetral* (2016) and *The Harbour* (O Porto, 2013) in relation to the Perimetral Elevated Highway; and *Iracema* (Iracema – Uma Transa Amazônica, 1974–81) in relation to the Trans-Amazonian Highway.

The modern project that was not accomplished by the *cepalista* school in the 1960s has certainly also failed under the promises of the neoliberal regime that grew stronger from the 1980s onwards. 'The Cold War might have ended but not the development problems of the world system, let alone of the periphery and the poor,' as Kay (1993: 692) affirms. The author argues that he remains 'unconvinced that neoliberalism has the answer to the development problems of the Third World, if development is understood not only as entailing the elimination of poverty, but also the construction of a more equitable and participatory world system' (ibid.: 697). With this in mind, structuralists – who had been discredited after the rise of Thatcherism and Reaganomics – may have a second shot in the Latin American economic debate. 'Structuralism or its current neostructuralist version might even offer the seeds for an alternative to the still hegemonic, although much questioned, neoliberal paradigm' (Kay 2009: 164). Considering Lazzara and Unruh's (2009) perspective, the neoliberal paradigm is not only much questioned but also increasingly challenged by the figure of ruins *as a measure of the era's own structure of feeling and as a new interpretive path.*

The Cuban axis

As stated above, the phenomenon of underdevelopment and its concrete manifestations do not only impact on Brazil. In this sense, it should come as no surprise that the first Brazilian publication entirely dedicated to exploring the role played by ruins finds its theoretical axis in the Cuban experience, perhaps the most prominent case study in present-day Latin America. In *Ruinologias*, editors Ana Luiza Andrade, Rodrigo Lopes de Barros and Carlos Eduardo Schmidt Capela deliver an original array of essays aiming to produce 'a history forged from an investigative exercise and practice that contemplates, with the ruins, the opening of archives, images and other temporalities' (2016: 27), hence questioning the official version of history built upon traditional historicism. They are rather interested in the 'traces and symptoms of an inevitable transit towards a ruined modernity' (ibid.: 26). In this regard, the decaying old buildings of Havana pervade the book as the leading example of the editors' thesis, as they render visible 'the imbrication between economic vicissitudes and ruination' (ibid.: 20).

Much of their argument draws on Antonio José Ponte's short story 'An Art of Making Ruins', more specifically, the term *tugurización*[5] that the author coined to refer to the deterioration of the Cuban capital. In it, he criticizes what he calls the museification of Havana, that is, the conservation of its dereliction and desertification in the wake of the Cuban Revolution (1953–9) and US economic embargo. 'For Ponte, who defined himself as a ruinologist, Havana is mainly catastrophe and debris. Thus, the museification of the old city coexists with the ruins of its remaining part' (Barros 2013: 118). Critical of Fidel Castro's regime, Ponte then invents Tuguria as a counteraction. Tuguria is a fictional city below the soil, the underground of the actual city, a sort of upside-down reflection of what happens on the surface: every collapsing building above the ground reappears in Tuguria, as if preserved by memory. 'Havana is a bombarded city by a bombing that never took place. Thus, life goes underground. Tuguria, the submerged city, is however fully synchronized to the wasteland that grows on the surface.' (ibid.: 115). Ultimately, the notion of *tugurización* is 'pertinent for reflecting on the degradation of urban space in the present time' (Andrade, Barros and Capela 2016: 23) and illuminates the book as a whole. Moreover, this insightful argument enables a reflection that 'implies a deterritorialization and a reterritorialization which, in a joint operation, helps the configuration of a symbolic space' (ibid.: 25).

In this sense, moving images would have a central role in that reflection. In Florian Borchmeyer's *Habana – Arte Nuevo de Hacer Ruinas* (2006), a documentary focused on helpless Havana dwellers living in edifications left in a state of abandonment, one sees the contradiction of ruins functioning as home for the characters. According to Ponte (2007), this contradiction is not so easily assimilated by tourists and residents: the former seems to visit Havana in the search for a *solemn tourism* (and might not be particularly aware of the implications of the local reality), whereas the latter may have been turned into an apathetic resident in the face of political measures and urban decay. For this reason, Ponte bluntly affirms 'the real urban growth of these years …: the construction of ruins' (ibid.: 196). The author also participates in the documentary stating that the situation should be seen as scandalous rather than melancholic as other types of historical ruins are seen. Ponte gets to the point to say that the abandonment is a political strategy to justify the political regime.[6]

In her film analysis of *Suite Habana* (2003), Salomé Aguilera Skvirsky (2013) goes in a contrasting direction that nuances the debate. In this documentary, director Fernando Pérez makes an incursion into a day in the life of twelve Havana residents spanning in age from 10 to 97, resorting to another discursive strategy, according to Skvirsky's reading of the film. The scholar defends that the film contests the discourse of ruins commonly associated with Havana, as, for her, the so-called Havana ruins contradict the classical notion of ruins. 'Conventionally, ruins are uninhabited. People don't live in them, and that is what makes them haunting or uncanny. But the majority of Cuba's so-called ruins are still inhabited' (ibid.: 429). For Andrade, Barros and Capela, however, this situation actually 'reveals how, in Havana, the ruins occupied by the people acquire the power to suggest *a decisive contradiction*, and even a risk' (2016: 20, emphasis added). In this regard, the contradiction of living in ruins seems like an appropriate metaphor for ruins in Latin America, where 'this dynamic between economic and social flourishing and its inevitable decline is recurrent' (ibid.). Rather than respecting the classical definition of ruins, the authors are interested in expanding it when considering the particularities of the sociopolitical context.

For Skvirsky, Pérez is inspired by the city symphony film genre, but, instead of focusing on the city itself, he casts light on its citizens. Moreover, on how citizens manage to be creative and productive in their daily life, so that the film is able to challenge the discourse that there is no human activity in a city reportedly stuck in time. Nevertheless, when a commentator of the film finds an innovative paradigm in the fact that this is a city symphony film showing stagnation and decay rather than speed and modernity, Skvirsky seems to find the paradox unsuitable, arguing that 'if this assessment is right, how can we make sense of the film's almost continuous depiction of human activity?' (2013: 431). I would argue that the author's query might point to a second decisive contradiction that places the Cuban case study as a paramount one, instead of a sign of unsuitable paradox. There could well be stagnation, decay and human activity. The two imminent questions should be: Why is that and how can that be depicted on screen?

Apart from that, Skvirsky has a strong point when she seems intrigued by the fact that 'the Cuban ruin does not stand as a reproach of modernity, but on the contrary, as a sign of an unfinished or sidetracked modernity'. For her, what seems to be at stake 'is a discourse of developmentalism, not one against developmentalism. The failure of Cuban-style socialism has been the failure to make Cuba truly modern, that is, developed, and the ruin is the preferred index of this failure' (ibid.: 430). She argues that the 'post-war European ruin – as depicted in, for example, *Germany Year Zero* or *Paisá* – has never signified backwardness, belatedness, or an incomplete modernity'; rather, 'it has signified overdevelopment, the kind of overdevelopment associated with modern warfare and mechanized death'. Conscious of the readings a ruin may acquire, she infers that 'the association of the ruin with underdevelopment is unique to the postcolonial context' (ibid.) – and I would contend that that is one of the reasons why it deserves further investigation.

Walter Benjamin has also contributed to a sense of ruination that came to be associated with so-called underdeveloped nations, even though not investigating the postcolonial context. In 'Naples', an essay written in 1924 with his partner Asja Lacis, he tours the imperial ruins of Italy but writes instead about 'a present-day process of decay', as if 'the structuring boundaries of modern capitalism ... have not yet been established' (Buck-Morss 1989: 26). Susan Buck-Morss goes even further when claiming that, in their essay, 'one sees neither an ancient society nor a modern one, but an improvisatory culture released, and even nourished, by the city's rapid decay' (ibid.: 27). In other words, it is as if Benjamin and Lacis had singled out 'the specifically capitalist form of Naples' underdevelopment' (ibid.: 26–7) when looking at its caves, arcades, churches, courtyards and old tenement blocks. The authors create a chaotic yet enchanting depiction of the city. Quite surprisingly, I find in Benjamin and Lacis's 'Naples' an element that lies at the core of the conceptualization of the ruins within underdevelopment, shaped by the connection between Caetano Veloso and Claude Lévi-Strauss. If the Brazilian musician once sang 'Here everything seems/It is still under construction/And is already a ruin'[7] (Veloso 1991) citing the French anthropologist's view on the so-called New World, Benjamin and Lacis's reading of Naples strikes a similar note: 'In such corners one can scarcely discern where building is still in progress and where dilapidation has already set in.' (1979: 170). In addition, much like Brazil's lack of long-term planning, both authors also state that 'porosity results not only from the indolence of the Southern artisan, but also, above all, from the passion for improvisation' (ibid.).

Pessimistic views of progress

Brazilian singer, composer, musician and writer Caetano Veloso perhaps best synthesized ruins considering the national environment. To a great extent, guided by Lévi-Strauss's 'pessimistic view of progress' (Veloso 2017: 29), the above-mentioned lyrics of *Fora da Ordem* (Out of Order), a song released on the album *Circuladô* (1991), seem to emphasize the chronic unfeasibility of Brazil being able to come to terms as a nation and thrive. The dialogue between the Brazilian singer and the French anthropologist animates many of the former's contributions to the national cultural debate, as will be addressed in Chapter 9. Interestingly enough, *Tropical Truth*, the title of the singer's memoir, subtly refers to the anthropologist's classic work *Tristes Tropiques*, which had a great impact on the musician. Published in 1955, it was groundbreaking in the field of anthropology and mandatory for anyone wishing to investigate the foundations of Brazilian identity in the light of Native cultures. During his visits to Brazil (between 1935 and 1939), Lévi-Strauss spent months travelling to Paraná, Goiás, Mato Grosso, Mato Grosso do Sul and Amazonas, Brazilian states far from São Paulo (where he first arrived as a visiting lecturer at the University of São Paulo), in pursuance of making a comparative study of particular indigenous tribes. However, I argue that it was while in São Paulo and Rio de Janeiro that he came up with his seminal argument for the very idea of Brazilianness – namely, his impressions of the fresh decadence, or decayed freshness, embedded in the country's DNA.

Wandering in downtown São Paulo, it was as if Lévi-Strauss (1973) was able to capture two opposing yet complementary aspects of South America's largest city. First, he perceived a metropolis that strangely worshipped a past not of its own making. 'The Italian colony had erected a statue of Augustus Caesar,' he writes. 'It was a life-size bronze reproduction of an antique marble statue, of no great artistic significance, it is true, but deserving of some respect in a town where there was nothing to remind one of any historical event dating back to before the previous century' (ibid.: 128). On the other hand, he found time to stare at Praça da Sé, in the old town of São Paulo, as if realizing that a degenerate past was unfolding right there in the present, a past that the city itself seemed unable to acknowledge. 'There was the Praça da Sé, the cathedral square, *halfway between a building site and a ruin*' (ibid.: 121, emphasis added), at once, an idiosyncratic embodiment of both construction and deconstruction.

The Brazilian sense of ruination suggested by Lévi-Strauss's *pensée* was at the basis of the nation's formation, a crucial component of it. Shaped by countless economic booms and downfalls, hardcore exploitation and subsequent contractions, cycles of construction and destruction, it was as if the nation was doomed to failure. That is, progress was conceptualized as conquering territories, exploiting their natural resources and human labour force, and then leaving in order to conquer and exploit somewhere and someone else. What Lévi-Strauss noticed in the fragile urbanization of Brazilian metropolises was much in tune with that logic. Paying attention to architecture, he managed to understand what the spread of decaying buildings could reveal about a nation per se. For him, the towns of the New World, from the United States down to Brazil, 'pass from freshness to decay without ever being simply old' because 'the passing of years brings degeneration' to those towns, not enhancement, as is the case of most European ones. Instead, when new districts are created, 'they are more like stands in a fairground or the pavilions of some international exhibition, built to last only a few months'. In the loop of rotten modernization, 'the original layout disappears through the demolitions caused by some new building fever'. Impressed by the distinction between the Old and New Worlds, he believes that while 'certain European cities sink gently into a moribund torpor; those of the New World live feverishly in the grip of a *chronic disease*; they are perpetually young, yet never healthy' (ibid.: 118–19, emphasis added).

When he finally landed in Rio de Janeiro, Lévi-Strauss had an unexpected reaction to the then capital of Brazil. 'The tropics are less exotic than out of date' (ibid.: 106), he observed about its city centre. Not much impressed by the natural landscape that had made Rio internationally renowned, the scholar focused instead on the consequences of the unplanned urban fabric for social relations. 'Perhaps the problem has now been solved by urbanization, but in 1935 the altimeter unfailingly indicated the place each individual occupied in the social scale: the higher you lived, the lower your status,' he wisely perceived. 'The poor were perched high up on the hillsides, in favelas, where a population of Negroes clad in well-washed rags composed lively guitar-melodies which, at carnival time, came down from the hills and invaded the town, together with their inventors' (ibid.: 107). Nothing has changed. In fact, *favelas* have continued to sprout in Rio's hills as a confirmation of Lévi-Strauss's appropriately 'pessimistic view of progress' (Veloso 2017: 29), to return to this definition again.

Curiously, it is another French anthropologist who will directly link Lévi-Strauss to ruins. In *Time in Ruins*, Marc Augé writes that 'Lévi-Strauss felt the close relationship between ethnology and memory (or forgetting) and, beyond that, the analogy between remembrance and ruin' (2003: 13). Augé even mentions an excerpt from *Tristes Tropiques* to illustrate Lévi-Strauss's methodology, precisely built from the fragments he remembers from different fieldwork experiences and articulates – which resulted in his paradigmatic stance in the anthropology studies domain. On that note, Augé goes on to explore the role of anthropologists, 'the first observers of the transition from one century to another, or rather, of the passage from one era to another' (ibid.: 16–17). Augé argues that anthropologists today, located in a sort of wasteland, 'realize that the inventory of ruins is not an end in itself and that what counts is the invention, although subjected to terrible pressures …. Humanity is not in ruins, it is under construction. It still belongs to history. A frequently tragic history, always uneven, but hopelessly ordinary' (ibid.: 19). In a second moment, the imbrication between ruins and construction sites is also taken up in his analysis. In acknowledging urbanization projects, Augé affirms that a construction work or an urban lot attracts filmmakers, writers and poets because the two 'underline both the still palpable presence of a lost past and the uncertain imminence of what may happen' (ibid.: 106); they are promising, poetic spaces, he claims. According to him, although the contemporary city lives in an eternal present (as buildings can be quickly renovated or replaced), construction sites can be seen, at least for a while, as 'spaces in a waiting situation that also function, in a somewhat vague way at times, as evocative of memories. They reopen the temptation of the past and the future. They may be like ruins' (ibid.: 108). In contrast, Augé questions the very existence of ruins today, as it could be argued that 'buildings are not built to age' (ibid.) – a debatable statement, if one considers, for instance, the Lévi-Strauss-inspired lyrics of Caetano.

Although Lévi-Strauss's anthropological work seems decisive in establishing a theoretical approach to the topic, the sense of ruination within the national context had already been hinted at before, even if not directly articulated. Of particular note in the national imaginary are the following sociological works: Gilberto Freyre's *The Masters and the Slaves* (Casa-grande & Senzala, 1998), Sérgio Buarque de Holanda's *Roots of Brazil* (Raízes do Brasil, 1995) and Caio Prado Júnior's *The Colonial Background of Modern Brazil* (Formação do Brasil Contemporâneo, 1961) – all published before Lévi-Strauss's book, in

1933, 1936 and 1942, respectively. For Freyre, the very definition of luxury in Brazil, for instance, is contradictory as it contains its opposite within itself: a 'morbid, sickly, incomplete luxury', with 'excess in a few things, and this excess at the expense of debts; deficiencies in others' (1998: 38). Holanda focuses on the impression that deficiencies were, in fact, an expected outcome, as the 'exploitation of the tropics was not really a methodical and rational enterprise, nor did it emanate from a constructive and energetic will: it was rather done with sloppiness and a certain abandonment' (1995: 43). As Prado Júnior points out, Brazil was thought to be put together as a nation 'by cycles in time and space alternating between *prosperity and ruin*, which summarizes the economic history of colonial Brazil' (1961: 284, emphasis added). For instance, the monoculture of sugarcane in the Northeast, the exploitation of the gold mines in Minas Gerais state and the coffee plantations in the São Paulo region are regarded as classical examples of extractivism devoid of long-term planning, relying on enslaved black workers and resulting in the long-standing ruination of indigenous territories, my focus on Part Four. Although much of their interpretation of Brazil reverberates to date, it is important to underline that these writings have been under scrutiny in the light of contemporary revaluations of history, especially in relation to the myth of racial democracy.

Furthermore, Capela (2016) also stresses the contribution of writer Euclides da Cunha, widely known for the masterpiece *Os Sertões* published in 1902. Translated as *Rebellion in the Backlands*, it is a nonfiction book about the War of Canudos (1893–7), which took place in the Canudos settlement, Bahia. Led by the messianic figure of Antonio the Counsellor, the community formed by local farmers, former slaves and indigenous peoples rebelled against oppressive Republican values. Although a remarkable historical feat, Capela highlights how the rapid construction of the settlement also foresaw the precariousness of the same project: 'As for Canudos, the vertiginous process of growth of the "obscure settlement" … is characterized by the absence of planning. It would have been "made at random", so that "the new settlement would appear within a few weeks", and, paradoxically, "*it was already like ruins. Born old*"' (ibid.: 301, emphasis added). The imbrication between progress and ruination is also present in an array of Cunha's essays, including *Entre As Ruínas* (Amid the Ruins). In it, he specifically comments on the decadence of the coffee plantations in the once-thriving region of Vale do Paraíba, in São Paulo. For Cunha, that geography encapsulates both triumph and degradation, and serves as an emblem for the country as a whole. Capela gives a clear diagnosis about the apparent contradiction:

> Faith in progress, however, did not prevent the acknowledgement that civilizational advancement, in a way that seems only at first glance to be paradoxical, almost always implies destruction. The expansion and conquest of territories, with which the very notion of advancement is materialized, sow ruins. ... The catchphrase, therefore, demands to be translated: *progress means to overthrow*, it implies damage or a material rearrangement. (ibid.: 298, emphasis added)

Faith in progress definitely belongs to both discourse and praxis attuned with the premises of the modern project. Modernity as a time frame, an ideology, an experience or a process has been for long at the heart of the West's investigations about itself. Néstor García Canclini (2005) defines the modern project as an emancipating, expansive, renovating and democratizing one. His argument considers the secularization of cultural fields, the rationalization of social life, scientific discoveries, industrial development, constant innovation and specialized knowledge as intrinsic to that fourfold project. In Latin America, however, modernity is not only linked to the history of colonialism and imperialism but also moulded by their impact, which may lead one to wonder if the subcontinent has ever truly progressed. In looking at Latin America's modern trajectory from the independence movements of the nineteenth century up to the neoliberal policies of this century, Jorge Larraín identifies specific features 'which mark a contrast with other trajectories to modernity' (2014: 33): clientelism, traditionalism, authoritarianism, masked racism and weak civil society, among others. Critical diagnoses like those have fuelled discussions about what kind of modernity that would be and how it would be reflected in nations like Brazil.

According to Aníbal Quijano (1989), there is a key difference between how Latin America comprehends time and history and how Europe and the United States do so. 'In Latin America, what in these other histories is sequence, is a simultaneity. It does not cease being a sequence. But it is preeminently a simultaneity' (ibid.: 157). That is, it would make no sense to believe in a teleological path towards progress, once unpacking the particularities of modernity in the subcontinent, as things happen simultaneously rather than sequentially. Even within Latin America, one could not talk about a cohesive modern gesture, as 'maybe different bits of Latin America – the bits may be countries, regions, sectors, or subcultures – are moving in different directions: some are getting more "modern," some more "traditional" (or "antimodern"? or postmodern?)' (Knight 2007: 93). That diverse, complex scenario is relevant in many ways, considering that it affects both sides of the centre-periphery paradigm. 'The multiple modernities perspective not only allows scope for local creativity, adaptability, and resistance to dominant modes of thinking; it also explicitly highlights the potential for *two-way interactions* between Latin America and the main centers of modernity, and the engagement between different variants of modernity as they attempt to mirror Latin America's hybrid social realities' (Whitehead 2007: 197).

It is precisely through the notion of hybridity that Canclini (2005) addresses the modern project in Latin America. He famously suggests that modernity should be seen, above all, as the result of the multitemporal heterogeneity of each nation, a sort of peculiar hybridity that enables pre-industrial and modern technology, erudite and mass cultures, and indigenous, African and European heritages to chaotically coexist. For him, 'this *multitemporal heterogeneity* of modern culture is a consequence of a history in which modernization rarely operated through the substitution of the traditional and the ancient' (ibid.: 47). Regarding the Brazilian case, his view is that, in fact, 'from Oswald de Andrade to the construction of Brasília, the struggle for modernization was a movement for critically raising a nation opposed to what the oligarchic or conservative forces and the external dominators wanted' (ibid.: 52). Complementarily, his perception is also informed by the paradox of Latin America having 'an exuberant modernism with a deficient modernization' (ibid.: 41). Canclini sees 'modernization with restricted expansion of the market, democratization for minorities, renewal of ideas but with low effectiveness in social processes' and defends that 'the disparities between modernism and modernization are useful to the dominant classes in preserving their hegemony, and at times in not having to worry about justifying it, in order simply to be dominant classes' (ibid.: 42–3).

Drawing on Canclini's influential considerations, Ângela Prysthon discusses modernity in Brazil as *peripheral modernity*, that is, a nation marked by 'an adhesion (unequal, delayed, naive, but adhesion anyway) to modernity' (2002: 26). At the same time, she also considers the risk that a general idea of hybridity could end up facilitating the construction of nationalist discourses in the Latin American context, dismissing, for instance, minority and marginalized groups. Therefore, peripheral modernity lies, she argues, in an in-between situation. At the same time that it is seduced by modern European achievements, it finds itself well rooted in a very specific cultural legacy, as Canclini (2005) himself remarks. Hence, 'the inexorable Latin American experience: to be Other and Same, simultaneously, yet unable to fully be either' (Prysthon 2002: 24). Although Brazilian modernism had São Paulo as its preferred backdrop, Rio de Janeiro was the very first city to be transformed, not just by modern urban planning, but by the modern mindset underpinning it. In other words, the then capital of Brazil proudly embodied the discourse of progress and development propagated in the first half of the twentieth century, even though it could not cope with the contradictions it entailed. After all, *Belle Époque* Rio was 'urban, sophisticated and, at the same time, *decadent*' (ibid.: 35, emphasis added).

For Nelson Brissac Peixoto (2003), the urban environment is precisely a palimpsest, a sort of archaeological site constituted by different spaces and times. It bears the mark of the new and the outdated in similar doses – and that balance is what defines it. 'Paradoxically, the permanence of these landscapes is evidenced when its next disappearance is announced. It is when its destiny is confirmed: to become ruin. The majesty of the great city is accompanied by its decrepitude' (ibid.: 274). Commenting on the advent of the modern city and in reference to Benjamin, Peixoto describes it as 'the stage of ceaseless transformations, which reveal its precariousness'. Moreover, he argues that 'ruins and construction sites look alike', as if 'death has already taken over the buildings we are building' (ibid.: 275). In this sense, again it is impossible not to think of the Lévi-Strauss-inspired lyrics of Caetano as the epitome of modern logic. I argue, however, that *Fora da Ordem* expands that logic: it does not only signpost the destructive premise of modernity but also identifies *the fresh decadence or decayed freshness* in the failed modern city from a Brazilian point of view.

Somewhat sceptical of referring to the Brazilian experience of modernity as strictly unique, Sérgio Tavolaro contends that 'dealing with contemporary

Brazil as an example of "semimodernity", "peripheral modernity", or even as a "singular case of modernity" (terms that may infer an idea of deviation) reinforces not only frozen and "essentializing" images of the Brazilian experience itself, but also of the dynamics of societies that are unequivocally located in the "center of modernity"' (2005: 18). A symptom of contemporary times, that paradigm is under constant scrutiny. 'The centers and peripheries move about, are rearticulated, and exhibit differing aspects,' Heinz Sonntag, Miguel Contreras and Javier Biardeau (2001: 244) point out. In this sense, they remind one that 'a growing number of scholars agree with the need to look for alternatives to development, to create and recreate new spaces, through the expansion and innovation of sociocultural practices which are persistent and resistant to the different colonizing mechanisms of development' (ibid.). That happens, they argue, because societies 'are living in a period in which the old formulae, such as "the future belongs to us" or "we must continue along this path," have collapsed and scientific thought is focused on complexity' (ibid.: 246). What Quijano once called 'the delusive chimera of modernity without revolution' (1989: 154) could only be overcome, therefore, with societies looking for alternatives to development in order to recover from that collapse. Already immersed in neoliberal constraints, Canclini highlights the importance of considering 'the nonsubstantialist reconstruction of a social critique and the questioning of technocratic neoliberalism's claims to become the dogma of modernity', and, more importantly, wondering 'how to be radical without being fundamentalist' (2005: 281) – something that contemporary Brazilian filmmakers seem to be aware of in their visual elaborations.

Cinematic ruins: Theoretical notes

As highlighted in the introduction, progress and destruction are necessarily intertwined in the reading of modernity from a Benjaminian perspective. Following on from that, Tim Edensor (2005) relates that sort of imbrication to the late capitalist crisis, famously materialized in the industrial ruins, for instance, of towns in Northern England and the city of Detroit in the United States. 'The production of spaces of ruination and dereliction are an inevitable result of capitalist development and the relentless search for profit' (ibid.: 4). Edensor, however, is particularly 'interested in re-evaluating industrial ruins in order to critique the negative connotations with which they are associated in official and common sense thought' (ibid.: 17), that is, before capitalism transforms them anew into something profitable. In this regard, it is not difficult to associate his critical viewpoint with the ruins of Machu Picchu, Chichen Itza and even those of downtown Havana, all turned into tourist attractions, historical areas which are now completely integrated into transnational capitalist profitability. Edensor, aware of how the capitalist system works, pursues an exploration of ruins prior to them becoming commodities in neoliberal times 'because they can't be commodified without being entirely transformed, they contrast with the spectacles of the postmodern, themed city, and can stimulate imaginative, alternative practices which bring forth alternative and critical forms of consciousness' (ibid.: 95). For Augé, when ruins 'escape the transformation of the present into spectacle, they are, like art, an invitation to experience time' (2003: 113). More significantly, 'it is incumbent on art to save what is most precious in the ruins and in the works of the past: a sense of time that is all the more provocative and moving because it cannot be reduced to history, because it is an awareness of a lack, expression of an absence, *pure desire*' (ibid.: 116, emphasis added).

The cinema, the modern artistic invention par excellence, certainly plays an important role in exploring possibilities for representation, including for ruins. As Edensor suggests, 'the representation of industrial ruins in films exposes, and is imbricated within, certain cultural assumptions about the negative qualities of contemporary cities and urban processes, particularly proffering dystopian visions of a bleak future' (2005: 35), which may lead to critiques and the development of new courses of action. Considering such a dystopian vision, one can easily identify cinematic ruins in action sequences and sci-fi landscapes as reminders of the end of the world as we know it. On the other hand, Edensor also claims that ruins can be positioned 'in a celebratory fashion, so that ruins are free from the gloomy constraints of a melancholic imagination, and can equally represent the *fecund*' (ibid.: 15, emphasis added). For instance, if ruins can serve as locations for subjects whose identities and activities are historically marginalized, they can also be depicted as sites of resistance and reclaiming. The very structure of ruins is open to interpretation, which potentially means being open to the fecund as well. Cinema, thus, can take advantage of the fact that ruins 'contain manifold unruly resources with which people can construct meaning, stories and practices' (ibid.: 62) – as put into practice by the filmmakers discussed in Parts Two, Three and Four.

With that in mind, Johannes von Moltke's (2010) contribution to cinematic ruins is central. In *Ruin Cinema*, he begins his essay by mentioning the Lumière brothers' *The Demolition of a Wall* (Démolition d'un Mur, 1896). The single-shot film shows workers demolishing a brick wall. A few moments later, the brick wall suddenly collapses. Moltke nonetheless says that the real appeal of the film was when the exhibitors ran the projector backwards to amaze the audience by the brick wall reassembling. This anecdote suggests a fascination with modernity through both the cinema, the archetypal modern medium, and the ruins, the inevitable outcome of modern (de)construction fever. As Moltke argues, 'the cinema and the ruin plough common epistemological ground: as peculiarly modern forms of grasping contingency and temporality, they activate ways of knowing the past and its relation to the present' (ibid.: 396). Evoking a Benjaminian view of the cinema spectator as a ruin traveller, Moltke compares the cinema with ruins in the sense that 'ruins represent and activate temporalities every bit as complex as those of the cinema as an indexical medium with the ability to (re)structure and reverse linear time' (ibid.: 398), as seen in the Lumière brothers' film.

By looking closely at the history of cinema, Moltke affirms that 'rather than ancient ruins or even the nostalgic ruin of romanticism, it is the quintessentially modern ruin produced by aerial bombing that holds pride of place in the ruin iconography of the cinema' (ibid.: 403). In this sense, Italian Neorealism and German Trümmerfilm, post-war cinematic movements deeply influenced not only by aerial bombings but also the whole deadly atmosphere of the time, stand as the foremost cinematic imaginary of ruination. According to Moltke, 'alongside the patent mythologization of ruins, the cinema's specific contribution to a postwar ruin aesthetic must also be sought in a more general effect of the transformation of rubble into representation' (ibid.: 405). Finally, he also recognizes the sci-fi genre as being in close dialogue with the aesthetics of ruins, as Edensor (2005) previously pointed out. 'Operating in the future anterior, the genre of science fiction projects the temporality of the ruin into the future,' explains Moltke (2010: 409). For him, sci-fi ruins can operate through a variety of approaches, such as the suspicious development of artificial intelligence, the aftermath of nuclear proliferation and even environmental damage. To a certain extent, the contamination of documentaries by aesthetic and discursive sci-fi strategies revisits that argument in Part Two.

Interestingly, André Habib's (2008) very original contribution to knowledge lies precisely in approaching ruins *in* films without disregarding the materiality of the media. After analysing the emergence of a cinematic regime of ruins (starting with post-war Italian Neorealism and German Trümmerfilm up to postmodern Jean-Luc Godard's *Germany Year 90 Nine Zero* [Allemagne Année 90 Neuf Zéro, 1991] and Wim Wenders's *Wings of Desire* [Der Himmel über Berlin, 1987]), Habib underlines the use of *decaying* film stock by artists Peter Delpeut, Bill Morrison, Angela Ricci Lucchi and Yervant Gianikian in their found footage and archive films. In creating original films out of old film fragments, those artists seem to tackle the essence of the ruin itself, as suggested by Hell and Schönle (2010): the end of something (in this case, the decaying film stock) and the beginning of something else (the brand-new narrative that emerges). Although Eurocentric, Habib's doctoral thesis *Le Temps Décomposé: Cinéma et Imaginaire de la Ruine* is a milestone in the field, as it specifically investigates the relationship between the cinema and the imagery/imaginary of ruins. While his focus is exploring film production from the post-war period to the aftermath of the fall of the Berlin Wall, Habib claims that the presence of ruins throughout the history of cinema could be divided into three broad categories to create a 'brief typology of ruin in cinema'[8] (2008: 121): travel, catastrophe and fantasy. That is, ruins are markedly present in travel films, war and period dramas, and sci-fi plots.

In his comparative study of Brazilian and Cuban artwork (cinema, painting, sculpture and literature), Barros (2013) pushes the ruin debate onto different ground, taking the particularities of the so-called Third World into account. In bringing that still underexplored relationship to the Latin American context, he addresses a sense of ruination in Brazilian cinema production, one not necessarily within Habib's brief typology. Barros chooses to shed light upon two landmark films from the 1960s, a decade in which national production saw the groundbreaking birth of Cinema Novo and Cinema Marginal. Glauber Rocha's *Entranced Earth* (Terra em Transe, 1967) and Rogério Sganzerla's *The Red Light Bandit* (O Bandido da Luz Vermelha, 1968) are put forward as cinematic attempts to visually translate the aftermath of the 1964 military coup d'état, emphasizing the underdeveloped condition of the country. For Barros, 'those are two films trying to make sense of the Third-World chaos' (ibid.: 57–8). He associates those films with the ruination of a country in crisis, drawing on Ismail Xavier's (2012) famous reading of their images as *allegories of underdevelopment*, as will be discussed in the next chapter. While this field of research is still in its early stages, two notions of ruins in the context of Brazilian cinema production seem to follow on from Barros's (2013) argument.

Denilson Lopes coined the term *poor ruins* to emphasize the role of ruins that 'are not monuments nor the master houses marked by gloomy decadence' (2016: 346). His essay is focused on Julia Murat's *Found Memories* (Histórias Que Só Existem Quando Lembradas, 2012), a fictional film about the arrival of a young photographer in a small village in Vale do Paraíba, a region historically marked by decaying coffee plantations, as mentioned earlier. Although demonstrating intimacy with narratives centred on great modern failures, some of them located in Vale do Paraíba itself, Lopes is more interested in what Murat's images of *poor ruins* have to say about the world we live in. 'Refusal of history? Certainly, refusal of great drama, great catastrophes. The focus is on the image and the image as a creator of atmosphere' (ibid.: 349). Complementarily, Prysthon's (2017) notion of *disappearing landscapes* relates to the critique of progress that this volume adresses in a more stratighforward way. Her analysis privileges films that denounce – sometimes directly, sometimes allegorically – the implications of socio-economic measures that have altered the landscapes of Northeastern Brazil, such as Gabriel Mascaro's *Defiant Brasília* (Avenida Brasília Formosa, 2010) and Kleber Mendonça Filho's *Neighbouring Sounds* (O Som Ao Redor, 2012). Prysthon acknowledges 'the production of images of transition that register the disappearance of forms of life, changes of the landscape and the ruins both of old ways of life and the novelties of predatory capitalism – that in some ways are born already obsolete' (ibid.: 16). Fascinatingly, Peixoto puts his trust in the filmmaker as someone with the means to capture and reflect on that kind of landscape: 'Lost in a world that one no longer recognizes and in a cinema whose conditions of production one does not control, the filmmaker tries once more to preserve what is ending, the images that seem to no longer exist, that have lost all sense' (1987: 191). Will the filmmaker be successful?

To a certain extent, Prysthon's (2017) view concurs with Barros's (2013) view of the process of ruination in the Third World environment. 'The Third World did not become a ruin. It was born a ruin. The Third World – as other significant phenomena of the twentieth century, especially modern warfare – contradicts the classical idea of ruins itself' (ibid.: 260), Barros concludes after discussing *Entranced Earth* and *The Red Light Bandit* alongside other Latin American artworks. His notion of *Third World ruins* exposes a contradiction that is precisely what makes the new investigation of ruins so challenging yet so fertile – one that features a 'radical potential', as Dillon (2011: 18) puts it. In this regard, the everlasting impact of the revolutionary 1960s on contemporary Brazilian cinema is crucial to investigate notions of progress and (under)development through moving images. Cinema Novo (alongside Tropicália and Cinema Marginal) was responsible for forging a certain idea of Brazilianness that resonates to this day, one that brought such controversial notions to the centre of the debate. The cinematic representation of the destructiveness of modernity figures as one of that movement's main features – something that contemporary filmmaking will recontextualize and relate to draconian neoliberal measures in the present. In the following chapter, I will discuss the contribution of Cinema Novo to establishing a sense of ruination within national production.

2

Cinema Novo: A country in crisis

Cinema Novo was not only a groundbreaking movement which challenged the discourse and the aesthetics of films being made at a specific time in history; its legacy turned out to be a paradigm, whether to be followed or deconstructed. Most importantly, Cinema Novo played a key role in questioning notions of progress and (under)development for the first time in Brazilian cinema, a critical stance that grew stronger in the wake of the election of left-wing President João Goulart in 1961. Indeed, that was a period that favoured the work of the leftist filmmakers who made up the movement – Glauber Rocha, Nelson Pereira dos Santos, Carlos Diegues, Leon Hirzsman, Joaquim Pedro de Andrade and Ruy Guerra, among others. In that same year, the episodic film *Favela X Five* (Cinco Vezes Favela, 1962), considered one of the first Cinema Novo outputs, was produced with the support of the newly formed Popular Culture Centre. Both Cinema Novo and Popular Culture Centre (under the umbrella of the socially committed Brazilian National Union of Students) were aimed at 'rethinking what popular culture was and how it could be expressed and channelled for revolutionary purposes' (Shaw and Dennison 2007: 82).

In that decade, Cinema Novo spread its iconoclastic, anti-imperialist discourse across an industry then satisfied by the popularity of the *chanchadas*[1] and the bourgeois drama of Vera Cruz,[2] cinematic reflections of a lack of political consciousness at the time. Mainly based in Rio de Janeiro, the *cinemanovistas* wanted to denounce social inequalities by shedding light upon the *favela* (the urban shantytowns) and the *sertão* (the Northeastern backlands), disregarded yet meaningful spaces where social contradictions were clearly visible. That spatial regime shift was one of their first and foremost achievements, one that provoked discussions around the representation of the people and the underdeveloped condition to which the masses were subjected. As Zuzana M. Pick claims, 'the movement asserted the creation of new expressive spaces' (1993: 190) that finally enabled those discussions to take place. Film space finally went beyond the urban paradigms of cinematic representation, challenging fixed notions of identity and forging new utopias. 'Through an oppositional notion of popular cinema, the New Latin American cinema has explored social experiences marginalized and excluded from class-based and homogeneous representation of nationhood' (ibid.: 8). With that in mind, spatial representation becomes key for *cinemanovistas* to expose and reflect upon the failures of 'a modernity based on self-confident promises of progress' (ibid.: 194) that were never kept.

Needless to say, Cinema Novo was part of a *continental project*, a major phenomenon concerning the underdeveloped condition of Latin America, as Pick famously put it with regard to the New Latin American Cinema.[3] Apart from the films produced in countries such as Argentina, Bolivia, Chile and Cuba, many filmmakers also wrote manifestos addressing that condition. In 1962, Argentinian Fernando Birri stated that the kind of cinema that the underdeveloped peoples of Latin America needed was 'a cinema which develops them', that is, 'which helps the passage from underdevelopment to development, from sub-stomach to stomach, from sub-culture to culture, from sub-happiness to happiness, from sub-life to *life*' (2014: 211). After the Cuban Revolution (1953–9), Latin American artists felt that an ideological agenda could be developed through the cinema, considering the political potential of the medium, 'a weapon against social alienation' (Pick 1993: 101). In 1969, Argentinians Fernando Solanas and Octavio Getino underlined underdevelopment itself as a hindrance to regional filmmaking: 'Some of the circumstances that delayed the use of films as a revolutionary tool until a short time ago were lack of equipment, technical difficulties, the compulsory specialization of each phase of work, and high costs' (1997: 44). Once that cinema became viable, however, it was to undertake a key double mission. 'The cinema of the revolution is at the same time one of *destruction and construction*: destruction of the image that neocolonialism has created of itself and of us, and construction of a throbbing, living reality which recaptures truth in any of its expressions' (ibid.: 46).

In terms of aesthetics, Cinema Novo set new rules for depicting reality in both fictional and nonfictional realms; moreover, it contributed to blurring the boundaries between the two domains, a key characteristic heavily explored in contemporary production. To a certain extent, this set of new rules was influenced by the post-war Italian Neorealism and French New Wave cinema. All three had in common the aim to subvert the bourgeois, classical narrative in vogue. The French New Wave, in particular, inspired *cinemanovistas* by its *politique des auteurs* developed by François Truffaut and his peers, positioning the filmmaker as the author of the film. Glauber, however, related the *politique des auteurs* to cultural politics being subjected to economic underdevelopment, shying away from authorship as no more than an aesthetic concern. 'He placed authorship at the center of an oppositional practice capable of contesting the thematics and politics of modernization and nationalization' (Pick 1993: 40). Cinema Novo had a closer relationship with Italian Neorealism, in the use of real locations and non-professional actors, strategies that, for instance, were not related to the popular *chanchadas*. Also, as Johannes von Moltke (2010) stressed, Italian Neorealism has an intrinsic link to cinematic ruination due to the context wherein it was born and the endeavour to film the ruined reality outdoors. Unsurprisingly, that stance resonates with *cinemanovistas* and their willingness to make films marked by their specific context and whose stories were shaped by the local reality, one deeply affected by economic underdevelopment and the ruinous consequences thus engendered.

Technically speaking, much of the innovative aesthetics of Cinema Novo relied on the limited conditions of the mode of production, which influenced the use of the camera and sound system, indeed, much like Italian Neorealism. In this sense, films tried to transmit the experience of specific places not only registering them but also using specific technical devices to heighten that experience in the film aesthetics. One of the best examples of that equation might be Nelson Pereira dos Santos's *Barren Lives* (Vidas Secas, 1963). Filming in the *sertão*, the director of photography Luiz Carlos Barreto innovatively opted for using no filter, so that the camera would allow the audience to witness the harsh, bright light of the region. Following the same purpose, the sound had no additional orchestral soundtrack added in post-production. Instead, the sounds captured *in loco*, like the creaking wheels of an ox cart, were used as diegetic (accompanying the image of an ox cart per se) but also as non-diegetic sound (creating an innovative soundtrack from it). Though the film uses sounds captured *in loco*, the voices in it are all dubbed. Based on Graciliano Ramos's 1938 classic novel of the same name, the film charts the story of a poverty-stricken family in the backlands of Brazil. Along with Ruy Guerra's *The Guns* (Os Fuzis, 1964) and Glauber's *Black God, White Devil* (Deus e o Diabo na Terra do Sol, 1964), they form 'the memorable trilogy of the arid northeast' (Stam and Xavier 1997: 299).

In this sense, the bleak scenarios depicting inequality and roughness in many Cinema Novo outputs were partly a thematic choice and partly the result of the precarious mode of production. That is, both the form and the content bear the marks of underdevelopment. Even though more recent re-evaluations of Third Cinema foreground its exile and diaspora topics of filmmaking, challenging fixed notions of the centre and periphery, East and West, developed and underdeveloped (Naficy 2001), the initial years of the movement were quite clear about what to target and whom to blame in the context of the 1960s. As previously mentioned, in Brazil, economist Celso Furtado's body of work is deemed a landmark in the reading of underdevelopment. Furthermore, his critical thinking gradually took account of the imbrication between the economy and culture and how that imbrication was the key for Brazil to overcome its underdeveloped condition. Later in his career, Furtado even became Minister of Culture and was involved in a series of projects to enable cultural initiatives to be carried forward. For him, 'overcoming the structural impasse that is at the root of our crisis will only be achieved if future development leads to a growing homogenization of our society and the opening up of space for the realization of the potential of our culture' (Furtado 2012: 33). Furtado's timely contribution was therefore in tune with the discourse that *cinemanovistas* were about to propagate through moving images.

The notion of underdevelopment as intrinsic not only to Cinema Novo but also to Brazilian cinema production as a whole was widely explored by Paulo Emílio Salles[4] Gomes (1996).[5] Written in 1973, 'Cinema: A Trajectory within Underdevelopment' is an essay specifically addressing underdevelopment through and within Brazilian cinema history. To achieve that, Paulo Emílio had already analysed that history in previous essays, from the arrival of the cinematograph up to the then newly emerged Cinema Novo (1896–1966) to the infrastructural limitations of Brazil. He tells of the endeavours to make films in spite of a complete lack of technical and economic support, irrespective of the international development of industrial technology. The advent of cinema, 'this fruit of the acceleration of technical and scientific progress found Brazil stagnating in underdevelopment' (ibid.: 8), as Rio de Janeiro, the then federal capital, did not even have a stable electricity supply. Also, he complains that the way Brazilians deal so carelessly with their past makes it impossible to overcome the condition of underdevelopment. 'The sloppiness about the past explains not only the abandonment of the national archives but the impossibility of creating a cinematheque' (ibid.: 7). When it comes to analysing film production per se, Paulo Emílio emphasizes the role of the cultural colonialism imposed by Hollywood films in Brazil. Because of being subjected to 'one of the laws of underdevelopment: the premature decays' (ibid.: 10), every time national production came to a halt, foreign production had the advantage to attract an audience.

In 'Cinema: A Trajectory within Underdevelopment' itself, Paulo Emílio underlines the dichotomy between the occupant and the occupied to refer to the way Brazilian society was forged. His thesis defends that it is a tension that also pervades national cinema production in what happens behind the camera and on screen. 'We are not Europeans nor North-Americans, but devoid of original culture, nothing is foreign to us, because everything is. The painful construction of ourselves unfolds in the rarefied dialectic between the non-being and being the other' (ibid.: 90). When the audience moved away from Cinema Novo films and replaced them with foreign ones, Paulo Emílio identified a concrete example of his theory. 'In reality, they find only a false compensation, a diversion that prevents them from recognizing their frustration, the first step in overcoming it' (ibid.: 110). Caught between the passivity of the bourgeois audience and the financial issues preventing production from rebounding, 'Brazilian cinema does not have the strength to escape underdevelopment' (ibid.: 111). After analysing the national cinema trajectory, he ends up paraphrasing Furtado's guidelines: 'In cinema, underdevelopment is not a phase, a stage, but a state: films from developed countries never went through that situation, whereas others tend to settle into it' (ibid.: 85). On the other hand, it was that somewhat ruinous scenario which allowed Cinema Novo to thrive in both its discourse and aesthetics, as pointed out. One could think of, for instance, Linduarte Noronha's short documentary *Aruanda* (1960), precisely 'the eloquent expression of a cinema that triumphs from underdevelopment' (Bernardet 2003: 221), in one of the very first gestures of the movement. According to Fernão Pessoa Ramos, 'there is no way one can deny that the precarious image goes hand in hand with the rough and poor reality in which the film is made' (2013: 326), referring to the technical limitations that led cinematographer Rucker Vieira to use natural light, which ended up giving the film an unusual burst of cinematography, similar to what occured to *Barren Lives*, as mentioned earlier.

Having lived in France for almost ten years split into two different occasions, it could be argued that Paulo Emílio was much under a Eurocentric influence by the time he started writing his first essays. His reading of Brazilian cinema trajectory within underdevelopment, however, seems less an inferiority complex than a desire for cultural emancipation. Carlos Augusto Calil affirms that '"Cinema: A Trajectory within Underdevelopment" (1973) is the ambitious crowning of the process of decolonization to which Paulo Emílio submitted himself' (2016: 503), since the publication of his article 'A Colonial Situation?' in 1960. For Calil, Paulo Emílio 'gives an account of the historical understanding of the colonial heritage, which submits culture because it submits the economy, and inserts cinema in the perspective of the struggle for political emancipation, combating conformism, dependence, the crossed interests between colonizers and colonized' (ibid.: 501). In addition, Ismail Xavier says that the ' "colonial situation", in short, was the expression of an already secular asymmetry, as cinema was the ground where the division between central and peripheral countries was clear. ... The emphasis that the critic gives to this situation ... is linked to his fight for a cultural life as a dialogue without hierarchies' (2016: 17). In this sense, when Paulo Emílio postulates that Brazilian cinema bears 'the cruel mark of underdevelopment' (Salles Gomes 2016a: 48), it makes one wonder if national production was ever able to fully develop and, more importantly, maintain an ongoing industry.

It is also worth noting that Paulo Emílio meditated on his trajectory as a film critic through his own writings.[6] 'I try to be understanding with much of what I read and hear about Brazilian cinema. I have great reasons to be nice: I do not know anyone as fully colonized as I was. ... I remain convinced that if I could be decolonized, then it is because that grace of liberation is available to any of us' (Salles Gomes 2016b: 493), he wrote in one of his final essays. Above all a Brazilian cinema enthusiast, Paulo Emílio became unequivocally sharp about it: 'I am convinced that "Brazilian cinema" is a subject capable of satisfying a lifetime. The viewer stimulated by the foreign product died in me and I see that this is not a personal phenomenon. The symptom is good' (Salles Gomes 2016c: 340). At the same time that he was aware of the limitations, the critic was able to see a bright side: 'Underdevelopment is tedious, but its conscience is creative' (ibid.: 341). His enthusiasm found in the creation of the Brazilian Cinematheque in São Paulo one of his best achievements. Paulo Emílio was closely involved in the foundation of the institution devoted to preserving films for future generations. Back then, neglect was already an issue. 'If the neglect of film preservation remains, the celebrations of the centenary of Brazilian cinema will certainly be disturbed by the presence of an unimaginable, squalid and accusing cinematheque' (Salles Gomes 2016b: 496).[7]

In tune with Paulo Emílio's rhetoric, the background of turmoil wherein Brazilian cinema/Cinema Novo developed was quintessentially captured by Glauber[8] in his 'Aesthetics of Hunger' manifesto, originally published in 1965. 'For the European observer, the processes of artistic creation in the underdeveloped world are of interest only insofar as they satisfy his nostalgia for primitivism; and this primitivism is ... poorly understood since it is imposed by colonial conditioning' (Rocha 2017). In forging a genuine cinematic language, the *cinemanovista* understands hunger not as a symptom but as the essence of Brazilian society, and that Cinema Novo films were able to transform social criticism into a central political issue. 'From *Aruanda* to *Vidas Secas* [*Barren Lives*], Cinema Novo narrated, described, poetized, discoursed, analyzed, aroused the themes of hunger .... What has made Cinema Novo a phenomenon of international relevance is precisely its deep engagement with the truth, its miserabilism' (ibid.). Aware of the conditions of production, that is, aware of the underdevelopment attached to Cinema Novo, he explains:

> We know – since we made these ugly, sad films, these screaming, desperate films in which reason has not always prevailed – that this hunger will not be cured by moderate government reforms, and that the cloak of technicolor cannot hide but rather aggravates its tumors. Therefore, only a culture of hunger, by undermining and destroying its own structures, can qualitatively surpass itself. The most noble cultural manifestation of hunger is violence. ... Cinema Novo, on the international level, demanded nothing; it fought the violence of its images and sounds in twenty-two international festivals.

The *ugly films* of Cinema Novo, as famously defined by the director, acknowledged the failures of Brazil as a nation, while conceiving of the urgent social revolution that their images could yield. Six years after writing 'Aesthetics of Hunger', however, he reassessed his account of the mid-1960s and stepped back from the more explicitly political discourse against underdevelopment in the 'Aesthetics of Dreaming'.[9] 'Between the internal repression and the international repercussion, I learned the best of lessons: artists must always keep their freedom above all circumstances'. His second manifesto emphasizes his Afro-Indian sensibility and defends popular culture as the people's 'language of a permanent, historical rebellion'. If his first manifesto was his 'rational comprehension of poverty', Glauber then invested in a mystical approach to combat domination. 'Dreaming is the only right that cannot be forbidden' (ibid.).

This complex debate was the main focus of film scholar Xavier (2012) when addressing the *allegories of underdevelopment* turned visible in Cinema Novo and Cinema Marginal films. His film analyses were more than a critical account of what Brazilian society was undergoing as framed by filmmakers; his work brought to the attention the motif of underdevelopment as a common thread in those films and placed it as central to an understanding of Brazil. For him, 'underdevelopment as a dramatic condition should come to the fore in films fighting the rules of spectacle and market culture, factors seen as part of a reproductive system of poverty and inequality' (ibid.: 14). In his interpretation of the political moment in which Cinema Novo came to prominence, he argues that

> the cinema discussion, when politicizing itself, assimilated the equation of poverty and social inequality as expressed in the notion of underdevelopment which, formulated in the economic sphere, assumed the principle that that was not just a new description of the distance between the poor and the rich, centre and periphery, but the elucidation of a structure to be fought. (ibid.)

Considering that *zeitgeist*, filmmakers were to elaborate on the tension between industrialization and emancipation in the wake of the 1964 military coup d'état and even more so after the Institutional Act N°5 (AI-5) issued in 1968, which suspended any constitutional guarantees to citizens – a coup within the coup. In this sense, what emerges on screen is 'a field of reflection detached from the conservative tradition, but mistrustful of progress, its organizational elements, its power structure' (ibid.: 447). In other words, films were to deny the 'heroic of development' and rather invest in the 'urban experience within the framework of underdevelopment' (ibid.: 450). According to Xavier, they do so by resorting to visual allegories, a strategy that found adepts in the arts of the 1960s and 1970s. Drawing on Walter Benjamin's defence of allegories as acknowledging the dissociation between man and nature (i.e. the human experience free from preconceived truths and open to the circumstances of an historical period), Xavier is precisely interested in exploring the fractures that that dissociation brings about. The allegorical discourse is made of gaps that not only require to be filled but that also ultimately expose the fragmentary aspect of history. History *as* catastrophe. Therefore, 'the allegorical sensibility – in the sense of fragmentary vision – has a revolutionary role: it faces a crisis masked by the bourgeois optimism of progress. (The revolutionary class is one that sees the bourgeois achievements of today as already ruins)' (ibid.: 474).

As soon as President João Goulart was ousted by the military coup, not only was the country dragged into a crisis but so were the *cinemanovistas*. As a collateral effect, the coup rendered explicit the 'contradictions embodied in the winners as progress, continuity, and the defeated as disaster, discontinuity' (ibid.: 15), as Xavier stresses. In his analysis of the *allegories of underdevelopment*, he thoroughly covers the double shift provoked by reality: the teleological crisis regarding the project of national liberation over international dependency, and the teleological crisis faced by avant-garde programs, such as Cinema Novo itself. In that scenario, films had to adjust to the new reality of the country by inventing allegories to cope with that same reality. Xavier then scrutinizes productions that brought a sense of catastrophe to the fore when unpacked, 'an allegorical place marked by an array of iniquities, inconsistencies, anomie, violence, fragmentation or constitutive incompetence' (ibid.: 17). He analyses a group of films released between 1967 and 1970 in order to identify the different forms of narrating the chaos installed, which emerged as three: the breakdown of traditional teleology marked by the installation of the military dictatorship (*Black God, White Devil, Entranced Earth, The Red Light Bandit*); the emergence of antiteleological themes, albeit with a teleological representation (*Brazil Year 2000* [Brasil Ano 2000, 1969], *Macunaíma* [1969], *Antonio das Mortes* [O

Dragão da Maldade Contra o Santo Guerreiro, 1969]); and finally the radical, antiteleological mode of representation (*Killed the Family and Went to the Movies* [Matou a Família e Foi ao Cinema, 1969], *The Angel Was Born* [O Anjo Nasceu, 1969], *Bang Bang* [1971]).

Xavier's point of departure is Glauber's[10] *Black God, White Devil*, the foremost example attempting to translate the mood of the early 1960s, framing a pre-military-coup society in which the oppressed have a vocation for freedom. The film articulates a classic teleology in the sense that the narrative embodies a utopian national project, leaving the rotten past behind and looking at a revolutionary future ('the *sertão* will turn into the sea, the sea will turn into the *sertão*'[11]). The people, represented by Manuel (Geraldo Del Rey) and Rosa (Yoná Magalhães), fight to overcome oppression and misery. The coup, of course, interrupts that utopian national liberation project. The imposed mindset shift can be first noted in the director's next film, *Entranced Earth*, when classical teleology is fractured in the face of the failure. The political crisis thus prompts a crisis in the narrative, here represented by Paulo Martins (Jardel Filho), a tormented left-wing poet. A Cinema Novo leading light, Glauber changed his approach to cinematic representation when writing 'Aesthetics of Dreaming', as noted above. Leaving the aesthetics of hunger behind, the director maximizes his allegorical, baroque strategies in *The Age of the Earth* (A Idade da Terra, 1980), his final film,[12] as I will discuss in Chapter 6.

Presumably, the allegorical take had a central role during that period due to censorship, but Xavier goes beyond that more obvious explanation. For him, 'apart from programmed schemes of communication and disguise, each work studied has an expressive dimension: it is capable of condensing a reflection, sometimes implicit, of the filmmaker in the face of the crisis' (ibid.: 31). Furthermore, each allegory 'has a specific way of articulating two temporalities: that of the historical experience narrated and that of the film itself in its internal arrangement' (ibid.: 34). In contemporary Brazilian cinema, however, criticism and creativity are not necessarily indebted to the allegorical discourse but, rather, to aesthetic experimentation. Although the will to politically intervene in society has not vanished, Xavier himself argues that that will is now pervaded by scepticism and doubt regarding the effectiveness of interventions. 'This is a problem that everyone shares, those who lived in the 60s and 70s and the filmmakers of the new generations, whose relationship with the past – as a source of inspiration or refusal – has a strong point of reference in modern cinema' (ibid.: 8), as the selected corpus in this book demonstrates.

Identifying less with traditional militancy and subsidized through unique modes of financing, present-day films resonate that tradition especially 'when the relations between aesthetics and politics, conventions and ruptures, insertion in the parameters of the cultural industry or affirmation of alternative languages are on the agenda' (ibid.: 9). For Xavier, 'the documentary, sometimes on the frontier of the essay film, has affirmed itself as a pool of creativity whose research methods drive the more dense, critical reflection about new forms of representation or question the image as representation' (ibid.: 10), as Chapter 3 will point out. In this regard, my analysis is precisely interested in that crop of films: films that relate to the 1960s and 1970s tradition – *as a source of inspiration or refusal* – and which resort to the documentary mode to render visible the ruins of Brazil. Here, I am not devoted to reading potential allegories into those films; rather, I focus my analysis on the film strategies used to render ruins visible and why present-day filmmakers aim to shed light on them as a way to articulate their critique of progress and (under)development.

Documentary impulse as revolutionary cinema

Undeniably, the nonfictional aspect of filmmaking became a central issue for many Cinema Novo/New Latin American Cinema directors, as Julianne Burton (1990) argues. Besides Italian Neorealism and French New Wave, innovations led by North American Direct Cinema and French Cinéma Vérité also affected how *cinemanovistas* addressed reality. Direct Cinema brought the fly-on-the-wall, observational mode while Cinéma Vérité introduced an interactive, participatory mode of representation, as categorized by Bill Nichols (1991). 'Socially committed filmmakers embraced documentary approaches as their primary tool in the search to discover and define the submerged, denied, devalued realities of an intricate palimpsest of cultures and castes' (Burton 1990: 6), that palimpsest being the boundaries of Latin America. 'This documentary impulse,' she insists, 'and the frequent aesthetic preference for a raw realism that replicated the compelling immediacy of certain techniques of reportage, has marked much of the fictional production throughout the region' (ibid.), similar to what Luiz Carlos Barreto, a news photographer, used in *Barren Lives*. By raw realism or critical realism, she means an attempt to frame reality by immersion into a specific environment, unlike the *chanchadas* of Atlântida or the classical cinema of Vera Cruz. Burton stresses the pioneering work of Argentinian Fernando Birri, whose Documentary School of Santa Fe famously put into action the 'documentary impulse – to record the unrecorded as it "really was" – with fictive strategies – a narrative and poetic recreation of events' (ibid.: 408), what would become a symbol of the New Latin American Cinema.

Indeed, Birri addressed documentary-making in his manifesto about cinema and underdevelopment, with the latter being the outcome of colonialism, 'both external and internal' (2014: 217). For him, 'the cinema of our countries shares the same general characteristics of this superstructure, of this kind of society, and presents us with a false image of both society and our people'. It is in this sense that the documentary mode comes to the fore in his argument as a way of engaging with reality and providing real images of it at last. 'By testifying, critically, to this reality – sub-reality, this misery – cinema refuses it. It rejects it. It denounces, judges, criticises and deconstructs it.' Of course, one should bear in mind that the documentary mode was taken as a conveyor of reality without necessarily incurring discussions about viewpoints, perspectives, subjectivity or even the concept of reality itself – something that would be seen as intrinsic to that mode in contemporary production. At the time, however, the alternative was 'a cinema which makes itself the accomplice of underdevelopment' (ibid.). In a similar vein, Solanas and Getino (1997) added weight to nonfictional strategies. 'The cinema known as documentary, with all the vastness that the concept has today, from educational films to the reconstruction of a fact or a historical event, is perhaps the main basis of revolutionary filmmaking' (ibid.: 46). To a certain degree, they had already taken account of filmmaking's capacity for *interacting* with so-called reality, as 'revolutionary cinema is not fundamentally one which illustrates, documents, or passively establishes a situation: *rather, it attempts to intervene in the situation as an element providing thrust or rectification*' (ibid.: 47) – a critical stance that realizes the documentary's power to elaborate on what is usually taken for granted.

In his analysis of the sense of ruination related to the rise of a new cinema in Latin America (especially in Brazil and Cuba), Rodrigo Lopes de Barros (2013) emphasizes the documentary mode as a pivotal point to be tackled. He understands that new cinema as 'a machine of establishment of stories that intend to be officialized', being 'the documentary the perfect weapon for that, for it is based on a presupposition that is the capture of a certain exteriority of the world' (ibid.: 29). For instance, the author mentions the use of scenes in *Entranced Earth* that were shot during the electoral campaign of José Sarney, who decades later would become president of Brazil. Those scenes were originally shown in *Maranhão 66* (1966), a short documentary directed by Glauber. In fact, his body of work salutes the documentary mode on different occasions, from *Amazonas, Amazonas* (1965), his debut short documentary, up to *Di Cavalcanti* (1977), about the death of the legendary Brazilian painter, Di Cavalcanti. For Barros, 'the new cinema, the revolutionary cinema or the cinema of the revolution, is nothing but an invasion of the documentary into fictional work' (ibid.).

With that in mind, it goes without saying that the origins of Cinema Novo already had close ties to nonfictional values, such as the use of real locations, natural light, non-professional actors and an in-depth concern with social issues. Considered the germ of the movement, Nelson Pereira dos Santos's *Rio, 40 Degrees* (Rio, 40 Graus, 1955) subverts classical fiction by incorporating nonfictional elements into its narrative, deeply influenced by Italian Neorealism. It was one of the first times[13] that a film crew had gone up into the hills of Rio de Janeiro to film a real *favela*, an achievement that has influenced Brazilian filmmaking to date. The camera follows five boys who live in the *favela* but make a living out of selling peanuts around the upper-class neighbourhood of Copacabana. In a semi-documentary style, *Rio, 40 Degrees* foregrounded the cinematic representation of ordinary people and the tension between them and the elite, which would later constitute a central point in the discourse of *cinemanovistas* (Ramos 1987a). By the end of the 1950s, two short documentaries contributed to the debate around the representation of the people. Although still in tune with classical documentary grammar via the traditional voice-over, Mário Carneiro and Paulo César Saraceni's *Arraial do Cabo* (1959), and Noronha's *Aruanda* (1960, but produced in 1959) moved away from the urban environment in the search to unveil another Brazil.

In *Arraial do Cabo*, the scene is a small fishing village whose fishing livelihood is menaced by the arrival of an industrial factory, causing human and environmental damage to the area. In *Aruanda*, the population in the Quilombo da Talhada, a former black hub of resistance during the time of slavery in the Northeastern state of Paraíba, lives in precarious conditions while the country is being rapidly industrialized in faraway urban areas. According to Jean-Claude Bernardet (2003), it was precisely in the 1950s that that sense of concern, from what he calls *critical short films*, was first aroused on screen. Both documentaries shed light upon and seem to question notions of progress and (under)development defended by both the Brazilian State and a certain Brazilian elite. Most importantly, they produce images of the people.[14] '*Aruanda* and *Arraial do Cabo* are already fully attuned to the sensitivity of the new cinema, but their narrative form is still classical' (Ramos 2013: 324). What *Rio, 40 Degrees*, *Arraial do Cabo* and *Aruanda* introduced was to be developed in subsequent documentaries produced from the 1960s onwards. The desire to frame the *other*, so that the real Brazil could be revealed; the depiction of different spatialities underlining the state of negligence affecting the people; and the assimilation of technical precariousness into aesthetics formed the basis for the new production to take over. While not specifically relying on decaying film stocks, as André Habib (2008) might have expected, the idea of precarity here suggests a cinematic domain that anticipates many of the discussions concerning the imagery/imaginary of ruins.

Nevertheless, documentary-makers would inevitably face controversy in their attempts to depict that *other*. The controversy lies in the tension caused by the fact that filmmakers were not exactly part of the *other*; on the contrary, they belonged to the middle class or even upper class, different from the people they wanted to frame. The contradiction between wanting to film the world (going out onto the streets, interviewing the people, being open at random) and, at the same time, wanting to voice their concerns as filmmakers (the use of the didactic voice-over) characterized what Bernardet (2003) famously defined as a *sociological model* of documentary. According to him, documentary-makers resorted to individual interviews making general statements about a given topic, as if a personal opinion could stand as official discourse. Therefore, 'cinematic images of the people cannot be considered their expression, but the manifestation of the relationship between filmmakers and the people in those films' (ibid.: 9), as Bernardet affirms. Even though that model went through changes and ruptures throughout the 1960s and 1970s, Bernardet argues that the so-called *other* would still be the *other* until the day when he/she truly takes ownership of the means of production to interpret the failures of underdevelopment and other matters.

In effect, Bernardet's criticism of Cinema Novo's middle-class stance is well known and materialized in his famous analysis of the character, Antonio das Mortes, in *Black God, White Devil* and *Antonio das Mortes*. Antonio das Mortes represents the *bad conscience* of the middle class, that is, the *bad conscience* of Glauber and, in the end, of all leftist, progressive intellectuals at that time – including Bernardet himself. Antonio das Mortes is a contradiction (he is *for* the people but not *of* the people) which reveals what Bernardet deemed to be an illusion: 'Brazilian cinema is not a popular cinema; it is a cinema of the middle class that searches for its political, social, cultural and cinematic way' (2007: 184). Ultimately, Bernardet, then a young film critic and scholar, audaciously reflects on those films in the heat of the moment, wondering what sort of cinema it was that only had white middle-class men, a 'cinema without tradition and born in an underdeveloped country', and where it was heading to, now that words like 'imperialism' and 'nationalism' were in vogue. 'What directions does it take? What forms does it create? What reality does it focus on?' (ibid.: 35). It seems those remain open questions.

Branching to Tropicália and Cinema Marginal

Cinema Novo, however, was not the only cultural movement that erupted in modern Brazil to tackle the country's contradictions. Xavier (2012) looks at Cinema Novo as a phenomenon in consonance with the emergence of Tropicália in the 1960s. Tropicália, also known as Tropicalismo, was a trailblazing artistic movement aimed at mixing traditional elements from national culture and foreign influences. Therefore, discussions focused on the highbrow and the lowbrow, the avant-garde and the kitsch, the folklore and the pop. Tropicália was the symbol of a newly urbanized Brazil, the rise of mass culture and the participation of youngsters in the arts and politics, as I will address in Chapter 9. This cultural uprising was greatly inspired by modernist writer Oswald de Andrade's 'Cannibalist Manifesto' (Manifesto Antropófago), dating back to 1928. For Andrade, cultural anthropophagy was the only possible answer to external domination. In the 1960s, tropicalist music, for instance, renewed Andrade's desire to mobilize foreign elements in favour of a genuine national manifestation. The lyrics of Caetano Veloso, Tropicália's leading man, were modern and subversive. Simultaneously, they managed to respect national tradition and propose a new sound. Most importantly, Tropicália, along with Cinema Novo, was aware of the crossroads at which Brazil was standing: the modernization of the country resulting in no political liberation and no social improvements.

Arguably, Cinema Marginal,[15] the underground or experimental cinema movement which responded to Cinema Novo's self-congratulatory revolutionary stamina with mockery and humour, could get even closer to the tropicalist imagery through films like Rogério Sganzerla's *The Red Light Bandit*, a postmodern, suicidal house burglar who challenges both morality and conservatism. As a sort of branch of Cinema Novo, Cinema Marginal relied on what became known as the *aesthetics of garbage*. Apart from Sganzerla, Júlio Bressane, Neville D'Almeida and Andrea Tonacci, to name but a few, represented a sort of cinematic counterculture at a time when some Rio-based *cinemanovistas* were aiming to make concessions to reach a wider audience. Cinema Marginal radicalized Cinema Novo's endeavour to create an imagery for Brazil; filmmakers addressed prostitution, promiscuity, alternative lifestyles and drug abuse in their films. Mainly based in downtown São Paulo, in a rundown area called Boca do Lixo (literally, Mouth of Garbage), the movement assimilated national *chanchadas* and Hollywood references into its aesthetics in order to play out the crisis. It is no coincidence that Xavier's (2012) examples of antiteleological films, in both form and content, are Bressane's *The Angel Was Born* and *Killed the Family and Went to the Movies*, and Tonacci's *Bang Bang*. If Cinema Novo had already turned 'scarcity into a signifier' (Stam and Xavier 1997: 303), Cinema Marginal bolstered 'an approach in which garbage provides the emblem of the social world portrayed and the key to the film's discursive procedures: the chaotic piling up of residue and detritus' (ibid.: 305).

Taking account of Cinema Novo and its ramifications can never be a simple task. As I have briefly demonstrated, the movement prompted discussions on a wide range of topics that have ended up inventing what Brazilian cinema would become known for. The wish to be part of a continental project; the need to incite a social revolution through moving images; the blurring of boundaries between fictional and nonfictional narratives; the urgency to expose the Brazilian reality on screen; the framing of the people as a means of embodying the nation; all were topics taken up by filmmakers making use of different aesthetic strategies. My understanding is that the articulation of controversial notions of progress and (under)development underpins such concerns. First, it permeates discussions relating to the extra-diegetic domain (the political aims of the movement, the pursued raise of awareness, the ideological battle, etc.); and second, it fulfils the diegetic space as well (from the themes underpinning the narrative to the technical limitations rendered visible on screen). I argue that it is precisely that articulation that set the ground for an imagery/imaginary of ruins to emerge, taking into account the aesthetics of hunger and garbage, dialoguing with Italian Neorealism and the anti-imperialist New Latin American Cinema revolution.

As a movement, Cinema Novo had dissolved by the mid-1970s. According to Randal Johnson and Robert Stam, apart from a preparatory period from 1954 to 1960, Cinema Novo can be divided into three main phases: 'a first phase going from 1960 to 1964, the date of the first coup d'état; from 1964 to 1968, the date of the second coup-within-the-coup; and from 1968 to 1972' (1982: 31–2). Filmmakers, however, carried on with their work as individuals. Likewise, Tropicália and Cinema Marginal did not last long. As 'premature decays' (Salles Gomes 1996: 10), to draw on Paulo Emílio, they collapsed in the face of the military dictatorship and the retraction of the cultural industry. Unlike any other cinematic movement in Brazil, however, Cinema Novo was successful in encapsulating the social inequality and political alienation that underpinned the underdeveloped condition of the country at the time. Those films were critical in depicting the growing tension that Xavier (2012) referred to as a sense of catastrophe and, more recently, Barros (2013) read as a sense of ruination, when shedding light on two of the flagship films of the 1960s. By the end of the 1980s, the economic crisis, foreign competition and corruption scandals deeply affected cinematic production. It took some time before filmmakers, producers and distributors were able to reset the industry and resume their duties, not until the mid-1990s. The legacy of Cinema Novo inevitably returned to the fore, with new filmmakers attempting to come to terms with the nation.

3

Documentary in the wake of Cinema da Retomada

The rebirth or revival of Brazilian cinema production during the 1990s is commonly known as Cinema da Retomada. At the same time it emerged in a radically different historical context from that of the recent past, its production mode, growing assimilation of technology and openness to the international market would resonate in the near future, enabling the consolidation of present-day filmmaking. Considered a decade of extremes, the 1990s started with the shutdown of Embrafilme[1] (Brazilian Film Company) in 1990 and witnessed a growing number of films being released from 1995 onwards due to new investment and funding policies. The impact of Embrafilme being dismantled was truly a milestone in the industry, as the State-body company had been successfully responsible for production and distribution nationwide since 1969. According to Lisa Shaw and Stephanie Dennison (2007), its importance was due to generous financial support, exhibition quotas, market reserves and effective film distribution. However, drowning in bribery scandals, weakened credibility and not in tune with the neoliberal plans of the time, the company was swallowed by foreign capital speculation and an internal economic recession that strongly affected its marketing performance. In 1990, the then president, Fernando Collor de Mello (1990–2), decided to close it down, freezing production completely.

Documentaries, however, did not suffer as much as feature films in terms of having their production interrupted. As Jean-Claude Bernardet (2003) pointed out, from the 1960s to the 1980s (i.e. including the Embrafilme period), documentary films were mainly short documentaries, therefore they took up less space in the industry and had less impact on the economy. During the heyday of Embrafilme in the 1970s, there was also a lot of competition among filmmakers, producers and distributors, all trying to benefit from the company's funding politics, which overshadowed documentary projects. Despite that, Tunico Amancio (2000) underlines two important measures that helped documentary production to carry under those circumstances: the foundation of the Brazilian Documentarist Association (Associação Brasileira de Documentaristas) in 1973, pushing for exhibitors to safeguard the showing of short films (including nonfictional ones) before every feature-film session, and the creation of the Brazilian Cinema Foundation (Fundação do Cinema Brasileiro) in 1988, emphasizing the cultural side of cinematic activities, thus taking into account short documentaries. Even if off the radar, these were strategies that managed to keep production alive.

Considered a 'minor genre' throughout the 1980s, documentary was mostly produced in video format at that time. In order to survive, it actually 'remained strongly attached to social movements which emerged or regained ground with the redemocratization of the country, but with few showings outside festivals, associations, Unions and communitarian TV networks', as Consuelo Lins and Cláudia Mesquita (2011: 11) argue. Many of the young documentary-makers also found themselves devoted to video art activities, which expanded the field of documentary into the visual arts domain. Lins and Mesquita argue that such documentaries 'renew themselves from strategies extracted from contemporary art and provide other ways to relate to moving images, redefining temporality, space, narrative and imposing modifications to the interaction with the viewer' (ibid.: 58). What Lins and Mesquita call the 'experimentalist impetus' (ibid.: 67) then became an important crop of documentary films produced from early 2000s onwards, such as Marília Rocha's *Cattle Callers* (Aboio, 2005), Clarissa Campolina and Helvécio Marins Jr.'s *Passage* (Trecho, 2006), and Cao Guimarães's *Two Way Street* (Rua de Mão Dupla, 2004) and *Drifter* (Andarilho, 2006) – the last two exhibited at the traditional São Paulo Art Biennial. 'Documentary cinema finds itself expanded by experimental video, video art, genre films, confronted with its limits' (França 2006: 50). Equally important, 'video artists also sought a dialogue with the cinema of the 1960s; a cinema that, both in the field of documentary and of fiction, began a whole new problematization about images of the world' (ibid.), as I demonstrated in the previous chapter. It is no coincidence that the majority of documentaries analysed in Parts Two and Three can be considered experimental or hybrid documentaries in dialogue with the visual arts and Cinema Novo/Cinema Marginal/Tropicália values.

After the collapse of the industry, the context that allowed Brazilian fictional film production to recover consequently provided the tools for documentary to develop as well. In terms of policy strategy and implementation, the advent of new laws to reverse the cinematic chaos had a much more positive effect on documentary production than Embrafilme ever had. For instance, the passing of the Rouanet Law (Lei Rouanet) and the Audiovisual Law (Lei do Audiovisual) in 1991 and 1993, respectively.[2] Likewise, since 2001, the National Film Agency (Agência Nacional do Cinema, known as Ancine) has been regulating, supervising and reporting on feature films and documentaries in equal measure. To a certain degree, the first two decades of the new millennium consolidated those public policies, which made many believe that Brazilian cinema's trajectory within underdevelopment (Salles Gomes 1996) would come to an end.

According to Ancine (2017), 430 Brazilian documentaries were released between 1995 and 2015. Moreover, the graphs show that production had been steadily increasing throughout the period. In 1995, for instance, only three documentaries were released in cinema theatres, whereas in 2015, the number went up to fifty. If during the Embrafilme age documentaries were mainly of short and medium length, Cinema da Retomada documentaries are longer and finally reach commercial cinema theatres.[3] Conscious of this singular moment in history, critics and academics then started to refer to that period as a time for resuming cinema production – hence the term *Retomada* is appropriate, as it refers to the renaissance of Brazilian cinema.[4] In parallel with the political context, the advent of new technology played a crucial part in providing the necessary means for documentary-makers to carry on experimenting. Digital equipment had technical, economic and aesthetic advantages over analogue, enabling established filmmakers and the younger generation to invest in documentary filmmaking at a relatively low cost. Apart from the available federal funding policies, independent documentary-makers were now also able to make films without the financial support of major investors. A landmark example is the work done by director Marcelo Masagão in *Here We Are, Waiting for You* (Nós que Aqui Estamos por Vós Esperamos, 1999), a documentary whose archival material editing was done by the director himself using Windows in his personal computer.

Until 1999, at É Tudo Verdade (It's All Truth), Brazil's first and foremost documentary film festival since 1996, only documentaries shot on film were exhibited. In 1999, digital documentaries could be submitted, and 130 documentaries applied, in comparison with an average of 15 documentaries in previous editions, as Lins and Mesquita (2011) point out. Apart from É Tudo Verdade, many other documentary film festivals were founded in the wake of Cinema da Retomada, such as forumdoc.bh (1997), CineDocumenta (2003) and CachoeiraDoc (2010). Most importantly, these events helped to deepen the discussion about the limits of documentary-making, the prominence of ethnographic films and the assimilation of visual arts into film practice. As an outcome of digital technology, the industry also acquired greater diversity in terms of modes of production and geographical localities outside Rio and São Paulo. Following on from that, an important factor to be taken into account is the consolidation of alternative programs willing not only to boost documentary production but also to democratize it (Lins and Mesquita 2011). DOCTV, for instance, is a governmental scheme linked to the former Ministry of Culture whose goal is to select documentary proposals to be produced and exhibited on public TV channels. Apart from supporting independent documentary-makers, the initiative covers the twenty-seven federative units of Brazil, which means production is not restricted to big cities. Revelando os Brasis strikes a similar note; it is a cultural project developed by a non-governmental organization (NGO), Instituto Marlin Azul, which used to be sponsored by Petrobras and supported by the Ministry of Culture as well. In this case, any Brazilian over eighteen years old living in a municipality of up to twenty thousand inhabitants is entitled to submit a film proposal. Those who are selected take part in filmmaking workshops and actually shoot in their hometowns. The final cut is exhibited in many Brazilian cities, plus on TV. In sum, such projects attempted to decentralize investment and ensure that documentary production can be seen by viewers in other parts of the country. The implementation of similar programmes was halted after the election of President Jair Bolsonaro, fiercely against cultural initiatives. The Ministry of Culture, for instance, was shut down as soon as he took the office in 2019.

In this sense, it is impossible not to highlight the work done by Vídeo nas Aldeias (VNA), an NGO aimed at supporting the indigenous fight for rights and providing filmmaking workshops in indigenous villages in Brazil. As will be discussed in Part Four, VNA members use the documentary as a political tool to reclaim indigenous territories under threat. At the same time, it enables indigenous people to become professional filmmakers and eventually fill the gap where indigenous self-representation in Brazilian documentaries was lacking. Those are initiatives that 'point to other roles for the documentary today: a place of production of "minimal" images, making self-representation films, affirmation of the diversity of experiences, identities and languages' (ibid.: 13). Similar projects can be found in postcolonial nations like Mexico, Bolivia, Colombia and Ecuador, especially because the 'indigenous media contest a process of colonial subalternization that has denied indigenous communities participation in the dominant discourses and practices that have shaped Latin American societies', as Freya Schiwy (2009: 9) puts it. The incorporation of diverse voices, historically left aside, into the cinematic production is certainly one of the most relevant characteristics of the post-Retomada crop of films – the indigenous case being under the spotlight here.

Considering a broader angle, Lúcia Nagib (2007) finds a way to relate the very emergence of Cinema da Retomada to the global picture. Nagib points out that the fall of the Berlin Wall in 1989 put an end not only to the socialist utopia but also to cinema as we knew it. In the new context, cinema production came to be identified with nostalgia, citation, parody and simulacra (Jameson 1991). Interestingly, she mentions Jean-Luc Godard's *Germany Year 90 Nine Zero* (1991), a postmodern film referencing Roberto Rossellini's *Germany Year Zero* (Germania Anno Zero, 1948) and evoking 'the ruins of narrative and the death of cinema itself' (Nagib 2007: xvii). The timely link between the ruins of the Berlin Wall and those of the Second World War depicted by Italian Neorealism hint at the ground zero in which both society and cinema found themselves. 'In Brazil, 1990 was cinema's real year zero. It saw the sudden closure of Embrafilme, the state film company, by the newly elected President, Fernando Collor de Mello, which brought film production to a halt for the following two years' (ibid.: xvii–xviii), as discussed. When President Fernando Henrique Cardoso (1995–2002) took over, Nagib remarks that filmmakers were successful in catching a glimpse of a belief in Brazil as a viable nation, a sense brought about by the economic improvements that had been lost since the initial years of Cinema Novo. Most importantly, however, she states that 'this new utopia never attained full development, subjected as it was to another realistic tendency which pointed to the continuation of the country's historical problems' (ibid.: xix).

Proposed by Cinema Novo, the utopian gesture towards social revolution depicted in Glauber Rocha's *Black God, White Devil* turned out to be a hopeless plan, as pointed out in the previous chapter. Therefore, not only did the *sertão* not turn into the sea, but people also would not triumph over underdevelopment any time soon. Hence, filmmakers from the mid-1990s onwards had to make sense of the country by reflecting on the failures of the nation once dreamed of by Cinema Novo. At this time, unlike *cinemanovistas*, filmmakers were not united in support of a political-cultural project standing up to socio-economic issues. There was no cohesive movement or any agenda to be followed. In fact, many had to deal with the very erosion of the potential of any such project while attempting to come to terms with the nation. In this regard, I draw attention to Fernão Pessoa Ramos's argument about the depiction of the new Brazil, a country constituted by what he calls a 'statute of incompetence' (2003: 66). According to him, filmmakers would turn against the country itself, depicting it as incapable of rising above profound historical problems. As a consequence, 'the constant demonstration of incompetence exacerbates the feeling of chaos' (ibid.) – and to a certain extent, it turns out that new Brazil is the same as old Brazil. Indeed, even if progressing in terms of audiovisual policies under Fernando Henrique Cardoso's (1995–2002), Luiz Inácio Lula da Silva's (2003–10) and Dilma Rousseff's (2011–16) presidential mandates, historical problems were not sorted once and for all. Under Michel Temer's (2016–18) government and especially with the election of Jair Bolsonaro, the scenario went downhill. Not only were audiovisual policies suspended but historical problems also worsened, adding new contours to Paulo Emílio Salles Gomes's interpretation of Brazilian cinema's hindrances (1996).

The contemporary documentary within the *unviable nation*

As mentioned above, present-day filmmaking directly results from the favourable setup of Cinema da Retomada, hence the relevance of unpacking it.

Although part of a post-Retomada corpus, the documentaries under analysis carry forward the effervescence of the nonfiction realm – developing and including new issues to be tackled. Ramos's critical standpoint detects the shift from the utopian yet failed desire of *cinemanovistas* to the corrupt and fragmented society depicted by a new generation of filmmakers. If 'to betray or not to betray the people is a dilemma that appears constantly in Brazilian films of the 1960s', it could be said that 'the 1990s, however, provide no fuel for the existential-political tragedy. Political action with the power to transform no longer appears on the horizon, giving way instead to the sordid and the incompetent'. This scenario led Ramos to coin the term *unviable nation* to encapsulate the impossibility of Brazil overcoming its historical problems, something that gave filmmakers room to explore these chronic issues as 'narcissism turned inside out' (ibid.: 67). Instead of a clear enemy, the author claims that 'the true villain has now become the nation as a whole, without further distinctions being made' (ibid.: 66). Rendered visible on screen, this institutional crisis stretches from the police department to the public health service, proving that Brazil has neither met Cinema Novo's expectations for revolution nor designed a new project to make it viable.

Films like *Central Station* (Central do Brasil, 1998), *Midnight* (O Primeiro Dia, 1999) and *Chronically Unfeasible* (Cronicamente Inviável, 1999) present the State as shredded, sordid and corrupt, as if confirming 'the unviability of the nation by showing up its incompetence' (ibid.: 72). Recycling Bernardet's (2007) pioneering discussion on the class tension between the middle-class *cinemanovistas* and those whom they filmed, Ramos (2003) makes use of his term *bad conscience* when investigating the representation of the populace. 'As a rule, it is made up of low self-esteem born of a feeling of responsibility for the terrible living conditions endured by the country's poor (identified as the "popular" section of society) who lend their voices to the middle-class filmmaker' (ibid.: 66). Ramos contends this is still the case, as the so-called populace has never actually owned the means of production to speak for themselves. In accordance with Ramos's viewpoint, I would argue that Brazilian cinema, in some measure, portrays the unfeasibility of actual development to take place, as if the country had become rather attached to a chronic condition.

Regarding the documentary, both the notion of the *unviable nation* and the tension attached to the *bad conscience* seem to echo in what Ramos calls the figure of 'the criminalized populace' (2013: 207). A cinematic concern since Cinema Novo, the representation of the people becomes increasingly linked to violence and misery in the most acclaimed documentaries: João Moreira Salles and Kátia Lund's *News from a Private War* (Notícias de uma Guerra Particular, 1999), José Padilha's *Bus 174* (Ônibus 174, 2002) and Paulo Sacramento's *The Prisoner of the Iron Bars* (O Prisioneiro da Grade de Ferro, 2003), productions that emphasize the feeling of chaos pointed out earlier by Ramos. In his definition, *the criminalized populace* is not just a matter of describing social types for (poor) people; it includes the spaces which those people occupy, namely *favelas* and prisons in the above examples. Needless to say, the attempt to seize a given reality links to Cinema Novo on different levels, establishing 'a form of dialogue that happens to be an update, at the beginning of the 21st century, of the acute existential exasperations with the relationship with the people that moved our main directors in the 1960s' (Ramos 2003: 246). This inescapable update is the backdrop from which contemporary production can arise. More specifically, what can documentaries do to direct the nation's attention towards itself in a precise yet creative fashion?

In this sense, the impetus for coping with national reality not only refers back to Cinema Novo but also experiments with the new possibilities available to frame the tangible world. Documentary thus found ground to flourish as a means of finding a reality and reflecting on its visual elaboration. In contemporary Brazilian cinema, Shaw and Dennison (2007) interestingly point out that many fiction films resort to documentary strategies, whereas many nonfiction films incorporate techniques associated with fictional narratives. Even though the dialogue between fiction and nonfiction films has been a constant in Brazilian cinema history (here one could refer to Cinema Novo again), Amir Labaki is aware that the 'boundaries between genres became even more permeable. In some cases, documentary and fiction are found in the same film, even, albeit rarely, in the same scene' (2003: 98). He claims that 'there are fewer certainties, fixed models and definitive explanations', so 'the challenge is no longer to give right answers but to present new questions' (ibid.: 104). Writing at the threshold of the 2000s, Labaki believes that, after having already expanded its thematic diversity, the documentary was then positioned to explore its stylistic diversity in the following years, confronting 'the challenge of reinvigorating itself as an aesthetic principle' (ibid.: 99).

Indeed, contemporary Brazilian documentary-makers have been exploring different ways of registering reality, as 'their films are aesthetically challenging, their methods are unorthodox, and their understanding of their contexts is multifaceted' (Navarro and Rodríguez 2014: 4). Formal innovation, personal filmmaking and self-reflexive strategies have allowed the documentary to problematize its own practice, opening up a discussion about documentary 'cinema's capacity for delivering such social diagnosis' (Andermann and Fernández-Bravo 2013: 2). For Cezar Migliorin, 'the place of documentary is that of undefinition' (2010: 9), that is, it should be understood precisely as 'the search for a way to approach the world' (ibid.: 10). In this regard, Eduardo Coutinho's *Playing* (Jogo de Cena, 2007) might stand at the forefront of that thought-provoking branch. In it, the director invites women (famous actresses, non-famous actresses and non-actresses) to tell their intimate stories to the camera. Challenging ideas of truth and authenticity, the documentary mixes up their statements to the point that the spectator is not capable of distinguishing which one is actually acting. One could also think of João Moreira Salles's *Santiago* (2007) and Petra Costa's *Elena* (2012), highly subjective documentaries centred on the directors' personal relationships with Salles's aristocratic family's butler and Costa's sister who committed suicide at a young age, respectively. Other documentaries, such as Sandra Kogut's *A Hungarian Passport* (Um Passaporte Húngaro, 2001), Kiko Goifman's *33* (2002), Marcelo Pedroso's *Pacific* (2009) and Gabriel Mascaro's *Housemaids* (Doméstica, 2012), also invest in formal innovation, personal filmmaking and self-reflexive strategies to deliver original perspectives of the world.

Common-sense audience has generally related to documentary *sensu stricto*, though. Mainly taken as impartial and devoted to explaining the facts, there is a set of tenets usually associated with regular, traditional or conventional documentaries. For Bill Nichols, 'the use of a voice-of-God commentary, interviews, location sound recording, cutaways from a given scene to provide images that illustrate or complicate stated points, and a reliance on social actors, or people, who present themselves in their everyday roles and activities, are among the conventions common to many documentaries' (2010: 21). Albeit there being a growing sense of experimentalism in nonfiction production, it is quite revealing that 'this genre still shares a tradition of sobriety in its determination to make a difference in how we regard the world and proceed within it' (ibid.: 38). In her analysis of documentary's principles, Patricia Aufderheide (2007) hints at what underpins the nonfiction structure. 'All documentary conventions – that is, habits or clichés in the formal choices of expression – arise from the need to convince viewers of the authenticity of what they are being told. For instance, experts vouch for the truthfulness of analysis; dignified male narrators signify authority for many viewers; classical music connotes seriousness' (ibid.: 33). In critically dealing with those principles, she explains that if, on the one hand, conventions 'work well to command attention, facilitate storytelling, and share a maker's perspective with audiences', on the other hand, they can 'disguise the assumptions that makers bring to the project, and make the presentation of the particular facts and scenes seem both inevitable and complete' (ibid.: 34).

Therefore, it is not so surprising that many invoke TV reportage and news broadcasting as examples of documentary-making. Dave Saunders (2010) will point out that their goals, however, are not quite the same. 'The news – influenced though its slant has often been by network ratings chasing, ideological concerns and corporate pressure – should *ideally* maintain an aloof position outside the sphere of partial political or social activism', whereas documentary film 'acceptably may walk a fine line between polemic and propaganda, machinate to make the everyday dramatic, accentuate, amplify, distil, and render poetic the unspeakable' (ibid.: 17–18). In terms of rendering poetic the unspeakable, Aufderheide observes that in the occasions where 'the market pressures of attracting audiences have led many filmmakers to employ familiar conventions, artists working outside the film and video marketplaces have sought to go beyond them. They are frontline innovators and experimenters' (2007: 35–6). As a consequence, those kinds of 'experiments have greatly expanded the repertoire of formal approaches for documentary filmmakers. At the same time, these experiments provide a sharp contrast to the most common conventions, those usually used in broadcast television' (ibid.: 39). It is precisely the conflation of conventional documentary-makers and frontline innovators that creates this enriching lineage. After all a 'fuzzy genre' (Chanan 2007: vi), by now one should be familiar with the fact that the documentary 'is not the simple reflection of reality, but an act of reflection upon it' (ibid.: 196).

In this sense, Migliorin (2010) argues for a documentary that unveils stories in an uncertain, fluid way, ready to invent a new space and time. 'In these aesthetic inventions lies the documentary as a political force that claims neither the indignation of the spectator nor guilt, but participation' (ibid.: 24–5), a step further in relation to Ramos's diagnosis. As Stella Bruzzi points out, what has come up in contemporary production is precisely an update of the definition of authenticity, 'one that eschews the traditional adherence to observation or to a Bazinian notion of transparency of film and replaces this with a multi-layered, performative exchange between subjects, film-makers/apparatus and spectators' (2006: 10). Alternatively, Erika Balsom and Hila Peleg remind us that the documentary, traditionally, 'has always been one of uncertainty, contamination, and contestation' (2016: 18), as its definition is not something set in stone. Nichols seems to agree with them and reiterates that 'the established story of documentary's beginnings continues to perpetuate a false division between the avant-garde and documentary that obscures their necessary proximity' (2001: 581). For him, in fact, 'documentary, like avant-garde film, cast the familiar in a new light' (ibid.: 583). Throughout the 1920s, for instance, the poetic experimentation in cinema played a central part in the consolidation of the documentary voice, as seen in Walter Ruttmann's *Berlin: Symphony of a Great City* (1927) and Dziga Vertov's *The Man with a Movie Camera* (1929). 'It was within the avant-garde that the sense of a distinct point of view or voice took shape' (Nichols 2010: 129). Moreover, in assimilating that influence, the 'indexical images of a recognizable world quickly veered in directions other than fidelity to the object and realism as a style' (ibid.).

At the same time that the dispute over what is *real* has shaken 'the viewer's belief in the images of the world' (Lins and Mesquita 2011: 69), it permitted other angles and perspectives to arise and contaminate the viewer's perception of reality. Gustavo Procopio Furtado suggests 'that the documentary's relative marginality and the resulting fact that it is not entirely bound by market logic offers it a degree of freedom to experiment with forms, dramaturgies, topics, temporalities, and modes of production sharply distinct from the mainstream' (2019: 3). As part of a *post-industrial cinema*, as Migliorin (2011) puts it, contemporary documentaries no longer follow the industrial capitalist logic centred on market profits and multiplex exhibition circuits. Rather, these new films (experimental, hybrid and blurred films) subvert the Fordist logic by relying on independent modes of production, collaborative projects, festival recognition and online exhibitions – strategies that indeed gave new contours to national production. Dellani Lima and Marcelo Ikeda (2011) coined the term *garage cinema* to refer to the innovative group of films emerging in the first decade of the new century. Bluntly put, the term encompasses not only low-budget films, as it might seem, but also films aimed at suggesting new aesthetics, ethics and politics concerning imagery and life. Most importantly, these are films questioning the world while inventing 'another way of being in the world, of connecting with the world from the audiovisual field' (Ikeda 2014: 12). Their goal, I would suggest: making the *unviable nation* – sooner or later, somehow, finally – viable.

Documentaries produced in Brazil find much of their power in this new ground that has been cultivated from the creative treatment of reality in experimental nonfiction films to the politicized pro-indigenous output. According to Ismail Xavier (2012), many of the concerns that shaped Cinema Novo as a daring movement were bequeathed to contemporary documentary production. In this sense, that heritage is underlined when the intended dialogue between Cinema Novo films and present-day documentaries takes place in this monograph – the mixture of fiction and nonfiction outputs as a clear evidence of its complexity. Regardless of contextual differences, Xavier believes that 'each one, interrogating its own condition in culture and politics, restores concerns about the status of art and the intellectual in this violent and fractured society, whether in the period of military government or in the current coalition presidency'. He contends that it is 'on the boundary between the documentary and the essay film that today's experience connects in a special way with the discussion in question' (ibid.: 27), one interested in scrutinizing reality through its disputes and ambiguities. It is via the documentary mode that contemporary production questions the conventional representation of reality and, consequently, our perception of the world.

For Nichols (2010), when it comes to documentary, there would be actually six modes available – not necessarily mutually excluded. His categorization is widely known in film studies and has been extensively referred to in academic works focused on investigating the genealogy of documentary, which is not particularly the case here. Considering the expository, observational, participatory, reflexive, poetic and performative modes of documenting reality, it is reasonably easy to infer that the former might allude to a more conventional style, whereas the latter may even blur the boundaries with the essay film. In his passionate defence of the essay film, Timothy Corrigan says that a lot of 'recent labels attempt, for instance, to recover the essay film in categories such as "meta-documentaries," "reflexive documentaries," or "personal or subjective documentaries." None of these, however, strikes me as entirely adequate (although Bill Nichols's notion of performative documentary suggestively intersects with some of the central features of my argument)' (2011: 5) – and that is because Nichols believes that the 'world as represented by performative documentaries becomes, however, suffused by evocative tones and expressive shadings that constantly remind us that the world is more than the sum of the visible evidence we derive from it' (2010: 206). For Corrigan, 'the essay film suggests an appropriation of certain avant-garde and documentary practices in a way different from the early historical practices of both, just as it tends to invert and restructure the relations between the essayistic and narrative to subsume narrative within that public expression' (2011: 51). In 'using the camera as a pen', as suggested by Laura Rascaroli (2017: 4), the essay film could be seen as a 'freer form of documentary' (ibid.: 3), 'a new type of documentary' or 'one of the liveliest expressions of international documentary filmmaking, one in constant growth and expansion' (ibid.: 4), according to the author. A self-reflective type of cinema, Alan Resnais's *Night and Fog* (Nuit et Brouillard, 1955), Chris Marker's *Letter from Siberia* (Lettre de Sibérie, 1957) and Agnès Varda's *Diary of a Pregnant Woman* (L'Opéra-mouffe, 1958) are usually cited as classic examples. Rascaroli even mentions Fernando Solanas and Octavio Getino's *The Hour of the Furnaces* (La Hora de los Hornos, 1968), which signals the dispute over the definition of essay film and/or documentary. Many of the films under analysis in this book, for instance, could be deemed experimental documentaries or even essayistic documentaries – the case of Ana Vaz's *The Age of Stone* and Luisa Marques's *Tropical Curse*.

The essay film points to an intimate dialogue between fictional and nonfictional elements, something that has become key in contemporary culture regardless of how one wants to name it. Balsom affirms that 'fiction and documentary, modalities previously problematized in artists' employments of the moving image, have become central to artistic production since the widespread embrace of video projection in the early 1990s' (2013: 24), just as Lins and Mesquita (2011) have argued considering the Brazilian context. Curiously, Balsom stresses a two-sided phenomenon in present-day audiovisual production. 'Fictional practices have emerged that explore the new possibilities for storytelling afforded by the multiple projection environments of the gallery space, while a whole host of critical and curatorial projects have explored what has been called the "documentary turn" of contemporary art' (2013: 157). Most importantly, we 'must attend to the documentary image with the attention that it demands, seeing in it neither the truth of the event nor a simulacrum, but a material image to be confronted, questioned, and considered' (ibid.: 182). As Furtado sums up: 'Documentary, narrative fiction, and experimental film are not entirely separate domains but overlapping and mutually influencing. Narrative is germane to documentary and fiction alike, and the documentary is no stranger either to the formal experimentations of the avant-garde or to fictional invention and dramatization' (2019: 8). Published in 2019, Furtado's *Documentary Filmmaking in Contemporary Brazil: Cinematic Archives of the Present* was considered the first book in English on contemporary Brazilian documentary. Stimulatingly, the author addresses Vincent Carelli's *Corumbiara* and Adirley Queirós's *White Out, Black In* in regards to their connection with the notion of the archive, two of the films I also look at in my study.

In this volume, all the documentaries under analysis have in common that they challenge the official narrative built upon historically biased truths. Therefore, contemporary Brazilian documentary has enabled controversial notions of progress and (under)development to be scrutinized in the light of a new context. The advent of digital technology, the decentralization of production, the scrutiny of what makes reality, the dialogue with the visual arts and the consolidation of alternative programs are some of the characteristics of present-day documentary-making. As Andréa França wonders, 'what can be the images of Brazil when one does not resort to the totalizing narrative …? Why carry out documentary filmmaking in Brazil?' (2006: 57). The answer to the first question might be implicit in the second one: I would argue that contemporary documentary filmmaking produces images of Brazil without relying on a narrative closed in on itself. With particular interest in documentary-makers who aimed at investigating progress and (under) development through images of ruination, the following pages delve into these images, not to fully capture them, but to illuminate some of their many nuances. As will be discussed, these images of ruins acknowledge desolation in the face of the unviability of the nation, but they also enable the emergence of new imagery and critical storytelling that diversely engages with the legacy of the revolutionary 1960s and 1970s.

Part Two

The other side of progress: Cinematic (re)constructions of Brasília

First stop: Brasília. In Part Two, I will explore the cinematic (re)construction of the federal capital via the experimental cinema of Ana Vaz and Adirley Queirós. Although adopting different film methodologies, Vaz's *The Age of Stone* (A Idade da Pedra, 2013) and Queirós's *White Out, Black In* (Branco Sai, Preto Fica, 2014) both claim to be sci-fi documentaries in their attempts to move far away from conventional documentary filmmaking. In doing so, both artists challenge the official narrative that underpins so-called reality and propose new imagery and critical storytelling to address the origins of Brasília as well as the consequences for society. Furthermore, both sci-fi documentaries seem to set up a dialogue with Cinema Novo/Cinema Marginal's visual legacy, either as its counterpoint or as its complement, as will be discussed. In this respect, I argue that their visual depictions frame the complexities of (under) development through images of ruins.

Divided into four chapters, Chapter 4 provides a brief discussion of the invention of Brasília itself in order to introduce the controversial spatiality of the capital and its subsequent cinematic translations. Chapter 5 tackles the current trend within Brazilian cinema that seems sceptical of realism as the most appropriate means to depict national issues. In this sense, Queirós's and Vaz's sci-fi documentaries can be read as fitting examples of that tendency. Chapters 6 and 7 relate their productions to Cinema Novo/Cinema Marginal: more specifically, the sixth focuses on the link between *The Age of Stone* and Glauber Rocha's *The Age of the Earth* (A Idade da Terra,

1980), whereas the seventh sheds light on *White Out, Black In* and Rogério Sganzerla's *The Red Light Bandit* (O Bandido da Luz Vermelha, 1968), paying special attention to their groundbreaking discussions on progress and (under)development. Here, the role of Queirós's and Vaz's images of ruins will be highlighted as a unique tool to enable the directors to cope with the premises and paradoxes of Brasília.

4

A controversial spatiality: Myth and apartheid

The city of Brasília encapsulates the cinematic discussion of space and society in a very particular way, as it could be argued that it was genuinely conceived for spatial segregation and subsequent social control. Built from ground zero, it took four years for the city to be inaugurated by President Juscelino Kubitschek (JK, 1956–61). From 1956 to 1960, the Central Plateau in the Brazilian state of Goiás was a continuous construction site. Part of JK's development project, known as '50 Years in 5', referring to the time of his presidency as a period of industrial and rampant modernization), the construction of the new capital of the country was its most ambitious aspect. Much influenced by State-directed industrialization, the building of Brasília was conceived as the means to create national integration (from the coastline to the Central Plateau) as well as regional development (its creation was to strengthen the infrastructure in a geographically undervalued area). Of course, sectors of society were critical of the plan, seeing it as a strategy to isolate political power in the middle of the Plateau, far from the most active and populated cities. Many also feared that JK's pharaonic plan would not be completed on time. 'They reasoned that the city's construction would never be continued by the succeeding administration and that it would remain an incomplete and *fabulously expensive ruin*' (Holston 1989: 20, emphasis added).

Under the guidance of urban planner Lúcio Costa and architect Oscar Niemeyer, the invention of Brasília was the main modernist achievement in Brazil. Following Le Corbusier's guidelines, the city gave form to the manifestos announced at the seminal Congrès Internationaux d'Architecture Moderne (CIAM), in which modern architecture and planning were deemed 'the means to create new forms of collective association, personal habit, and daily life' (ibid.: 31). Originally aimed at solving the crisis Western capitalist societies had created through architecture, the modernist city, however, could not cope with this mission in the Brazilian context. As one of the premises of modernist cities is an absolute break with the past – for the past had led society to a chaotic present of inequality – Costa and Niemeyer had to deny the historical background of Brazil when planning and designing Brasília. That is, they followed dehistoricizing and decontextualizing principles in order to propose new forms of perception through architecture. The strategy Costa found to dehistoricize and decontextualize the yet-to-come city, however, was somewhat controversial. He opted for building Brasília using the foundation myth[1] rhetoric, as if it had been 'divinely inspired' (ibid.: 65). In fact, this mythical aspect would later be found in a variety of literary excerpts addressing the character of the city, especially in writer Clarice Lispector's two tales, *Brasília* (1999a) and *Five Days in Brasília* (1999b, originally *Brasília: Esplendor*), written on the occasions she visited the capital in 1962 and 1974.

Not by coincidence, Ernesto Silva, a military man and bureaucrat in Brasília, wrote right at the beginning of his *History of Brasília* a mythical yet strategic comparison between Rome and Brasília, since both cities were founded on 21 April, with a twenty-seven-century break in between. 'On 21 April, 753 B.C., Romulus founded, on the Palatine Hill, a city that would be the mark of a new era in the Pagan World – the Rome of the Caesars,' Silva goes. 'On the same day, 27 centuries later, Divine Providence willed that a pleiad [i.e., a group] of valiant men should give Brasília to Brazil' (Silva cited in Holston 1989: 72). Although in a much more complex and sophisticated way, Clarice (Lispector 1999a) resorted to the same comparison in order to simultaneously stress the greatness of the construction and also a certain sense of failure (the Roman Empire collapsed, after all) that this greatness inevitably would inherit. 'I look at Brasília the way I look at Rome: Brasília began with a final simplification of ruins. The ivy has not yet grown' (ibid.: 41).

The dualities of Brasília as a project (the greatness and the great failure, a two-way street) have gone far beyond the mythological aspect that helped Costa's urban plan to win the government's competition back in the 1950s. The modernist values embedded in Costa and Niemeyer's approach to JK's mandate gave it the foregrounding it needed. Modernism and modernization were then ready to go hand in hand to make a new Brazil. While architects and politics seemingly agreed on the building of that utopian city, the modernism of the former and the modernization of the latter did not necessarily merge. Contradictory as it was, the conflict of intention and interpretation bequeathed Brasília the paradox of being socialist-modernist yet national-developmentalist. After all, the contradictions in its formulations have forged Brasília into what it is. 'I adore Brasília. Is it contradictory? But what is not contradictory?' (Lispector 1999b: 47).

The vast, empty outdoor spaces; the collapse of the distinction between public and private; the end of the culture of the street and the square – none of that communicated to Brasília's population in a positive way. Nevertheless, the most significant aspect evoked by the architecture of Brasília ended up being the segregation and social control that modernism was unable to prevent. While the Pilot Plan does make a clear distinction between the centre and the periphery, it is worth noting that the idea of stratification was present even before its inauguration. Coming mainly from the Northeastern states of Brazil, the labour force that erected Brasília had no function other than to build the city – a city only for politicians, bureaucrats and businessmen. 'While "the creators of Brasília", the architects and politicians, were exalted, the workers, who actually gave their blood to build the city, were "honoured" by their removal to several satellite cities soon after the completion of the works in which they were engaged in the Pilot Plan' (Gouvêa 1995: 65).

The contentious capital on screen

The dynamics of spatiality, with their strong links to power and privilege, influenced more than just the geography of Brasília. The controversies resonate with the way Brazilian cinema frames the space of the capital, as if the spatial politics led to the spatial aesthetics. Eduardo de Jesus particularly emphasizes that spatial/social tension in film. Despite propaganda newsreels[2] produced before Brasília's inauguration, there is a group of documentaries that do take into consideration the paradox that surrounds the construction of the city. In this sense, Vladimir Carvalho's *Old-Time Veteran Countrymen* (Conterrâneos Velhos de Guerra, 1990) is a critical landmark, a call to pay attention to what the official narrative has deliberately obliterated. The documentary gives an in-depth view of urban planning and its social consequences, mainly from the perspective of the *candangos*, the Northeastern migrants. Produced over the course of twenty years, the documentary interweaves archival footage with interviews, 'with the dusty desert spaces of the new capital shown in wide open shots denouncing the policy of segregation and the almost uncontrolled spread of suburbs that would end up housing the migrant builders', as de Jesus (2017: 46) puts it. Here, one sees the very origins of Ceilândia, as the documentary, according to Gustavo Procopio Furtado, 'includes footage of the Vila do IAPI, the shantytown that grew on the edge of the city after its construction, and of the early years of the decrepit unpaved streets of Ceilândia, to which the inhabitants of the IAPI were forcibly relocated in 1971' (2019: 121). The eviction was to be addressed by Adirley Queirós, himself an admirer of Carvalho's work, in his first documentary feature, as will be pointed out. In fact, Carvalho's really critical approach to the federal capital had been already felt in his short documentary *Brasília Segundo Feldman* (1979), in which he uses historical images produced by North American artist Eugene Feldman – instead of official archive imagery – in order to shine a light on the controversies of the construction, as Jean-Claude Bernardet (2003) claims.

Previously, Joaquim Pedro de Andrade's *Brasília: Contradictions of a New City* (Brasília: Contradições de Uma Cidade Nova, 1967) had already attempted to expose the other side of the capital, just seven years after its establishment. The Olivetti company, which had commissioned a short documentary about the city, turned out to be unhappy with the final cut, as it exposed the contradictions mentioned in the title. In the first part, the documentary presents Brasília through an explanatory voice-over narration and a moving, instrumental soundtrack – the official Brasília on-screen. In the second part, however, the documentary foregrounds interviews with the *candangos* in the satellite cities – the unofficial Brasília invades the on-screen domain. Facing censorship by its own sponsors and the military dictatorship, Andrade's documentary was never released, in particular because focusing on *candangos* 'shows the other side of Brasília, which, contrary to what had been planned, became a Brazilian city like any other, divided and socially segregated by the ways space was occupied' (de Jesus 2017: 47).

'From underdevelopment to the incongruously modern' – that is how Holston (1989: 3) coherently defined the birth of Brasília. His comment says much, not only about the capital but the country as a whole – a country in which space and status have gone hand in hand since its foundation, followed by three centuries of extractive colonialism. The aim to pass from an underdeveloped to a modern nation was more of a utopian dream than a project – hence, the debacle. At the same time, Holston suggests 'that without a utopian factor, plans remain locked in the prison-house of existing conditions' (ibid.: 317). Caught between the past and the future, the premise and the paradox, the intention and the interpretation, the spatiality of Brasília does not facilitate the cinematic endeavour to depict it. 'What possibilities are left for intellectual and artistic production that wants to retain an image of a better or different world with which to point to an emergent future?' (ibid.), Holston wonders.

In this sense, perhaps the cinema of experimentation of Queirós and Ana Vaz sets out new ways to investigate the controversial spatiality of Brasília famously addressed by Holston. De Jesus (2017) has hinted that recent productions may seem to be interested in subverting rather than representing reality. 'Contemporary Brazilian cinema seems to have noticed these forms of domination directed toward space and shows us other visions of the city, induced by more vigorous and libertarian representations' (ibid.: 42). Both Queirós's *White Out, Black In* and Vaz's *The Age of Stone* propose new film methods and critical angles from which to reflect upon how the capital was shaped and how its contradictions dictate the way it is today. Interestingly, the directors chose to construct an image of Brasília by filming outside Brasília. Queirós's production takes place in Ceilândia, a satellite city on the outskirts of the capital, whereas Vaz's is filmed in two different regions of the Goiás state, north and west of Brasília.

In *White Out, Black In*, Queirós deliberately mixes fiction and nonfiction elements to address a police shooting that happened in Ceilândia in 1986. On that occasion, Marquim do Tropa and Shokito, friends with the director and non-professional actors in the film, were attending a party at the Quarentão, a famous nightclub at the time and a place known for its black music culture. The brutal event injured both friends, leaving Marquim in a wheelchair and Shokito in need of a prosthetic to replace one of his legs. Shouting 'white people can leave the place, but black people stay in!', the police act of violence not only left scars on them both but also emphasized the racial and social apartheid still perceivable today. Instead of retelling the story through conventional documentary methods, Queirós decided, alongside Marquim and Shokito, to create a sci-fi documentary feature that interestingly moves away from reality but, at the same time, addresses it with fierceness and poignancy.

In *The Age of Stone*, Vaz follows a similar journey in terms of not giving in to conventional documentary methods, like her contemporary Queirós. The director also plays with fictitious and non-fictitious elements in the attempt to put on screen a different version of what Brasília might look like. Her short film invites the audience to discover a monumental structure in the form of a ruin placed in the heart of the Central Plateau, an allusion to Brasília itself. Shying away from a teleological narrative, Vaz invests in building up the spatial concept through images and sounds, mobilizing just a few characters, but more importantly, letting the camera roam through and extract meaning from that specific region. In brief, the film could be said to be an investigation of the origins of the city. The monument seems to hypnotize both the characters and the spectators, confronted by the fact that no kind of certainty seems available to them.

Most importantly, both filmmakers resort to the imagery of ruins to deliver original insights into the history of Brasília and the way it has traditionally been presented. This is specifically what makes these productions artistic outputs that urgently need to be considered: by relying on the imagery of ruins, these films seem keen to invest in the multiple narrative possibilities of history, as if inspired by the multiple possibilities that a ruin contains within itself. Even though commonly associated with the collapse of something, Brian Dillon remarks that 'the most enigmatic aspect of the time of ruination is the manner in which it points towards the future, rather than the past, or rather uses the ruined resources of the past to imagine, or reimagine, the future' (2011: 18).

5

Realism under erasure or not quite: New imagery and storytelling

The concept of the *unviable nation* (Ramos 2003) relating to the unlikeliness of Brazil becoming a stable and prosperous nation has been widely explored by Brazilian filmmakers since Cinema da Retomada's early years, as pointed out in Chapter 3. In depicting the social, economic, political and cultural turmoil of contemporary Brazil, these films usually resort to realism as a strategy for conveying urgency and credibility to the audience. *Central Station* (Central do Brasil, 1998), *City of God* (Cidade de Deus, 2002) and *Elite Squad* (Tropa de Elite, 2007), three of the most internationally successful Brazilian films, have relied on this strategy to the fullest, frequently reaching into the nonfiction domain by the use of non-professional actors and real locations. If one considers documentary production itself, *News from a Private War* (Notícias de Uma Guerra Particular, 1999), *Bus 174* (Ônibus 174, 2002) and *The Prisoner of the Iron Bars* (O Prisioneiro da Grade de Ferro, 2003) also shed light on national issues, especially the *favela* and prison environments.

Ângela Prysthon, however, claims that present-day production might go in a different direction. If Brazilian cinema, from the first decade of 2000, has been heavily marked by a belief that realism is the most appropriate means to portray and scrutinize national issues, Prysthon (2015: 68) suggests that many present-day films are devoted to what she refers to as 'realism under erasure', a cinematic language that plays with the very idea of what real means by focusing on more ambiguous and thought-provoking narratives. She is not necessarily labelling the strategy as a new one but underlining it as a prominent characteristic of the ongoing approach to reality. Her perspective focuses the attention on the 'deliberate shock between realism and an excess of artifice that disarticulates and destabilizes the effects of real' (ibid.) in many films, the excessive artifice achieved through the revitalization of film genres, such as horror or science fiction, within national production.

The assumption that genres normally associated with mainstream cinema could be a powerful, critical means of addressing Brazilian reality then led Prysthon to coin the term 'furious frivolity' (ibid.: 69). In other words, the sense of so-called frivolity attached to the horror or sci-fi genre embraces furious as an adjective, for those films would also contain an inevitable fury in their storytelling due to the problematic reality they are actually attempting to emulate. As Eduardo de Jesus claims, those could be films with 'more vigorous and libertarian representations' (2017: 42) of what we understand by reality. One could think of André Antônio's *The Cult* (A Seita, 2015), Anita Rocha da Silveira's *Kill Me Please* (Mate-me, Por Favor, 2015), Juliana Rojas and Marco Dutra's *Good Manners* (As Boas Maneiras, 2017), and Marcelo Pedroso's *Brasil S/A* (2014), to name but a few. In this regard, Prysthon (2015) highlights a branch of contemporary production that could also be in tune with the notions of *post-industrial cinema* (Migliorin 2011) or *garage cinema* (Lima and Ikeda 2011) mentioned in Chapter 3 – theoretical efforts that try to pin down not only the context in which this crop of contemporary production lies but also the belief that the new context allows for the creation of images detached from convention.

Nevertheless, the idea of *realism under erasure* is less a negation of realism than 'a more complex exploration of its possibilities' (Prysthon 2015: 74). Thoroughly explored by Lúcia Nagib (2011, 2017b), her discussion of cinematic realism goes beyond classic elaborations on the topic, such as André Bazin's (1967) ontology of the photographic image or Gilles Deleuze's (1989) movement-image and time-image concepts, whose discussions took greatly into account a Eurocentric perspective marked by the Second World War and the rise of modern cinema. While paying tribute to their seminal contributions, Nagib is less interested in their 'evolutionist model' (2017b: 312) than in a 'timeless view of realism' (ibid.: 313). Also, rather than reaffirming World Cinema[1] as a term born from realistic strategies developed from Italian Neorealism onwards, as postulated by Thomas Elsaesser (2009), Nagib defends a realist cinema in itself, 'which is defined by an ethics of the real that has bound world films together across history and geography at cinema's most creative peaks' (2017b: 311). On that note, she advocates an ethics of realism attached to, most importantly, a 'realist mode of production and address' (Nagib 2011: 10). That is, instead of embracing a somewhat worn-out debate about reality and simulation, the author sees it as 'a moral question, but one which concerns casts and crews alone in their drive to merge with the phenomenological real, and this is why the stress on modes of production and address is here of the essence' (ibid.). In this sense, the scholar believes in 'the realism of the medium' (ibid.: 125), one less concerned with narrative mimesis than with what Alain Badiou calls 'an active fidelity to the event of truth' (2006: xiii).

Furthermore, Nagib (2017b) proposes a taxonomy of cinematic realism encompassing modes of production, address, exhibition and reception. In terms of modes of production, she lists 'the physical engagement on the part of crew and cast with the profilmic event; the near identity between the cast and their roles; real location shooting; the audiovisual medium's inherent indexical property; and the engagement with works of art in progress within the film' (ibid.: 316). These are characteristics attached to the work of Adirley Queirós and Ana Vaz – whose outputs are not straightforwardly associated with a conventional idea of realism but could be associated with what Nagib refers to as an ethics of realism. 'In films resulting from this mode of production, the illusionistic fictional thread (if existing) interweaves with documentary footage and/or approach, as well as with crew and cast's direct interference with the historical world' (ibid.). Moreover, she argues that it is 'aimed not only at highlighting the reality of the medium but also at producing, as well as reproducing, social and historical reality' (ibid.). In *White Out, Black In* and *The Age of Stone*, both filmmakers choose to approach Brasília by resorting to sci-fi elements, although genuinely referring to reality. In this sense, the documentary mode present in the construction of their narratives turns out to be penetrated by unexpected artifices – an undertaking that rivals conventional nonfiction attempts to capture reality.

The sci-fi way into reality

Having thoroughly analysed the role of science fiction, Fredric Jameson (2005) raises awareness of a key point that seems crucial for understanding the use of the genre in relation to realism: science fiction is about what is happening here and now. In this regard, it stands as a genre willing 'not to give us "images" of the future ... but rather to defamiliarize and restructure our experience of our own *present*' (ibid.: 286). By doing so, science fiction can elaborate on the present by enriching the cityscape with imaginary futures. The resulting unfamiliar present, in this sense, is devoted to what Vivian Sobchack (1987) has suggested as the speculative or the extrapolative realm. Her groundbreaking study addresses sci-fi films as nothing less than the visuality of postmodernity, a meaningful product of the cultural logic of late capitalism (Jameson 1991). 'Of all narrative film genres, science fiction has been most concerned with poetically mapping those transformations of spatiality, temporality, and subjectivity informed and/or constituted by new technologies' (Sobchack 2016: 127), which flourished in the second half of the twentieth century. Most importantly for this chapter, Sobchack's understanding of science fiction is not a disbelief in the real but a suspension of belief in realism (in its definition *sensu stricto*), 'a rejection of the transparency of such belief in "realism" and a recognition that our access to the real is always mediated and epistemologically partial' (ibid.: 124). It is precisely this approach that seems to characterize Queirós's and Vaz's outputs about their Brasília.[2]

According to Jeffrey Skoller, what makes experimental or avant-garde films like theirs 'important departures from conventional historicism is the incorporation of what is imagined or remains unrealized in a given historical moment but returns as potential within these works of art' (2005: xli). In (re)constructing Brasília by defying the official discourse about the city, Queirós and Vaz invest in experimental narratives to see how far they can defamiliarize themselves with their present and restructure it. Willing to create new imagery and critical storytelling, both artists seem to find in the realm of science fiction the opportunity to subvert the official narrative and its traditional form of representation. Considering their sci-fi documentaries, it is like 'the representational apparatus of Science Fiction ... sends back more reliable information about the contemporary world than an exhausted realism' (Jameson 2005: 384). Following this perspective, Prysthon affirms that what she calls frivolity in film does 'not necessarily mean escapism; rather, it is a matter of conceiving the most interesting forms of escaping' (2015: 74) from a problematic reality in order to propose a fresh concept of it.

Worth mentioning at this point, in his pioneering research,[3] Alfredo Suppia (2007) investigates the presence of the sci-fi genre within Brazilian cinema. In terms of the unusual conflation of sci-fi and documentary,[4] he highlights Marcos Bertoni's *Sangue de Tatu* (1986) and Jorge Furtado's *Barbosa* (1988), two short films that add nonfictional elements (interviews and real footage) to their futuristic plots. Notably, both films are short films; Suppia claims that experimental films like these are more commonly short and medium-length productions. More interestingly, however, are his mentions of films with Brasília as a backdrop. First, Suppia mentions Tadao Miaqui's *Projeto Pulex* (1991), a short animation set in the Brasília of June 2013.[5] In the story, the Brazilian government intends to exterminate the poor in the population to achieve 'acceptable' levels, in a sort of capitalist eugenics. In a more recent past, Santiago Dellape's *Nada Consta* (2006) depicted Brasília in a live-action short film taking place in 2017. In it, the protagonist needs the government to issue an official document allowing him to travel to the moon. The only obstacle is his participation in a march against the Robotic World Government, years before, which obstructs the approval he needs. The black-and-white cinematography explores the modernist lines of Brasília Airport and the University of Brasília in order to create the sci-fi atmosphere. Significantly, Suppia points out that, in the majority of Brazilian sci-fi films, 'the theme of underdevelopment and the Third World discourse seem impregnated – even when one tries to deny them' (2007: 248). The theme of underdevelopment and the Third World discourse, although through different film methodologies, could be said to be part of Queirós's and Vaz's outputs about Brasília. As Gustavo Procopio Furtado claims, the sci-fi genre 'is less commonly used in the countries of the Global South – and is an anomaly in marginal and underdeveloped locales such as Ceilândia' (2019: 131). In specifically referring to Queirós's film, 'the failed project of modernity embodied by the Federal District, mired in the contradictions of ambitious modernization combined with dire segregation and uneven development, makes dystopian science fiction a perfect aesthetic framework' (ibid.).

As Ella Shohat and Robert Stam (1994) famously suggest, discussions with regard to Third World issues should not be taken as homogeneous at all. By using the term *Third World* in order to delve into what has become known as the Third World Cinema, the authors do not express any empathy towards it;

quite the contrary, they believe the term 'not only flattens heterogeneity, masks contradictions, and elides differences, it also obscures similarities' (ibid.: 26). Considering the (dis)similarities between Queirós and Vaz, in particular, what interests me in the combination of historiographic revisionism and innovative language present in their sci-fi documentaries is the cinematic will to challenge the narrative paradigm, which is historically 'enlisted to serve teleological notions of national progress and manifest destiny' (ibid.: 118). When they break that chain, they render visible their criticism in relation to both the teleological narrative and the so-called national progress itself. Coming from quite different backgrounds, Queirós and Vaz are drawn to discuss the advent of Brasília as the other side (or the underside) of that so-called national progress. Both filmmakers are conscious of the importance of investigating Brasília in terms of its construction and the consequences of it: Why build a capital city from scratch? How did the capital city come to be populated? What kind of government policies shaped Brasília as it is today? What sort of imaginary was invented to cope with its construction? The cinematic gaze of Vaz and Queirós reflects upon these questions in *The Age of Stone* and *White Out, Black In*, respectively – the former being more interested in the origins of the mythical city and the latter in the aftermath of its construction.

6

The Age of Stone: The uchronic mode of a monument

The crafting of *The Age of Stone* results from both Ana Vaz's experience in her two previous short films and her dialectical engagement with Glauber Rocha's filmography, specifically *The Age of the Earth*. *The Age of Stone* could be said to be a journey into the far west of Brazil, an immersion into the flora, fauna and textures of geography, a voyage that leads the audience to discover a mysterious, monumental structure in the middle of nowhere. It is never quite clear if the monument found in the Central Plateau stands as the foundation of Brasília or the debris of what was once the federal capital. That monument is an invention, a kind of foreign body in the region, quite like Brasília was at the time of its invention. Filmed in the Chapada dos Veadeiros' wild nature and in a Pirenópolis quarry (areas surrounding the capital), one witnesses the building of a purposely unspecified space through visual and sensorial pillars. The location is inhabited by a few characters who never share the screen: a teenage girl, a black *boiadeiro* (or a cowherd) and a group of quarry workers, as I will discuss in greater detail below. They are characters but also real people who live and/or work in the region, exemplifying Lúcia Nagib's (2017b) ethics of realism as one that, among other assets, underlines near identity between the cast and their roles. In this case, Vaz had travelled a few times to those cities to meet the locals and eventually cast some of them. The teenage girl is Ivonete dos Santos Moraes,[1] with whom Vaz ended up establishing a friendly professional relationship; the black *boiadeiro* is Seu Chico Preto, and when he rides his horse on screen he is doing nothing different from what he does in daily life; and the workers are simply doing their ordinary work shift in front of the camera.

Nevertheless, one could say that the main character is indeed that mysterious, monumental structure resembling a ruin, although it is only seen in its entirety in the final third of the film. Before that, the camera just shows fragments of it, unveiling particular parts through carefully selected angles. As mentioned, the monument itself plays with uncertainty: one never knows if it is a ruin from ancient times or a visionary image of the future. Sometimes, it is integrated into the massive rocks of the region; at other times, it is clearly an architectonic outsider, so the viewer wonders if it really can be found in the Central Plateau or is crafted by the film crew. None of these possibilities are correct, as the monument is actually a CGI monument developed by French sculptress Anne-Charlotte Yver. In collaboration with Vaz, Yver's artwork is a structure much greater than human scale, sprouting from the arid terrain yet falling from the blue sky. It seems composed of giant concrete slabs, right angles, sand colour. Workers unearth an archaeological find and/or erect a monumental memorial. It is therefore about to collapse and, at the same time, about to be established. The monument is Brasília. Full of dualities (like the actual city), the monument is both an allegory of progress and of its underside, as it can be understood as a spectacle or a catastrophe. In Clarice Lispector's words, it is 'the failure of the most spectacular success' (1999b: 46).

Figure 6.1: The timid first appearance of a fragment of the monument.

The very idea of imagining a brand new starting point or a tragic ending for Brasília came into being while Vaz was making *Entre Temps* (2011), a short film focused on the demolition of ZUP[2] buildings, a controversial project aimed at constructing public housing complexes between 1959 and 1967 in France, some of which collapsed due to poor construction and inadequate finance provided by government policies in the subsequent decades. Looking at the debris from the ZUP implosions, Vaz found herself thinking that 'in the middle of that destruction camp, there would and *should* be a parallel universe in which things could be redefined in another way' (2017a), she affirms in the interview I did with her. In this sense, she is faithful to Gilles Deleuze and Félix Guattari's (1987) critical thinking in terms of breaking the chains of a dogmatic, dualist understanding of the world. By contrast, the rhizome philosophy proposed by both authors in *A Thousand Plateaus* finds import in multiple, non-hierarchical interpretations of reality, as 'any point of a rhizome can be connected to anything other, and must be', which 'is very different from the tree or root, which plots a point, fixes an order' (ibid.: 7). In other words, the image of the rhizome translates into the freedom to articulate potential connections within reality. And this could only work by taking language and 'decentering it onto other dimensions and other registers' (ibid.: 8). Moreover, it is a matter of defending a model 'perpetually in construction or collapsing' (ibid.: 20), as the CGI monument seems to embody.

Considering Vaz's body of work, *Entre Temps* and *The Age of Stone* are closely related as both discuss the power of architecture as a sign of history and the passage of time. *The Age of Stone*, however, is more interested in nineteenth-century French philosopher Charles Renouvier's (1988) coining of 'uchronia', a neologism derived from utopia, replacing *topos* (place) with *chronos* (time). The concept is commonly associated with the idea of alternate or alternative history – a widely deployed narrative strategy in sci-fi outputs, 'in which history as we know it is changed for dramatic and often ironic effect' (Duncan 2003: 209). Uchronia refers to a hypothetical time in history, mainly unspecified to the reader/viewer. When Vaz started the project, she decided it was not an appropriate time to address Brasília through an iconoclastic gesture that could spoil the complexity of her approach to her hometown. The iconoclastic gesture towards Brasília could have led to a pointless binarism, as if by destroying whoever/whatever the enemy is, one is actually reaffirming the supremacy of that enemy. Rather, the film opts for (re)imagining the beginning (or the ending) of Brasília in uchronic mode. There is no clear information about whether Chapada dos Veadeiros or Pirenópolis are the settings, nor in which year the story unfolds. Therefore, the film seems to implicitly ask: What *if* history was told from a different perspective? That is, what *if* one could redefine time and space via imagery?

In *The Age of Stone*, there is no past, no present, no future; rather, all exist at the same time, as the Benjaminian, dialectical relation to time suggests. As a matter of fact, Vaz refers less to Walter Benjamin (1968) than she does to Clarice (Lispector 1999a,b) when it comes to challenging temporal accuracy. In this regard, the legacy of Clarice's two tales, *Brasília* and *Five Days in Brasília*, plays a clear role, as the writer defines Brasília as 'a future that happened in the past' (Lispector 1999b: 50), obstructing attempts to specify the imaginary of the capital. In this sense, the building of time and space in the narrative of *The Age of Stone* (or, perhaps, the blurring of them) works as a visual translation of Clarice's genuine impressions: 'I am so lost. But it is indeed like this one lives: lost in time and space' (ibid.: 63). Interestingly, the impact of Clarice on Vaz's work has actually been part of Vaz's artistic practice since her first short film, *Sacris Pulso* (2008). Having lived abroad since the age of seventeen,[3] *Sacris Pulso* was Vaz's first attempt to cinematically return to her hometown. The short film is a very personal meditation on *Brasiliários*, a 1986 short film directed by Sérgio Bazi and Zuleica Porto based on Clarice's tales, assembled with a body of 8mm found footage depicting rituals of travel and family. Vaz's connection to *Brasiliários* is vital, as her mother, Cláudia Pereira, is the actress who plays Clarice on screen, and her father, Guilherme Vaz,[4] is the sound designer and music composer of the film. Her parents actually met during the shooting and, nine months later, Vaz was born. She then comes not only from a family of artists but also metaphorically from a film set in and based on Brasília itself. *Sacris Pulso* is an attempt to unravel her origins as a daughter of artists as well as an artist herself in order to access her hometown through moving images. In this sense, *Sacris Pulso* can be read as her encounter with a ghost city, a city that never actually existed. It is rather an investigation of the Brasília of her memories, of her parents and of Clarice. According to Vaz in her interview, 'Clarice re-imagines the city as a ruin from a far-away future or a really old past' (2017a), creating an imaginary which deliberately plays with time and space. *Sacris Pulso*, *Entre Temps* and *The Age of Stone* make up what Vaz has called her 'Trilogy of Utopias'.

In analysing Vaz's cinema, Raquel Schefer (2016) sees two main strategies, each overlapping the other. First, the author points out 'questions related to the multi-temporality of the event (experience, recollection, multiple interpretations and multiplied perspectives)' (ibid.: 2). That is, she identifies Vaz's concern with reimagining history as a means of shedding light on its obscurities – or, rather, suggesting *another* history. The first aspect, therefore, stands as a theoretical one, a question of content. Second, Schefer notes 'a demystification not only of the history of modernism, but also of its visual forms, the essentially architectural and filmic (mainly New Latin American Cinema and, in particular, Brazilian Cinema Novo)'. Here, it is Vaz's endeavour to respond to or to dialogue with the visual forms of modern Brazilian cinema which is at issue. Particularly, the scholar rather emphasizes the artist's ability to produce original imagery whilst proposing *another* history. In this sense, this aspect is a practical question concerned with form. Nevertheless, in highlighting both work-defining characteristics of Vaz's cinema, Schefer claims that form and content are not and should not be taken as separate domains in her artistic practice. Rather, they are intrinsically linked, acting and reacting in relation to each other. 'If the motives of Vaz's cinema are the engine of its formal inventiveness, the latter gives rise to new perspectives of the present, history, as well as representational forms' (ibid.).

The Earth and the Stone: Brasília is delirium

Bearing that in mind, Vaz's Deleuzian intellectual porosity concerning critical thinking stands as an alternative to pregiven information about the tangible world. As an artist, she is less interested in finding certainties than in questioning them. Not surprisingly, Vaz critically takes account of the Marxist approach that influenced moving images from the late 1950s onwards in Brazil. Even though such principles were a common theme in the work of Cinema Novo filmmakers, Vaz specifically refers to Glauber. His disruptive 1965 manifesto, 'Aesthetics of Hunger', is a summary of his aims as the militant artist that he was. As such, Vaz (2017a) seems sceptical of an approach like his, which she considers a sort of cinematic pamphlet. 'Latin America has suffered a hangover from Marxism, which is not a communitarian but a communist booklet' (ibid.), she observes in her interview. The so-called radical, Latin American militancy of the 1960s that she refers to has never come to terms, for instance, with two core historical mistakes it somehow endorsed: a profound machismo in relation not only to women but also to the complexity of the idea of the other in general, and a disdain for ethnicities and their fundamental relevance in the search for a sense of Brazilianness, she argues.

In 1971, however, Glauber wrote 'Aesthetics of Dreaming', marking a conceptual shift in filmmaking that aims for a much more complex political strategy through moving images. 'Glauber goes from hunger to the delirium of the hungry, from realism to surrealism, making brutality and dreaming the basis of a new thinking' (Bentes 2002: 91). Mainly on account of the military coup d'état that took place in 1964, Glauber reprocessed the idea of underdevelopment in a Third World nation, rejecting the rational, sociological approach and choosing instead a mystical, sensible one. Influenced by anthropophagic Brazilian Modernism, Latin American Magical Realism and European Surrealism, he acknowledged that neither can hunger be 'comprehended' nor can revolution be 'rationalized'. 'What Glauber seems to be saying is that no historical, sociological, Marxist, or capitalist explanation can account for the complexity and tragedy of the experience of poverty, something for him of the order of the "unknowable", the "unthinkable", and the "intolerable"' (ibid.: 92). It is precisely the 'mystical politics' (ibid.: 94) of that new Glauber that attracts Vaz as both a spectator and an artist, particularly epitomized in his last film, *The Age of the Earth*. 'It breaks away from a Marxist script, because it resurrects the dimension of dreaming, the dimension of the ritual that it so inconspicuously represses' (Vaz 2017b: 217).

Produced in 1980, Glauber's final cinematic contribution symbolizes best the mystical politics that the 'Aesthetics of Dreaming' manifesto advocates. In this film, the allegorical takes the stage in order to re-elaborate the mythical, religious and prophetic aspects of Brazilian/Latin American identity. 'On the day that Pasolini, the great Italian poet, was murdered, I thought of filming the life of Christ in the Third World,' says Glauber in voice-over. Charting the story (or the anti-story, as Glauber himself says, the film has no teleological thread) of four Christs (a black Christ, an indigenous Christ, a military Christ and a guerrilla Christ), the film questions Western imperialism in relation to the spiritual as well as the mundane domains. Profoundly criticized by the Italian press on the occasion of its premiere at the 1980 Venice Film Festival, *The Age of the Earth* is less a film than a manifesto in itself in proposing a Latin American perspective of (neo)colonialism and an allegorical Christianism which rejects the martyr and celebrates a Christ made of 'destabilizing forces' (Bentes 2002: 9).

As a manifesto, *The Age of the Earth* challenges the bourgeois cinema to the fullest. The anti-stories of the four Christs were shot separately as four distinct blocks and were edited by three editors working individually. Ricardo Miranda, Raul Soares and Carlos Cox were responsible for editing sequences filmed in Rio de Janeiro, Brasília and Bahia, respectively. Consequently, each city block bears a unique editing style. 'Glauber did not formulate a specific aesthetic approach, a unique stimulus for all of us: he would say something different to each one of us,' says Miranda, interviewed by scholar Albert Elduque (2017: 197). Put together, the four blocks (Rio has two different settings which counts as two separate blocks) first resulted in six hours of material, but the theatrical version was 160 minutes long, the director's longest output. Once it was made, Glauber wanted it to be screened on the walls of buildings and public squares, breaking down the exhibition circuit. Also, as his final intervention, he required the projectionist to assemble the film's reels in any order, offering no chance of logical narrative. Commercially speaking, the film has circulated in just one version as far as one knows. Curated by Stefan Solomon, Tate Modern film season *Tropicália and Beyond: Dialogues in Brazilian Film History* followed Glauber's initial idea when screening the film in 2017.

With no title or credits, the shooting was mostly impromptu, as no script was provided to cast and crew. Whether filmed on the beach, in a Carnival parade, during a *candomblé* ceremony or in the streets of the modernist capital, the hallucinatory sequences lead to the confrontation between the Christs and Johan Brahms, a ruthless foreign businessman, the representation of the imperialist mindset. It goes without saying that the film was not conceived for one to follow their journey but to witness 'a cinematic trance through hand-held camera and montage' (Bentes 2002: 8). As Glauber himself claims, 'it is a film that the viewer should watch as if in a bed, in a party, a strike or a revolution. It is a new cinema, anti-literary and metatheatrical, that will be enjoyed, and not seen and heard like the cinema out there' (cited in Freitas 2008: 1). According to Ismail Xavier, in *The Age of the Earth*, Glauber finally achieves a 'syncretic way of thinking of Brazil as a peripheral country within the decadence of imperialism' (2001: 108). His achievement is deeply attached to the film's formal aspects (the long take, the free camera movement, the non-teleological montage), which gave him the means to transfer the sociopolitical crisis of representation to the cinema.

The Age of Stone is Vaz's animist answer to Glauber's *The Age of the Earth*. Instead of four Christs vociferating entranced words, Vaz's 29-minute short film sheds light upon nature, light, silence and colour, allowing her human characters to merge with the geography. It is an elaboration of the possibilities of contemporary Brazilian cinema opening a dialogue with tradition, 'beyond the canonical, but alongside the canonical', as Vaz (2017a) states in her interview. Screened together for the first time as part of the above-mentioned Tate Modern film season, one film seems to echo the other, with delirium as a common theme. That delirium was Glauber's rupture with any kind of cinematic rule. Vaz herself pays tribute to *The Age of the Earth* as 'one of the most rebellious gestures of the Cinema Novo' in the programme's catalogue: 'because it refuses the discipline of any militant agenda and situates its militancy elsewhere, in the shadows of a hallucination, in the body of its characters, in the breakdown of industrious narrative structures' (2017b: 214), as discussed earlier. In *The Age of Stone*, delirium is conducted by the uchronic mode of the film, as this is 'a cinema that seeks images of other possible worlds' (ibid.: 223). On screen, Brasília is a delirium, as it is not Brasília that one sees but its fractured, CGI monumental version. In common, both outputs seem to be interested in the image in flux, in the montage as an experience, in cinema as the building of different spatial-temporal dimensions. They both seem to take 'the incorporation of what is imagined or remains unrealized' (Skoller 2005: xli) as their guideline.

There are differences, though. While the title of Glauber's film refers to the Earth (in Portuguese, earth also means land, or one's motherland) as a stage for characters to explore, Vaz's opts for referring to an age of Stone, that is, a primitive age still full of possibilities. More than questioning the world as we know it (precisely what Glauber does), she is questioning the very origins of the world/Brasília. Apart from the title, Vaz's experimental way of documenting that age also cites Glauber's work in its opening sequence. In his film, the first sequence (perhaps the most iconic of late Cinema Novo) is a circular panoramic scene which frames the sun rising above the Palácio da Alvorada (Palace of Dawn, the president's official residence in Brasília). While the sun rises over the modernist palace, Naná Vasconcelos's music score underlines Amerindian and African sonorities through human chants and percussive instruments referring to national roots. For Vaz, 'the sequence incarnates at once the mythic birth of the city of Brasília as a totem of modern prophecy whilst also revealing the messianic mysticism of its foundations. … Brasília emerges as both fever and prayer – totem and taboo' (2017b: 213). *The Age of the Earth* being concerned with establishing a Brazilian/Latin American identity, the sequence plays a crucial role as it portrays Brasília as the embodiment of the contradictions of the country.

Schefer explains the use of circular panoramic view in Cinema Novo (and other emerging Latin American cinemas of the 1950s and 1960s) as an emancipatory film strategy: 'a formal expression of an extensive understanding of the process of decolonization (political, cultural, aesthetic, perceptual and cognitive decolonization)' (2016: 6). In other words, the camera movement embodies a dual representation: one's view about the world itself, and, more specifically, the vision of the observed covering those who have been historically observing – 'a non-European cosmovision' (ibid.). While aiming

Figure 6.2: The sun rising above the Palácio da Alvorada in *The Age of the Earth*.

for national liberation, by resorting to this strategy, she argues, *cinemanovistas* have ended up reproducing the binary relationship of the colonized and colonizer. In Vaz's take, the circular panorama gives way to a zoomed-in camera shot, as if attempting to unravel that paradoxical strategy. According to Schefer, her camera movement is aimed at breaking the separation between the subject filming and the object filmed, as well as replacing the representation by the interpretation of reality. Rather than decolonizing, Vaz is interested in exploring the possibilities of not being colonized in the first place.

In this sense, she sides with scholar Suely Rolnik's intellectual mission for a permanent decolonization of the unconscious and its creative irruptions. Art is not the fire exit for a political agenda; 'rather it is a space for calling upon that which has been taken away from us, what Suely Rolnik calls the body-that-knows, the body that has been domesticated, colonized, and needs to vibrate again' (Ramos 2016: 256). Hence, Vaz's camera is an extension of the body, much in tune with Maya Deren's cinema tradition of exploring visual representation through the body. The zoom-in 'is a movement that the human eye is not able to make. It is the camera-body that is able to do so,' Vaz states in her interview. Besides being a union between camera and body, 'it is as if the camera movement itself could insinuate the construction and destruction of the landscape, as if the camera were inserting the movements of those sculpting that landscape, as if the camera could also carve that landscape' (2017a). Influenced by the North American avant-garde feminism, her camera is a subjective prosthesis of the body, a tool to explore a range of (psycho) geography. *The Age of Stone*'s opening sequence, therefore, deconstructs that of *The Age of the Earth* in merging subject and object, turning the camera into an element of nature. Interestingly, Xavier (2012) briefly remarks that, although initially inspired by Italian Neorealism and French New Wave, modern Brazilian cinema then went on to flirt with North American experimental productions, inaugurated in 1947 by Deren herself.

While Vaz's sensorial camera movement zooms in, there is no Palace of Dawn on the horizon but dawn itself, as if the film was exploring a space-time prior to the existence of the human-made construction or one that will never lead to it. The dynamic is enhanced by the sound design. The use of sound marks a second difference with regards to Glauber's sequence. Designed by Arno Ledoux and Vaz herself, the sound departs from natural to artificial

Figure 6.3: The uchronic sunrise in the Central Plateau in *The Age of Stone*.

sound, following the director's approach to reality as construction. At first sight, the soundtrack can be taken as purely diegetic, as it was indeed fully captured *in loco* by Chico Bororo. However, while the sun rises and the camera zooms in, that diegetic sound (wind blowing, birds singing) is intensified to the extent it becomes fake, almost electronic, *naturally artificial*. Again, Vaz plays with the blurring of nature and artificiality in order to question what one acknowledges as reality. The images that match those blurred sounds are framed by Vaz herself and Jacques Cheuiche. As if coming full circle, her partnership with Cheuiche is quite a meaningful one, as he was the director of photography in *Brasiliários* – in a way, where all this started.

Indeed, *The Age of Stone* is a comeback. Personally, it is Vaz's comeback to her hometown, in a journey that, significantly enough, takes place outside her hometown. The federal capital is not there because it has never actually been – only in Vaz's imagination. After addressing Brasília in *Sacris Pulso* through archival material, *The Age of Stone* imposed itself as an invitation for her to finally travel and give meaning to her imagined Brasília. Cinematically, it is her return to images, sounds and texts that have haunted and fascinated her for years: from *Brasiliários* and Clarice's two tales to *Sacris Pulso* and *Entre Temps*, an artistic thread that found in Glauber's iconic *The Age of the Earth* a friction that had to be explored. Influenced by the monumentality of modernist Brasília and in dialogue with Brazilian cinema tradition, Vaz builds a narrative interested in deconstructing (or reconstructing alongside) the references. Her sci-fi documentary, the outcome of her speculations on reality, is not only a voyage into the far west of Brazil but also an attempt to redefine national history and (hi)storytelling through cinematic friction.

The science *friction* documentary of Ana Vaz

'Brasília is science fiction,' as Clarice (Lispector 1999b: 59) categorically affirmed. Her impressions of the country's new capital are still today what best encapsulates the mixture of astonishment and strangeness that arises in those who set eyes on Brasília. 'Brasília is a strictly perfect and error-free joke. And what only saves me is the error' (ibid.: 44). In other words, the perfection acquired by the architecture has forgotten to take account of the imperfections of reality. Errors not only save (or better, define) Clarice but all of us as well. 'I never cried in Brasília. There was no place to' (Lispector 1999a: 42), she confessed referring to the lack of corners, streets and squares the modernist city wanted to avoid constructing. Interestingly, the void of modernist architecture became, after all, the emptiness that had a decisive impact upon Clarice's outlook. 'If it is not populated, or rather overpopulated, it will be too late: there will be no place for people' (ibid.). It is a hyperbole, but one that subtly points to the lack of human presence in the Pilot Plan. The sophisticated stream of consciousness dear to Clarice's literature beautifully permeates the two tales she wrote, as the above-mentioned extracts demonstrate. Fascinated by the inaccuracy of time and space that only Brasília bears, Clarice felt, indeed, like a 'space traveller' (Lispector 1999b: 52), who had 'finally got off the flying saucer' (ibid.: 53), and was quite overwhelmed by 'writing in the past, in the present and in the future' (ibid.: 46).

In *The Age of Stone*, science fiction is not straightforwardly a projection of the future. That is, it is not evident if what one sees on screen is set in a distant future per se. Rather, the film is more the visual conflation of Clarice's past, present and future, interested in the friction with so-called reality. Like the Brasília of Clarice, the Brasília of Vaz 'is the place where space resembles time more' (Lispector 1999a: 43). In other words, space is constructed through the exploration of the possibilities of cinematic time. As the Deleuzian time-image, Vaz's visual tapestry evokes temporalities that go beyond the image itself, as 'the image itself is the system of the relationships of its elements, that is, a set of relationships of time from which the variable present only flows' (Deleuze 1989: xii). Much in tune with the idea of uchronia (Renouvier 1988), one could be seeing either the origins of Brasília or its final days. The element which conveys this sense of multiple spatial temporalities is precisely an allegorical ruin. This choice is quite significant, as the ruin has the ability to 'embody a set of temporal and historical paradoxes' (Dillon 2011: 11). It seems to bear past, present and future within itself. It is physically in the present; it is a reminder of what has now gone and invites conjecture about what is to come.

As mentioned earlier, the monument-ruin in its entirety is only seen in the third part of the film. Until then, the ambience is composed by an exploration of other human and non-human elements. The construction of the surroundings of the ruin is directly linked to the use of sound, which marks the first turning point in the film. For nine minutes, the landscape is that of Chapada dos Veadeiros.[5] The camera explores the fauna and flora, and the geological site slowly unfolds as a black *boiadeiro* rides his horse across the frame. At a given moment, part of the monument is seen at relative distance, without further explanation. In a close-up shot, the *boiadeiro* gazes steadily at the horizon. The camera frames the mountains covered in green vegetation. As the camera zooms in, the crescendo of sound resumes its artificial timbre, similar to what happens in the opening sequence, as discussed earlier. Cut. And what one then sees is a quarry in Pirenópolis. The sound becomes purely diegetic again. In the quarry, workers and stones share the same environment. Amid them, fragments of the monument start to appear regularly, albeit never entirely.

What I call a second turning point in the film is the appearance of Ivonete dos Santos Moraes, a young girl Vaz had met during her location research. Ivonete's figure appears like a sort of ghost, the daughter of miscegenation and offspring of that (psycho)geography. Originally from that locality, the film plays with the fragility and strength that Ivonete contains within herself. Some might see her as a fragile teenager subjected to that arid atmosphere, but others see her as a strong force in constant interaction with nature. In many of the close-ups Ivonete seems to be looking at the horizon, as the reverse-angle shot shows the impressive landscape – and stays there for more than

Figures 6.4, 6.5 and 6.6: From Chapada dos Veadeiros to Pirenópolis through the gaze of the *boiadeiro*.

just a few seconds. Therefore, one has the impression that Ivonete is not only looking at the landscape, but the landscape is also looking back at her. In tune with Deleuze and Guattari's (1987) exploration of the earth/Earth's limits, the Brasília of Vaz *is* the solid yet disoriented Central Plateau. Full of holes, recesses and textures, the topography could be that of the moon or Mars – the earth/Earth is indeed another planet – the rhizomatic plateau 'a continuous, self-vibrating region of intensities whose development avoids any orientation toward a culmination point or external end' (ibid.: 21–2). If a rhizome is made of plateaus, as both authors claim, then Brasília, located in the Central Plateau, appropriately matches the concept.

In clear opposition to Glauber's verbiage in *The Age of the Earth*, silence is definitely part of the soundtrack in *The Age of Stone*. Characters, from the black *boiadeiro* to Ivonete and the workers, do not say much. In fact, only Ivonete speaks to the camera. She recites literary extracts from Machado de Assis, Hilda Hilst and, not surprisingly, Clarice Lispector, transforming them into a prosaic yet mythical speech. Interestingly, when Clarice's words are uttered, something quite significant happens. 'It was as artificial as the world must have been when it was created,' says Ivonete, looking at the camera/spectator. Not coincidentally, Clarice's famous sentence referring to Brasília's natural-artificial aspects is the same sentence used by Vaz to underline the natural-artificial in cinema as well. Ivonete breaks the cinematic fourth wall precisely by pronouncing these words. Declaiming in an amateur fashion, her own acting seems artificial in itself, she ends up giving another dimension to Clarice's words. More than characters, Ivonete, Seu Chico Preto and the diggers are spectral figures, uchronic announcers of people who might have once been there. Although allowing itself some distance from Cinema Novo, the use of non-professional actors in this film is worth mentioning, an element often present in the 1960s cinematic movement that continues to the present (Adirley Queirós's films are examples of that, too).

In that dreamlike scenario, the enormous size and power of the ruin/Brasília strikes one when it is finally shown in its entirety. In a circular panoramic shot that lasts two minutes, we see the structure from a privileged point of view (the camera is positioned in the centre of the quarry), equally acknowledging its extension and oddness. In the frame, there is a man, one of the diggers, crossing the site, tiny in comparison with the monument.

106 Brazilian Cinema and the Aesthetics of Ruins

Figures 6.7 and 6.8: Ivonete looks at the horizon, and the horizon looks back at Ivonete.

There is also a little house made of stones as small as his human stature. The nomadic thought (to make use of a Deleuzian term) of Vaz prevents us from fully decoding those elements. Again, a suspicion arises. The monument is not only an object of science fiction but also the outcome of the friction between reality and speculation. Interested in merging with Clarice and Glauber, past

The Age of Stone

Figure 6.9: Ivonete recites Clarice to the camera.

Figures 6.10 and 6.11: The monument-Brasília.

and future, Brasília and outside Brasília, it turns out to be an object of science *friction*. Near the end, it vanishes. The camera moves toward the blue sky and the monument is no longer there. If development has not yet come, the ruins resulting from underdevelopment have already disappeared. 'Brasília is a future that happened in the past. Eternal as a stone' (Lispector 1999b: 50).

7

White Out, Black In: Exploding the Third World from a *laje* point of view

To a certain extent, the Brasília of *The Age of the Earth* runs in parallel with the Brasília of *White Out, Black In*. According to Ismail Xavier (2001), although fragmentary, the discourse of Glauber Rocha and his four Christs is underpinned by violence and exclusion as issues deeply attached to national history. In Glauber's film, the foreigner, capitalist conqueror arrives in Brasília bragging about his superiority over the decadent elite of that piece of land. In these sequences, Glauber explores the threads linking business, corruption and oppression, with the urban, modernist space of Brasília as the setting. 'The greater metaphor of imperial exploration crystallizes in the biblical image of the enslaved people working on the building of tombs – this is the connotation that acquires the monumental architecture of Brasília' (ibid.: 126), as the local labour force is seen in a similar situation. In voice-over, that spatial-political oppression makes Glauber no longer believe in socialism and capitalism as separate domains but as imbricated ideologies that do not help solve social problems. Above all, he is *for* the people. 'Democracy is not socialist, communist, nor capitalist. Democracy is the reign of the people. De-mo-cra-cy is the *un*-reign of the people,' he shouts at a given moment.

The Brasília of *White Out, Black In* is, indeed, one of violence and exclusion, but Adirley Queirós's discourse as a filmmaker is less fragmentary. Glauber's sense of being politically adrift in 1980 is replaced by a renewed leftist discourse in Queirós's experimental documentary. It is noteworthy that Queirós's political stance has been mostly in tune with left-wing federal governments through the mandates of President Luiz Inácio Lula da Silva (2003–10) and President Dilma Rousseff (2011–16) – the latter's second mandate was interrupted by a controversial impeachment process that many believe to be a political coup d'état orchestrated by the right-wing sector of her presidency, including her vice president Michel Temer. Though always critical of the role played by the State, the director is an enthusiastic supporter of the anti-poverty programs and affirmative action policies developed by the Partido dos Trabalhadores (Workers' Party), such as university quotas for minorities. In a sense, his documentaries quite directly open a dialogue with that leftist debate, as his body of work sheds light upon the poor black communities targeted by those policies. His political concerns were to come to the fore perhaps in a more explicit way in *Once There Was Brasília* (Era Uma Vez Brasília, 2017), an experimental feature film released right in the wake of Rousseff's dismissal. In it, WA4 (Wellington Abreu), an agent travelling from another planet, was supposed to come to Earth to kill President Juscelino Kubitschek in 1960 but ends up landing in 2016, the year Rousseff was impeached. Real audios from Rousseff and Temer themselves underline the political fact in the narrative, even though the film seems more interested in the allegorical mode that had already been crafted in Queirós's previous film project, which I will discuss.

The concern with discourse and aesthetics goes hand in hand with his cinema. The cinematic elaboration of Brasília's segregated society gives form and content the same level of importance, although doing that is constantly questioned, he complains. 'They only want to relate the people of the periphery to discursive matters. It is funny how when we deal with aesthetic and formal areas, these are ignored, as if we don't have the capacity to think about form in cinema,' affirms Queirós in a Canal E (2014) interview. In that powerful statement, 'they' could be interpreted as the mainstream, the industry, the system, whilst 'we' means him and his crew from Coletivo de Cinema em Ceilândia (Ceicine), the Ceilândia-based film collective founded by him. The director complains that 'they' expect documentaries to be 'serious' and stress that it is important 'to mess things up, by which he does not mean having no responsibility' (ibid.). In Portuguese, he uses the word *avacalhar*, which approximately translates into 'mess up' or 'screw up', unsettling or discomposing something, but it has a rougher and more popular sense in the original.

The segregation between Brasília and its satellite cities indeed fuels Queirós's politically charged documentaries about the consequences of that institutionalized social fissure. Before *White Out, Black In*, Queirós directed *Rap: The Song of Ceilândia* (Rap: O Canto da Ceilândia, 2005), *Strike Days*

(Dias de Greve, 2009), *Off the Field* (Fora de Campo, 2010) and *Is the City Only One?* (A Cidade É Uma Só?, 2011). In *Is the City Only One?*, he shows how the governmental strategy to control citizens via urban planning is far from restricted to the late 1950s. The film focuses on the displacement from the city centre of the vulnerable population who helped to build the capital. In the 1970s, the dictatorial military government managed to evict the remaining *favelas* of the downtown area when putting forward the Invasion Eradication Campaign (Campanha de Erradicação de Invasões, widely known as CEI). The population was removed from Vila do IAPI to the recently created Ceilândia. Founded in 1971, its name comes from CEI itself, its meaning referring to CEI land. The traumatic displacement is precisely the plot of the documentary, whose title alludes to the lyrics of a political jingle promoted by the military government in order to brainwash people about the fact that the removal was the best option at hand. '*Você que tem um bom lugar pra morar/Nos dê a mão/Ajude a construir nosso lar/Para que possamos dizer juntos/"A cidade é uma só"*'. In English: 'You who have a good place to live/ Give us your hand/Help to build our home/So we can say together/"The city is one only"', children used to naively sing without noting the cynism embedded in those lyrics. According to Luiz Alberto de Campos Gouvêa (1995), between 1970 and 1976, 118,453 residents in *favelas* and communities within the Pilot Plan were displaced. In the meantime, 43,985 new lots were developed in the satellite cities and its surrounding areas.

Here, one could easily identify film strategies that were going to be radicalized in *White Out, Black In*, his second documentary feature. *Is the City Only One?* does not simply draw on remembering the traumatic event. As Cláudia Mesquita (2011a) explains, first there is an impulse to shed light on the memories of those who were/are marginalized in society. In this case, Queirós questions Brasília's official narrative while putting under scrutiny the general belief in the official archive imagery. In searching for a counter-discourse, the film interviews Nancy Araújo – back in the 1970s one of the children who participated in the recording of the infamous political jingle. As Gustavo Procopio Furtado argues, 'Queirós views with suspicion and may indeed have intended to destabilize our faith in authoritative documents by fabricating one. … Faced with the absence of an archival proof for the remembered event, Queirós opts for simulation as a gesture of commitment to marginalized subjects and their memories' (2019: 126). Through Araújo's mediation, *Is the City Only One?* critically engages with the fake visual archive to unpack its meaning. 'Just as singing the old jingle on the radio puts it back into circulation in the lived world, the reenactment of the jingle gathers together a group of girls from a present-day, under-served public school in a commemoration of the social or group memory or marginalization,' Furtado affirms. 'More than a reflection about the past, the filmmaking process is a vehicle for tactical interventions in the present' (ibid.). Second, the documentary departs from a memorialist tone to unexpectedly reach the fictional domain in a more open way. Dildu, for instance, is a fictional character played by non-professional actor Dilmar Durães, who was born and lives in Ceilândia, just as his character. In the film, Dildu is supposedly running for election in the federal capital. In blurring the boundaries between fiction and nonfiction, he wanders around the city interacting with people and places, in a very different mood in comparison with Araújo's sequences. Worth mentioning, his collaboration with Queirós will happen again in Queirós's second feature.

In *White Out, Black In*, the aggression towards Brasília is so strong that the capital does not even appear in the frame, as the narrative's point of view comes from the satellite city. The documentary charts the story of Marquim do Tropa and Shokito, survivors of police violence at the locally popular Quarentão nightclub in 1986.[1] In acknowledging how painful it would be to register the traumatic events in documentary mode alone, Queirós opted to work through sci-fi fabulation with them. Through constant interaction, all decisions were made collectively. For instance, Queirós says they would normally shoot according to the will and availability of the non-professional actors on the day: if they were not in the mood to shoot a particular heavy sequence, they would do something else instead. Because they were the characters themselves, that kind of dynamics was crucial for setting the very specific tone of a film centred on a traumatic event. Again, Lúcia Nagib's (2017b) ethics of realism can be mobilized in relation to the mode of production. Marquim and Shokito (Sartana, in the film), although in a fictional context, identify with their roles in a quite literal way here. As mentioned above, the non-professional actors actually play themselves, not only merging with but also mirroring the phenomenological real. They have known each other for a long time, they experienced the same violent episode, they are residents in Ceilândia – and the film uses all of that to support the narrative. As characters in a sci-fi documentary, they plan to explode a sonic-atomic bomb over Brasília, the conjunction of music,[2] sounds and noises collected on the streets of Ceilândia and integrated into a futuristic contraption. Interestingly, the allegorical bomb is a musical one, as the crime took place in a black music nightclub.

The capital is constructed as an off-screen space. Brasília is absent, unreachable, not there. Rather, it gains meaning through the marginalized spatial architecture of Ceilândia, subjected to the capital's tyrannical pomposity in both the film and reality. In a way, it seems that there is no need for the white, wealthy Brasília to be shown. First, because its official version has already been exhaustively mediated; and second, because cast and crew want it to vanish for good. The best symbol of its off-screen presence comes in the shape of a passport, a key element for the film to convey the sense of apartheid in the Ceilândia/Brasília equation. More than just an object, the passport raises awareness of the boundaries that exist between the two localities. To access Brasília, one needs to have this document. 'If you are listening to this track, it is because you are in the controlled area of the city of Brasília. Please have your passport with you,' advises the announcer, as if referring to Michel Foucault's (1995) disciplinary panoptic. In another moment, the characters listen to a curfew announcement through urban loudspeakers: 'Citizen, the social welfare police are starting their night round. We urge everyone to remove children from the streets and return to their homes. Have your documents to hand. One hundred and three days have passed without a record of any attacks in our city. A better government is an alert government.' Both the need for a passport to enter the capital city and the control curfew define the kind of space the characters live in for the audience.

The sci-fi documentary, therefore, sets its perspective at a distance from the capital, although from a 'privileged' viewpoint, or a *'laje* point of view', as César Guimarães (2014: 198) suggests. Literally a paving slab in English, the word *laje* also has a social connotation in Portuguese. If someone lives or parties on a *laje*, this is a reference to the open-to-the-air first floor of a poor house, or a *favela* shack. In this sense, the perspective of the film finds a correlation in the set design per se, as Marquim and Sartana have a sort of *laje* in their houses in Ceilândia. As a matter of fact, the way the characters' houses were designed (collectively constructed especially for the shoot) also emphasizes their personal relationships to Ceilândia/Brasília. For Mesquita, 'in the film, Ceilândia is figured less as the fulfillment of the utopian "good place" than as a ruined, dusky setting in a state of melancholy' (2018: 73), very different from Brasília. In the case of Marquim, there are two opposite yet oppressive scenarios. Marquim goes to the basement to work in his subversive radio station, a sort of bunker in which he plays songs and elaborates on his memories for potential listeners. Going up to the first floor, the bunker is exchanged for a balcony surrounded by iron bars. When he is up there, he seems to be set apart, isolated from the street, almost imprisoned; paradoxically, he also feels the city is much closer there, as he can gaze upon the urban horizon from his own *laje* viewpoint. The city also invades the house of Sartana, a house that seems to have no walls. Many sequences take place in his *laje*, a mixture of inside and outside, as if the place was either under construction or being demolished.

When he is not at home drawing or taking digital-camera pictures, Sartana is framed in a sort of junkyard, where he is surrounded by mechanical debris, including prosthetics like the one he himself uses. Sartana was so badly injured after being trodden on by police horses that he lost one of his legs. The shocking police onslaught had consequences for Marquim's mobility as well – today, he is in a wheelchair. Thus, the cinematic space not only reveals the materialization of social apartheid but also the characters/people's own fractured bodies, the intimate space they inhabit, bearing the consequences of it. In fracturing their bodies, the police violence also fractured their urban experience within the city. Tatiana Hora calls both Marquim and Sartana 'cyborgs of the past' (2016: 14), referring to the meaning of their bodies in Queirós's sci-fi documentary. Half human, half machine, the cyborg, here, is the aftermath of State violence. Interestingly, there is an opposition between the bodies in the Brasília newsreels of the 1950s and the ones in his film, as 'instead of the bodies capable of tireless and accelerated work to erect the new capital presented in the official films, *White Out, Black In* shows the bodies of the city mutilated by urban control' (ibid.: 14–15). In an interview with me, Queirós (2018) affirms that 'the characters are amputated, just as the city is amputated. And where there are bodies amputated in an amputated territory, there is a state of permanent war'. Alternatively, the director claims that the state of permanent war also allows reaction, one that fiercely refuses the status quo and aims at other possibilities.

Figure 7.1: Marquim on the *laje*.

Figure 7.2: Sartana in the no-wall house.

Two cyborgs of the past against one Red Light bandit

As pointed out in Chapter 2, Cinema Marginal was a response to the deep consciousness of Cinema Novo films. Exploring an *aesthetics of garbage*, it emerged as an underground movement resorting to a radical discourse fuelled by irony and humour, as Rogério Sganzerla's *The Red Light Bandit* emblematically demonstrates. Jorge the bandit, played by actor Paulo Villaça, is essentially an outlaw in crisis: he steals and attacks women, while questioning his identity and life. He is an aggressive, frustrated anti-hero who wanders in Boca do Lixo, the red-light district of São Paulo, and whose unpredictable political action is precisely to *avacalhar*. At one point, he even says: 'When we can do nothing, we can only *avacalhar*.' That is, make a fool of oneself, or more appropriately, to let oneself collapse. The irony and humour engendered in the precarious sci-fi aesthetics of *White Out, Black In* bring Queirós's film closer to Cinema Marginal than to Cinema Novo, as the director believes that the former had a greater impact on his filmmaking. As Queirós himself has said, the will of *avacalhar*, or to mess things up, gives his film the freedom to play with sci-fi elements and yet address current reality, much in tune with the idea of *furious frivolity* evoked by Ângela Prysthon (2015). Unsurprisingly, sci-fi elements are also an essential part of the imagery of Sganzerla's film as a means of conveying a powerful social critique. If Sganzerla's film is devoted to an aesthetics of garbage, many of the sequences in Queirós's film take place in a junkyard, bringing together and rendering visible the sense of ruination that pervades both films.

Looking closely at *The Red Light Bandit* might help unpack *White Out, Black In*'s strategies by taking account of their differences. Whereas the bandit is the portrait of the failed, tedious criminal man, Marquim and Sartana are proactive victims in face of the crisis. There is no way out for the bandit; and there is revolution for the cyborgs of the past. It is Queirós himself, however, who seems to address the reality of his characters/actors by resorting to a strategy similar to Sganzerla's inventiveness. Even the term *avacalhar* is mobilized by both Queirós and Sganzerla's protagonist. 'The worst place for cinema is that of the politically correct. The politically correct is an incredible place for the political, democratic, and party's needs. The politically correct character in the films is a reactionary,' says Queirós in an Itaú Cultural Encontros de Cinema interview (2015). In an angry film like this one, 'a vengeful film' (ibid.) as the director defines it, Marquim and Sartana's aim to blow up Brasília comes as a political statement in the storytelling. Indeed, the politically correct as a dramaturgical element is not an option here.

Although working with different cinematic styles, the freshness of the narrative position of both films produces a sort of dialogue. Sganzerla's film is essentially a fictitious film, but not just that. At twenty-one years old, the director was mocking Cinema Novo's seriousness in investigating national issues by shedding light on a collage of references. The urban culture of the red-light district resulted in an aesthetics of garbage in opposition to an already disseminated aesthetics of hunger – even though Sganzerla had Glauber as one of his references alongside Sergei Eisenstein, Orson Welles and Jean-Luc Godard. 'My film is a Western about the Third World. That is to say, a fusion and a blending of various genres. I made a somatic film; a western, but also a musical, a *documentary*, a cop film, a comedy (or is that slap-stick?), and *science fiction*' (Sganzerla 2017: 81, emphases added). As claimed by Xavier (2017), the tropicalist tone of *The Red Light Bandit*, that of mixing national and international references in a pop, parodic mode, is the film's most prominent feature. Instead of imitating Cinema Novo's search for an authentic national cinema, Sganzerla opts for subverting the idea of the national, questioning progress and (under)development through self-mockery and countless citations. For instance, whereas the use of African percussion sounds in Glauber's *Entranced Earth* (Terra em Transe, 1967) intends to shed light on Brazil's African roots, in Sganzerla's film, the same African percussion sounds are intertwined with Jimi Hendrix's guitar, very much in tune with Tropicália aesthetics. The dialogue between Sganzerla/*The Red Light Bandit* and Glauber/*Entranced Earth* confirms both films as 'an allegory of national underdevelopment' (Xavier 2012: 176), though resorting to different cinematic strategies based on how Cinema Marginal and Cinema Novo decided to tackle the topic.

Sganzerla reaches the sci-fi domain through citing Welles's classic radio adaptation of H. G. Wells's *The War of the Worlds*. In the film, the voice-over narrators seem to be working at a radio station per se, as they announce all sorts of information with a sensationalist vibe. Again, it is the tropicalist tone that comes to the foreground. Additionally, the image of flying saucers frequently occurs throughout the film, playing a central role in the dialogue with science fiction. More than a homage to the genre, Xavier (2012) suggests that repetition is the key to the fragmentation of *The Red Light Bandit*. In a first moment, a flying saucer appears in the film the bandit is watching, that is, as an element outside the bandit's tangible world; later on, however, it reappears inserted into the bandit's film narrative per se. That is to say, the flying saucer creates a sense of chaos that not only pervades the film the bandit is watching but also the one the audience is watching. Sganzerla does this without a trace of intellectual seriousness. On the contrary, according to Alfredo Suppia, *The Red Light Bandit* 'is perhaps the apex of the parody attitude of Brazilian cinema in relation to science fiction'[3] (2007: 122).

In the final sequence, the bandit succumbs to the crisis and commits suicide after being chased by the farcical police, in a clear reference to Godard's *Pierrot Le Fou* (1965) ending. Next, flying saucers, called UFOs by the voice-over narrators, unexpectedly float above the Boca do Lixo sky. Creating an apocalyptic atmosphere, the flying saucers, accompanied by images of Afro-Brazilian carnival dancers and radio announcements about general disorder, finally hit the ground at a single moment. At this point, the death of the bandit has already been set aside by the film, and the exploding flying saucer becomes the climax of the narrative. The explosion is a sign of failure, defeat, finality. The voice-over narrators, however, refuse to attribute meaning to this frenetic sequence. Although in allusion to the Wells/Welles narration, any dramatic sense is completely absent. Intentionally, there is no moral in the conclusion; rather, there is a sense of catastrophe which attempts to communicate the political environment of the off-screen world at that time. Captivatingly, Rodrigo Lopes de Barros (2013) relates the sense of catastrophe to ruination in his reading of the film. For him, the city is in a state of siege – and the bandit is a tropical outsider that refuses to cooperate. He is the underdeveloped criminal, 'the one who could not stand the frustration humanity and devolved into a destructive form of indiscriminate violence' (ibid.: 62–3).

In his unconventional documentary film, Queirós's output brings to the fore the mix of genres seen in Sganzerla's classic, deeply drawing on science fiction, as pointed out. A big fan of Hollywood sci-fi, the director has said on several occasions that his dream was to film his own *Mad Max* (1979) or *Blade Runner* (1982). As such, documentary and science fiction fulfil the narrative needs at similar levels, playing with the blurring of boundaries but, most importantly, using sci-fi elements to paradoxically enhance the characters/director's approach to reality. As mentioned, the irony and humour in the use of these elements bring Queirós's and Sganzerla's projects closer together, as the sense of *avacalhar* seems to guide the political discourse of both projects. Like Vaz, Queirós acknowledges Glauber's manifestos as key to Brazilian cinematic history and influential in his cinema practice (Furtado

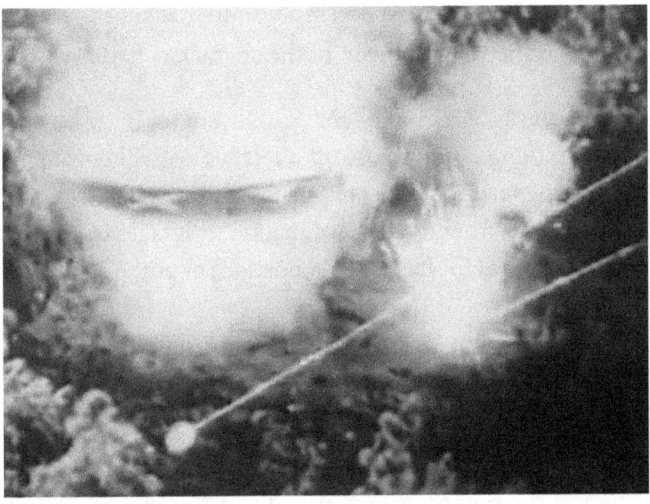

Figure 7.3: Flying saucers hit Boca do Lixo in the closing sequence of *The Red Light Bandit*.

2017). Not surprisingly, however, he highlights the work of Cinema Marginal filmmakers, such as Sganzerla and Andrea Tonacci, as aesthetically closer to himself: 'Not only because of the *avacalhação*, but mainly due to the fact that Cinema Marginal appeared at a time when Cinema Novo was becoming an institution, making concessions and presenting an average Brazil on screen,' Queirós (2018) observes in his interview with me. For him, the risk his cinema and the cinema of some of his contemporaries are proud of taking refers back to the risk that Cinema Marginal (and, to a lesser extent, Cinema Novo) once had in the past.

Nevertheless, the central point of *White Out, Black In* differs from that of *The Red Light Bandit*. Whereas the latter shows a protagonist in search of his own identity ('Who am I?', he questions throughout), the former creates self-assured characters, conscious of their place in society and willing to overthrow the current social structure. In this sense, if the bandit is an allegory of a man/country immersed in chaos, Queirós's sci-fi documentary is the visualization of the aftermath, the post-apocalyptic environment, the ruined Third World. Its characters, however, are not finished but ready to revolt. Here, the explosion planned by Marquim and Sartana is an allegory of rebellion, achievement, a new beginning. The final sequence of *White Out, Black In* is a drawing sequence showing a spaceship bomb-attacking the main political hub of Brasília, as if the vengeful plan of the characters had finally succeeded.

> The barbarians' invasion is imminent … they are ten seconds away from Brasília … everything is suffused with a terrible red light, no one can tell what is going to happen … the people are invading the public parks … only a miracle can save us from total extermination … it takes only one obscure individual in the crowd to shake the foundations of power in the world.

The above quotation could belong to Queirós's sci-fi documentary, but it is actually one of Sganzerla's film's final voice-over announcements. The bandit is dead, the police are miserable, the dancers seem entranced, a flying saucer is in the air, the Third World is about to explode. This chaotic scenario is underlined by the radio announcers' parody, as Xavier (2017) argues. There is a sense of Cold War paranoia when the speakers claim the flying saucers arrived from the East, meaning it does not matter whether they are Reds or Yellows. The news billboard informs us the marines have landed in Bahia in order to defend Brazil, while the Martian fantasy invasion is taking place at the same time. Xavier calls attention to 'the image of the "survivors of the Third World" conducting their Afro-Brazilian carnival in the realm of trash … turning itself into an emblem, a kind of nightmarish vision threatening the conservative mind' (ibid.: 100). The closing sequence takes place in São Paulo but, as the speakers say, could be ten seconds away from Brasília, where Marquim and Sartana would inevitably be found. Their bomb does not come from the East but from the outskirts. They are not Cold War paranoia sufferers but present-day oppressed. They are not dancing amid the trash but surviving out of the trash.

The science *non*fiction documentary of Adirley Queirós

Instead of prompting a meditation on the origins (or the collapse) of Brasília as seen in *The Age of Stone*, the role played by ruins in *White Out, Black In* goes in a different direction, as Queirós finds redemption in exploding the bomb in the Pilot Plan. In other words, the image of a ruined Brasília is the director's way of shedding light upon and condemning the capital's history of segregation and social control (Gouvêa 1995). In fact, the destruction of the capital represents the destruction of the oppressive regime that sustains society as a whole. Although aiming to rewrite history through science fiction, the nonfictional aspects of the narrative are implied by a range of documentary strategies. The traumatic event itself is unveiled mainly through voice-over statements by Marquim and Sartana. These passages are objective and descriptive, compared to the more loose and playful aspects of the narrative. At one point, there are even talking-head interviews with Marquim and Sartana. Here, it seems as if the documentary mode has imposed itself on the narrative. That may be true until the moment when a reverse angle shot shows Dimas Cravalanças (Dilmar Durães), the time-traveller agent, watching the interviews projected inside his precarious spaceship (in reality, a container). All of a sudden, one is brought back to science fiction. Dimas is an agent from the future who time-travels in order to collect evidence of crimes committed by the State.

In addition to the commentary (via voice-over or talking-head interviews), the viewer also gets the chance to see archival photos that evoke the atmosphere of the Quarentão nightclub, alluding to more conventional documentary storytelling. It is precisely the indexicality of the photos (or the ontology of the image, to mention André Bazin's (1967) famous concept) that prevents the film from moving away from realism completely. Nevertheless, when these images are on screen, Marquim is not giving any interview whatsoever. Rather, he recounts the event from his bunker/radio station while putting on records. Again, the film suspends conventional documentary mode, exploring new possibilities of conceiving reality in film by adding sci-fi elements to empirical evidence. Most importantly, this sort of fiction and nonfiction overlapping reveals that, no matter how science-fictional this documentary seems, there is a pulse of reality in each of its frames. In this sense, it is rather a science *non*fiction than a science fiction per se, hence the term *sci-fi documentary*. In this sense, Suppia (2015) reads the film as an example of *borderlands science fiction*,[4] as it is precisely located in an in-between cinematic situation. It is a documentary and, at the same time, a Third World cyberpunk or a *garbage-punk film*, as the author claims. For Mesquita, 'by contaminating fiction with the introduction of features pertaining to the domain of documentary and by parodying the genre's conventions, he inhibits the possibility of an alternative utopia' (2018: 74). Furthermore, when the film opposes 'precarious

Figures 7.4 and 7.5: Sartana/Shokito speaks to the camera in the documentary, whereas Dimas Cravalanças watches him speaking in the sci-fi film.

contraptions (his spaceship is an old container of construction work) to the faith in progress and machinery once shed on the creation of Brasília, a kind of "anti-future," and also a "scientific anti-fiction" is affirmed, marked by scarcity, debris, and obsolescence' (ibid.).

In this case, the conventional documentary form could not ever be applied because 'it cannot handle telling a class story, that is, the story of a Brazilian periphery, in the sense that it cannot overcome the documentary form itself', Queirós (2018) affirms in the interview I did with him. For the director, every time conventional documentaries aim to tell a story like the one of *White Out, Black In*, they fail. 'It is as if the documentary betrays the characters. The revenge that is supposed to happen does not happen. The documentary presents these characters as victims and turns the everyday event, or even an extraordinary one, into an extremely exotic thing'. To put it differently, 'the memory remains the memory of the oppressor's eye over the oppressed. This is what the classic documentary does: it gives the memory of suffered oppression' (ibid.). It is no coincidence that in the final credits of the sci-fi documentary Queirós's comment appears: '*Da nossa memória fabulamos nóis mesmos*' ('Our memory, we ourselves make fables', in loose translation). Interested in reassessing history through memory, he argues that once one acquires power over the narration, new layers of politics, interventions, possibilities and territories are created and have to be taken into account. With this in mind, the ruinous cinematic atmosphere is key, as Tim Edensor reminds us of 'the allegorical power of ruins to interrogate memory, look at the stimulation of involuntary memories, and identify the numerous ghosts which inhabit the haunted space of the ruin' (2005: 139).

According to Mesquita (2015), *White Out, Black In* engenders its own regime of historicity, regardless of any institutional attempt to define temporal phases. Referring to Queirós's documentaries, she believes his 'works evoke the past, but in relation to the present (and sometimes to the future)' (ibid.: 3). Although the actual crime took place in 1986, the film is quite vague about the year in which the action takes place. The viewer knows the time-traveller agent has come from a 2070s society and that for three years he has been in the 'territory of the past'. In the opening credits, a board informs the viewer that the story is set in Old Ceilândia, Federal District, but gives no further information. The spatial-temporal vagueness is so that Dimas can receive a message from the future telling him that, after three years away, he might actually be lost: 'We don't know of your whereabouts and there is the suspicion that you have disintegrated in time and space'. The disintegration that the message refers to helps Queirós to purposely puzzle our perception. When Dimas wanders into the so-called 'territory of the past', for instance, he strolls through vast, empty spaces that could be a sort of wasteland or ground ready to receive high-rise buildings.

In this sense, Hora (2017) claims that Dimas's precarious spaceship-container plays a key role in the construction of time – or within its own regime of historicity. 'Anachronistic scenic object par excellence, the time machine, a construction container, is an apparatus of the future, but also an allegory of the past of Brasília's construction and of the present of the capital's growth.' (ibid.: 73). That is, the container refers to an idea of Brasília being a construction-site type of city, from its modernist invention to current real estate speculation. As a sci-fi element, the time-travel machine is therefore a contradictory *novum* in the narrative. According to Darko Suvin (1979), *novum* (Latin for 'new thing') is the defining characteristic of a sci-fi narrative. The term is used to describe the scientifically plausible innovations that allow the story to be developed in a sci-fi mode. At the same time that the time-travel machine is used as a means of bringing justice from the future, it encompasses the controversies of past and present times. Interestingly, Hora creates an opposition between the machine and the bomb, the film's second *novum*. While both objects are sci-fi objects, they have opposite meanings in the storytelling. 'If the time machine is the anachronistic element par excellence that promotes the multiple plots between different temporalities, the weapon of mass destruction is the element that implodes the very historical time and that crystallizes progress as a catastrophe' (ibid.: 77), in a true Benjaminian fashion.

The second half of the sci-fi documentary focuses on the second *novum*. The bomb is going to be launched into the future; the characters stress, calling attention to the division between the space-time of (Old) Ceilândia and Brasília. Not by coincidence is the bomb heading into the future, as Brasília has forever been considered the city of the future. There is a sense of naivety in this vindictive plan, very much in tune with the fable tone of the story. While Marquim is responsible for collecting and mixing the atomic sound, Sartana takes pictures of Brasília (from quite a distance) and draws something which will only be understood at the end of the film (as his drawings become the ending of the film per se). As Furtado underlines, Sartana's drawings 'constitute an alternative visuality and a secret or shadow form of record' (2019: 136). Nothing is known at this stage, but Sartana, just like Marquim, is cooperating with the final explosive sequence.[5] The sentence that wraps up the film points out: 'Our memory, we ourselves make fables.' Indeed, revenge comes in the

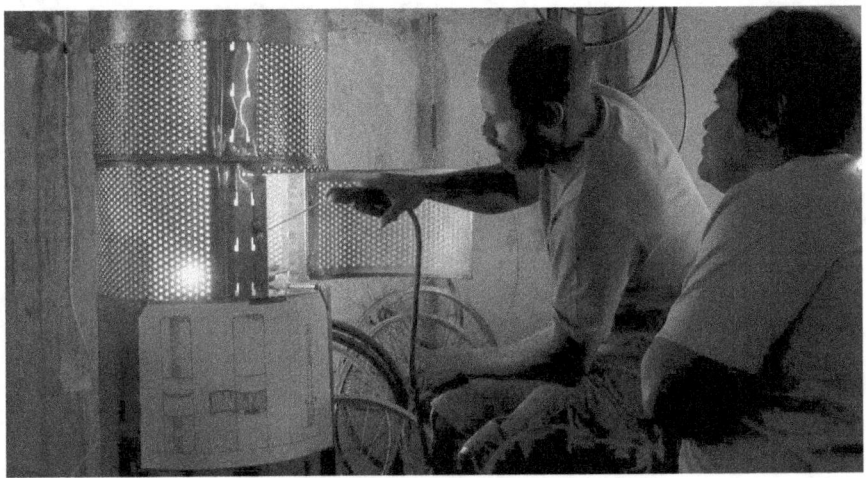

Figure 7.6: Marquim (right) and Sartana assemble the sonic-atomic bomb.

shape of art. Fulfilled by music and depicted through drawings, the closing sequence shows the collapse of the white, wealthy Brasília, the modernist design under attack, the capital in ruins. The use of drawings is particularly interesting as it stresses the fable/fabrication aspect of the narrative, a fantasy created by the draftsman (and the director). Moreover, there seems to be an implicit analogy here: if the drawings are a sci-fi invention in the film, Brasília itself is a modernist invention in the real world.

Apart from *The Red Light Bandit*'s dystopic ending, the final sequence of *White Out, Black In* seems to open an involuntary dialogue with *Projeto Pulex*, Tadao Miaqui's short animation film. As mentioned earlier, *Projeto Pulex* shows a Brasília ruled by politicians aimed at exterminating the poor population. In it, a man of the people attempts to stop the plan. He invades the meeting where the government is explaining the project in order to shoot them. The security system, however, identifies his presence and murders him first. In a sense, Marquim and Sartana, men of the people, carry on with that failed plan. Their successful plan is put into action through drawings, an explicit link between both films, as *Projeto Pulex* is an animation per se. For Suppia (2007), dystopia in the short film is a reflection of a general social indignation which was aroused in the wake of the neoliberal presidency of the late 1980s, just after the end of the military dictatorship.[6] In *White Out, Black In*, the crime under scrutiny took place in 1986, a time link between

Figures 7.7, 7.8 and 7.9: Brasília under attack.

the films. This time, however, dystopia turns into revolution as Marquim and Sartana succeed in their plan. In this sense, they stand as an empowering Afrofuturist Brazilian narrative, as Antonio Cordoba (2017) suggests, bearing both a deconstructive and reparative tone, and making use of technology in favour of black storytelling. In addition, Furtado sees a reference to the dichotomy between past and future, modernization and ruination, in the figure of construction scaffoldings in disarray that appears on screen after the explosion. 'Following Sartana's sketches of the terrorist attack, the shot can be seen as a post-apocalyptic representation of Brasilia after the explosion of Marquim's bomb,' he (2019: 138) affirms. On the other hand, he also argues 'that the scaffoldings are meant to evoke the memory of the city's construction. Although the human costs and tremendous violence necessary for the building of Brasilia were never fully acknowledged, documented, or divulged by the state, the city's construction was widely publicized as a heroic, epic modernization project' (ibid.: 138–9). For Furtado, 'the film's final shot of scaffoldings in ruin suggests the ruination of Brasilia as un unfinished, future-oriented project' (ibid.: 139).

Finally, Daniel Herwitz reminds us that 'Le Corbusier's cities aim for permanence' and that 'it is hardly an easy thing to imagine dismantling Brasilia or Chandigarh now' (2010: 236). At the same time that he believes that 'the presumption of such radical change would simply be a perpetuation of the thinking of the utopian planner, like Le Corbusier, or the apartheid administrator', he does not think that we 'must accept the human or urban landscape exactly as it is'. For Herwitz, 'velvet revolutions are often about tearing down the icons of authoritarian monumentality, and most of us have seen images of crowds gleefully ripping down Berlin Wall or a statue of Lenin' (ibid.), so perhaps it is indeed about time for us to see the images created by Queirós. His ruins question viewing Brasília as an untouchable icon. As a UNESCO World Heritage Site, the modernist Pilot Plan does not allow urban interventions at any cost. 'Brasília is a city that can't be touched. You can't change her physical structure. The surroundings, they can explode,' says Queirós in the Canal E (2014) interview. Hence, the situation is reversed in *White Out, Black In*.

The bomb will not only touch but also explode the modernist symbols of the Pilot Plan. Most of the drawings show the emblematic Plaza of the Three

Powers being squashed, while furious, funk-music lyrics by MC Dodô loudly play in the soundtrack ('Bomb explodes in the head ripping thief apart/Frying quickly the neuron that pacifies reason/I will collect the debt and for sure the war I will win').[7] 'Social transition required a symbolic break from the monuments of the past, giving their complicity in forms of hegemonic power,' Herwitz (2010: 238) claims, but those could also be Queirós's words. 'These styles of monumentalization were written in the script of the settler. They speak to the excluded majority only as confirmations of its exclusion' (ibid.). At last, the monument is torn down. So-called progress is undone, though not as a regression. As one knows, ruins have the ability to be the end of one cycle and, at the same time, the promising starting point of something else.

The heterotopic Brasília

As discussed, reality in *White Out, Black In* and *The Age of Stone* takes place in spaces other than Brasília itself. In the case of *White Out, Black In*, the absence of the capital has a strong political sense, as Queirós rejects the white, wealthy Brasília – for him, a symbol of oppression. Therefore, Ceilândia, home of the director, 30 km from Brasília, is his cinematic viewpoint. With regard to *The Age of Stone*, sequences were filmed in Chapada dos Veadeiros, 230 km north of the capital, and Pirenópolis, 150 km west of the capital. In proposing a new spatiality for Brasília, the director suggests mystery instead of understanding, as neither Chapada dos Veadeiros nor Pirenópolis are even identified as such. Vaz decentralizes the historical perspective of Brasília through decentralizing its space. These places, however, should not be taken as unreal; they are more 'like counter-sites, a kind of effectively enacted utopia in which the real sites, all the other real sites that can be found within the culture, are simultaneously represented, contested, and inverted', as Foucault (1986: 24) defines *heterotopia*. Furthermore, the Brasília of Queirós and Vaz, like the counter-sites of Foucault, 'are most often linked to slices in time ..., a sort of absolute break with their traditional time' (ibid.: 26), in other words, a spatial-temporal experimentation attempting to flee the authoritarianism of society.

In this sense, the connection between Brasília and ruins in the directors' outputs are no coincidence. As Edensor claims, 'ruins are exemplary spaces of this sort of heterotopia. The affective, peculiar sensations experienced in the ruin slip away from those normative procedures through which space is represented and categorised' (2005: 63). Drawing on the Foucauldian *heterotopia*, Vaz and Queirós seem to entail this concept in their cinematic (re)constructions of Brasília. In so doing, both filmmakers propose *another* perspective of the capital. Their alternative worlds rely on sci-fi elements as a detour from the official narrative. First, this is because the genre per se is based on the invention of alternative worlds as 'the exploration of all the constraints thrown up by history itself – the web of counterfinalities and anti-dialectics which human production has itself produced' (Jameson 2005: 66). Second, and perhaps more importantly, because the sci-fi imaginary is mobilized with regard to the idea propagated of Brasília being the city of the future – the modernist city was meant to create genuine, 'new forms of collective association, personal habit, and daily life' (Holston 1989: 31).

Significantly, neither *The Age of Stone* nor *White Out, Black In* are labelled as sci-fi films but as sci-fi documentaries, by the directors themselves. That is, apart from the sci-fi realm, there is a genuine concern in locating both outputs within the field of documentary. My hypothesis is that their attempts to suggest an original approach to reality gain credibility if linked to cinema's most realistic strategy: the documentary film, the professed visual document of one's historical time. Nevertheless, the connection with the documentary mode also seems very keen to play with the false certainties usually attached to it. That is, both films appropriate (or, better yet, resituate) the values of the documentary film in order to problematize the idea of reality. Plus, they resort to defamiliarizing the present (Jameson 2005) through science fiction by aiming to redefine that same reality. Thereby, both films encompass a dual plea: in questioning the official narrative of Brasília, they find it impossible not to question the traditional means of narrating it – content and form under inspection.

Unlike Vaz's *The Age of Stone*, *White Out, Black In* targets a new representation of Brasília as a clear enemy to be destroyed. It is precisely that iconoclastic gesture that sets Queirós and Vaz apart. Whereas Vaz believes that defining the enemy so assuredly actually empowers it, Queirós seems to follow a more Marxist way of reading social relations, underlining hierarchical positions in Brasília's spatiality and society. The oppressed characters in his fable-documentary plan to drop a sonic-atomic bomb on the white, wealthy Brasília, the political hub created by modernism. That Brasília is Queirós's and the film's enemy. By resorting to sci-fi elements, the director is able to cinematically destroy it, as the awaited explosion can finally turn that Brasília to ruins. The constant interaction and division between Queirós and Vaz's film methodologies provides at least one certainty: there should be nothing like a fixed notion or pregiven reading of what Brasília is.

Their artistic aims and original schemes put the very meaning of the capital city into narrative dispute alongside previous attempts to depict national progress and (under)development, such as *The Age of the Earth* and *The Red Light Bandit*. That dispute implies a place of tension that houses creative initiatives aimed at destabilizing the status quo instead of finding easy solutions. Even though Queirós seems to be firm in his left-wing political stance, he openly welcomes contradiction as a quintessential element of his filmmaking. He says *White Out, Black In* is a contradictory film or a film that works through contradiction. For instance, the film crew, though cohesive and friendly, is immersed in contradiction themselves, disagreeing and coping with their distinct subjectivities. He mentions that, at the same time that he is a *white* director representing (though he dislikes that word) *black*-community demands, he feels he can legitimately talk about territorial issues in Ceilândia as he has always lived there. 'The only thing that makes us move is contradiction. It can advance with us or implode on us,' Queirós states in the Canal E (2014) interview. In terms of methods, one could relate Queirós's fondness for contradiction to Vaz's Deleuzian intellectual porosity concerning critical thinking and filmmaking. Their heterotopic Brasília, therefore, is the aftermath of contradiction and porosity.

***

In 1964, Oscar Niemeyer was in Paris when the military coup d'état took the federal capital by storm. Haunted by the prognosis of what was to come, he painted two oil paintings straightforwardly titled *Ruins of Brasília*. The man who once designed the genesis of the city also painted his modernist columns lying on a dark horizon in an expressionist tone. Highly obscure and to date left out of the national imaginary, the two paintings came to public view in 2017 in an exhibition celebrating the 110th anniversary of the architect's birth – one of them for the very first time.[8] His prophecy was realized in motion. As if in the climax of ruin or a cinematic trance, Dimas shouts, pretending to have an imaginary gun in his hands: 'Take this, progress-toady! … Racist who will never change; it's going to stay the same! … Take this, hell of Europe; take this, everyone!' He is insanely mad in his own science *non*fiction act, as if opening a time-travelling dialogue with *The Red Light Bandit*. 'The Third World will explode! … The solution for Brazil is extermination!,' exclaims the little poet man in Sganzerla's frenetic film debut. The black Christ of Glauber does not shy away either. He welcomes the bomb in the theatrical tone of *The Age of the Earth*: 'Blessed be the misery, because one day they will break free! Blessed be the atomic bomb, the prostitute of Babylon, blessed be the criminals!' The diggers of the quarry are sculpting the bomb. Or collecting the remnants. Between fear and fascination, Clarice ensures that 'Brasília is broken glass on the street floor. Shards' (Lispector 1999b: 56). How long will it take for the shattered pieces to be gathered? Amid the ruins of underdevelopment, Brasília is still breathing.

Part Three

Constructing ruins in Rio de Janeiro: An intermedial visualization of failing projects

Before Brasília was crowned capital of Brazil, Rio de Janeiro had been the country's leading city for almost two centuries. It was in Rio that Hélio Oiticica exhibited *Tropicália* for the first time and that Caetano Veloso first saw Glauber Rocha's *Entranced Earth* (Terra em Transe, 1967), a catalyst for Tropicália to erupt as a movement in 1967. In Part Three, I consider the city as an ongoing (de)construction site, from the standpoint of the experimental documentaries that question the modern and neoliberal consequences embedded in the urban space. I argue that they apply an intermedial aesthetics to the documentary mode to visualize ruins in Rio.

Chapter 8 draws on the intermedial emergence of Tropicália (Solomon 2017) in the wake of Cinema Novo, underlining its countercultural attitude of unpacking national issues and the risk of that being commodified under the yoke of the neoliberal regime (Rolnik 2006, 2011). In the face of that risk, I reason that the films I analyse fight against the loss of the radical power of art precisely by exposing the architectural failures of the city. Chapter 9 offers the World Cup and the Olympic (de)construction works as emblematic images of the present-day dynamics of capitalist extraction, as explored in Daniel Santos's *ExPerimetral* (2016) and Clarissa Campolina, Julia de Simone, Luiz Pretti and Ricardo Pretti's *The Harbour* (O Porto, 2013), two experimental short documentaries on the Elevado da Perimetral, a 5.5-km elevated highway located in Rio's harbour zone, that make use of intermedial tactics and help me prepare the ground for analyses in the two chapters that follow.

Chapter 10 is completely focused on Luisa Marques's *Tropical Curse* (A Maldição Tropical, 2016), an experimental short documentary intermingling visual arts and performance. It starts with the abandoned Carmen Miranda Museum to question national development through both Mirandas, the commodified Portuguese-Brazilian artist and the decaying, modernist building. In Chapter 11, I look at Joana Traub Csekö and Pedro Urano's exploration of the intermedial, multi-sensorial documentary aesthetic that reflexively references the country's historical architectural modernism in *HU Enigma* (HU, 2011). The documentary feature investigates the last days of the university hospital of the Federal University of Rio de Janeiro – in fact, half of the building's final days, as the other half still functions as a fragile public hospital. Four visual constructions of failing projects that frame ruins (an elevated highway, a museum and a hospital) are presented as a means of addressing Rio's (and Brazil's, by extension) (under)development. In doing so, the filmmakers' belief that the ruin in Brazil is not the work of chance but a project in itself establishes a dialogue with the 1960s tropicalist intermediality.

8

Tropicália: An intermedial counterculture

In *Tropical Truth: A Story of Music and Revolution in Brazil*,[1] a blending of autobiographical episodes intermingled with commentaries on Brazilian culture, Caetano Veloso (2017) delivers an exquisite mosaic to unpack issues related to national identity. He explores the 1964 military coup d'état, modernist anthropophagy and, most importantly, Tropicália itself – the innovative intermedial movement that originally mixed national and international references to create an authentic image of the turmoils of late 1960s' Brazil. In the book (which had a revised and amplified second edition in 2017, twenty years after its original release), Caetano delves into the politically charged decades of the 1960s and 1970s, left and right-wing debates, capitalist and socialist ideologies, to articulate his particular viewpoint – or, rather, his tropical truth. Accused by the traditional left of being alienated, and criticized by the conservative right of being subversive, Caetano's stance is indeed hard to label. Tropicália, in that sense, was his means of expressing through music the dualities, nuances and contradictions of what it felt like to be young, progressive and Brazilian, at that specific moment in time.

As briefly pointed out in Chapter 2, it is worth considering Caetano's tribute to Claude Lévi-Strauss's writings in his fifty-year body of work, one of particular relevance to this study. The conflation of the Brazilian *tropicalista* and the French anthropologist, the popular artist and the foreigner lecturer, the singer-thinker and the European-Indigenist, took shape better when the former wrote the lyrics of *Fora da Ordem* (Out of Order), a song for his album *Circuladô* (1991). Inspired by the paradoxes of Brazilian progress suggested by Lévi-Strauss, he evokes the French author, singing: '*Aqui tudo parece/Que é ainda construção/E já é ruína.*' In English: 'Here everything seems/It is still under construction/And is already a ruin.' Full of dialectic images, the song plays with the idea of the country being a construction site whose work will never be completed. This conclusion presents itself in the following: '*O asfalto, a ponte, o viaduto/Ganindo pra lua/Nada continua*' ('The asphalt, the bridge, the viaduct/Howling at the moon/Nothing continues'). In another excerpt, there is even an implicit relationship between the devastated landscape and the socio-economic wreckage of Brazil: '*Um mero serviçal/Do narcotráfico/ Foi encontrado na ruína/De uma escola em construção*' ('A mere servant/ Of drug trafficking/Was found in the ruin/Of a school under construction') (Veloso 1991).

Fascinatingly, that perception attunes with North American artist Robert Smithson's notion of *ruins in reverse*, which has served as a conceptual umbrella for many contemporary artists. In his 1967 essay 'The Monuments of Passaic' (the year of publication is a symptomatic coincidence here), Smithson wanders in his New Jersey hometown and notices that 'that zero panorama seemed to contain ruins in reverse, that is – all the new construction that would eventually be built. This is the opposite of the "romantic ruin" because the buildings don't fall into ruin after they are built but rather rise as ruins before they are built' (1996: 72). As Brian Dillon claims, the concept 'reminds us that the ruin is always dynamic and in process, giving rise to what Smithson calls "dialectical landscapes" that hover between the deep geological past and a catastrophic future' (2011: 14). Seemingly inspired by both Caetano's and Smithson's critical viewpoints, Welsh visual artist Cerith Wyn Evans directly embraced the argument. In 2004, he displayed a major installation called *Aqui Tudo Parece Que É Ainda Construção e Já É Ruína, A Partir de Fora da Ordem*[2] (Here Everything Seems That It Is Still under Construction and It Is Already a Ruin, from Out of Order), a sort of ephemeral firework sculpture. In the artwork, the famous sentence borrowed from Caetano's song shines in a precarious wooden outdoor structure – a luminous event that lasts less than two minutes to underline its transient nature.

More recently, for instance, Brazilian visual artist Andrey Zignnatto reappropriated the concept in his installation *Tudo É Sempre Construção, e Também Ruínas*[3] (Everything Is Always Construction, and Also Ruins). Here, Zignnatto plays with a wall made of broken bricks, emphasizing the logic of (de)construction, and making use of a single object to depict the duality. Notably, the dialogue established between literature, music and installation art not only points to the kind of productions Tropicália might have inspired but also refers to its very origins as a movement. As will be discussed throughout Part Three, the tropicalist critical reading of national (under)development had intermediality as its main driving force, an artistic strategy that blurred the boundaries within the cultural scene at the time and resonates to this day. Multimedia artist Caetano himself has also been involved in the visual arts, particularly film.[4] In 1986, he directed *O Cinema Falado*[5] (loosely translated as The Talkies), a fragmented, experimental collage of literary references, from Guimarães Rosa to Thomas Mann, whose texts were brought to life by friends and family members.

Having said that, his connection to Brazilian cinema actually goes back to the conception of Tropicália itself. The trigger for the movement to erupt took place when he first saw Glauber Rocha's *Entranced Earth*. 'One powerful image after another confirmed my impression that unconscious aspects of our reality were on the verge of being revealed' (Veloso 2017: 35). The contradictions that Glauber managed to visually represent on screen had a decisive impact on Caetano. What struck Caetano most was Glauber's emphatic discourse on the death of populism, questioning the traditional leftist approach in the middle of a right-wing military dictatorship that lasted from 1964 to 1985. In the film, the protagonist is a haunted left-wing poet in crisis with his own political beliefs – and Glauber radically addresses that topic in one of the film's many iconic sequences. 'During a mass demonstration, the poet, who is among those making speeches, calls forward a unionized worker and, to show how unprepared the worker is to fight for his rights, violently covers his mouth, shouting at the other (and at the audience), "This is the People! Idiots, illiterate, no politics!"', Caetano recalls. 'It was a hecatomb that I was facing. … *Tropicalismo* would never have come into being but for that traumatic moment' (ibid.: 39).

The birth of Cinema Novo was itself a hecatomb. It ruthlessly destroyed what people – from intellectuals to a general audience – had understood about national cinema up to then. Aiming to construct a genuine Brazilian identity from moving images, Glauber, alongside Nelson Pereira dos Santos, Ruy Guerra, Joaquim Pedro de Andrade and many others, sought to evolve out of the standard cinematic output of Atlântida and Vera Cruz studios by bringing to the foreground the contradictions of underdevelopment in which the country was immersed. In other words, the complexities of Brazil as a Third World nation, more specifically, after the military coup d'état, became the very motto for that generation of artists to work on – something that Caetano would put into action through Tropicália sonorities. According to Ismail Xavier, that was actually 'a moment of strong transition – political, cultural, aesthetic – where cinema, theatre, the visual arts and popular music, together and in constant interaction, defined a time and a debate of rare intensity' (2012: 7). Particularly thinking of the cinema, Xavier regards the films of that period as filled with allegorical strategies marked by a sense of history as catastrophe, as discussed in Chapter 2.

In the recently published *Tropicália and Beyond: Dialogues in Brazilian Film History*, Stefan Solomon (2017) attempts to reassess that legacy in order to evaluate the resonances of the Tropicália era in the present-day artistic scene, especially considering its intermedial aspect. Both in the book he edited and in the film season he organized, Solomon sheds light on particular strands of that cinema and on more recent productions in dialogue with that tradition. Celebrating *Entranced Earth*'s fiftieth anniversary, he points out: 'We are now a full fifty years from the film's release, but its concerns seem just as pressing today as they were then; indeed, one cannot help but consider the way that the political crisis depicted in *Terra em Transe* mirrors the abject failure of politics in Brazil circa 2017' (ibid.: 20), referring to President Dilma Rousseff's controversial impeachment and the political and economic turmoil that damaged national democracy afterwards. According to a Lévi-Straussian pessimistic view of progress (Veloso 2017), the failure of development has been contingent upon the cyclical phases of economic boom and downfall, hardcore exploitation and subsequent contraction, cycles of construction and subsequent destruction, as previously mentioned.

Discussions of cinema and intermediality, in particular, play a central role in the work of scholar Ágnes Pethő (2010, 2011), whose research delves into a variety of intermedial approaches to cinema and advocates intermediality as a consistent branch of film studies. Rather than a compilation of overlapping media expressions, her work revisits and expands the realm of filmmaking, taking into account 'cinema's non-discursive domains and more sensual modes of perception' (Pethő 2010: 65) through the fusion, not the accumulation, of film and other art forms. It seems to be, after all, an opportunity to scrutinize, once again, the ubiquitous Bazinian enquiry: *What is cinema?* As Lúcia Nagib and Anne Jerslev (2014) point out, the Bazinian tone is indeed a crucial part of intermedia's genealogy, since Bazin's 'Pour un Cinéma Impur: Défense de l'Adaptation'[6] addressed the debated relationship between cinema and literature in the early 1950s in France. For Nagib and Jerslev, a so-called impure cinema should be seen not as an object but as a method 'capable of understanding cinema beyond the constraints of the medium's specificity' (ibid.: xxi). In this sense, an intermedial approach to film relates to a theory that 'is focused on relationships, rather than structures, on something that "happens" in-between media' (Pethő 2011: 2).

As stated above, Solomon (2017) draws on that intermedial method in his reassessment of Tropicália against the contemporary cinema backdrop. Focusing on the Brazilian artistic experience, he underlines the implicit analogy between intermediality and cultural anthropophagy in a country marked by cannibalistic rhetoric. As Caetano once stated, 'Tropicalismo is a neo-Anthropophagism' (Veloso cited in Campos 1974: 207). Solomon appeals to Brazilian scholar Jairo Ferreira's timely reading of 'cinema as an *anthropophagic* art, polarised and transcendental in the way it synthesises all six previous arts and metamorphoses itself into an uneasiness about its future' (2006, emphasis added). Nagib and Jerslev (2014) strike a similar note when simultaneously relating intermedial and intercultural approaches to film: 'From Lumière's travelling the globe with the *cinématographe*, the moving image as well as the moving camera have been crossing cultural boundaries in the same way that they cannibalized pre-existing arts and media' (ibid.: xxiv). The intercultural aspect (or the cultural anthropophagic aspect) of intermediality has also been tackled by Robert Stam in his analyses of the 'multicultural nature of artistic intertextuality' (2005: 3).

Ultimately, Nagib and Jerslev emphasize another aspect of intermedial practice that seems to mirror tropicalist-like values. Rather than 'ascribing, in principle, a politically progressive, "modern" and/or experimental character to films which expose in form and content their cross-border intentions', both authors are interested in such films precisely 'because, among other things, they push intermediality to its ultimate boundary, which is the division between art and life' (2014: xxiv). Certainly, the blurring of boundaries between art and life itself was one of Hélio Oiticica's (1999a) main goals in defending his *anti-art*, an art intrinsically linked to everyday experience, centred on the multi-sensorial mode of human interaction with the world. According to Pethő, intermediality has 'a kind of sensual mode', one that invites the audience 'to literally get in touch with a world portrayed not at a distance but at the proximity of entangled synesthetic sensations, and resulting in a cinema that can be perceived in the terms of music, painting, architectural forms or haptic textures' (2011: 5). Bluntly put, as Oiticica's multisensory *Penetrable PN2* encapsulated in its title: *"Purity Is a Myth"*.

In this context, Solomon places intermediality as the defining aspect of the countercultural 1960s movement, as '*tropicalismo* offered itself as a banner under which the purity and particularity of any given art form could become compromised, giving rise to something new by ignoring its own institutional confines' (2017: 16). In his study, intermediality encompasses Tropicália as a whole, from the intermingling of the cinematic and visual arts to the multitasking kind of artist – like Oiticica himself, who experimented with painting, sculpture, performance and film (with filmmakers Neville D'Almeida and Ivan Cardoso). When investigating its resonances in contemporary cinema, Solomon is less interested in tropicalist films per se than in films that have 'at least some connection with *tropicalismo* as a strategy or an idea' (ibid.: 19). According to Nagib and Solomon, 'Tropicália collected and made sense of the debris of the left-wing revolutionary utopia shattered by the military coup in Brazil in 1964' (2019: 123). More fundamentally, 'Tropicália artists took the political catastrophe as an opportunity to dismiss hierarchies and break the boundaries', as 'their outputs and interventions recognized no frontiers between the established arts and media but circulated freely across them' (ibid.).

Following that argument, I focus on the intermedial aspect of experimental documentary-making as one of the everlasting resonances of Tropicália in present-day culture. The return to Tropicália via a contemporary version of intermediality can be read as the execution of intermedial aesthetics in the documentary mode to visualize ruins. The dialogue with that tradition and the openness to experiment seem in tune with Cezar Migliorin's argument affirming that today 'the place of documentary is that of undefinition' (2010: 9). If since Cinema da Retomada, 'there have been fewer certainties, fixed models and definitive explanations' in Brazilian documentary, as Amir Labaki (2003: 104) suggests, contemporary production seems to be at ease exploring the boundaries of cinema, visual arts and other art practices. In Brazil, the proximity between documentary and video art, for instance, echoes the 1980s, as Consuelo Lins and Cláudia Mesquita (2011) point out. That crop of nonfiction production was consolidated after the digital revolution, while fostering connections with both the contemporary art circuit and the 1960s revolutionary cinema, as Andréa França (2006) contends in Chapter 3.

The anthropophagic tropicalist appearance

Considered the Tropicália leader alongside his music partner Gilberto Gil, one cannot dismiss the role of other art practices (cinema, visual arts, theatre)[7] in the music of Caetano and his comrades. In this regard, the mix partially resulted from the way Caetano related to Oswald de Andrade's 'Cannibalist Manifesto'[8] (1928), released in the wake of controversies provoked by the 1922 São Paulo Modern Art Week. His tropicalist conceptualization was much influenced by Andrade's anthropophagic approach to art and culture, one inspired by the Tupinambá cannibalism in order to allegorically digest foreign influences in favour of developing a Brazilian art. Tropicália drew inspiration from the modernist movement of the 1920s, at the same time maintaining a stimulating interchange with contemporary artists in the 1960s. In mixing bossa nova and rock and roll, high art and pop culture, music and visual arts, it proposed a new look at the condition of underdevelopment, updating Cinema Novo's early days and establishing a dialogue with Cinema Marginal films. Honouring the intermedial aspect, the movement was actually baptized after Oiticica's installation *Tropicália, Penetrable PN2 "Purity Is a Myth" and PN3 "Imagetic"*, displayed as part of a major exhibition *New Brazilian Objectivity* (1967), at the Museum of Modern Art in Rio de Janeiro – the first time the word *Tropicália* was used.

Inferring connections between Oiticica's artwork and one of Caetano's early songs, cinematographer and producer Luiz Carlos Barreto suggested the title *Tropicália* for the songwriter's lyrics. It is no coincidence that *Tropicália*, the song, a sort of unofficial anthem, contains an intermedial discourse unlike in any other lyrics, playing with references ranging from filmmaker Glauber to singer Tom Jobim and writer José de Alencar.[9] In *Tropical Truth*, the composer affirms that the song 'was the closest I could get to what it had been suggested to me by *Entranced Earth*' (Veloso 2017: 204).[10]

In this sense, it becomes clear that the movement had its origins in the visual arts realm. In fact, Cynthia Canejo (2004) shifts the focus away from Caetano, claiming the prominence of Oiticica in promoting Tropicália as both an artistic practice and form of critical thinking – a fact commonly overlooked, she argues in her essay. Canejo takes issue with Caetano not knowing Oiticica's influential work at the time, as 'considering the intercommunication within the fairly compact art world in Brazil and the impact that Oiticica's Tropicália stirred, it is possible that Caetano had not seen Oiticica's work personally, but almost certainly he would have heard of it through the media' (ibid.: 66). Oiticica's installation invited the public to walk through a labyrinth of a garden of sand intermingled with clichéd tropical signs attached to a certain idea of Brazilian identity. In parallel, the structure brought the precarious architecture of Rio's *favelas* to the fore while TV images situated the oeuvre in a technological, postmodern context. Mobilizing the cultural anthropophagy proposed by Andrade (and later absorbed by Caetano), both *penetrables* 'are multi-sensory installations surrounded by stereotypically emblematic Brazilian elements' (ibid.: 65). For Oiticica, *Tropicália*, the artwork, was 'the very first objectively conscious attempt to impose an obviously "Brazilian" image on the current context of the avant-garde and the manifestations of national art in general', he wrote back in 1968.[11] Focusing on the liminality between art and life, he advocated an *anti-art*, one that should be sensorial, turn passive spectators into active participants and consider the world out there as the true museum (Oiticica 1999a). In *General Scheme of the New Objectivity*, the catalogue text for the exhibition, he sees the artist as a proposer, and wonders: 'In Brazil, the roles take on the following pattern: how to, in an underdeveloped country, explain and justify the appearance of an avant-garde, not as a symptom of alienation, but as a decisive factor in its collective progress?' (Oiticica 1999b: 41).

Certainly not by the commodification of such praxis, Oiticica would contend. His concern about Tropicália being itself devoured by consumerism was part of the game since the threshold of tropicalist debates. One year after the *New Brazilian Objectivity* show, the artist-proposer was confronting market-oriented art consumption: 'And now what does one see? Bourgeois, sub-intellectuals, cretins of all kinds, preaching Tropicalism, tropicália (turned into fashion) – in short, transforming something that they don't really know what it is into consumption' (Oiticica no date). Canejo immediately singles out his approach by affirming that 'Oiticica's use of tropical elements was different from the strictly marketable colourful banana and mango creations that began to appear' (2004: 66). In drawing on Andrade's cultural anthropophagy, the scholar argues that Oiticica took a step further in pursuing the deconstruction of the myth of a Brazilian tropical paradise under the yoke of a rising capitalist economy. Interestingly, Nagib reminds one that Andrade himself, after committing to the communist ideology, was soon to put his cultural strategy under scrutiny in the early 1930s, 'rejecting his youthful enthusiasm for anthropophagy' (2017a: 8).

In the art history domain, Oiticica is usually associated with the Neo-Concrete Movement that took place in Rio de Janeiro, with a manifesto signed by Reynaldo Jardim, Ferreira Gullar, Theon Spanudis, Amílcar de Castro, Franz Weissman, Lygia Clark and Lygia Pape in 1959. The Neo-Concrete Movement is known as Rio's answer to São Paulo's Concrete Movement. In common, they both had the constructivist art's 'evolutionary reading of art history, fidelity to the geometric abstraction language and the proposal for social insertion' (Zilio 2009: 123). The Neo-Concrete artists, however, started questioning that art process from within and became interested in establishing a connection with the audience. 'While Concretism, linked to constructive orthodoxy, would be a kind of positivism in art, Neoconcretism, linked to phenomenological idealism, sees man as a being in the world, resuming a concentration of totality that restores expressiveness as legitimate in art' (ibid.). After that decisive period, Oiticica was to develop an art (or an *anti-art*) of his own. With his *penetrables*,[12] Oiticica's work moved towards what would be called *environmental art*, taken as the starting point of contemporary art in Brazil. Particularly with *Tropicália*, he wanted to 'provoke the explosion of the obvious' or 'the rupture with the attempts to update national and popular ideology' (ibid.: 128). As stated, he became very critical of the way the work as a whole was apprehended and later co-opted. 'All these things with an obvious image of tropicality, which had macaw, plants, sand, were not to be taken as a school, as something to be followed afterwards, everything that became pineapple and Carmen Miranda became a symbol of tropicalism, the exact opposite of what I wanted. *Tropicália* was exactly to end this' (Oiticica cited in Zilio 2009: 128–9). Even though 'Tropicália or Tropicalismo was never a declared movement in the plastic arts' (Canejo 2004: 66), Canejo sees 'Oiticica as not only the father of the movement but also a critical motivator and participant, especially during the initial stages' (ibid.: 61). She mentions his friendship with Caetano and Gil as an evidence of their similar mindset – Caetano wore one of his *parangolés* and exhibited Oiticica's *Be Marginal, Be a Hero* silk-screened banner in one of his concerts. On the other hand, she will contend that 'to place Oiticica's work inside the closed context of anthropophagy (whether it is an international form or one specifically Brazilian) without clarifying his contributions or the trajectory of his entire work is to deny his individuality and extremely limit his importance' (ibid.: 68). Because Tropicália, the movement, was fed by *Tropicália*, the penetrable, it became impossible not to relate Oiticica's anthropophagic, intermedial and multi-sensorial art to tropicalist-like values, even if to underline internal tensions.

Beyond anthropophagy: Commodification and neoliberalization

Prior to discussing the risk of Tropicália being turned into a commodity, Marxist critic Roberto Schwarz (2005) famously took issue with the conceptual genesis of the movement. For him, Tropicália's ability to blend political and aesthetic issues hindered the fight for national liberation, because 'lack of food and lack of style can hardly be of the same order of inconvenience' (ibid.: 294). To a certain degree, one could say Schwarz identified and anticipated that risk from the outset:

> Once this anachronistic conjunction has been produced, along with the conventional idea that this is Brazil, the 'ready-made' images of the patriarchal world and of imbecilic consumerism start signifying on their own, in a shameless, unaestheticized fashion, over and over again suggesting their stifled, frustrated lives, which we will never get to know. The tropicalist image encloses the past in the form of images that are active, or that might come back to life, and suggests that they are our destiny, which is the reason why we can't stop looking at them. (ibid.: 295)

Regardless of Schwarz's sceptical understanding of the tropicalist allegory, Christopher Dunn claims that the critic did recognize its potential but 'was troubled by its propensity to advance a fatalistic "atemporal idea of Brazil" that seemed to negate any potential for social transformation' (2001: 4). In an attempt to clarify its ambiguous nature, the author resorts to a hypothetical distinction between the terminologies 'Tropicália' and 'Tropicalismo'.[13] 'Since the late 1960s, critics have argued that Tropicália represented the moment of invention and innovation, while Tropicalismo denoted a subsequent moment of dilution, stereotype, and massification' (Dunn 2016: 21). Wisely pointing out the two sides of the same coin, Ivana Bentes encapsulates the contradiction in what she calls 'anthropophagy in the era of technical reproducibility', an alternative way to perhaps unpack 'certain practices of Tropicalism' (2005: 100). For Carlos Basualdo, the cultural anthropophagy nurtured by the likes of Andrade, Oiticica and Caetano – one translated into Tropicália poetics and aesthetics – will exist 'as long as there is the possibility that creative work will not be completely absorbed by the logic of capital and converted into alienating labor' (2005: 23).

Unsurprisingly, the debate that took place amid the rotten military modernization of Brazil reached its peak in the neoliberal period. Much in tune with that debate, perhaps no other scholar has been so emphatically critical of the dangerous neoliberal tactics in relation to cultural anthropophagy than Suely Rolnik (2006, 2011). She contends that the politics of subjectivity and cultural production of the 1960s and 1970s were co-opted by transnational finance capitalism. Furthermore, in countries like Brazil, 'paralyzed by the micropolitics of dictatorships, such experimentalism was reactivated with the establishment of cultural capitalism only to be directly channeled into the market' (Rolnik 2011). As paradoxical as it may seem, if the tropicalist anthropophagy 'played a role in the radicality of the counter-cultural experience of young Brazilians in the 1960s and 70s, it now tends to contribute to a soft adaptation of the neoliberal environment'. This is partly because when cultural capitalism enthusiasts seem to celebrate notions of fluidity, flexibility and hybridization, they are actually undermining the creative forces that used to depend on that triad, 'since it came to constitute the dominant logic of neoliberalism and its society of control'. On that note, it is the unexpected reverse that takes place: 'Creation can result from a refusal to listen to chaos and the effects of otherness on our body', hence what could prevail is 'the consumption of ready-made ideas and images' (ibid.).

In 1998, conscious of the role of post-coloniality within the globalization of the art world, the 24th São Paulo Biennial focused on investigating the Brazilian notion of anthropophagy as a concept and a method while challenging the Western European canon by using the rhetoric of cannibalism. In spite of conflicting reviews, the event was a watershed in terms of rethinking and resituating anthropophagy as a cultural strategy, one that could be even more controversial in the wake of the crumbling of the Berlin Wall, as Lisette Lagnado and Pablo Lafuente (2015) point out. According to Mirtes Marins de Oliveira, both the press and academia identified a *polarity* in the exhibition curated by Paulo Herkenhoff: 'its insertion in an anthropophagic order and, through it, in an order promoted by the international circuit of exhibitions that, in the 1980s and 90s, proposed a revision of the idea of the "primitive" and its modern appropriation' (2015: 176). Oliveira's essay on the event mentions historian Annateresa Fabris's account of the conceptual crossroads, as she problematized 'whether the "Manifesto antropófago", decontextualised from its modernist origins, could articulate a contemporary vision'. Moreover, Oliveira asks, 'Was adopting a concept defined in relation to a national identity appropriate in a moment of redefining the national under the pressure of globalisation?' (ibid.: 184). It is symptomatic, however, that the debate only drew widespread attention some ten years after the 24th Biennial took place – proof of its relevance and potential to reverberate, but also proof of neoliberal power and consolidation.

Writer and visual artist Pedro Neves Marques (2014) has recently taken up the argument considering the turning of cultural anthropophagy into a neoliberal commodity per se. Moreover, Tropicália turned into a shallow, if not empty, image of Brazil, interested in the *other* just to nullify its *difference* in the name of the so-called anthropophagy. 'Commodified, it becomes synonymous with a Neo-Darwinist mode of predation, precarious, and individualistic' (ibid.: 65), losing its collective strength. Indeed, his view mirrors Rolnik's critique, when she blames the country's elites and middle classes for giving in to the neoliberal regime, which succeeded in truly 'making its inhabitants, especially the city-dwellers, into veritable anthropophagic zombies' (2006). For her, the legacy of the 1960s and 1970s can still be helpful if only to problematize the contradictions of progress and (under)development today, 'but not to guarantee their access to the imaginary paradises of capital' (ibid.) – a reassessment that Solomon (2017) recently attempted.

Following on from that, the next chapters dwell on present-day experimental documentary films which potentially reverberate tropicalist-like values. To some extent, the films under analysis seem to hint at those values, though in very different ways, to reflect upon the contradictions of progress and (under)development in Rio de Janeiro, the city where Oiticica exhibited his *penetrables*, Glauber screened *Entranced Earth* and Caetano was irreversibly impacted.[14] More specifically, they do this by rendering visible an architecture of failing projects dating back to the rotten military modernization up until the neoliberalization of construction sites. In this sense, I argue that filmmakers also seem to echo Lévi-Strauss's attitude towards the city's social and urban planning, an attitude that Caetano himself mobilizes in his own work, as discussed.

The ruinous Brazil that Lévi-Strauss (1973) so poignantly describes through the façades of the New World, as highlighted in Chapter 1, resonates with contemporary filmmakers keen to scrutinize Rio as a paramount case study. Curiously, Lévi-Strauss was most unimpressed when he arrived in Rio. 'Despite his mental efforts, the scenario offended his sense of classical proportions. The Sugar Loaf and the Corcovado mountain were too big in relation to their surroundings, like "stumps ... in a toothless mouth", as if nature had left behind an unfinished, lopsided terrain' (Wilcken 2010: 47). In fact, Caetano (Veloso 1989) straightforwardly referred to Lévi-Strauss's infamous first impression in another of his songs, *O Estrangeiro* (The Foreigner): '*O antropólogo Claude Lévi-Strauss detestou a Baía de Guanabara/Pareceu-lhe uma boca banguela*' ('The anthropologist Claude Lévi-Strauss hated Guanabara Bay/It seemed to him like a toothless mouth').

Less concerned with the natural landscape, contemporary filmmakers, rather, seem to focus on the human-made landscape subject to the cycles of excitement and depression in a city like Rio. Thus, when Rolnik poses the question of 'how to reactivate in our times, in each situation, the political potential inherent in artistic activity, its power to unleash possibles' (2006), I reason that these diverse yet in-dialogue outputs find a way out precisely by exposing the ruins on screen. These images thus articulate a critique of the modern and neoliberal processes which result in architectural failures. If Glauber once said that 'Tropicalism is the acceptance, the rise of underdevelopment' (Rocha 2005: 277), what are then the resonances of its intermedial, multi-sensorial aspects in conceptualizing an aesthetics of ruins in contemporary cinema? Even more, what are these ruins capable of doing, if anything, to take back the radical power of artistic contribution?

9

The rubble as the legacy: A ruin for the World Cup and the Olympics

Rio de Janeiro has been at the forefront of political measures driven by the neoliberal regime, very much criticized by Suely Rolnik (2006, 2011) and marked by foreign capital interests and strong real estate speculation which transformed the landscape. Stemming from a critical perspective on that socio-economic model, current visual elaborations depict the city as an ongoing (de)construction site. Seemingly echoing a Lévi-Straussian conception, contemporary filmmakers have shed light on failing projects as a means of questioning controversial notions of progress and (under)development. In this case, a (de)construction site is not to be regarded as a mere metaphor. As soon as Brazil was elected to host the 2014 FIFA World Cup (in 2007) and Rio de Janeiro was chosen to host the 2016 Olympic Games (in 2009), the city immediately found itself at the centre of gigantic projects.[1] At the time, State Governor Sérgio Cabral[2] (2007–14, currently in prison for corruption) along with Mayor Eduardo Paes (2009–16 and elected again in 2020) started a neoliberal crusade to prepare the city to welcome the world, with an outdated discourse of modernization.

Throughout the twentieth century, that same endeavour towards the new and the modern was the excuse for certain government policies to be implemented. Mayor Pereira Passos (1902–6), for instance, was responsible for allowing what became historically known as Bota-abaixo (literally, Tear-down), a policy that displaced people from the city centre to allow the government to build a Parisian-inspired Central Avenue to please the growing *carioca* bourgeoisie. For that to happen, many of the displaced working class had to move to the hillside (namely, the *favelas*) or the distant suburbs – once again, placing the wreckage as a synonym for progress in Benjaminian terms.

As suggested by the lyrics of Caetano Veloso (1971) in *Maria Bethânia*, written while exiled in London during the military dictatorship: 'Everybody knows/ That our cities were built/To be destroyed.'

Focusing on the advent of modernity in the then capital of Brazil, Maite Conde (2012) relates its modern landscape to division. 'Social relations were expressed through the very space of the city: Rio's urban redevelopment articulated the divisive nature of Brazil's modern identity' (ibid.: 65). On that note, she sees the arrival of the cinema[3] – the modern artistic invention par excellence – as a means of questioning that division. In her view, 'the cinema was inextricably linked to changes taking place in the country's social and urban landscape, articulating and responding to transformations taking place in everyday life' (ibid.: 95). Conde points out the contribution of iconic early-twentieth-century chronicler, João do Rio, who understood modern man as *homus cinematographicus*, relating modernity's unstoppable cycles of construction and deconstruction to cinema's ability to frenetically cut and juxtapose images. 'Far from a negative characteristic, the cinema's superficiality and absence of memory are seen by João do Rio as ideally suited to the new urban environment, with its rapid transformation and *destruction* of the past' (ibid.: 42, emphasis added). Cinema, thus, if not completely, was able to find ways to embed this kind of discussion, as 'what was needed was another narrative of modernity, one that could forge a different relationship between the past and the future, between Brazil and the rest of the world' (ibid.: 168) – a role that contemporary artists seem to take upon themselves.

Bearing Rio's obsession with altering its divided landscape in mind, it comes as no surprise that, precisely one hundred years after Bota-abaixo, the local government resorted to similar strategies to deliver a modern Rio 'to the world'. In 2015, *El País Brasil*'s website, for instance, posted an investigative article written by journalist Felipe Betim about the displacement of families from Vila Autódromo, a neighbourhood on the outskirts of Rio, so that the local government could start building part of the Olympic complex. 'Most of the houses seem to have been bombed – and in this case, by City Hall itself. ... Today, living in rubble, in a war scenario, 192 families (about 800 people) promise to fight until the end so they do not have to leave Vila Autódromo,' Betim reported. 'The history of Vila Autódromo symbolizes a legacy of removals and expropriations left by the organizers of the Rio de Janeiro Olympics' (Betim

2015). Similarly, *Agência Pública* published an award-winning story called '100', reporting '100 stories, 100 removals, 100 houses destroyed by the Olympic Games'. Like a journalistic marathon, according to the news agency, '100' aims to shed light on what the mainstream media seems to leave out and let the people themselves tell their own stories through videos and podcasts. Quotes like 'They broke my entire house into pieces in front of me' or 'Like with all progress, someone always has to lose for someone else to win' are comments made by interviewees targeted by a City Hall wanting to start construction work as soon as possible. The strategies used, however, were not always honest. Architect and urban planner Lucas Faulhauber listed suspicious City Hall strategies to make the removals happen more efficiently. 'The visit of undercover government agents, under pretexts invented to measure and photograph the house and interview people; the repression of the municipal guard against residents; the demolition of houses which had already been negotiated, leaving the community a wreck,' *Agência Pública* (2016) reported.

Another ramification of this problem considers what happens when construction is approved and yet not completed. In this sense, one could argue that the art circuit was also somehow affected by this building impulse. 'As Rio geared up for the Olympics, three huge new public museums also went into construction,' says art critic Silas Martí (2016), referring to what could initially be seen as a positive aspect of the mood of the city. 'The Museu de Arte do Rio and starchitect Santiago Calatrava's Museu do Amanhã (Museum of Tomorrow) arose along the city's revamped old port. The Museu da Imagem e do Som, designed by New York firm Diller Scofidio + Renfro, also started to take shape on Copacabana Beach,' commenting on the promising projects. Nevertheless, having also researched the relationship between urban ruins and contemporary art in his MPhil project (2017), Martí points out the other side of those building promises. At the same time as the construction projects were very much part of the urban planning, it was as if they had brought a sense of decay within themselves.

> On the surface, ... things appear normal. But the rapidly decaying situation of museums in Brazil, especially the public institutions battling for the leftovers of contracting state budgets, seems to confirm the troubling pertinence of an observation Claude Lévi-Strauss made in the 1930s. ... Indeed, even before Santiago Calatrava's Museu do Amanhã opened in Rio, parts of its

tortoise-like metallic shell had already rusted, like a corpse decomposing under the sun. Not far from there, in Copacabana, the Museu da Imagem e do Som's Rio outpost was said to be sinking into the soft ground near the beach before its top floors were even completed. (Martí 2016)

In this context, artists themselves endorsed the view of Rio's sloppiness and abandonment. 'In Brazil we have this modern syndrome which praises the new and abandons heritage. In Rio one can see this very clearly,' claims director Luisa Marques (2018) in interview with me. 'Rio has these layers of institutional destruction and unstoppable construction; the whole twentieth century was like that. And it happened again in recent years due to the World Cup and the Olympics. I guess that debate touched many people' (ibid.); she is referring to filmmakers, artists and curators all absorbed in rethinking the city. Intermixing a documentary instinct with her visual arts background, Marques addresses Rio's spatiality in *Tropical Curse* as the outcome of that sloppiness and abandonment. In her meditation on the Carmen Miranda Museum, the Flamengo Park, where the museum is located, is another example of Rio's construction obsession. Built in the early 1960s, the project required the destruction of the Castelo, Querosene and Santo Antônio hills, so that they could be used to fill in the terrain where the park was to be constructed. Oddly enough, the park was opened to the public in 1965, but not quite – since the original project was never fully completed, the park was never officially inaugurated. The director plays around with the idea of *developing* an area, a museum, or even a persona (Miranda herself) as part of that modern syndrome, as will be discussed.

Director Joana Traub Csekö (2017) concurs with Marques about the current spatial debate reaching the domain of the arts in the interview I did with her. 'Thinking of Rio de Janeiro and, in particular, the recent mega-events that took place in the city (World Cup and Olympics) which have left a trail of corruption and obsolete buildings as their main legacy, we realize that underdevelopment and its power games are still issues we need to deal with.' As a visual artist and filmmaker, she dealt with that tension first through a series of photographs of the Federal University hospital and, later, by directing *HU Enigma* along with Pedro Urano, a documentary about the unfinished yet crumbling hospital, as will be pointed out. In Csekö's words, '*HU Enigma* aims to investigate an emblematic case through which … we witness this monumental building deeply immersed in underdevelopment. It seemed necessary to trace this story back to us, so that we, as Brazilians, can reflect on how we will not fall into the same traps again' (ibid.). Both in her photo series and their documentary feature, there is common ground that invites one to question the construction impulse embedded in projects like HU. Even if the capacity for preservation does not exist, one might wonder here if it is possible to at least finish the proposed building plans.

Imploding the Perimetral in *ExPerimetral*

More recently, the collapse of the Perimetral certainly represented the most dramatic change in Rio's human-made landscape, as part of the (de) construction work for the international sports events. Although discussed in many articles and TV reportage, it is in *ExPerimetral* that the Perimetral and its debris actually come to the fore. 'During the work for the World Cup and the Olympics, the city turned out to be a massive construction site, installing chaos on public roadways,' says director Daniel Santos (2017) in an interview with me about the elevated highway. 'And the curious thing is that the community involved in the history of these places does not benefit from the works; in fact, they end up being harmed and excluded' (ibid.). The debris from the Perimetral is the image that Santos uses to encapsulate the harm and exclusion brought about by government policies. Right in the opening credits, one hears the sound of trumpets, like the sound of the trumpets of the apocalypse heralding the beginning of the end. What next appears could be the debris of war and the remaining shells of bombed-out buildings. The camera of Santos wanders amid the rubble, filming fallen walls and damaged earth. Not until the last minute does the camera's gaze leave the debris behind and turn to the surroundings of that ruined place. An urban landscape appears, a horizon of standing buildings, an actual city. Rio de Janeiro is revealed.

In the frame, there is also an excavator, showing that that city is not precisely at war but under (de)construction. 'Rio is a war scenario; and the conflict is evident in many spheres, not only in the *favelas*, where the conflict is permanent.' On the other hand, the war scenario shaped by, among many other factors, the implosion of the elevated highway should not be seen as

Figure 9.1: Excavation work in *ExPerimetral*.

an asset restricted to Rio. 'The city appears just at the end because I see these redevelopment projects, mainly present in historical areas of cities, as a global phenomenon' (ibid.). As they usually take place in historical areas, such redevelopment projects often end up facing history itself. During the work in the harbour zone, for instance, archaeologists found many African amulets and religious objects dating back to the eighteenth and nineteenth centuries. Cais do Valongo (Valongo Wharf),[4] as the area was then known, gave anchorage to many ships bringing enslaved Africans to the New World at that time.

In *ExPerimetral*, Santos highlights the past through a graffiti inscription captured amid the rubble, which reads '*nossa senzala*' ('our *senzala*', a slave camp in colonial Brazil). The contemporary graffiti amid the rubble actually points to a past that some have tried to bury deep down but literally returns from the ashes, urging to be included in the account of history. 'I only noticed that image during the editing. It was quite symbolic, as the process of colonization started in that region, a territory crossed by many enslaved men and women' (ibid.). His approach to the topic is much influenced by the work on race and history of black British artists Isaac Julien and John Akomfrah because of the way they play with the boundaries of cinema itself. In a sense, the collapse of that structure is also the collapse of African history in the country. In addition to the iconic concrete music of Iannis Xenakis, the percussive sound that invades the screen refers to African culture. The tangle of red, crumbling iron structures resembles human veins, while the tangle of rusty iron structures

Figures 9.2 and 9.3: The veins and the roots: The first image shows '*nossa senzala*' graffiti at the bottom left.

looks like tree roots emerging from the ground: black blood, black roots. The debris turns into 'the veins that connect, the roots that were ripped out and exposed to sunlight' (ibid.), as Santos metaphorically puts it.

The imagery itself might be sufficient for one to grasp the atmosphere of warlike Rio. Nevertheless, Santos's decision to add Mayor Eduardo Paes's speeches from the official TED Conference,[5] in 2012, and the Columbia

Global Debates,[6] in 2013, increases the critical potential of the nine-minute experimental documentary. Talking about the significant role played by mayors in shaping people's lives, Paes's discourse ends up having an awkwardly unplanned tragicomic effect, as his words do not match reality. 'We call Rio a very democratic city, with great open spaces where people can meet and you cannot see the social differences when you go to the streets or to the beach in Rio,' he says whilst one sees a Rio immersed in rubble. 'With his *tupiniquim* brand of English, ... he was there to be praised and not questioned about his project, ... showing his commitment to private initiative rather than public management' (ibid.).

That specific situation seems to acutely echo what Idelber Avelar (2009) refers to as *neoliberal ruin*, when claiming that social life has become a commodity followed by the economic and political collapse that it entails. That is, multilayered wreckage based on the conflation of public and suspect private interests, the wreckage that takes centre stage in today's society. The Porto Maravilha Urban Operation,[7] one of the main reasons for the Perimetral to be imploded, was presented by the former mayor as the most fitting project to revitalize the Port Region of Rio de Janeiro – and is also the most fitting example of the relationship between private initiatives and local government. In *ExPerimetral*, a sort of response to 'the destructive utopia of privatization' (ibid.: 192), as Avelar puts it, Santos's imagery encompasses the contradictions of (de)construction through the debris of the Perimetral. In this regard, the World Cup and the Olympic (de)construction works can be read as emblematic images of the present-day dynamic of capitalist extraction, at the same time embodying a 'palimpsest of multiple historical events and representations', as Andreas Huyssen's (2006: 8) imaginary of ruins is famously defined.

In a sense, the neoliberal ruins of Avelar (2009) seem to be the next stage for the notion of *creative destruction* originally developed by Joseph Schumpeter (1976) in the context of 1940s modernity. Drawing on Marxist theory, the need for construction, deconstruction and then reconstruction could be the very motto of capitalism, a dynamic that would maintain the system's relevance. Since then, this notion has been explored by many scholars, from David Harvey (1989) to Manuel Castells (2009), and expanded to the present context. Already immersed in the neoliberal era, those authors reflect on the profitability of that dynamic and the implications for the built environment and social relations. Evoking this prime contradiction of classical capitalism in the title of his influential book *All That Is Solid Melts into Air*, Marshall Berman could have been referring to the Porto Maravilha Urban Operation when he says:

> 'All that is solid' – from the clothes on our backs to the looms and mills that weave them, to the men and women who work the machines, to the houses and neighborhoods the workers live in, to the firms and corporations that exploit the workers, to the towns and cities and whole regions and even nations that embrace them all – all these are made to be broken tomorrow, smashed or shredded or pulverized or dissolved, so they can be recycled or replaced next week, and the whole process can go on again and again, hopefully forever, in ever more profitable forms. (1983: 99)

The Perimetral's original construction per se was not devoid of contradiction. Developed in stages between the 1950s and 1970s, it became an easy target for political (and architectural) debate. Built in the harbour zone, its presence blocked the views from the land; neither could ship crews see the land properly. A car-oriented development, it symbolized the modernity that the 1950s and 1960s wanted to emulate, regardless of the pedestrian experience in public spaces. By the end of the twentieth century, the Perimetral had lost its *raison d'être* at the same time as traffic became unbearable due to the growing number of vehicles on the highway. Outdated as a project, 'like stands in a fairground or the pavilions of some international exhibition, built to last only a few months' (Lévi-Strauss 1973: 118), the solution was to simply replace it rather than try to find a new purpose for it. Demolished in stages between 2013 and 2014, its tearing down was, in reality, intrinsically related to the Porto Maravilha Urban Operation, a highly criticized gentrified project for a so-called degraded area. 'These projects cause the gentrification of historical areas, putting local history at the service of tourism and of the capital for entertainment', as Santos (2017) claims in his interview.

Born and raised in the outskirts of Campinas, in the state of São Paulo, Santos has been involved in projects mixing cinema with performance and sound art. Aware of the effects of that blurring in his creative process, Santos claims that, above all, his work 'points to the hybridity of languages and artistic tools'. The *ExPerimetral* project, for instance, started not as an experimental documentary but as what he calls a live performance experience. 'At the time, I already had the idea of making the film, but wanted to explore other exhibition platforms for the same project.' In art galleries, he put together scaffolding, covered with voile fabric to serve as a screen for images to be projected on. Interested in exploring sound art as well, the soundtrack for the art gallery was a mixed acoustic-electronic piece created by the De Repente Acidente collective, of which he was part at the time. 'I have a lot of interest in sound narrative and I see it as an infinite possibility in the perception of ideas, an open possibility for the free interpretation of the viewer' (ibid.). Moving from gallery space to the cinema screen, the director then incorporated the concrete music influence of Xenakis into the soundtrack. The Greek-French composer, who was also a civil engineer, worked with the modernist, Le Corbusier, and absorbed many of his architectural concepts into later compositions. Symptomatically, Xenakis's body of work was mobilized in a project devoted to questioning the dynamics of (de)construction in Rio. *ExPerimetral* is a timid yet appropriate way into this discussion: while it is located at the core of urban transformations derived from a neoliberal mindset based on the modernization discourse, it emerges from different media practices to shine a light on the rubble.

An alternative anchorage in *The Harbour*

The port, therefore, became a symbol encapsulating the ever-changing atmosphere of Rio, with the debris of the Perimetral as the debris of the city. Throughout the last decade, the harbour has been visualized as a controversial cinematic space in projects like *ExPerimetral* and others connected with concerns that come into play in Santos's output. With the most straightforward title, *The Harbour*, for instance, is a collective experimental production directed by Clarissa Campolina, Julia de Simone, Luiz Pretti and Ricardo Pretti on the eve of the Olympics. As in *ExPerimetral*, it uses the indexicality of Rio's harbour zone to create an alternative perception of reality via manipulation of image and sound. More than actual ruins, *The Harbour* constructs a dreamy atmosphere that may lead to or be the result of ruination. The port is the scenario for the exploration of a city lost in time, perhaps emerging from opposite Guanabara Bay.[8] In this sense, the insertion of the Porto Maravilha

Figure 9.4: Digitally, the Elevado da Perimetral gives way to aseptic trees in *The Harbour*.

Urban Operation digital mock-up enhances the nightmarish tone: the virtual renovation of the harbour zone *is* the ruination per se. In other words, the asepticism of the technology points to a project clearly detached from reality that will turn the area into a neoliberal commodity, or better still, a *neoliberal ruin* (Avelar 2009).

Although even more experimental than *ExPerimetral*, *The Harbour* is very much a commentary on the transformations of the real Rio. In an interview with me, Ricardo Pretti (2019) argues that there is a sense of exhaustion with regards our models of city and society, with no room for new ideas to emerge. 'The problem is that this repetition becomes a lower copy of the past. We live in a sloppy copy of the past, and so we bury the true past. Even the ruins already have an air of copy' (ibid.). The ruins of the Valongo Wharf come to the fore again as an image of that exhaustion, an overlooked historical area soon to be swallowed by the Porto Maravilha. The harbour that used to anchor slave ships in the past is the same one that now welcomes luxury transatlantic cruise ships, as a sequence filmed from the Perimetral viewpoint reveals – perhaps one of the last ones before the elevated highway was swallowed, too. The camera takes nothing for granted; rather, it frames everything as if discovering another space-time dimension. 'Filming in Rio de Janeiro becomes much more interesting when you extract your excessive familiarity, to let what is unusual remain. Rio can be unusual' (ibid.).

In *The Harbour*, the dialogue with the visual arts is very much present on the surface of the image, as the film threads experimental shots exploring the harbour zone, with no voice-over or any other kind of verbal information. In addition, it could be argued this dialogue might be prompted by co-director Clarissa Campolina's own artistic experimentation. In 2010, she exhibited *Traces: The Landscape Fills In* (Rastros: A Paisagem Invade), a video installation about the human relationship to the city environment. Purposely displayed in a gallery located in a former fabric factory, the artwork condensed many of the concerns reverberating in *The Harbour*, from the urban space topic to the intermedial approach to the arts.[9] As in *ExPerimetral*, the image of the city is also directly constructed through the use of sound, as if image and sound were not combined but rather merged into one another. Here, the anthropophagic aspect is fed by a *carioca* funk beat alongside the experimental work of Swedish saxophonist Mats Gustafsson. The outcome is a mysterious soundscape that reaches its peak during the appearance of the Porto Maravilha Urban Operation digital mock-up.

Incidentally, at the film's climax, that sequence plays with a videogame-like aesthetics and its aseptic trees. Nevertheless, more than simply drawing on another media, the digital mock-up is brought to the fore as a critical means of commenting on the neoliberalization of public spaces, as discussed above. It is the aseptic animation that conveys the lack of engagement with the local communities and their actual needs. Hence, it is not about an accumulation of media but an intermedial fusion per se (Pethő 2010). More than a fusion, for Pretti, albeit not purposefully, there could be a tropicalist flavour in 'the cinematographic apparatus being *devoured* by other apparatuses, means and sensibilities', something that seems 'necessary to make our cinema breathe better' (2019, emphasis added), as he underlines in his interview. To a certain extent, one could argue that the tropicalist flavour materializes in two of the film's sequences in which carnivalesque allegorical cars move down the road located beneath the elevated highway. Seemingly out of service, those cars gain a phantasmagorical appearance as being completely out of place in the harbour zone. If Tropicália used to reference popular national iconography via the use of signs, colours and textures, the precarious parade under the Perimetral flirts

Figures 9.5 and 9.6: Phantasmagoric carnival parade in the harbour zone.

with a faded version of Tropicalism, one framed in the light of the harbour zone's ruination. More relevant than direct referencing, experimental short documentaries like those analysed in this chapter signal the power of art in dealing with the remains.

10

The Carmen Miranda ruinous spaceship in *Tropical Curse*

Luisa Marques's *Tropical Curse* engages with the tropicalist intermediality in a much more explicit way than *ExPerimetral* and *The Harbour*. Like Daniel Santos, Marques is based in Rio, but she is not originally from there. Her family comes from Fortaleza, Northeast of Brazil, where she was born. Living in Rio for more than a decade now, she still considers herself more of an observer than a local. Furthermore, both directors were students at the Escola de Artes Visuais do Parque Lage, a well-established visual arts school in Rio. Although a cinema graduate (having worked at the Museum of Modern Art Cinematheque), Marques's trajectory also overlapped with the visual arts.[1] In 2011, she went to Amsterdam to study fine arts at the Gerrit Rietveld Academie – a turning point in her artistic development. 'Since then I think I have made video experiments more inclined towards the domain of the visual arts than to Cinema with a capital C,' Marques (2018) said in her interview.

Indeed, her early works *Manassés* (2009), *Star Power Ready* (2011) and *Toda Cor Abandonada É Violenta* (2014) were already within the video art and experimental cinema tradition. In this sense, Marques also draws on international references to conceive a work whose aim is to dwell on quintessential national tropes. North American filmmaker Kenneth Anger, for instance, has left an imprint by her blurring of cinematic boundaries. She mentions *Scorpio Rising* (1963) and *Lucifer Rising* (1972) as major references in the crafting of *Tropical Curse*. 'In *Lucifer Rising* there are pyramids, and I thought that the modernist, brutalist constructions were types of unidentified objects. They are kind of mysterious like the pyramids' (ibid.), Marques says, referring to the modernist style of the Carmen Miranda Museum, the backdrop for *Tropical Curse* to unfold.

In her experimental documentary, the Carmen Miranda Museum, a spaceship-like project designed by Affonso Reidy landed in the middle of Flamengo Park,[2] represents a sort of contradiction. While this museum should represent Brazilian modernism through architectonic forms, its history is one of sloppiness and abandonment. In reality, the modernist construction erected in the mid-twentieth century was not planned to house a museum but to be a sort of playroom, a recreational space within the park designed by the famous self-taught Brazilian architect Lota de Macedo Soares. The initial plan, however, did not quite work out. The building ended by being abandoned until the idea of paying tribute to Carmen Miranda came up in the mid-1970s. In 1976, the museum was inaugurated, but again it was never really part of the dynamics of the park or the cultural life of the city. Abandoned for a second time, it was finally shut down in 2013. The current promise is to transfer the archives to the new Museum of Image and Sound – which has been under construction since 2011, although it was expected to be completed in time for the Olympics, as mentioned earlier by Silas Martí (2016). 'Here everything seems/It is still under construction/And is already a ruin,' Caetano Veloso (1991) echoes in a loop. The museum is an example of architecture that failed somehow – *Tropical Curse*, the visualization of that failure.

The construction itself came to the fore as a consequence of Marques's interest in researching national identity and gender issues through the figure of Carmen Miranda. No coincidence, she says, that her interest became stronger while studying abroad. 'I felt quite uncomfortable with a certain stigma of what it is to be a "Brazilian woman" (and in my case, non-White) in Europe. So, this cliché pops up into our heads, right? Because Carmen Miranda – although not Brazilian, or precisely because of that – incorporates all these contradictions,' says Marques (2018). Originally from Portugal, Carmen Miranda[3] moved to Brazil at the age of one. She is historically regarded as the most successful Brazilian artist of all time in Hollywood, being its highest-paid actress by the mid-1940s (Los Angeles Times website, with her obituary originally published in 1955). On the other hand, her image has always been controversial. Considered a product of the Good Neighbour Policy implemented by the United States towards Latin American countries, she was consequently accused of commercializing a stereotypical Brazilian woman. Presenting a debateable Brazilian/Latin American identity to the world, her artistic persona, whether genuine or fabricated, has been widely associated with the fruit-covered hat outfit she wore in her most celebrated films and concerts. 'More than her biography, it is her image and what it carries that interests me' (ibid.), Marques underlines.

Therefore, *Tropical Curse* illustrates the friction between two nation-building projects forged for a country aiming to finally be seen as modern and developed, drawing on Tropicália references in order to question the failures of Brazilian modernism/modernity. Marques manages to explore the modernist building she was already familiar with as a Rio resident, in light of Carmen Miranda's contradictions. The imagery of her experimental documentary plays with the double modern iconography through overlapping the modernist architectural forms with the singer's scenographic tropical fruits. On screen, one sees archival photographs of the Flamengo Park construction site, with pineapples and bananas superimposed upon it. The manipulation of light and colours helps to build a dreamlike, retro-futuristic atmosphere. In this sense, North American visual artist Paul Sharits's *T,O,U,C,H,I,N,G* (1968) contributed a great deal. Marques digests his film to use its colour and strobe effects to create a different texture for her psychedelic narrative. Undoubtedly, the building of a cinematic texture is at the core of Marques's filmmaking. As the vast majority of the images come from archives (she only shot a few additional scenes), *Tropical Curse* is mostly a montage film. Marques, a film editor herself, overlaps different bits of films gathered online (from searches at Creative Commons and Archive.Org, for instance), in order to play with the materiality of those archives. 'The layers of time and history are in a landscape through which the film wanders with delusional intensity but are also in the materiality of the images. The files that have come to me have been somewhat distorted, compressed, lost some features and gained others,' she contends in her interview (2018).

Significant to Marques's film practice is the debate about art and moving images in the digital age. More specifically interested in the intersection of cinema and archival practice, Domietta Torlasco has focused on 'the relation between memory and creation – between the persistence of the past and the emergence of the new – in films and installations that adopt digital technology and simultaneously appropriate analog materials' (2013: xi). Her interest precisely mirrors Marques's strategy to refer to and update Tropicália via the

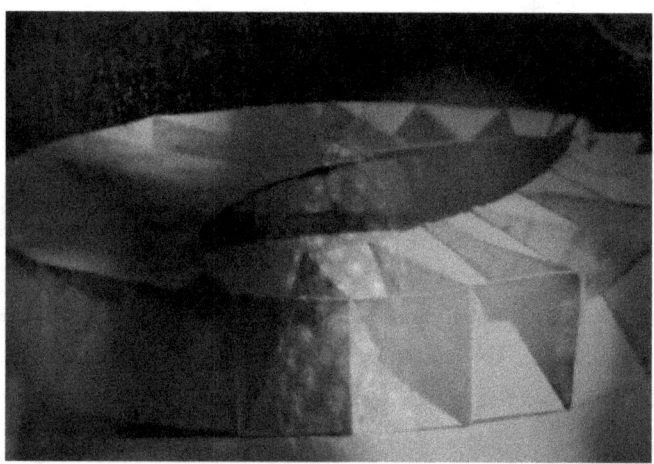

Figures 10.1 and 10.2: Colours, textures and superimpositions in *Tropical Curse*.

digital manipulation of colours, textures and superimpositions. In gathering different bits of films online, Marques deals with two different aspects of artistic practice in the digital age: first, the attractive possibility of dealing with old analogue material that had been digitalized; and, second, her own digital use of that material combined with other techniques. Marques's practice only relies on the archive to resignify it, attesting to '"archiving" as intervention – not the systematic preservation of film materials but the creative reelaboration of cinema's aesthetic and ideological complexities' (ibid.: xiii).

Tropicalist intermedial flavour: Flying saucers, ghosts and *gringos*

As pointed out earlier, Carmen Miranda became a sort of Tropicália darling, as her figure was attuned to the tropicalist desire to activate colourful national symbols in a cheerful yet critical fashion. Marcelo Ikeda (2017) underlines Marques's appropriation of Tropicália in the way the director addresses the legendary artist, puzzlingly halfway between homage and parody. 'What is at stake is a re-reading of the tradition of Brazilian modernism and the updating of Carmen's presence by the Tropicalism of the 1960s and 1970s' (ibid.). In many occasions, Caetano himself has expressed the importance of Carmen Miranda as an image/imaginary for the tropicalist attitude. In *Tropical Truth*, he refers to her as 'a tropicalist emblem, a sign overwhelmed by contradictory affects' (Veloso 2017: 279). *Tropicália*, the song, for instance, carries her name in its vast number of references. 'I imagined putting side by side ideas, images and entities of the Brazilian tragicomedy, of the adventure at the same time frustrating and glittering of being Brazilian' (ibid.: 201). In the new version of his book, there is an additional chapter entitled 'Carmen Miranda Não Sabia Sambar'[4] (In English, 'Carmen Miranda Did Not Know How to Samba'). In it, Caetano points out that, until the revolutionary 1960s, singers, actresses and middle-class girls did not know the samba dance – Carmen Miranda, the great star, included. The anecdote is less a critique of her artistic skills than an observation about the power of popular culture (Tropicália, Cinema Novo, Cinema Marginal, etc.) from the 1960s onwards, and how it has profoundly impacted on national culture. In any case, once again, Carmen Miranda's figure is mobilized to embody the contradiction of being the most famous Brazilian artist yet not knowing how to dance to the most Brazilian of rhythms.

The assimilation of performance art plays a key role in the visualization of contradictions in the film. The above-mentioned homage-parody in-between situation becomes visually represented by Darks Miranda,[5] a persona created and performed by Marques herself, covered in white fabric and dancing outside the museum. The first time she performed as Darks Miranda was for the video art installation *Equilíbrio de Frutas Sobre a Cabeça, Sob os Olhares de Carmen Miranda* (Fruit Balance Over the Head, Under the Eyes of Carmen Miranda, 2012–2013), exhibited at Galeria de Arte Ibeu, in Rio. In the film, the performance attempts to emulate the spirit of Carmen Miranda – hence the pineapple on her head. This sort of Third World, precarious ghost image leaves a bittersweet impression, adding a tone of parody to the sequence. Also, light and colour effects enhance the B-movie atmosphere. In fact, the hints of B-movie culture brought into play here form a bridge to a song called *Carmen Miranda's Ghost* (1985) by another North American artist, the anarchist musician Leslie Fish. In the song, Carmen Miranda is, indeed, a phantasmagorical figure in a sort of sci-fi musical tale, a song Marques herself had listened to *ad nauseam*. 'Carmen Miranda's ghost is haunting Space Station Three/Not that we're complaining, since the fresh fruit all comes free' (Weyrdmusicman, 2011), the lyrics humorously indicate. As if in an out-of-space, artistic partnership between creator and creature, Darks Miranda is also credited as director alongside Marques, which emphasizes the performative aspect of *Tropical Curse*.

The tropicalist tone that Ikeda (2017) notes finds a parallel in Rogério Sganzerla's output, a cinema in tune with the reverberations of Tropicália, as Ismail Xavier (2012) famously suggests. The sense of chaos and dissonance found in the montage of Sílvio Renoldi in Sganzerla's *The Red Light Bandit* (O Bandido da Luz Vermelha, 1968) is echoed in Marques's editing role in her ability to build a narrative through fragments of sounds and images. Worth noting, the images of flying saucers seen in the final sequence of *The Red Light Bandit* (turning Sganzerla's film into a collage of parodic sci-fi and B-movie references all at the same time, as mentioned in comparison with Adirley Queirós's *White Out, Black In*, in Chapter 7) also make a special appearance in *Tropical Curse*. While Marques's experimental documentary points to that same cinematic universe, her flying saucers play with the imaginary of futurism in a film aimed at discussing, with somewhat humorous elements, the future of Rio de Janeiro – or precisely the past of a future that has never arrived.

Here, she forges a dialogue with Sganzerla's film through the insertion of random flying saucers found in her online excavation, giving them a different cinematic meaning. Seemingly drawing on Torlasco again, in her case, 'any gesture of interpretation entails assuming a position that is internal to and transformative of the very relational network posited as object – it requires opening the past of the archive to mutations that belong to the future' (2013: xiv). The films were screened together as part of Stefan Solomon's

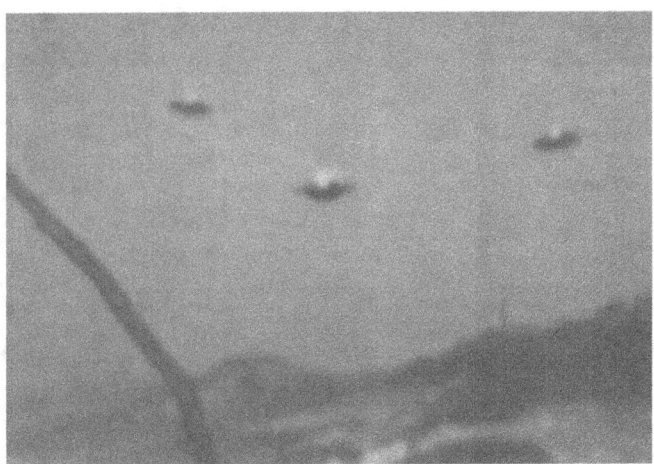

Figures 10.3 and 10.4: Flying saucers: From *The Red Light Bandit* to *Tropical Curse*.

(2017) Tate Modern film season *Tropicália and Beyond: Dialogues in Brazilian Film History*, underlining their connections by alluding to the contradictions in both Rio and São Paulo (the setting of Sganzerla's directorial debut).

Apart from that, I argue that the Third World, precarious ghost performed by Marques/Darks Miranda might represent another echo of Sganzerla's filmography. In *Copacabana Mon Amour* (1970), Sônia Silk, played by famous Cinema Novo/Cinema Marginal actress Helena Ignez, is a tormented prostitute followed by a ghost on the beach in Copacabana. Much like Marques's ghost,

Figures 10.5 and 10.6: A Third World ghost in *Copacabana Mon Amour* and *Tropical Curse*.

the phantasmagorical figure is almost childlike. There is a man playing with a piece of long, white fabric over his head, provoking less fear than indifference in his human target. While Silk walks around Copacabana, with the miserable ghost just behind her; the voice-over says a few words about a person's underdeveloped condition being related to a necessary madness in order to deal with reality: 'The sun of Copacabana drives Brazilians like us crazy in a very few seconds, leaving us completely perverted, astonished and silly; the supernatural forces paralyse us, the hungry ghosts of the planet.' In her interview, Marques (2018) claims there was no intention to evoke that specific sequence in *Tropical Curse* but acknowledges that her unconscious might have done a good job.

In his brief yet insightful commentary on the short film, Ikeda (2017), however, links *Tropical Curse* to Sganzerla's legacy in a more direct way. He points out that the director's trilogy about Orson Welles[6] was a similar exercise to Marques's handling of Carmen Miranda's public figure. 'For both, these artists are a way of talking about the contradictions of a project of progress in our own country' (ibid.). Furthermore, if one thinks of *All is Brazil* (Tudo é Brasil, 1997), the last instalment of Sganzerla's documentary series, Welles and Carmen Miranda even have an on-screen encounter. They appear in constant interaction through the juxtaposition of photographs and the use of a radio broadcast made by Welles, when he was American cultural ambassador to Latin America, from Rio de Janeiro's Cassino da Urca, in 1942, and in conversation with the Brazilian starlet. Apart from exploring the manipulation of cultural stereotypes, the film uses the dialogue between Welles and Carmen Miranda to emphasize what their personas bear in common: a trigger for investigating Brazilian identity, especially from the point of view of the foreigner or outsider.

Similarly, Carmen Miranda appears in another documentary from the 1990s whose historical background is set in the 1940s, except this time, she is the main subject of the film. One of the few female Cinema Novo directors, Helena Solberg,[7] made *Carmen Miranda: Bananas is My Business* (1995) as a means of going behind the scenes to unmask the myth for the film audience. Solberg mixes conventional, talking-head documentary with fantasy sequences performed by Eric Barreto, who was famously known as a drag queen who portrayed the singer. One of his performances in the documentary was chosen by Marques for use in the audiovisual thread that *Tropical Curse* is. It is no coincidence that performance is again mobilized (this time through the montage) as an intrinsic element of the experimental documentary. Significantly, this is a sequence filmed inside the Carmen Miranda Museum, still in operation at the time. Barreto plays a Carmen Miranda mannequin that comes to life and flees the museum. The ghost (Darks Miranda) then appears

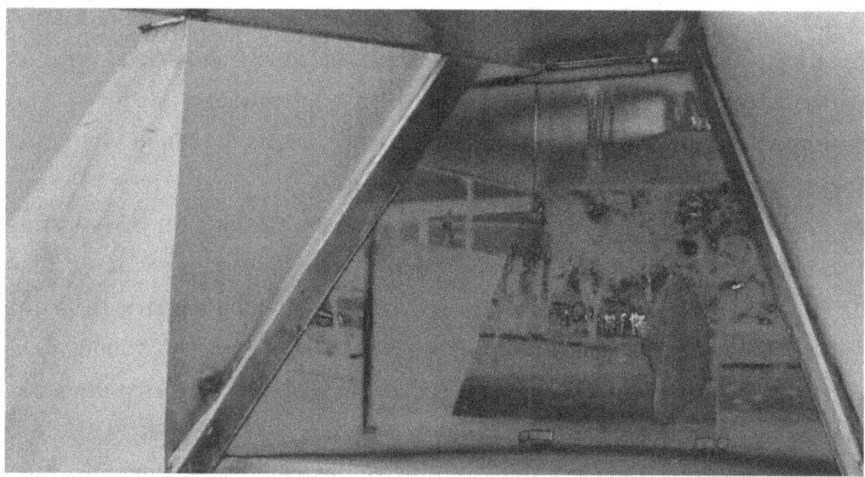

Figures 10.7 and 10.8: Montage effect: Carmen Miranda/Darks Miranda escapes the modernist museum.

dancing in the gardens, as if freed from the gallery in which it was kept. The narrative effect here comes from the original sequence suggested by Marques's montage.

In viewing the contradictions of Carmen Miranda's persona through Brazilian modernist architecture, the above-mentioned foreign viewpoint inevitably becomes a central issue. From Le Corbusier's modernist guidelines to a Portuguese-Brazilian-Hollywood star, the story told by Marques seems to come from an outsider perspective throughout. Brazilian progress and development at the mercy of either European colonizers, North American imperialists or flying saucers from a faraway galaxy. It is precisely in this sense that the director makes use of literary excerpts from Claude Lévi-Strauss, Pablo León de la Barra and Dominique Gonzalez-Foerster in the film. In fact, she freely alters the originals, creating her own meaning *from* what they have written. 'No wonder these are texts written by three *gringos* who somehow had a relationship with Brazil and whose imaginaries were also formed by this country. This "foreignism" is in the text and in the film. It is in Carmen Miranda, in science fiction, in the beings from other planets and unidentified objects,' Marques (2018) argues. Literature plays a dual role here: it is mobilized as both a source of knowledge and a sort of raw material for Marques to elaborate upon. Moreover, the assimilation of literary excerpts goes hand in hand with the assimilation of visual arts and performance elements into this intermedial experimental documentary. In this regard, it is the tropicalist intermediality that renders visible this ruin of underdevelopment: a museum hovering between sloppiness and abandonment, the rotten modernization that erected it and the neoliberal regime that cannot sustain it.

Of the three *gringos*, the contribution of Lévi-Strauss matters greatly. 'Doubtlessly we are on the other side of the Atlantic and the Equator, and quite near the tropics' is one of the sentences borrowed from Lévi-Strauss's *Tristes Tropiques* in the voice-over. Though a minimal citation, it carries the sense of location that underpins the anthropologist's study and his transatlantic arrival at *the fresh decadence or decayed freshness*, of the New World, as discussed in Chapter 1. This time, there would be no ship's crew to lead the way. Travelling on one of those flying saucers, Lévi-Strauss would land in a tropical, ultramodern construction site, with viaducts, bananas, stairs and pineapples. Forms and curves, flora and fauna. Wandering in the green area, the small, concrete spaceship in the middle of Flamengo Park would presumably catch his attention. A spaceship from the past, an abandoned museum, a forgotten playroom. A ruin from the future. If he does not feel frightened by the hungry ghosts from this planet, perhaps he might even glimpse Carmen Miranda dancing to a Caetano Veloso song. But definitely not a samba.

11

A lame-leg architecture: Half-hospital, half-ruin in *HU Enigma*

As mentioned earlier, Joana Traub Csekö has much in common with Daniel Santos and Luisa Marques. She is also a Rio-based artist originally from elsewhere – Csekö was born in Denver, United States, into a Brazilian family of European origins. To a certain degree, she therefore situates herself as an insider-outsider practitioner – not so much because of her origins (in fact, she moved to Rio aged two) but because she claims it is impossible for one person to fully grasp any kind of city. Like her peers, she seems to be interested in exploring the boundaries between cinema and the visual arts, particularly the intersection of documentary and photography, in the making of *HU Enigma*. A visual artist herself, the documentary feature she co-directed with Pedro Urano was initially a photographic series developed as part of an MPhil degree at the Federal University of Rio de Janeiro, in 2008. As will be discussed in this chapter, her photographic series deeply influenced the documentary's aesthetics of resorting to the use of photography as an intermedial strategy. In a way, as her MPhil included practice-led research, the project was also the outcome of another liminality, this time between artistic practice and academic research.

Her MPhil project aimed at discussing the notion of *point of view* in art production. She began her investigation from two specific and familiar viewpoints: her own personal perspective as a contemporary Brazilian artist, and the geographical location of Ilha do Fundão, the area designated for her photographic experiment to take place. The Ilha do Fundão environment is an artificial island located in Ilha do Governador, a suburb in Rio's North Zone. Like the area of Flamengo Park, the island is the result of an earthworks process (1949–52) led by the then president, Getúlio Vargas. The work joined up eight existing islands to literally create the terrain for the construction of the future Federal University. It is where the Hospital Universitário Clementino Fraga Filho, the university hospital commonly referred to as HU, is located. As the most outstanding yet unfinished modernist building in the region, Csekö's perspective relies on a key element of its construction: the fact that half of it is a hospital and the other half is empty, 'condemned to be forever simultaneously *construction and ruin*' (Csekö 2008: 38, emphasis added), echoing Claude Lévi-Strauss's perception of São Paulo's Praça da Sé, 'the cathedral square, halfway between a building site and a ruin' (1973: 121), as mentioned in Chapter 1.

According to Celeste Olalquiaga and Lisa Blackmore (2017, 2018), Latin American mid-twentieth-century modernist architecture has the potential to embody the contradictions of underdeveloped nations, as 'while urban design gave material expression to development, the twentieth century's uneven urbanization, rapid population growth, and spasmodic economy all ran contrary to modern planning' (2017). The paradoxical condition of HU – partly a hospital in operation, partly a crumbling building – is a key example of the authors' point. Once planned to be an outstanding modernist achievement, HU and, in fact, other 'iconic modern designs were repeatedly undercut by contingency and precariousness, leading them to take unexpected detours' (ibid.). In this sense, one could also think of failed projects like the Perimetral (inaugurated in 1960 and expanded in 1978) and the Carmen Miranda Museum (opened to the public in 1976). The authors also shed light on the construction of Brasília and its mix of formal (Le Corbusier style) and informal (satellite city style) architecture, as extensively explored in Part Two. For them, these projects are *living ruins*, a type of construction 'lapsing into the very opposite of its futuristic thrust as the sites turned either into unplanned spaces or outright ruins' (ibid.). From an artistic viewpoint, Robert Smithson referred to this paradox as *ruins in reverse*, anti-picturesque ruins part of 'a kind of self-destroying postcard world' (1996: 72), as highlighted at the opening of Part Three.

Now Csekö's own viewpoint as a contemporary Brazilian artist was to find inspiration in the first wave of postmodern art made in Brazil – to a certain extent, an art that examined the certainties of modernism. Interested in mobilizing perspectives related to the establishment of a national territory for art, she inevitably draws on the contribution of Tropicália and Cinema

Novo. As discussed in Chapter 2, this is a territory eagerly explored by Glauber Rocha, a filmmaker and intellectual concerned with scrutinizing underdevelopment and its manifold manifestations. Rather than merely arguing for a national cinema, Glauber believes that Brazilian malaise (hunger, misery, violence) must be turned inside out in order to conceive a genuine national cinema – a painful yet urgent artistic process that the tropicalist trigger *Entranced Earth*, for instance, attempts to accomplish. Csekö, therefore, acknowledges Glauber's effort to give birth to a national viewpoint within underdevelopment, something she pursues in her practice, more specifically in the still and moving images relating to HU. 'How can we handle, transmute, approach the Brazilian reality from which to produce art, when shortcuts, precariousness, adversity, poverty, immediacy, celerity are often impeding or overpowering factors, and can easily lead to feelings of despair or impotence?' (Csekö 2008: 26).

Unsurprisingly, Csekö then heavily draws on Hélio Oiticica's perspective. What strikes her most is his keenness that the role of the artist is to be an active, social body within a given reality, as elaborated in his *General Scheme of the New Objectivity*. In other words, the artist should engage with society and contribute to establishing a national point of view (which by no means should be an isolated point of view, but one in dialogue with international strands, in a very tropicalist methodology). As pointed out above, Oiticica also wondered 'how to, in an underdeveloped country, explain and justify the appearance of an avant-garde, not as a symptom of alienation, but as a decisive factor in its collective progress?' (1999b: 41), a question that resonates with Csekö's visualization of underdevelopment through the ruination of HU. For both Oiticica and Csekö, that visualization lies in the contact between art and life, as in Oiticica's famous proposition. 'I propose here to move it, update it, articulate it to other thoughts and stances, aiming to give free continuity to this attempt to come, which is to think how the artist can participate in his/her era (in his/her time, in his/her reality)' (Csekö 2008: 28). Bearing this in mind, *HU*, her photographic series, covers two major aspects: first, it dissects and exposes the underdeveloped condition (Glauber's Brazilian malaise) materialized through failed architecture (the hospital building itself); second, it considers what a visual regime (photographic, cinematic, artistic) is able to articulate and effectively communicate (as Oiticica pondered). Furthermore,

I also argue that *HU Enigma* takes a great deal from Oiticica's multi-sensorial intermediality to expose the HU condition.

Intrinsically attached to the photographic series, the conceptualization of *HU Enigma* was built upon what Csekö had already articulated in her still images: a critique of the modern(ist) project and the emphasis on the overlap between imagery and architecture. The photographic series-documentary connection points to a true fusion, not an accumulation, of media expressions drawing on Ágnes Pethő's (2010) definition of intermediality. Urano, filmmaker and her friend, decided to push forward a documentary project about HU after finding out about the research study she was conducting at university. Initially, the project was a medium-length documentary sponsored by DOCTV, an important government scheme linked to the Ministry of Culture that helped support independent audiovisual productions, as mentioned in Chapter 3. Later on, it was turned into a full-length documentary – the final cut version under analysis here.[1] Considering the language Csekö had developed in her photographic work, their basic choice of dividing the screen in half comes from the way Csekö conceived her diptychs in the gallery. Thus, the documentary image has an unusual 2:1 aspect ratio, that is, the width of the frame is exactly double the height of the frame.

To deal with two square-format screens in most of the sequences, Urano and Csekö had to take extra care in positioning the interviewees for the camera. Right in the middle of the frame, they appear with the highest headroom possible for photographic framing so the directors can create an analogy and visually refer to the modernist architecture where they were actually filming. On that note, apart from photography, it could be argued that architecture itself plays a fundamental role in the documentary-making, enhancing Pethő's approach to intermediality as a 'sensual mode' that entices the viewer to also perceive a film through its 'architectural forms and haptic textures' (2011: 5). In this sense, *HU*, the documentary, is also a reflection of HU, the building, as the latter directly influences the contours of the former. Ultimately, the visual composition makes it easier to feel the power of institution over individuals, something that becomes visible through the interview *mise en scène*. In an interview with me, Urano (2017) also suggests that that cinematic approach somehow wanted to challenge the role of the interview[2] as a means of creating intimacy between interviewer and interviewee, something that was much in vogue at the time.

The history of HU, the building, dates back to 1950, when construction started. Designed by modernist architect Jorge Machado Moreira, the new university hospital had been planned to be Latin America's largest hospital of 220,000 m² to replace the former hospital building located in Rio's South Zone, far from Ilha do Fundão. When President Getúlio Vargas committed suicide in 1954, the construction came to a halt due to the subsequent political crisis. With Brasília about to be inaugurated as the country's new capital, Rio (and in this case, HU) felt the impact of a lack of investment. Work only resumed in 1972, taking six more years for HU to finally function as an operating hospital (Oliveira 2005). Ironically, it took twenty-eight years for a single building to be constructed, whereas Brasília was built from scratch in less than five, as discussed in Part Two. In fact, the building was never fully constructed, as one half remained unfinished, hence abandoned. In a clumsy attempt to raise money for the construction to be concluded, the government authorized the demolition of the former hospital, so the land could be sold off (Rocha 2003). Consequently, Rio lost one of the city's foremost neoclassical architectural examples – and HU was never finished.

Figure 11.1: Split-screen interviews in *HU Enigma*.

A fractured building is a fractured ethos

The 1970s' modernist fever definitely had a dual impact on the urbanism of Rio, providing evidence of both its prestige and subsequent dereliction in the much-delayed inauguration of HU. Focusing on the paradox of being a monument yet a ruin, *HU Enigma* encapsulates 'the decrepitude of the new' (Jaguaribe 1998: 101) that Brazilian modernism would be, sooner or later, forced to acknowledge. The discussion proposed by Beatriz Jaguaribe accords with that of Mexican scholar, Rubén Gallo, when he argues 'many modernist projects have not aged well and have now become architectural ruins themselves' (2009: 108) in the context of Mexican society, one also devoted to countless cycles of tearing down and rebuilding throughout history. When Jaguaribe makes a similar claim, she also considers the Gustavo Capanema Palace, the former Ministry of Education and Health headquarters in Rio. Designed by Lúcio Costa and supervised by Le Corbusier, the project is considered to be the first public modernist building in Brazil. Apart from its modernist style per se, Jaguaribe claims that both the Gustavo Capanema Palace and the Ilha do Fundão building complex sadly share a similar state of abandonment. They are both 'allegorical ruins of the modernist collapse' (Jaguaribe 1998: 112), or the *living ruins* of Olalquiaga and Blackmore (2017).

More significantly, Jaguaribe links the decayed architecture to the fractured ethos of a country that has not come to terms with itself. Those were buildings planned to embody a sense of nationalism so it was quite unexpected yet meaningful that they were abandoned – or even left incomplete. The modernist utopia resulting in the modernist ruin. In this sense, Jaguaribe (1998) refers to the conceptual analogy *building/Nation* coined by Maurício Lissovsky and Paulo Sérgio Moraes de Sá (1996), when investigating the ideological disputes before the approval of architectural projects, especially in the 1930s and 1940s, a period marked by elaborations of what a sense of Brazilianness meant. The duality of a decayed architecture and a fractured ethos is even more prominent in *HU Enigma*, which Csekö had already addressed in her dissertation. The documentary explores the fact that half the building actually operated as a hospital to provide a commentary on that fractured ethos. Even though doctors do the best they can and manage to attend to patients, Urano and

Figure 11.2: Two square-format screens: Two halves of the HU building.

Csekö underline the precarious situation the hospital actually faces. The lack of investment and the overcrowded corridors create a hellish environment. If, at first sight, the split-screen strategy seemed to emphasize the opposing halves of the same building, a second look allows one to catch the subtle commentary. The hospital-half actually mirrors the emptied-half – or the lame-leg, as people refer to the abandoned area. They are both in the process of ruination. In this case, the *asymmetric symmetry* (Csekö 2008) that the camera angles and the juxtaposition of images use give the impression that the decaying architecture *is* the fractured ethos.

In fact, the HU is depicted not only as the materialization of that fractured ethos but also as an organism representing the nation itself. The parallel between the concrete structure and the human body is activated right from the opening sequence. First, one sees a surgical team preparing to operate on a patient. The surgery starts. An endoscopic procedure allows the doctors (and the audience) to see inside the patient's body. Sequentially, another camera (Urano's camera, as he is also the cinematographer) wanders in a dark room. There are lots of long, rusty pipes, water leaking, a little mouse running across the frame. Now, one is seeing the innards of the building-body. This association comes and goes throughout the documentary. At another moment, for instance, medical students attend a lecture in one of the building's auditoriums. The professor shows images of skin diseases and the following scene presents details of peeling, muddy walls; the skin of the HU. The idea of exposing these elements of the building is also a cinematic strategy to reveal its decaying structure. The inside-out revelation tactic is highlighted by Tim Edensor in his analyses of the state of post-industrial ruins:

> Ruination produces a defamiliarized landscape in which the formerly hidden emerges; the tricks that make a building a coherent ensemble are revealed, exposing the magic of construction. The internal organs, pipes, veins, wiring and tubes – the guts of a building – spill out, as informal and official asset-strippers remove key materials such as tiles and lead. The key points of tension become visible, and the skeleton – the infrastructure on which all else hangs – the pillars, keystones, support walls and beams stand while less sturdy material – the clothing or flesh of the building – peels off. And the hidden networks are laid open, released from their confinement behind walls and under floors. (2005: 109–110)

This sick part of the building-body is treated as a restricted zone in the documentary, as if the lame-leg really forbids access to the general public. The enhanced sense of a thriller atmosphere here draws on Andrei Tarkovsky's *Stalker* (1979), a major reference for Urano and Csekö and considered by André Habib to be 'the most original, complex and radical formulation of ruins in Tarkovsky's filmography' (2008: 269). Johannes von Moltke also sheds light on Tarkovsky via Hartmut Böhme's argument that 'ruins are "the aesthetic center of his films"' (2010: 412). In this Soviet, sci-fi tale (loosely inspired by the sci-fi novel of Arkady and Boris Strugatsky, *Roadside Picnic, Tale of the Troika*), a guide leads two men through an area known as the Zone, when they seek a room that has the capacity to grant their innermost wishes. The Zone, however, is an area of quarantined land. Filmed during the Cold War, it is a forbidden area controlled by the government and covered with industrial debris in a post-apocalyptic scenario. It bears a sense of mystery and interdiction that fascinates Urano and Csekö, which translates into the way they approach the HU's lame-leg. Provocatively, they film and interview people (from medical students to architects) inside the restricted zone, as if testing the limits of the ruined area.

With grass growing and birds randomly flying around the restricted zone, nature takes over a human-made landscape, as if illustrating a Georg Simmel prophecy. In this regard, it is worth mentioning the contribution of the German sociologist who famously discusses the central role played

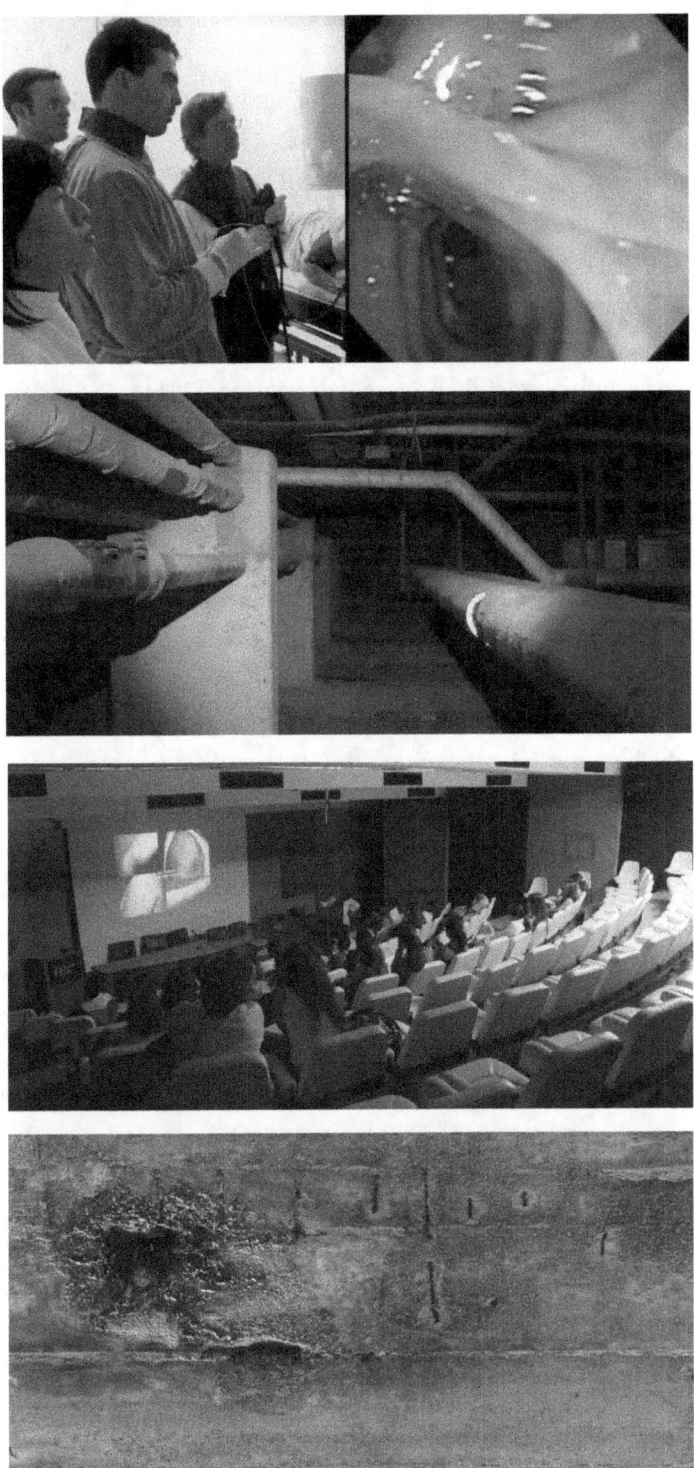

Figures 11.3, 11.4, 11.5 and 11.6: The human body, the HU body.

by nature in the process of ruination of human-made landscapes in his landmark essay 'The Ruin', originally published in 1911. Albeit 'in some ways still a Romantic conception of the ruin' (2011: 13), as Brian Dillon ponders, Simmel's argument saw architecture as 'the only art in which the great struggle between the will of the spirit and the necessity of nature issues into real peace' (1965: 259), materializing the equilibrium of all contradictions. Nevertheless, nature is expected to take control eventually, providing 'a certain imaginative perspectivism in its hopeful and tragic dimension' (2011), as Svetlana Boym puts it. That is, Simmel's ruins unfold what *should have been* that has no chance of being, hence the neoromantic prospect is still latent. From a postmodern perspective, Dillon (2005–6), however, questions that approach. 'The ruin is not the triumph of nature, but an intermediate moment, a fragile equilibrium between persistence and decay' (ibid.). Striking a similar note, Boym argues that 'present-day ruinophilia is not merely a neoromantic malaise and a reflection of our inner landscapes. Rediscovered, off-modern ruins are not only symptoms but also sites for a new exploration and production of meanings' (2011), which seems to be the case with Urano and Csekö's exploration of the documentary.

If Tarkovsky's *Stalker* already hinted at Csekö and Urano's endeavour to mobilize international references, the influence of North American artist Gordon Matta-Clark underlines the relevance of that kind of mobilization even more. In this case, there is a digest not only of foreign art but also of other types of art practices. This is a strong echo of Oiticica's multi-sensorial approach to the arts domain. In fact, Oiticica and Matta-Clark were collaborators in 1970s New York, when the Brazilian was in exile for seven years there. Struggling to formulate the category of the subterranean, Oiticica wrote *Subterrania* in 1971, a book made of fifteen sections dedicated to North and South American artists especially devoted to urban engagement. Matta-Clark was one of those artists. As in Rio, in New York, Oiticica 'subverted the supremacy of the museum/gallery as the defining space of the art object, and, instead, brought work to the streets' (Sussman 2016: 132), hence 'the affinity with Matta-Clark's inventive play and experimentation, paramount opportunities for knowledge and experience available to the body in action' (ibid.: 137).

With a relevant body of work ranging from performance to film and photography, Matta-Clark became notorious for his 'building cuts'

Figure 11.7: Nature takes over: A woman wanders amid the ruins.

interventions in existing abandoned buildings, mainly in New York. He would slice into and literally open the building up, as if transforming it into a walk-through sculpture to challenge the human perception of things and relationships. Coming from an architectural background, he saw himself as an *anarchitect*,[3] derived from the term *anarchitecture*, coined by the artist himself to refer to both his architectural expertise and site-specific artworks. The camera in *HU Enigma* latently pays homage to the relationship between architecture and contemporary art developed by Matta-Clark. In fact, his influence was such that Urano and Csekö made a sort of epilogue or follow-up to *HU Enigma*. *Tribute to Matta-Clark*[4] (Homenagem a Matta-Clark, 2015) is a short documentary exclusively focused on the engineering work that had to be done after the structural failure had compromised the building as a whole. In 2010, the structural failure urgently demanded the physical separation of the north and south wings. Over the course of four months, a twenty-meter-wide section of the monumental concrete structure was demolished – heavy work that the directors filmed making a clear allusion to Matta-Clark's famous 'building cuts'.

Installation art has thus also established an intermedial dialogue through Csekö and Urano's moving images. To a certain extent, the soundscape of *HU Enigma* refers to Brazilian conceptual artist Cildo Meireles's *Através* (Through),[5] conceived between 1983 and 1989. In the wake of the Neo-Concrete generation formed by Hélio Oiticica, Ferreira Gullar, Lygia Clark and Lygia Pape, to name but a few, Meireles's artistic practice became world-renowned. This famous piece is a beautifully crafted installation made of prison bars, curtains and fences – barriers to be overcome. On the floor, shattered glass for one to walk upon creates a nerve-wrecking, destructive sound. In his interview, Urano (2017) links it to the work of sound editor, Edson Secco, in charge of capturing diegetic sound in *HU Enigma*. Secco is also a musician and recorded the sound of rusty bits of iron found in his wanderings around the lame-leg. The melodic piece ended up being used as extra-diegetic sound for sequences where the characters walk as if in a restricted zone. For the director, the combination of sound and image here creates a bridge to Meireles's artwork. The use of sound, however, is paradoxical in one of the final sequences when there is actually no sound whatsoever. When HU's south wing finally collapses, the sequence is shown mute. Only after a minute or so, when the screen goes completely dark, is the aggressive noise of the building's implosion heard. The climax is a blank space. 'This temporal disjunction of sound and image concerns my experience of the event. The image captured by the camera played at normal speed and synchronized with the sound didn't resemble the experience of the implosion that I had in my mind' (ibid.). After the screen goes back to normal, dark smoke spreads across the city sky.

Framed by the modernist glass window of HU, the Rio de Janeiro which appears on the horizon is nothing but an unattainable postcard. The dreams of modernism never succeeded in keeping up with the so-called Marvellous City that the broken window frame reveals. Whilst walking through the lame-leg, architect Margareth Pereira wonders where modernist architecture went wrong if the HU project balances light and shadow, among other assets. In this sense, it is quite meaningful to hear one of the medical students regretting the misuse of the hospital while visiting the lame-leg. 'We don't really need more hospitals ... There are too many already,' he says in an ironic, unhappy tone. The paradoxical 'this is way too big' is what he hears as the answer from one of his peers. Restorative nostalgia (Boym 2001) has no room and it is also trashed by Urano in his interview when he criticizes the *tabula rasa* logic of modernism: 'There is no way of fixing Brazil by ignoring its past' (2017). Indeed, as discussed in Chapter 4, James Holston (1989) explains that one of the main features of the modernist pattern is to dismiss the national colonial past and think of a revolutionary architecture starting from ground zero, a strategy that

Figure 11.8: The final collapse of the lame-leg.

turned out to be both controversial and unsatisfactory. 'The ruin, not only of the HU, but also of public health and education in Brazil, is a project. Every day we spend a lot of energy, money and lives to keep our backwardness. It is not the work of chance, it is not an accident, it is a project. The point is asking ourselves: Who is benefiting from it?' Urano (2017) inquires.

In *HU Enigma*, as in *Tropical Curse*, *The Harbour* and *ExPerimetral*, contemporary filmmakers seem highly conscious of these controversies and dissatisfaction. Drawing on intermedial tactics, these experimental documentaries find their mission in exposing the precarious condition of an elevated highway, a museum and a hospital. They aimed at articulating a critique of the modern and neoliberal processes that resulted in failing projects, connecting these ruins in the same imagetic thread. They discuss an architecture that failed in Rio de Janeiro – a city that passes from freshness to decay without ever being simply old, a city to which the passage of time brings degeneration instead of improvement, a city perpetually young yet never healthy (Lévi-Strauss 1973). Furthermore, these artists question so-called progress and (under)development while shedding light on historical aspects usually not taken into consideration. On that note, I argue that this critique is precisely enhanced by the updating of tropicalist-like values through the fusion of multi-sensorial media expressions on screen, even though to different degrees. In contrast to the commodification of moving images in neoliberal times, their cinematic ruins of underdevelopment reclaim the radical power of artistic contributions, 'to reactivate in our times, in each situation, the political potential inherent in artistic activity, its power to unleash possibles', as Suely Rolnik (2006) hoped.

***

Rio de Janeiro, 1967. Caetano Veloso saw *Entranced Earth* for the first time. He had recently moved from Bahia to live there not long before. Glauber, who was originally from Bahia as well, was also living in Rio at the time. Likewise, visual artist Oiticica, a *carioca* himself, displayed his groundbreaking installation art at the city's Museum of Modern Art – the very first time the word *Tropicália* had been used. Rio was also one of the main settings of Cinema Novo films, including *Entranced Earth*. No longer the capital of Brazil, Rio has managed to remain the capital of Brazil as far as the world is concerned. Unlike any other Brazilian city, it paradoxically encapsulates beauty (despite Lévi-Strauss's indifference) and exclusion (*the higher you live, the lower your status*, to refer to the French anthropologist again). The city has witnessed innumerable demolitions and renovations, chasing first a Paris and then a New York kind of urbanism. Rio erected an elevated highway in 1960, a spaceship-like museum in 1976, the lame-leg hospital in 1978. The elevated highway collapsed, the museum closed, the hospital imploded. Ultimately, is it the Marvellous City or *a toothless mouth*?

Part Four

The long-standing ruination: Indigenous territory in dispute

Part Four compares the representation of indigenous territories in Cinema Novo films with that of the Vídeo nas Aldeias (VNA) project. In discussing a territory under threat, the visualization of indigenous land contains embedded layers of time echoing the past of colonization, the military modernization and present-day neoliberal agenda. I argue that that territorial dispute is rendered visible precisely through images of ruins in this context. In Chapter 12, I delve into the contribution of Cinema Novo in addressing indigenous imagery as damaged territory as a critique of so-called progress and (under)development in the wake of the military coup d'état. Next, I introduce the VNA project born amid the emergence of indigenous media elsewhere, with a special focus on reclaiming land boundaries through politically committed documentary-making, by both non-indigenous and indigenous affiliated directors, in Chapter 13. This is a necessary survey as it explains how that specific crop of documentary-making is structured and how that structure influences the way ruined areas may be depicted.

Chapters 14 and 15 explore documentaries specifically centred on images of ruins as a means of exposing the historical struggle. The former is focused on VNA leader Vincent Carelli's *Corumbiara: They Shoot Indians, Don't They?* (Corumbiara, 2009) and how it constructs its spatial representation while wandering amid devastated indigenous villages; and the latter explores collaborative indigenous documentaries *Tava, The House of Stone* (Tava, A Casa de Pedra, 2012), *Two Villages, One Path* (Duas Aldeias, Uma Caminhada,

2008) and *Guarani Exile* (Desterro Guarani, 2011), films concerned with problematizing the Tava São Miguel tourist ruin complex and advocating a new understanding of history. Differently from Parts Two and Three, here the ruins are not modern(ist), urban failures like those of Brasília and Rio de Janeiro, but they are complementarily produced by the same suspicious developmentalist mindset, this time in rural areas.

Discussing the indigenous territory within Brazilian cinema necessarily means shedding light upon VNA, a seminal project founded in 1986 by anthropologist, activist and documentarist Vincent Carelli. As will be discussed, VNA is a non-governmental organization aimed at supporting the indigenous people's struggles to protect both their culture and territory using audiovisual resources. Since its creation, it has mapped, contacted and engaged with no less than forty indigenous groups in Brazil. In brief, special attention is given here to this initiative for two main reasons. In the first place is its impressively high productivity: more than eighty videos and films, half of them produced along with indigenous communities (Fulni-ô, Kuikuro, Mbyá-Guarani and Xavante, among others) as the outcome of filmmaking workshops provided by VNA members.

Second, but by no means less important, the political role of VNA in fighting for indigenous rights through moving image militancy, particularly with regard to the urgency of land demarcation for groups, such as the Guarani Kaiowá (in Mato Grosso do Sul state) and the Kanoê (in Rondônia state), to name but two. Land, indeed, has always been at the very heart of indigenous people's struggles. While violent territorial disputes can easily refer back to the arrival of Portuguese colonizers in 1500, it can also refer to ongoing quarrels between indigenous peoples and farmers, politicians and agribusiness entrepreneurs. In this sense, VNA advocates for Native peoples' rights to their ancestral territories through the documentary representation of these now damaged territories.

12

Setting the ground: Cinema Novo and indigenous representation

Early Brazilian cinema was not much interested in discussing indigenous issues. Fiction films, in fact, romanticized the Indian personae using idyllic adaptations of writer José de Alencar's books, such as *The Guarani* (1857), *Iracema* (1865) and *Ubirajara* (1874). Thus, the Indian was portrayed as a naïve yet brave warrior, the so-called noble savage, while the European characters appeared as peaceful conquerors. Their encounters consequently mythologized the narrative of nationhood[1] rather than problematizing it. Ironically enough, 'while the actually existing Indian was destroyed, marginalized, or eliminated through miscegenation, the remote Indian was idealized', as Robert Stam (2003: 209) points out. In terms of nonfiction, Luiz Thomaz Reis, military man and documentarist of the Rondon Commission[2] (1907–15), became well known for documenting evidence of indigenous groups at that time, as seen in his landmark documentary *Bororo Rituals and Feasts* (Rituais e Festas Bororo, 1917) and many others. 'The history of documentary cinema,' Gustavo Procopio Furtado argues, 'is enmeshed with the history of far-flung expeditions and the resulting contacts between western travelers and indigenous groups' (2019: 32), the exploration of the Brazilian territory being an example of that. Nonetheless, Furtado claims that Reis's work 'is closer to the status of the ethnographic "document" than the "documentary", meaning that the images he produced and accumulated over time were predominantly observational and only sparingly narrative' (ibid.: 33). In other words, even though key in the documentation of the indigenous people, 'Reis's images of contact with such people reflected the protectionist perspective of indigenist thought during the Rondón era' (ibid.). It is in this sense that, albeit also pointing out the ethnographic appeal in Reis's body of work, Fernando de Tacca (2001) believes that the actual aim was to construct an official Indian image for the recently unified Republican nation at the time. As Furtado wisely points out, with the passage of time, however, 'those films dealing with ethnographic contact move from the desire to record primal scenes to the accumulation of images and memories of destruction ..., records not of contact but of disease and devastation' (2019: 25).

Apart from at the threshold of the twentieth century, the portrayal of indigenous figures only properly re-emerged in the 1970s, as Brazilian cinema spent the decades of 1930s,[3] 1940s, 1950s and 1960s paying more attention to black than to Indian (mis)representation, as Stam (1997) claims. Interestingly, it is no coincidence that this cinematic hiatus was interrupted by the contribution of Cinema Novo, especially after 1968, when the military coup d'état of 1964 became more repressive with the advent of the Institutional Act Nº5, which pushed the country (and *cinemanovistas*) into an abyssal identity crisis, as pointed out in Chapter 2. Even though commonly referred to as a white, male-led movement, it was with Cinema Novo that the critique of progress and (under)development was visually articulated for the first time within national production. It was in this context that the indigenous imaginary was taken account of again as part of the problem brought about by the underdevelopment under investigation. When that kind of production came about, the romanticized Indian was appropriately left behind and State-oriented filmmaking was set to be challenged. Furthermore, indigenous groups were portrayed not only as a component of the country's identity, ready to be scrutinized, but as intrinsically affected by the destruction generated by 'progress' – two strong areas of interest to Cinema Novo.

In this sense, Joaquim Pedro de Andrade's *Macunaíma* (1969) successfully encapsulated part of that discussion. According to Ismail Xavier (2012), the director chose to acknowledge the crisis in which the country was immersed by adapting Mário de Andrade's novel of the same title. Praised as one of the main Brazilian modernist novels, *Macunaíma* (1928) the book was effective in articulating a narrative based on apparently opposing poles (the modern and the primitive, represented by the metropolis and the countryside) to hint at the formation of a modern national character. Both the writer Andrade and the filmmaker Andrade resort to a series of foundation myths, folklore objects and Afro-Brazilian references to produce a sense of Brazilianness – with the idea of modernization as a key part of that unveiled identity, as Ângela Prysthon (2002) underlined in her analysis of the novel. Although four decades separate each artwork, the assimilation of Mário de Andrade's novel into the film project was part of Cinema Novo/Tropicália's strategy to open a dialogue with the anthropophagy debate of the 1920s. In fact, the cultural rescue that Caetano Veloso and his contemporaries accomplished gave the modernist movement led by Oswald de Andrade[4] and Mário de Andrade (to mention but two of the leading artists involved in the 1922 São Paulo Modern Art Week) a kind of popularity it had not acquired before, as discussed in Chapter 8. For Ivana Bentes, there is a key difference between the 1920s and the 1960s: 'From Mário de Andrade's lyrical commotion we move on to debauchery and pessimism, tropicalism and dictatorship' (1996: 68). Even though the director did not see the film as directly linked to the Tropicália movement, Bentes places it as 'a reinterpretation of modernism, nationalism and tropicalism' that 'reconciled Cinema Novo with the public, the critics, the box office and the international market' (ibid.: 3).

In Ella Shohat and Stam's (1994) view, modernist *anthropophagy* (a word referring to the anthropophagic or cannibalistic indigenous ritual that famously characterized the Tupinambá people) is imbued with a double sense: at the same time that it advocates the decolonization of the mind (or de-*Vespuccization* of the Americas/de-*Cabralization* of Brazil), it finds the cultural interchange between the so-called centre and periphery inevitable. The result of that interaction, therefore, must be a cannibalist artistic stance: 'The artist in the dominated culture should not ignore the foreign presence but must swallow it, carnivalize it, recycle it for national ends' (ibid.: 307). In this regard, the alliance between the novel and the film (regardless of their dissimilarities) takes into account a particular idea of modernity interested in that continuous flow of references. That is, one interested in the *dialectics of cosmopolitanism* (Prysthon 2002) in the periphery of the Western world. 'Peripheral cosmopolitanism will be defined by the modernists precisely as this ability to assimilate and reprocess all the origins and cultural influences within the metropolis' (ibid.: 46). It is important to bear this in mind because the indigenous imaginary, particularly in this film, is articulated precisely in relation to the building of a critical (and commonly parodic) imagery for modern/modernized Brazil.

Even though indigenous origins and influences are not overtly present in the film,[5] *Macunaíma* decidedly mobilized elements of indigenous culture in an emblematic way at the end of the turbulent 1960s. Macunaíma, initially played by black actor Grande Otelo, soon smokes a magic cigarette[6] and turns into white actor Paulo José. The transformation will happen in another sequence, when Macunaíma/Grande Otelo takes a shower in a spring and turns into Macunaíma/Paulo José again – a powerful commentary on racism through irony. While the cast/characters allegorically point to the miscegenation factor attached to Brazil, neither of them is indigenous. His name, however, along with his brothers' names, Jiguê and Maanape, are. They live in the jungle, in an imprecise location, and their home is a *maloca*, a kind of community Indian hut, whose Tupi-Guarani definition is 'war house' or 'Indian ranch'. Furthermore, mother and children sleep in hammocks and spend the day surrounded by nature. Rather than designing an authentic indigenous environment, the construction of that atmosphere comes into being as the outcome of history itself. 'Colonization, economic expansion, migrations, extraction fronts, renewed conflicts between Aborigines and invaders, miscegenation, everything has already occurred and these processes have left their traces on the lands,' as Xavier (2012: 239) puts it. Certainly, the wrecked structure of that environment works as a reflection of Macunaíma's wrecked identity – *a hero without character*, as indicated by the novel's subtitle.

In tune with modernist-tropicalist references to cannibalism, Stam (1997) famously claims that *Macunaíma* explores the concept's negative aspect. In his influential analysis of the film, instead of emphasizing aboriginal matriarchy and utopian communalism, he believes Joaquim Pedro de Andrade 'made cannibalism a critical instrument for exposing the exploitative social Darwinism implicit in 'savage capitalism' and bourgeois civility' (ibid.: 239). The director's point of view considers the social, political, economic and work relationships established in the context of the 1960s' military dictatorship as relationships guided by power and consumerism, as if the nation was *devouring* its own people.[7] When Macunaíma flees to the big city in the second part of the film, these aspects are enhanced by the character's initial difficulty in relating to the metropolis' multiple machines and flashing lights. After some time, however, Macunaíma starts to benefit from living in a spacious apartment full of electrical goods representing the 'economic miracle' of the military regime. Surprisingly, it is as if his laziness and individualism fit perfectly into that shallow, modern environment. Aimless in the metropolis after acquiring the *muiraquitã* (a Tupi-Guarani word meaning stone-carved artefacts) talisman he was looking for, he decides to leave for good. Yet, Joaquim Pedro de Andrade refuses to allow him redemption on his return, as one might expect. The search for national identity is not found in the gesture towards nature; rather, a stand-off situation is produced. According to Xavier, in essence, 'the journey of Macunaíma ... is a parable of migration without return, of the contact between two worlds that exhibit the same rules for devouring' (2012: 262).

The failure of modern progress is not reserved to the metropolis alone, as the final sequences in the forest demonstrate. On their way back home, Macunaíma, along with his brothers and girlfriend, navigate a river. The boat is filled with electrical wares: a TV, fan, blender and an electric guitar, the legacy from his urban experience. As they sail along, he even carelessly suggests building a bridge to make people's lives easier, a comment that makes explicit his *nouveau-riche*, developmentalist mindset. Once ashore, they find their *maloca* has now become a *tapera* (an old house or abandoned village in Tupi-Guarani). Macunaíma seems unworried about his damaged territory. He lies down in a hammock, while the others go to catch fish and find birds to be hunted and corn cobs to be harvested. Nothing is found, though. Next morning, the three are gone and Macunaíma is all by himself. The *tapera* looks even more precarious, 'in complete abandonment', stresses the narrator. The thatched structure collapses. Naked in the jungle as an Indian would be (he actually covers himself with a green-military jacket, a modern national symbol at that time), there is not much he can do. His death is imminent and there is no one to mourn him but a parrot. When he finally disappears beneath the water in the river, after being attracted and eaten by the cannibalistic, mythological Uiara, his green-military jacket floats covered in his blood. In this closing sequence, the classical Villa-Lobos's *Desfile aos Heróis do Brasil* (Parade to the Heroes of Brazil) plays, but it is a joke. There is nothing patriotic about it; on the contrary, 'the end projects onto the back of Macunaíma all the burden of rejection of the nationalist myths appropriated by the military regime: the exaltation of nature and heroism, the myth of the tropical paradise and the great destiny of the nation' (ibid.: 265). It has all ended in ruin.

Figure 12.1: Macunaíma and the ruined *tapera*.

Instead of indigenous cooperation and harmony with nature, Macunaíma represents the exact opposite, just how ready he is to inhabit the modern world – that is the sad yet humorous conclusion. If the indigenous approach is limited inasmuch as there is no direct mention of the cause, the film, however, is clearly structured upon the conceptual duality of cannibalism/anthropophagy. Challenging the way the military dictatorship took possession of national symbols, Joaquim Pedro de Andrade uses the indigenous imaginary in his critique. Moreover, he makes use of the anthropophagic motif to question the national predatory class structure, as he himself states cited in Shohat and Stam: 'Cannibalism is an exemplary mode of consumerism adopted by underdeveloped peoples' (1994: 311). In this sense, the film invests in a debate very dear to the new left represented by the Tropicália movement at the time: the assimilation of consumer society values by a Third World nation like Brazil and what can be made of that. 'Macunaíma, cultural industry hero,' as Bentes (1996: 74) wisely puts it. Closing the 1960s by building up to that kind of discussion, *Macunaíma* was emblematic of this period's modernist tactic of playing around with an allegorical Brazilian figure which, as anthropophagy itself postulates, swallowed and recycled indigenous elements in order to critique the so-called progress and (under)development advocated at the time. Setting the scene, Joaquim Pedro de Andrade portrays indigenous lands invaded by rotten modernization, with a ruined *tapera* as its emblem.

The (absent) figure of the Indian

In the same year *Macunaíma* was released, Walter Lima Jr. depicted Brazil in the aftermath of a Third World War that had destroyed the Northern Hemisphere. In *Brazil Year 2000* (Brasil Ano 2000, 1969), the periphery was finally taking centre stage, but that did not bring redemption; on the contrary, it only reiterated national failure, according to Xavier (2012). In the film, a mother and her young son and daughter wander in the partially devastated landscape until they come across a city called I Forgot. There, preparation for a rocket launch mobilizes the remaining citizens, ironically unveiling the precarious infrastructure of the project. The apparent modernization proceeds, but filled with ineffectiveness. 'In an ironic way, the catastrophic consciousness of underdevelopment privileges here, as its target, the mystification of "the country of the future"' (ibid.: 232), a false belief in a future that would finally place Brazil in a privileged position, but, of course, this is a future that never comes. 'The parody of modernization slips into the diagnosis of general incompetence, as in *The Red Light Bandit*'[8] (ibid.: 224), with the fantasy of being a country predestined to progress, actually preventing it from overcoming underdevelopment.

In that post-apocalyptic yet satirical scenario, it is quite meaningful that the (absent) figure of the Indian plays a central role. In terms of space, in opposition to the rocket platform, there is an indigenous reserve. Nonetheless, if the rocket platform delivers underdevelopment rather than cutting-edge technology, the spatial representation of the indigenous reserve is also controversial. When the migrant family arrives at what used to be the Indian Education Service, they meet an indolent old employee moaning that although he 'educated' eighteen tribes throughout his career, they have all disappeared. The young son wants clarification and asks who the people are he is talking about. 'They are not people, they are Indians,' replies the old man. Because the general is coming to visit I Forgot (and the old man is afraid of losing his now pointless job), he makes an offer: if the family agrees to pretend to be Indians, they will have food and a roof over their heads. The farce makes visible the absence of Indians in the post-apocalyptic Brazil (i.e. in military Brazil of the 1960s – and one might argue in present-day Brazil as well). Moreover, the family's role-play renders the figure of the Indian a metaphor for inferiority.

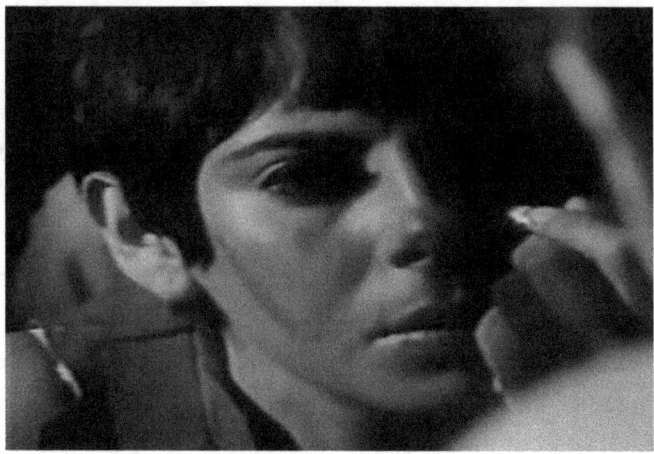

Figure 12.2: White turned into fake Indian in a devastated Brazil.

'Absent, unknown, an emblem of defeat on the level of history, he can only assume here the clichéd figure of another, unrecognized and stigmatized by the winner, but strong and pertinent as a ghost of origins' (ibid.: 231).

In *Brazil Year 2000*, one could argue there is no Indian and no indigenous reserve, as if they and their territory had been so badly damaged that they had vanished. Yet, Lima Jr. is not necessarily suggesting that as the outcome of the world war. Although speculating about a dystopic future, the film is commenting on that situation in the present of when it was made. 'In this sense, despite the imagined atomic catastrophe and the future crisis, it would be naïve to speak about ruins or fragments' (ibid.: 207), Xavier stresses. In other words, that situation depicted is not the result of a catastrophe but a permanent state. I would argue, however, that, precisely because it is a permanent state and not the result of catastrophe, speaking of ruins in that context could hint at something else. Other than an unexpected consequence, the ruined territory in both the fictional future and what was the current dictatorial present is, rather, the unchanging condition of underdevelopment. Embedded in that situation, the indigenous territory that had vanished in *Brazil Year 2000* was to reappear under similar circumstances in other Cinema Novo outputs. In Arnaldo Jabor's *Pindorama*[9] (1970), for instance, Pindorama is an allegorical land representing Brazil, where the indigenous territory is the target of an exploitative system and the Indians are exiles in their own land. In contrast,

Nelson Pereira dos Santos's *How Tasty Was My Little Frenchman* (Como Era Gostoso o Meu Francês, 1971) comments on that by cinematically subverting the oppression. Mainly spoken in Tupi-Guarani, here the Tupinambá people capture a French conqueror, and his tragic end represents historical redemption through an anthropophagic[10] critique of European colonialism.

The Coca-Cola-Indian allegory

Ultimately, that critique reached its peak in the mid-1970s with *Iracema*[11] (Iracema – Uma Transa Amazônica, 1974–81).[12] Jorge Bodanzky and Orlando Senna's production turned out to be a milestone film, mixing fiction and nonfiction in a kind of fictional documentary heavily drawing on Cinéma Vérité techniques. While the title might suggest yet another adaptation of Alencar's famous novel, the film actually plays with the literary reference to deconstruct the Romantic main character. Iracema is not a virgin Indian as in the novel. Played by Edna de Cássia, a non-professional actress, the character here is actually a young Indian woman working as a prostitute, displaced from a safe environment. Her European saviour is, in this case, a Brazilian truck driver called Tião Brasil Grande, played by professional actor Paulo César Pereio, who treats her as merely a sexual commodity. His character is the embodiment of a military, conservative Brazil, whose mindset follows the guidelines of developmentalism at any cost. Even his name (in English, Tião Big Brazil) refers to the depiction of the country as an unbeatable, oppressive nation. Although the interaction between them is fiction, his behaviour with others includes that of being a reporter or interviewer asking questions and provoking passers-by in an interactive documentary style.

Without a linear storyline, the narrative sews random events together as Tião and Iracema cut through the Trans-Amazonian Highway, an extensive and symbolic engineering project dear to the military 'economic miracle' discourse. 'Nature is the highway', as Tião sarcastically informs a local, while felled trees are being turned into sales products. In conversation with Iracema, Tião also states that he had cut through the highway before, in a faraway past in which 'one could fear the presence of Indians', as if he was referring to an extinct wild animal. Iracema, who denies being an Indian, lets it go. She sees herself as a white girl born to Brazilians. She lives in a *palafita*, a stilt house commonly built in the Amazon rainforest region. Iracema is the Indian of the *peripheral modernity* – if drawing on Prysthon's (2002) concept. She embodies the dialectics of cosmopolitanism in the sense that she is at once an Indian and a prostitute, natural and urban, idyllic and catastrophic. In one of the film's famous stills, Iracema/Edna is wearing a top and microshorts with the Coca-Cola logo, standing opposite a truck. The image encapsulates the desire for modernity while taking account of the marginalized subject who is part of that desire as well. This so-called modernity, therefore, comes in the shape of human degradation, but also deforestation (the truck is in the frame, after all), an ecological catastrophe mistakenly seen as imperative for modernization. As Stam claims, 'in *Iracema*, ecological disaster and social exploitation configure an institutionalized hell' (2003: 218).

On at least two occasions, the film frames massive areas affected by fire or industrial tractors: first, when the camera is positioned inside the truck, the damaged area is seen through the window; second, the point of view is from an airplane flying over the region. The truck and the airplane are two means of transportation symbolizing modernity and also happen to signify the film's own perspective. At the same time, these specific framings help make the association between modernity and deforestation, therefore implying a

Figure 12.3: Iracema and Tião Brasil Grande clamber over logs.

Figures 12.4 and 12.5: Views of destruction from the truck and airplane viewpoints.

critique of progress. The camera, however, is located inside the truck and the airplane, not exactly amid the debris. In pointing this out, I am not weakening Bodanzky and Senna's remarkable achievement but suggesting a gap in Cinema Novo's approach that perhaps only the emergence of an indigenous media would be able to fill. The initiative of Vídeo nas Aldeias (VNA), thus, could be deemed the first step in that direction. Apart from producing documentaries made by its non-indigenous members, VNA provides filmmaking workshops as a means of equipping indigenous people with the skills to produce their own films. Though these films are mainly made collaboratively by the indigenous and non-indigenous, VNA has also prompted the creation of authentic indigenous film collectives, such as Coletivo Mbyá-Guarani, Coletivo Kuikuro de Cinema and Coletivo Fulni-ô de Cinema, which are not the main focus of this particular study. Nevertheless, *Iracema* interestingly adds another layer to the depiction of indigenous territory: the film directs the discussion towards documentary strategies.

In their different ways, *Macunaíma*, *Brazil Year 2000* and *Iracema* worked to frame indigenous territories as territories damaged by the idea of development as advocated by modernity/modernization during the military dictatorship, as I have attempted to briefly demonstrate. *Macunaíma* intermixed cannibalism with the consumer society in order to articulate an overlap between indigenous motifs and rotten modernization – the final *tapera* encapsulating that tension. *Brazil Year 2000* is set nowhere else but in a post-apocalypse scenario, where the indigenous reserve has simply vanished and the (absent) Indian is both a sign of defeat and a reminder of the country's origins. *Iracema* portrayed ecological disaster and social exploitation as intrinsic to the Amazon forest environment, resorting to a Cinéma Vérité style, far from Alencar's romanticized tone. Through their critiques, *cinemanovistas* (not only in those films but also in others, including *Pindorama* and *How Tasty Was My Little Frenchman*, as mentioned above) brought to the fore an indigenous territory impacted by a (neo)colonialism stance disguised by a controversial development mentality, one that resonates to date. Characteristically, these films seem to mobilize the Indian figure through the allegorical register, that is, as an allegory of the imminent destruction of the nation itself. Macunaíma in his *tapera*, the white-family-turned-Indian, and the Coca-Cola Iracema are examples of that strategy. With this in mind, their contribution was responsible for forging an imaginary, not only to define how Cinema Novo narratively dealt with the topic, but also an imaginary redefined from the 1980s onwards,[13] as soon as social movements and video technology appeared as an alternative way to engage with the cause. This is the focus of the next chapter.

13

The Vídeo nas Aldeias case: For an indigenous media to emerge

Just as Cinema Novo was seen as part of a major phenomenon in Latin America under the umbrella of Third Cinema, the birth of Vídeo nas Aldeias (VNA) is intimately connected to a regional network that advanced the debate about the need for an indigenous media to rise from the wake of decolonial movements and video technology innovations. As Freya Schiwy explains, the 'indigenous media contest a process of colonial subalternization that has denied indigenous communities participation in the dominant discourses and practices that have shaped Latin American societies' (2009: 9), hence the urgency. Among those countries, Mexico[1] is considered one of the pioneers in terms of encouraging indigenous people to take part in the media field, especially in film and TV production. By the end of the 1980s, important bodies like the National Indigenist Institute, the Transfer of Audiovisual Media to Indigenous Communities and the Latin American Coordinating Council for Indigenous Film and Media had succeeded in decentralizing traditional film production by providing filmmaking workshops and granting greater visibility for that kind of initiative (Gleghorn 2017).

Nearer Brazil, Schiwy (2009) highlights, for instance, the prominence of the Bolivian situation.[2] In 1989, filmmaker and activist Iván Sanjinés created the Cinematography Education Production Centre, aimed at providing indigenous groups with video equipment and filmmaking skills. The members also worked closely with members of the Bolivian Indigenous Peoples' Audiovisual Council, an organization dedicated to broadening the scope of action for indigenous groups living in the valleys, lowlands and highlands in the country. Together, 'CEFREC[3] and CAIB[4] maintain a media network that connects over one hundred rural communities throughout Bolivia and in the transnational Amazon basin' (ibid.: 5), producing reportage and music videos to short fiction films and documentaries. Bolivia has indeed a certain tradition of ethnographic cinema. Jorge Ruiz's documentaries represent that tradition, in particular, *Come Back, Sebastiana* (Vuelve Sebastiana!, 1953), co-directed by Augusto Roca and considered the first indigenous film made in Latin America.

Retrospectively, Faye Ginsburg (2002a) cites the groundbreaking work of Sol Worth and John Adair, back in the 1960s, when they attempted to give film lessons to Navajo students for them to develop their own way of filming. According to Ginsburg, it could be argued, however, that it was a 'sterile and patronizing experiment' that did not succeed because 'Worth and Adair failed to consider seriously potential cultural differences in the social relations around image making and viewing' (ibid.: 214). From the 1970s onwards, apart from the conventions of cinematic representation, she argues that indigenous projects were also concerned with power control over the production and distribution of images, a key theme for projects like VNA and others. Nevertheless, *Navajo Film Themselves*, a 1966 series of seven short documentaries about the life of the Navajo Nation, inevitably stood as a reference for Latin American filmmakers to develop their own initiatives in the following decades (Córdova 2014).

It was in that context that VNA found fertile ground to grow in. Born to a Brazilian father and a French mother, Vincent Carelli moved from Paris to São Paulo aged five. A social sciences graduate, since 1973 he has been involved in projects supporting indigenous communities in Brazil. Initially, he worked for the National Indian Foundation (Fundação Nacional do Índio), a historically controversial State body 'positioned on the knife edge of assimilationist and protectionist measures' (Gleghorn 2017: 176) that had been founded in 1967, during the military dictatorship. Although aimed at protecting indigenous interests, many have argued that the National Indian Foundation has not been successful in preserving their culture and territory in the face of agribusiness harassment. In 1979, Carelli co-founded the independent, non-profit organization Centre for Indigenous Advocacy (Centro de Trabalho Indigenista). Alongside anthropologists and indigenous experts, the initiative sought to 'develop projects based on local demands, aiming to support indigenous peoples in taking effective control of their territories, helping them understand the State's role in their protection and the assurance of their constitutional rights' (Trabalho Indigenista website, no date). Within this context, Carelli went on to found VNA – in English, Video in the Villages – as a branch of the activities already underway. The year was 1986, the first democratic year after twenty-one years of military dictatorship. Since 2000, VNA has been a non-governmental organization (NGO) detached from the Centre for Indigenous Advocacy.

The main characteristic of VNA is to support the indigenous fight for rights through audiovisual resources. It started when Carelli visited the Nambikwara people, in Mato Grosso and Rondônia states, to film them with the purpose of making the material available for them to watch afterwards. That innovative strategy not only produced material that enabled them to reflect upon their everyday lives through images, but the material was also available to circulate to other tribes, so that following generations could access their traditions and perhaps keep them alive. In this first attempt, Carelli made *Girl's Celebration* (A Festa da Moça, 1987), a short documentary about a Nambikwara ritual about the celebration of a young girl's menarche. In seeing the images of the ritual, the Nambikwara suddenly realized they were carrying it out differently from how they used to. About thirty Indians had their lips pierced as they used to, something that had not happened for twenty years. After that, they decided to regain and follow tradition more closely, as if the film had provoked that kind of reaction – what Carelli calls the *mirror game* or *mirror effect* (Cesar 2013). *Girl's Celebration* pave the way to other documentaries be produced by other VNA members, such as Dominique Gallois, Virgínia Valadão, Tiago Campos Torres and Ernesto de Carvalho. In establishing a close relationship with those communities, VNA hoped to call attention to their vulnerable situation in face of the Brazilian State.

In 1997, there was a turning point in the VNA trajectory when the first filmmaking workshop took place in the Xingu Indigenous Park, in Mato Grosso state. Step by step, training programmes devoted to supporting indigenous peoples interested in developing filmmaking skills were implemented. 'VNA staff distributed display equipment and video cameras to these communities, which ended up creating a distribution circuit for the videos they were producing. That developed and generated new experiences, such as promoting the in person encounters of people who had met through video' (Vídeo nas Aldeias no date-a). In a way, that set up was enhanced after visual anthropologist, filmmaker and editor Mari Corrêa joined VNA in 1998. Having worked at the well-known Jean Rouch's Atelier Varan[5] in Paris, Corrêa helped to conduct both filming and editing workshops. VNA teams move to indigenous villages and stay there for approximately three weeks to explain technical know-how in the first week, start filming in the second and finishing up in the third.

In an interview with me, Carelli (2018) argues that three weeks is indeed the minimum amount of time needed to establish a sense of confidence between indigenous and non-indigenous participants. 'There is a language barrier and intimacy barrier. You arrive in a village and, even if you know the people, it takes a week for them to get used to your presence …. You're entering other worlds.' As there is no script, the themes are usually chosen by the trainees based on their daily life experience, and the facilitators encourage them to explore the topic and experiment with the camera. At the end of the day, the material shot is screened in the village so that everyone can discuss it and think about ways to improve it. The VNA teams return to the village a second time (usually for a month) to edit the material along with the villagers and eventually shoot additional sequences. 'That also changed when digital revolution came along. In the first workshops, production was still analog, so we had to take the people to edit at VNA headquarters. After the digital revolution, it becomes possible to edit in the villages' (ibid.). Once the material is ready, it is screened in the village and circulated to other villages, as VNA is interested in intertribal relationships and the effects on self-image. Some of the videos are also sent to schools, a strategy to support the incorporation of indigenous knowledge and make indigenous students feel represented in the classroom. 'Documentary filmmaking is not just an archival practice that produces lasting records of the indigenous world but an enabling medium that allows for and incites ongoing processes of self-reflection and change. The reparative mediations recurring in VNA films … sets these documentaries far apart from the feverish ethnographic films,' as Gustavo Procopio Furtado (2019: 82) affirms.

The workshop model has matured through years of practice and engagement. The first filmmaking workshop, for instance, had a nationwide appeal, gathering indigenous groups coming from a variety of Brazilian states. Later on, VNA experimented by offering regional workshops focusing on peoples living in the same territorial area. Finally, meetings started to happen in each village at a given time, allowing each group of participants to be fully immersed in the experience. In situ, places were offered to individuals previously selected by the local community. 'The participants are usually youngsters appointed by the community. ... In any case, there is the commitment to the collective, as the collective is the one that suggests,' Carelli (2018) affirms. However, sometimes attendees give up in the middle of the process when they realize the work is harder than they could have imagined. 'It is tough. It requires immersion in the project on their part. ... There are those guys who enjoy filming, but just once in a while. And there are those guys who make a profession out of it' (ibid.). Scholar Rodrigo Lacerda (2018) suggests that the learning process ends up being two-way procedure: non-indigenous trainers have high levels of technical and artistic knowledge but know much less about the community, whereas indigenous students may know nothing about filmmaking but know their own culture in depth. Consequently, it works out as an 'interlaced learning process' (ibid.: 4). It is worth pointing out that more than two decades after the first workshop, it has now become more common to have indigenous as trainers as well, such as Divino Tserewahú and Kamikia Kisedjê.

Initially, funding for the workshops (and the project as a whole) came mostly from international foundations, mainly North American ones (Guggenheim, MacArthur, Rockefeller, Ford) and also the Norwegian Agency for Development Cooperation. In the first decade of 2000, Brazilian public investments through the Ministry of Culture during President Luiz Inácio Lula da Silva's mandates (2003–10) gave VNA a boost in terms of productions and visibility. At that point, the production was a mix of VNA members' films and collaborative films made by indigenous and non-indigenous crews. At the same time, the output produced as the result of investment started to circulate in film festivals, reaching national and international audiences beyond the villages. These films were mainly interested in presenting indigenous cultures, like Komoi Panará's *Prîara Jõ – After the Egg, the War* (Prîara Jõ – Depois do Ovo, a Guerra, 2008), focusing on Panará indigenous children at play, and reclaiming territory, and Divino Tserewahú's *The Struggle Goes On* (Vamos à Luta!, 2002), centred on the recognition of the Makuxi Indian reserve. The project is still underway, although funding for VNA is currently scarce. Norway has stepped down and public investment, if any, relies on punctual financial compensation from big national corporations, such as Eletrobrás and Vale, due to the ongoing political crisis in Brazil. In 2018, for instance, VNA managed to launch an online platform (videonasaldeias.org.br/loja) for the renting and purchase of eighty-eight videos and films.

An *integral process* for *a kind of Faustian dilemma*

Apart from producing pro-indigenous documentaries directed by non-indigenous documentarists, VNA became internationally known for conducting filmmaking workshops for indigenous peoples who wanted to explore image-making as a political tool. Even though not an indigenous film collective per se, it could be argued that VNA democratizes access to digital technology and supports new perspectives of history through collaborative film projects. By having three key objectives – training, production and dissemination – 'Vídeo nas Aldeias provides technical and financial support for the emerging indigenous audiovisual production and its diffusion among indigenous peoples, as well as in the national and international media circuit' (Vídeo nas Aldeias no date-b). If the circulation of these images were already important in the context of local communities, crossing geographical boundaries enabled them to acquire an even stronger political meaning, as indeed 'indigenous media projects have often been a site for activist participation' (Ginsburg, Abu-Lughod and Larkin 2002: 8).

Curiously, when those images reach new audiences (more precisely, white audiences), they immediately create a debate that questions not only the political claims embedded in the images but the authenticity of the images themselves. Ginsburg has widely written on that topic, with the following provocation as a guideline: 'Is it indeed possible to develop an alternative practice and aesthetic using forms so identified with the political and economic imperatives of Western consumer culture and the institutions of mass society?' (2002a: 210). In response to her own question, Ginsburg argues that indigenous peoples inevitably face what she famously calls *a kind of Faustian dilemma*:

> On the one hand, they are finding new modes for expressing indigenous identity through media and gaining access to film and video to serve their own needs and ends. On the other hand, the spread of communications

technology such as home video and satellite downlinks threatens to be a final assault on culture, language, imagery, relationship between generations, and respect for traditional knowledge. (1991: 96)

In the face of such a dilemma, she sides with the first alternative. Ginsburg claims that 'indigenous people, scholars, and policymakers have been advocating indigenous use of media technology as a new opportunity for influence and self-expression' (ibid.: 97). Furthermore, the author resorts to a Freudian analogy to elaborate her argument. The term *screen memories*, originally used to describe how individuals tend to protect themselves from trauma by obfuscating memory, is subverted in the sense that 'indigenous people are using screen media not to mask but to recuperate their own collective stories and histories – some of them traumatic – that have been erased in the national narratives of the dominant culture' (Ginsburg 2002b: 40). Her claim does not limit the debate to being only a matter of narrative. Rather, the scope of her analysis takes serious account of the political economy and the commercial media scenario behind the indigenous peoples' struggle to control their own images.

Criticism in relation to the capacity of Indians to actually make films has been strenuously challenged by scholar Terence Turner[6] (2002). Interestingly, he first argues that it is not because an outsider hands over video cameras to Indians that their discourse will be univocal and free from controversy – that would be an understanding that implied all indigenous people think and act alike, overlooking their differences and particularities. 'The production of social and political reality, as well as the representations through which it is mediated by and to its producers, is a multivocal process in which the participants draw in different ways upon their common cultural stock of ideas, symbols, tropes, and values' (ibid.: 77). Turner finds it even more problematic that using a video camera is customarily seen as *a poison pill*, 'too much for "their" culture to withstand, while "we" remain robustly impervious (and indifferent) to all forms of cultural contact with "them"'. Apart from being ethnocentric, such a viewpoint seems to disregard the 'capacity for creativity and aesthetic judgement' (ibid.: 80) of an indigenous cameraperson and/or editor.

Bearing this in mind, Schiwy (2009) attempts to broaden the perception of this topic, which is commonly applied to indigenous image-making but seldom to other media domains. She argues that interest in the idea of joint authorship of projects is nothing new, as historically 'film is linked to industrial labor and the fragmentation of the creative process. Or, to put it in different terms, film has long been a collective enterprise that sits uneasily with the idea of authorship' (ibid.: 63). Even though she acknowledges the so-called cult of the author, usually embedded in the figure of the director, Schiwy reminds one that the producer frequently has the power to intervene. Therefore, she argues that 'the Hollywood industry, socialist and testimonial third cinema, as well as indigenous video share from the outset a certain disenfranchisement of the author as creator' (ibid.: 64). In order to face the idea of subalternity entailed in indigenous collaborative projects, Schiwy gives the example of Bolivian indigenous films, whose credits replace the term *director* with *responsible* or simply *producer*. 'Omitting the word director in the credits places emphasis on the *collaboration* between indigenous communities, CEFREC, and CAIB' (ibid.: 69, emphasis added).

Indigenous filmmaker Ariel Ortega, a VNA workshop attendee in 2007 and one of the names behind *Two Villages, One Path*, *Guarani Exile* and *Tava, The House of Stone*, understands that debate as symptomatically attuned with a Western point of view. 'It is a collective work and for the collective. It is very Western to push that question. Again, we will be talking about property, what is mine, what is my authorship, what is my idea. It is not very collective to think in this way,' Ortega (2018) observes in interview with me. Ortega feels uncomfortable claiming he is the director of any of the above documentaries. 'Everybody did a bit of everything. ... I can't simply put it down as something of mine or of my authorship because others may have the same point of view about the work.' Although credited as the director, he claims that sometimes he was responsible for operating the camera and even the sound recording equipment. In addition, 'I have always taken part in every editing. When Ernesto [de Carvalho, editor and member of VNA] could not come to the village, I would go to Olinda, in Pernambuco [head office of VNA], and stay there for a couple of weeks, mainly to help translate the material' (ibid.).

In his interview, Carelli (2018) agrees with Ortega about the authorship question. 'If this is an issue, it is always an issue on our side', referring to the non-indigenous side. 'They think VNA workshop films are too good to be true. Like a fake diamond. I don't know what is the interest in that discussion, but anyway' (ibid.). In a sense, Carelli's comment is an answer to those who criticize the initiative and try to undermine it by being suspicious of the collaborative process. More importantly, he believes that VNA's dynamics comprise a variety of 'inputs that run in a very open and fluid way' (ibid.), which is not to say free of tension and nuance. When analysing VNA's hybrid dynamics, Lacerda claims that 'collaboration is not a technique, it is not even a methodology. It is, above all, an aesthetic-ethic that relies on human (and non-human) relationships, including affections and dislikes, and openness to new situations and proposals' (2018: 10). This approach is at the very basis of VNA workshop practice. Lacerda explains that a workshop usually consists of six to eight trainees selected by the community. The facilitators usually suggest each participant chooses a resident in the village 'to follow' with the camera for two main reasons. First, it is a practical strategy to encourage students to make choices and develop a cinematic focus; and second, it prompts interaction between residents and allows them to see a bigger picture of the topic initially selected. In this respect, 'the film is constructed from these various narratives and relationships that often intersect and give rise to an inner picture of the community and the village' (ibid.: 6).

On that note, Schiwy (2009) suggests that cases like VNA should be seen as an *integral process*, since the word *integral* has a sense of collectivity in itself. 'The *proceso integral* strives to tie communities, video makers, and independent filmmakers into relations of reciprocity and a research ethos of accountability', hence it 'points to a new conceptualization of collaborative epistemic processes that has its historical roots in indigenous scholarship' (ibid.: 69). In arguing this, Schiwy not only opens a discussion that may relate to many indigenous collaborative projects, such as VNA in Brazil, but, most importantly, positions the Indians as agents, not passive.

> The media activists utilize their nonindigenous collaborators while also taking their advice into account. This is not the same as submitting to the guidance of an educated elite. Similarly, the communities make use of the video makers' ability to filmically address issues of concern. Again, this shift in epistemic agency did not occur spontaneously but correlates with the growing importance of indigenous scholarship and social movements. (ibid.: 73)

In this sense, the discussion about authorship and collaboration was crucial to the establishment of the cinema of the 1960s and 1970s (i.e. Cinema Novo) and contemporary output (i.e. VNA) as two distinct forms for representing indigenous territories on screen. Although both cinematic initiatives can be taken as politically charged and concerned with society's hierarchical structure, Schiwy remarks that Third Cinema filmmakers 'did not permanently include members of the impoverished or indigenous communities they worked with' (ibid.: 74), that is, collaboration was not necessarily the premise for their filmmaking. On the other hand, the belief in an authorial cinema was greatly in vogue at that time. 'Third cinema filmmakers and film critics continued to ascribe creative and critical force to the director, or at least to the production crew' (ibid.). On the other hand, Charlotte Gleghorn (2017) highlights the unique contribution of Bolivian Jorge Sanjinés and the Grupo Ukamau, as well as Colombians Marta Rodríguez and Jorge Silva. Gleghorn claims that although they had 'embraced discourses of revolution' of Third Cinema, 'from their respective contexts these directors engaged with reformulating the idea of the national, which crucially acknowledged Indigenous populations' (ibid.: 170), in films like *Blood of the Condor* (Yawar Mallku, 1969) and *Planas: Testimony about an Ethnocide* (Planas: Testimonio de un Etnocidio, 1971), respectively. Worth mentioning, Jorge Sanjinés is the father of Iván Sanjinés, filmmaker and activist that, twenty years after the release of *Blood of the Condor*, founded indigenous media projects, as mentioned earlier.

Juan Salazar and Amalia Córdova go deeper into that topic by specifically relating Julio García Espinosa's notion of *imperfect cinema* – discussed in his 1969 'For an Imperfect Cinema' manifesto – to the contemporary indigenous media, as 'imperfect media is about the constant search for new languages, languages unconcerned with technical perfection or conventional rules and modes of representation and narrativization' (2008: 50). Salazar and Córdova argue, however, that the contemporary indigenous media is not strictly against nor subject to mainstream cinema, as Third Cinema certainly was in the past. In fact, that duality obscures the complexities of this emerging mode of production. Rather, Latin American indigenous output looks for a representational space of its own, positioning itself 'as a signifying practice separate from national cinemas, popular and community video, and tactical media practices' (ibid.: 43). In this sense, its interest is in creating 'parallel circuits of production, dissemination, and reception of cultural materials, which for some indicate the end of the hegemony of the literate and the beginning of a decolonization of the intellect' (ibid.). Whilst contemporary mainstream Latin American cinema has shied away from many of the progressive discussions prompted by the revolutionary cinema of the 1960s and 1970s, projects like VNA and the indigenous film collectives that emerged due to its support seem to be taking up that role.[7]

Un Indien, Tonacci and Cowell

Although documentaries made collaboratively have gained considerable attention, like *Bicycles of Nhanderu* (Bicicletas de Nhanderú, 2011) and *I've Already Become an Image* (Já me Transformei em Imagem, 2008), it could be argued that two of VNA's most successful productions are Carelli's documentary feature films, *Corumbiara* and *Martyrdom* (Martírio, 2017, co-directed by Ernesto de Carvalho and Tatiana Almeida). Both films won prestigious awards[8] and helped VNA to become highly regarded as an important branch of contemporary Brazilian cinema. In acquiring this sort of recognition, VNA's reputation for supporting indigenous communities through moving images gained prominence nationwide – its unusual participation in the 32nd São Paulo Biennial[9] best symbolizes that achievement. Not by coincidence, the main topic of both documentaries is the ownership of indigenous land. That is, both narratives follow indigenous groups' struggles to defend their ancestral territories – the Kanoê in Rondônia state and the Guarani-Kaiowá in Mato Grosso do Sul state. In *Corumbiara*, Carelli explores violent episodes suffered by the Kanoê in the context of the wood extraction industry of the 1980s up to the soy production beginning in the 2000s. In *Martyrdom*, the directors have a more ambitious mission: to cover the historical territorial struggle of the Guarani-Kaiowá from colonial times up to the agribusiness era of today. That is, at the core of both projects is the dispute over land and the will to reclaim ancestral territories. As Córdova claims, 'the documentary has proven to be by far the weapon of choice for recording subaltern histories, contesting multinational extraction and development projects, and denouncing human rights violations on Native lands and bodies' (2014: 124).

Carelli is both an anthropologist and activist. His connection to documentary-making was developed simultaneously with the setting up of VNA as a project. 'My learning of the cinematographic language occurred at the same time as I offered the chance to register and access images of other peoples and leaders that I admired for their vision of the future, for their discourse of resistance,' Carelli (2004) explains in a confessional text entitled 'Moi, un Indien',[10] an attempt to bring himself and the Indian figure closer together. 'I learned by doing, intuitively' (ibid.), he adds. Also, Italian-Brazilian filmmaker Andrea Tonacci[11] greatly influenced Carelli's work and contributed to a change in how indigenous peoples were depicted in Brazilian documentaries. In the late 1970s, the director contacted Carelli when he was already involved in the Centre for Indigenous Advocacy to develop a video project named 'Inter Povos'. Tonacci's idea was to enable the exchange of images produced by Indians, that is, 'an intertribal communication project through video' (Carelli 2011: 46). Because of the low-level technology available back then, Inter Povos did not come about. However, Tonacci's genuine interest in exploring what would be the Indian way of seeing inspired Carelli to pursue a video project in the near future. Even though Inter Povos had to be suspended, Tonacci did release three productions whose impact has been remarkable to date: *Conversas no Maranhão*, a documentary feature filmed in 1977 and released in 1983; *Os Arara*, a three-episode TV series made in 1980; and *Hills of Disorder*[12](Serras da Desordem, 2006), his last cinematic contribution to the indigenous debate.

The documentary tells the story of Carapiru, an indigenous man who survived the massacre of his tribe in 1978, and who had been wandering in the hills of Central Brazil for a decade. Playing with re-enactment and archive imagery, Tonacci invited Carapiru to participate in the film as himself to relive key events. It is most certainly a multilayered approach to his (hi)story, but Carelli found something was lacking. 'I think it is lovely! But there are things I don't understand: Why does Carapiru have no voice?' (Carelli cited in Brasil et al. 2017: 256). Although a range of documentary methods were explored to portray Carapiru's journey, *Hills of Disorder* apparently did not tackle the matter of the *place of speech* that Carelli had envisioned. Of course, the problem of (self)representation has been critically explored in documentaries like Sylvio Back's *Our Indians* (Yndio do Brasil, 1995), Sérgio Bianchi's *Should I Kill Them?* (Mato Eles?, 1982) or even Arthur Omar's *Triste Trópico* (1974), this one permeated by the anthropophagy tension between Natives and conquerors. It is the territorial issue, thus, that stands as a common theme among Tonacci's and Carelli's efforts, and that was put forward by VNA.

Apart from Tonacci's significant contribution, it is worth mentioning that the damaged indigenous territories were also at the core of Adrian Cowell's prolific documentary production – also commonly associated with the Villas Bôas brothers,[13] as he accompanied the famous Brazilian indigenists in their expedition to contact the Kreen-Akrore tribe. The Chinese-born British filmmaker spent the second half of the twentieth century registering the destructive impact of the State and private company projects upon the Amazon region. 'Progress, as ideology, was the enemy,' as Felipe Milanez (2013: 323) claims about Cowell's approach. Mainly sponsored by British TV channels, Cowell developed series of TV documentaries focused on the disastrous consequences of such initiatives – many of them shedding light on the indigenous situation amid the chaos, as in the emblematic three-part film series *The Last of the Hiding Tribes* (1999). Although not institutional, Cowell's approach was very informative (because it was devoted to the conventional television format) rather than an experiment in documentary-making. Years later, the VNA team used some of Cowell's documentaries to review the indigenous attitude to their devastated lands. For instance, Carelli and Corrêa's *Back to the Good Land* (De Volta à Terra Boa, 2008) draws on Cowell's *Returning from Extinction* (Fugindo da Extinção, 1999), part of *The Last of the Hiding Tribes*. 'If in *Returning from Extinction*, the testimonies make up Cowell's narrative, aiming to confer legibility to the history of the Panará, in *Back to the Good Land*, they seem to drive the narrative even more strongly, which works to construct an internal point of view' (Brasil 2016a: 81).

Coming full circle now, this VNA production could be said to be in dialectical position regarding Cinema Novo. While Cinema Novo set the ground for a critical representation of indigenous territories through allegorical Indian figures, there was no room to invite indigenous groups to be part of the artistic process taking place. Here, one might recall Jean-Claude Bernardet (2003) arguing that the so-called *other* will still be the *other* until the day he/she truly takes ownership of the means of production – a critical thinking articulated in the 1980s, when his famous book *Cineastas e Imagens do Povo* was first published, and still accurate. Though there is a long way ahead, VNA makes an important move in that direction by providing financial and technical support for an indigenous media to eventually emerge, as it was the case with Coletivo Mbyá-Guarani. Their collaborative documentaries could also be seen as partial progress in that sense. At the same time, it could be argued that Carelli's authorial voice as a documentarist (as mentioned above, in dialogue with the work of Tonacci, himself considered an author)[14] preserves a certain aura typical of Cinema Novo/Cinema Marginal directors, though to a different degree.

In pointing out the production mode of the 1960s and 1970s, I am by no means disregarding the historical context of these decades or the limited technology that barely enabled *cinemanovistas* themselves to film. Indeed, Cinema Novo has the merit of being a pioneer in covering a variety of national themes with social revolution as its motto. It was a movement formed by different filmmakers with different styles, whereas VNA has a very distinct NGO background and with very specific aims. In addition, Carelli's project benefitted from the advent of video and digital technologies, pivotal for offering filmmaking workshops to indigenous communities. As a consequence, there seems to have been a shift in the depiction of their damaged territory: instead of the allegorical Indian figure parodying the modernization of Brazil in Cinema Novo films, VNA documentaries shed light on what that rotten process left behind. In neoliberal times, VNA put the spotlight on damaged lands as ruins of underdevelopment. In a way, it was the effort of linking Cinema Novo fiction films to contemporary documentary that resulted in that illumination. In the end, what brings Cinema Novo and VNA closer together is their willingness to take on the critique of progress in relation to the indigenous territories and the understanding of film as a militant tool to change society.

14

'Here, in this scenario of destruction ...':
Territory of ruins in *Corumbiara*

Focusing on Vídeo nas Aldeias (VNA) documentaries specifically interested in illuminating the ruinous territorial dispute, my analysis will be divided into two chapters. In this one, I dwell on VNA leader Vincent Carelli's *Corumbiara*, a documentary feature film that interweaves his engagement in the project with the political struggle to reclaim the indigenous territories under threat. In the next, I will look at collaborative documentaries developed by indigenous and non-indigenous crew, the outcomes of VNA filmmaking workshops. All the projects have in common the aim to make images of ruins visible as a means of questioning notions of progress and (under)development in relation to the indigenous history of Brazil. In this sense, *Corumbiara* stands out as one of VNA's most relevant cinematic contributions, as previously mentioned. Even though Carelli had first called attention to the cause with his short *Girl's Celebration*, it was the award-winning documentary which consolidated both the reputation of VNA and its way of depicting indigenous territoriality as an area of conflict. 'In relation to the indigenous issue, everything is a dispute. Territory, resources, space, lands. This is the eternal struggle. Today the image has become a tool of dispute,' Carelli (2018) observes in his interview.

In fact, the development of the *Corumbiara* project is intrinsically linked to the *Girl's Celebration* as it was during the shooting of the latter that Carelli first heard of the massacre of the Kanoê and Akuntsu[1] groups in the Corumbiara territory, in Rondônia state, Northern Brazil. In the late 1960s, the military government auctioned off the lands within the territory of the Kanoê and Akuntsu to businessmen from São Paulo, all members of one family, at a derisory price. Since then, these groups have been reportedly hunted by gunmen hired by farmers interested in wood extraction in the region. In 1986, Carelli was informed of this situation by his friend, Marcelo Santos, a progressive voice within the National Indian Foundation. They arrived in the area and were able to confirm the destruction of the indigenous village but were prevented from proceeding with filming by the farmers' lawyer, Mr Flausino. The State did not carry out any investigation of the case. The documentary project was, thus, suspended.

In 2006, after being contacted by an international journalist to explain the case, Carelli decided to resume the project and finally complete the documentary. Between 1986 and 2006, the images he produced had a clear-cut purpose: to gather evidence of the existence of the Kanoê and Akuntsu in order to prove to the State that their roots were in that territory. Through voice-over narration, the director outlines a series of issues faced by the crew in attempting to contact the Indians as well as their dealings with politicians, farmers and agribusiness men from that region. Considered a *cinema-process*, a term coined by Cláudia Mesquita (2011b) to refer to films not only made over several years or even decades but also whose content is deeply affected by the passage of time, *Corumbiara* attests to that through Carelli's temporal reflections on the images and the way they acquired meaning over time. In this sense, the passage of time and his reflections upon it indicate both the engagement of the militant documentarist in the cause and the endless violence suffered by the Indians.

In its search for evidence, the film becomes a journey of devastation, from the Indians' *taperas* to the artefacts found along the way. Coincidentally, Argentinian Andrés Di Tella addressed this sort of approach in an essay which he starts by bluntly affirming: 'As a documentary filmmaker, I deal constantly with ruins' (2009: 87). This sentence refers to his nonfiction work on La Conquista del Desierto (or The Conquest of the Desert), an 1870s' military campaign that exterminated at least three thousand Indians in the Pampas and Patagonia regions of Argentina. 'The question for me was to find a way to make a documentary about how that world disappeared. The answer of course was: *ruins*' (ibid.: 88). The lack of proper 'observable ruins' (ibid.) prompted the director to develop a particular methodology for making (and writing about) his documentary *Land of the Devil* (El País del Diablo, 2008). He chose abandoned forts (actually, celebratory reconstructions made by subsequent governments and already decaying), Indian skulls (reading the skull as a human, Hamlet-like ruin), archival photography (the majority taken by military photographers of the time) and papers (rare official letters exchanged between *caciques* and representatives of the State). In addition, Di Tella calls attention to the fact that this is about a two-faced massacre – genocide and ethnocide – that is, the destruction of a people and their culture.

To a certain extent, Carelli's work resembles Di Tella's viewpoint, since both directors seem to wander over ruins struggling to cinematically address genocide and ethnocide as the consequences of 'progress', particularly with regards to land exploitation. André Brasil tackled this when analysing Carelli's latest documentary *Martyrdom*: 'In the well-known Benjaminian formula, there is no image of progress that is not at the same time an image of barbarism' (2016b: 147). Indeed, *Martyrdom*, Carelli's second documentary feature, is an attempt to didactically expose the mechanisms of barbaric progress so dear to Walter Benjamin's (1968) understanding of history. Simultaneously, the film performs an act of resistance in inviting the audience to stand up for the cause. *Martyrdom* demands justice for what happened to the Guarani-Kaiowá people, the subject of the film. In other words, in spite of the horror faced by the Guarani-Kaiowá, *Martyrdom* succeeds in standing up against that horror.[2] In contrast, the power of *Corumbiara* lies in telling a story of defeat while exploring territoriality as devastation – and this is precisely why I have chosen to focus on this particular film. As Carelli claims in an interview with Brasil et al., '*Corumbiara* is the end of the line. We arrived late. It is a people who can no longer reproduce …, it is extermination. They did not kill everyone, but little by little, everyone will disappear' (2017: 254).

In Victor Guimarães's reading of the documentary, 'after countless unsuccessful attempts to turn the images into evidence of the massacre suffered by the Indians, what was left for the film to do was to collect the fragments and to provide a possible narrative of a process that had lasted for twenty years' (2016). That is, all that was left for Carelli to do was to 'deal constantly with ruins', as suggested by Di Tella (2009: 87) in his essay. Interestingly, Guimarães (2016) then relates the editing work of VNA member Mari Corrêa to the ruins found throughout the film's production. In dealing with a time span of twenty years or so, Corrêa had to actually gather *fragments* of images (VNA previous videos, TV news and newspaper extracts) from different years to compose the two-hour nonfiction film. 'The fragmentary nature of the montage was based on the accumulation of ruins – ruins of the world, ruins of History – that the film aimed to gather' (ibid.). With this in mind, I would suggest *Corumbiara* is the epitome of the visualization of indigenous territory as damaged territory – an imaginary previously foregrounded by Cinema Novo, as discussed in Chapter 12. *Corumbiara* not only renders visible a territory made up of fragments but also seems to have its own documentary language structured upon them.

A four-sequence pilgrimage

To begin with, it could be argued that the dynamics of spatial representation in *Corumbiara* foreground the indigenous village framed as a destroyed and abandoned space. Indeed, this is the main staging of the documentary, where many of the sequences and most of the interaction take place. For analytical purposes, I will employ four of these sequences, as they add meaningful layers to what is being framed. After a brief voice-over introduction and the opening credits, the camera goes on to introduce Corumbiara territory. As previously mentioned, Carelli explains how the area was auctioned off by the military government to influential businessmen at the end of the 1960s. Since then, what used to be indigenous land has been turned into large private estates, mainly focused on wood extraction and livestock. On the margins of the road, deforestation and huge areas of felled timber are visible. Shortly after, Carelli asks and Marcelo Santos confirms that the road was built with the sole purpose of destroying the indigenous dwelling. Santos talks to both Carelli and the camera while pointing to the debris from the torn-down settlement. He even finds a broken piece of clay pot as evidence.

The Indian accompanying them walks through the area, an area so degraded that it seems indeed to have been targeted on purpose. In this regard, when the camera shows an airplane flying overhead, the viewer may even wonder if a bomb could drop from the sky at any moment. Mr Flausino, the farmers' lawyer, arrives and engages in debate, challenging the relevance of Carelli and Santos's claim as well as the prior existence of Indians in that area. They are forced to leave. According to Leandro Saraiva, *Corumbiara* has the 'ethics of political action' (2009: 43), that is, the documentary is precisely built upon an alliance of confrontational relationships in regard to the indigenous cause. It is overtly a documentary project centred on independent investigation,

Figure 14.1: The damaged indigenous territory as a consequence of so-called progress.

anthropological fieldwork, left-wing militancy and a crystal-clear political agenda. An ethics that, Saraiva claims, ends up shaping the film's aesthetics itself, as its political action is registered by the camera.

The above sequence was recorded in 1986 and many of its characteristics are revisited again throughout the documentary. That is, use of a handheld camera, dialogues between on-screen and off-screen characters (Carelli is doing the filming), voice-over comments providing explanatory information and, above all, what is left of the indigenous territory taking centre stage. Interestingly, the assumption that indigenous territory is damaged territory is supported by the brief sequence that comes after. In 2006, Carelli visited Santos. They are no longer amid the Corumbiara ruins but at Santos's house in Goiânia, Goiás state. The sequence starts with the prosaic yet meaningful comment made by Carelli to Santos and his wife: 'We tweak things a little here to set up the scenario.' To which she replies: 'Scenario?' And he says, referring to her husband: 'Yeah, we just have to put the victim there.' They laugh as friends in the comfort of a white-family domestic space, far from Corumbiara, even though profoundly connected to the subject matter. These prosaic comments are meaningful for two reasons: first, the reference to that specific space through the use of the word *scenario*, which appropriately, considering the filmic context, also bears within itself the sense of a film set; and second, it creates an ironic analogy as that they 'set up the scenario' in Santos's house, since they had been accused of creating a scenario of destruction in Corumbiara in the past. Most importantly, that safe, white-family domestic space appears in the documentary as a counterpoint to the indigenous villages constantly at risk.

From their encounter, one learns that the National Indian Foundation, a State body supposedly created to protect Indians and their cultures, has suspended both the investigation and the temporary prohibition of trespass the area, regardless of the evidence presented. A 1986 aerial shot gives an idea of the environmental damage caused in the territory. In the voice-over, Carelli, however, notes that, in spite of the heavy deforestation, the Indian crops bravely insist on sprouting. The camera shows small green areas from above, as if they were spreading and reclaiming their land. In this sense, Georg Simmel's (1965) famous interpretation of nature taking over architecture as a sign of ruination acquires an additional meaning: the takeover does not endorse a *what-could-have-been* discourse; instead, it praises nature as the opposite of decay. Here, it is not the return of architecture to nature, but the return of nature to nature itself.

After their meeting, Carelli and Santos decide to resume the project abandoned a few years before in order to complete the documentary. Non-chronologically, the film then moves back to 1995 to show their second visit to an indigenous village. Carelli and Santos are accompanied by Alemão, Santos's assistant, and two journalists. At that time, Santos was head of a federal programme aimed at protecting isolated Indian settlements and was therefore allowed to access private property. On a visit to one, the framing is similar to the earlier set-up, except for the absence of the Indian, who had since passed away. Wandering amid the deforested land, the camera zooms in closely on discovering what looks like an Indian *tapera*, a new element in the frame. They manage to get in and find a variety of artefacts, probably left behind in a hurry. What happens next adds another layer to the spatial representation. The team hears human sounds. Santos panics and wants to leave. Carelli persuades him to stay with the promise that they will wait for the Indians to approach them, not the other way around. This is a sequence that Clarisse Alvarenga (2017) has thoroughly analysed as a first-contact sequence between indigenous and white characters – an essential part of her broader investigation of *contact films*.

Figure 14.2: In the second sequence, a *tapera* is incorporated into the frame.

Her analysis focuses on mobilizing Eduardo Viveiros de Castro's (2004) concept of *equivocation* to unpack the on-screen encounter as one not just between two different world views, but two different worlds per se. For the Brazilian anthropologist, 'an equivocation is not an error, a mistake, or a deception. Instead, it is the foundation of the relation that implicates, and that is always a relation with an exteriority' (ibid.: 9). In essence, the equivocation lies in the difference that brings together distinct worlds, not as an issue but as the very basis of their interaction. Positively, the idea of equivocation implies that one needs 'to communicate by differences, instead of silencing the Other by presuming a univocality – the essential similarity – between what the Other and We are saying' (ibid.: 10). In fact, a vast and complex discussion comes from Viveiros de Castro's (2004, 2014) theory of Amerindian perspectivism.[3] The key concern in this specific filmic context is that the encounter between VNA members and indigenous individuals is nothing more than the opportunity to visually represent *equivocation*.

According to Alvarenga, 'the world that the Natives describe with their understanding is different and irreconcilable with the world the farmers describe. What divides them is not the way they understand, but the worlds their understandings foreground' (2017: 186). She mentions the lack of a common language to communicate and the inability, or better, that it was impossible for Carelli to film clearly the unexpected encounter (his unstable handheld camera fails to properly frame the Indians), two issues attached to the concept of *equivocation* in the scene. Although my focus is not this first-contact sequence, it is interesting to stress the role played by the Indians in that encounter. Like a spectral apparition, Tiramantu and Purá, two Kanoê brothers, slowly become visible in front of the camera lens. They walk towards the crew, as if to make clear who is in charge of that piece of land. They act like guards coming to inspect what is going on: Indian-guardians. If fear is the first feeling experienced by the crew, it fades away when the Indians take them by the hand and lead them to their village. Not far from there, the scene is bleak. The remaining *taperas* are surrounded by fire-ravaged trees. Carelli and his team found the Indians amid the debris and could not do much about it.

The third sequence in an indigenous village is marked by the presence of visiting anthropologists, including Carelli's wife, Virgínia Valadão. Together, they decide to explore the area surrounding the settlement where the film crew had installed a camping hub. The scene is warlike, already familiar to the audience. The diegetic sound is made up of bird calls, which somehow intensify the bleakness of that environment. Virgínia is getting along well with Tiramantu and Umoró, two female Indians. They offer her fruit and even play the flute. They all walk back to the white man's settlement. At this point, linguist

Figure 14.3: The Indian-guardians.

Inês Hargreaves tries to identify whether they speak Kanoê, so the language barrier could finally be lifted. Consequently, there is a sense of cordiality in the air, scenically enhanced by the vibrant yellow tarpaulins in the camp which help to convey a feeling of festive partnership. Upon arrival, the Indians keep touching Santos's arms as a sign of affection. They also interact with the linguist who shows them images in a book in attempting to communicate better. The sense of cordiality reaches a peak when Tiramantu inspects the camera with her own hands, and what the spectator sees is her face fairly close to the lens – an intimacy allowed by the cordiality of the encounter. Considering the specific spatial dynamics of this event, it is worth underlining how the white man's space provides a safe atmosphere here, even if in the middle of the decaying jungle. Once again, as happened in the sequence at Santos's house, the framing of that kind of space seems to re-endorse the indigenous territory as one in total opposition.

Later in the film, the fourth and final sequence I wish to discuss shifts from this virtually peaceful environment to perhaps the most tense. One year later, Carelli is informed that an indigenous *maloca* had been found 40 km from his settlement. An interesting decision is made: he invites members of the Kanoê people to accompany him in his field research as co-workers. What they encountered had never been seen or 'mentioned in the literature before', Carelli claims: the Indians of the hole. This is what he called them after finding a big hole carved out inside the *maloca*. There is no one there but plenty of evidence of their existence. In a nearby locality, the team discover not a single hole but dozens of them, both inside the *malocas* and scattered throughout the plantation. 'This was a village', the astonished Santos states. Deeply bothered by their presence on the land, a farmer sends his henchmen and the police to find out what they are doing there. Carelli explains they have legal permission to be there, but the police argue that the camera is a problem. Carelli is detained but released soon after the episode. This is but a prologue to the most tense moment yet.

Two years later, Carelli and Santos had their last chance to prove at least one Indian was living in that isolated area, before the farmers take over the land again. The remaining *maloca* they finally find is, in fact, a *tapera*, one that resembles many they had found before, about to collapse like the *tapera* of Macunaíma, isolated in the jungle and covered by a green-military jacket, in

Figures 14.4 and 14.5: Two frames, two realities: The white space and the indigenous space.

faraway 1969. Inside, there is no Macunaíma but a trapped Indian. The climax builds up to the confrontation between the solitary Indian inside the *tapera* and the film crew: the Indian with a bow and an arrow, Carelli with a camera. 'Unlike all other contacts with isolated Indians that are filmed in *Corumbiara*,

Figure 14.6: A conversation in the remains of the village.

the encounter with the Indian of the hole stands out for its incisive radicalism' (Alvarenga 2017: 202). The Indian of the hole establishes a limit to contact, as if trying to establish a boundary to the land. As a consequence, the documentary per se cannot access that space and turn it into an on-screen space. It is the end of the line. Moreover, the Indian personifies a boundary, not between two different cultures, but two different natures, as Viveiros de Castro (2004) would claim. After six hours of impasse, Carelli and his team give up and leave. Later on, they find out that the Indian vanished after the encounter, and they realized he was moving from place to place precisely because of their persistence. Apparently, by digging holes in the ground, the Indians were trying to hide from white men. In other words, through that unexpected act they were trying to hide from the violence and destruction generated by constant harassment from agribusiness. For Gustavo Procopio Furtado, 'Carelli follows the trail of the isolated Indians to attempt to document their presence and to advocate on their behalf. In this case, producing archival images of vanishing groups is in fact a true effort to stave off their destruction' (2019: 41). This is a generous view on Carelli's work, considering that Furtado has been critical of contact films in his own research.[4] He argues that 'the entry of indigenous people into the archive has signaled their destruction as a living people' (ibid.: 38), and that this may be the case with many ethnographic documentaries, even when indigenists and documentarists 'seemed to be guided by their best intentions' (ibid.: 39). By taking *Corumbiara* as an example, Furtado does not shy away from pointing out the risks involved: 'Filmmaking at this contact zone becomes increasingly burdened by the history of contact and implicated in its destructive violence.' (ibid.: 42).

If the ruined *tapera* calls *Macunaíma* to mind, one could argue that the roads in *Corumbiara* might allude to *Iracema*. In both documentaries, apart from the airplane viewpoint shots, roads are more than a means for the characters to travel along; they are significant in themselves. The difference in their meaning in each case, however, is sharp. Whereas in Jorge Bodanzky and Orlando Senna's Cinema Novo output roads are the means for Tião Brasil Grande to transport felled timber for sale, in Carelli's VNA project, they have quite the opposite function. Both Carelli and Santos drive from one place to another searching for evidence of criminal activity, so that wood extraction can come to an end. Roads, therefore, enable them to go into action. In addition, they function as a marker of time in the film. In most of the temporal jumps, the first image to appear on screen is a frame of the road from inside a vehicle. Interestingly, the glass window itself turns into a screen by allowing Carelli, Santos and the audience to catch glimpses of reality out there. In this sense, the sequence of the first visit to an indigenous village mentioned earlier does the same thing. As discussed, the window allows the viewer to witness the deforestation and more, from inside the car. In fact, this method of framing permeates the narrative as a whole. When the window screen reveals, for instance, an extensive, burned-out area, it connects *Corumbiara* to *Iracema* once again, as if showing the result of a long sequence of fires burning the trees in Bodanzky and Senna's film. The difference, however, is that *Corumbiara* also wanders amid the debris, in an effort to film from within and better develop its pro-indigenous perspective. In one of the scenes shot inside the vehicle, the radio is on and one particular song can be heard. *País Tropical*, a big national hit by popular singer Jorge Ben Jor has a strange, discomforting effect, as the lyrics '*Moro num país tropical/Abençoado por Deus/E bonito por natureza*' ('I live in a tropical country/Blessed by God/And beautiful by nature') by no means concur with what can be seen through the car windows.

Interestingly, the evidence found in the outside space reverberates inside the minds of both Carelli and Santos. It is no coincidence that the documentary

Figures 14.7 and 14.8: The views from the airplane and the 'window screen'.

makes two references to nightmares, reflecting the perils seen and lived by the pair. When they discovered the abandoned indigenous village in 1995, Santos had a bad dream that night of a tractor destroying the village they had found. An image one can easily picture could occur in the film when watching it. Later, in 1998, after Carelli was confronted by the Indian of the hole, the director dreamed of anaesthetizing that Indian in order to finally gain access to him and his *tapera*, a bad dream which represented his bad conscience about trying to force a contact that never happened. In this regard, Alvarenga wisely reads this sequence keeping in mind that 'the encounter of the camera with those who have remained at a distance – this intense moment[5] – defines not only the direction of the film but also the history of these other forms of life that *development and progress* ceaselessly try to annihilate, to put an end to them' (2017: 207, emphasis added). Unsurprisingly, it is also in the name of progress that Mr Flausino, the lawyer of one of the farmers in the Corumbiara territory, shockingly says at a certain point: 'What do you not do to develop a region? … Make an Indian reserve. Because the USA after killing all its Indians, wiping out its Indians in the West, in the Mississippi Valley, became the largest grain producer in the world.'

In her analysis of Peruvian territories, scholar Jill Lane stresses how 'national space has long been imagined as a geographical container for contiguous but separate regional ethnic identities' (2009: 137), referring to the division between indigenous and white social groups. Furthermore, she points out it is only when violence crosses spatial lines that divisions start to matter to everyone. In this sense, she is particularly interested in the use of space made by artwork projects as a reflection of the great importance of space for ethnic identities at risk. Lane understands 'the production of social memory as explicitly *embodied* and *social* practices, ones in which embodied performance negotiates and potentially alters the ways in which power, identity, and difference are spatially distributed' (ibid.: 136). That is, the space that stages action is key to conveying the dynamics of the historical struggles of indigenous groups, which *Corumbiara* insightfully renders visible. Filmmaker Di Tella claims that 'if ruins provoke meditation, it is because they are evidence of something that is no longer there' (2009: 94). Thinking of the ruins of the Kanoê people and conscious of the damaged space/staging in which he circulates, Carelli also manages to find beauty amid the degradation. His delight at finally having the chance to hear the rare call of the legendary uirapuru bird means more than luck. For him, it means hope in the prevailing of nature. 'Here, in this scenario of destruction, the bird used to come along every day at sunset to say goodbye.'

15

Made of stone and ruins: Indigenous filmmaking in *Tava, The House of Stone, Two Villages, One Path* and *Guarani Exile*

Corumbiara may be the epitome of Vídeo nas Aldeias's (VNA's) representation of indigenous territory as damaged territory, but it is definitely not the sole example. As a result of VNA filmmaking workshops, many collaborative projects also explore the territorial issue. Little by little, film critics and well-established directors started to pay attention to the 'breath of fresh air' those films represent, as Ruben Caixeta de Queiroz (2008: 101) claims. He argues that 'VNA films bring gestures and scenes of everyday life, they are not limited to interviews, they produce new ways of representing the 'other', reveal the other without exoticizing him/her' (ibid.). Caixeta de Queiroz endorses indigenous media scholarship, understanding VNA documentaries as a *cinema of co-authorship*. In this sense, he refers back to Jean Rouch's ethnographic outputs that transformed everything and everyone captured by the camera into subjects and co-authors of the projects in what became widely known as *shared or reflexive anthropology* (Stoller 1992; Henley 2010).

For Philipi Bandeira (2017),[1] *The Hyperwomen* (As Hipermulheres, 2011) is truly a milestone in this regard. Co-directed by non-Indians Carlos Fausto, Leonardo Sette and Indian Takumã Kuikuro, the documentary is the outcome of a VNA project in partnership with Coletivo Kuikuro de Cinema, a film collective created in 2002 and run by Kuikuro since 2011. Bandeira agrees that 'unlike the traditional Brazilian view – and imposition –, indigenous peoples are not just made the subjects, but themselves guard their respective autonomies (political regime) and authorship (aesthetic regime)' (ibid.: 136). Kuikuro's autonomy and authorship, for instance, is a well-regarded skill employed in *The Hyperwomen*, as in his subsequent film projects, such as

Karioka (2014) and *London as a Village* (2017). *The Hyperwomen* won Best Editing and the Special Jury Prize at the 2011 Gramado Film Festival, one of the most important film festivals in Brazil, in addition to other awards elsewhere.

In a way, the path opened up by this co-authored or collaborative indigenous cinema is the result of a complex historical dispute about representing indigenous peoples, which I have attempted to address throughout Part Four, with particular interest in the dynamics of indigenous spaces. At this point, the question posed by André Brasil seems to encapsulate the stage which this kind of production is at: 'What happens when the phenomenological machine of cinema meets the shamanic machine of the Amerindian peoples?' (2016c: 127), he wonders relating the experience of moving-imaging to that of shamanic trance. More importantly, this enquiry seems to acknowledge the originality of these documentaries within the context of Brazilian cinema. That is, whatever may come in future, they will inevitably function as a development (and perhaps as a response) to previous films with the problem of representing indigenous territories at their core. From Jorge Bodanzky and Orlando Senna's *Iracema* to Andrea Tonacci's *Hills of Disorder*, these and many other films mentioned above all question, in their particular ways, the place available for the voices of indigenous peoples to be heard within the Brazilian documentary, and how indigenous territories could then be visualized on screen. As Ivana Bentes claims, the place might be in 'the discovery of a form of audiovisual thinking, a global audiovisual village, in which the uniqueness of Brazilian Indians meets the uniqueness and vigor of documentary and of contemporary cinema issues' (2004).

When Caixeta de Queiroz (2008) decided to explore what could potentially become an indigenous cinema, he retrieved Claude Lévi-Strauss's *savage mind* dual argument.[2] While indigenous thought has been elaborated from fragments, residues, parts that, once mobilized, form a structure, it is also willing to constantly undo and then to redo itself. That is, 'savage because always ready to be constituted from the pieces of what was demolished or destroyed' (ibid.: 117). Caixeta de Queiroz then moves forward to compare this indigenous ontology to documentary-making itself, an artistic practice 'attentive to what happens in front of the camera, picking up pieces (that is, images) of a "whole" (material, corporeal) and an "everything" (an imaginary)' (ibid.: 118) – not forgetting that the montage itself can be read as a collection of loose ends. I would then argue that when it comes to representing indigenous territory, the idea of *pieces of what was demolished* and *picking up pieces of a whole* resonates with greater significance. A territory historically disputed is a territory in pieces that need to be reclaimed – and VNA collaborations represent a means to achieve that. With this in mind, it is not surprising that *Tava, The House of Stone* stands as an accurate example of these dynamics precisely because it places a tourist attraction ruin complex under scrutiny.

This 2012 documentary feature was co-directed by Indians Ariel Ortega and Patrícia Ferreira, former VNA trainees and now part of the Coletivo Mbyá-Guarani, and non-Indians Ernesto de Carvalho and Vincent Carelli, VNA facilitators. Ortega and Ferreira are married and live in Aldeia Koenju, an indigenous village in São Miguel das Missões, a town in Rio Grande do Sul state, Southern Brazil. They were introduced to VNA work back in 2007, when the National Historical and Artistic Heritage Institute (Instituto do Patrimônio Histórico e Artístico Nacional) commissioned VNA to make videos about historical landmarks in the region. Ortega then took part in the first workshop, with Ferreira accompanying him informally. 'In Guarani culture, there are things only for women and things only for men,' she explains in an interview to Itaú Cultural (2017). In 2008, however, she decided to push the boundaries and participate in the second workshop. 'I wanted to hold the camera and make films' (ibid.). A teacher in the village, today she is one of the few indigenous female filmmakers active in Brazil.[3] *Tava* is already her third documentary made alongside Ortega. It follows an investigation of the construction of *tavas*, grand stone-built sacred indigenous temples, and the ruins of these constructions, particularly in their hometown. Furthermore, the film uses this investigation into the origins of the *tavas* to shed light on the European-led colonization process, marked by violence and slavery, in the mid-seventeenth century in that specific region.

Ortega and Ferreira are co-directors but also on-screen presences in the film. They visit about seven indigenous villages (in Brazil and Argentina) to interview their Indian residents about historical events relating to the *tavas*, so that their version of events could be recorded. White historiography teaches that Europeans landed and found the indigenous peoples were willing to give up their beliefs, after being persuaded by Jesuit priests. As a consequence, indigenous peoples were recruited (not enslaved) to participate in the construction of these church-like structures. For Ortega, a Guarani, like Ferreira, the project was also an opportunity to revisit his own (hi)story. 'I always wondered if I was a descendant of the Guarani who stayed or the Guarani who fled to take shelter in the jungle,' says Ortega (2018) in his interview. Ortega and Ferreira, as well as their interviewees, question not only the official version but the invasion and capturing of indigenous territory by white people. In presenting new arguments and pushing for a new understanding of history, the main purpose of these indigenous-oriented moving images is to reclaim land demarcation. In this documentary and in others co-directed by Ortega, 'the main issue is territorial' (ibid.) indeed. In this respect, as Amalia Córdova claims, 'indigenous video productions are being used to rethink history, critically and creatively countering foundational narratives on indigeneity that emerged from the ethnographic documents since first contact' (2014: 123–4).

Fundamentally, *Tava* does this by disputing not only the narrative but the space itself. In this sense, it is quite emblematic that the space in dispute here is a ruin complex per se. A UNESCO World Heritage Site since 1983, the ruins of the Jesuit reduction[4] São Miguel Arcanjo is more than just a symbol of seventeenth-century colonial architecture. In truth, in its form, it should be seen as the outcome of indigenous slave labour, whereas its state signifies the result of destruction and abandonment in the wake of the Guarani War (or War of the Seven Reductions) in the mid-eighteenth century.[5] Not until the twentieth century did this area draw attention again: in the late 1930s, modernist architect Lúcio Costa (who later idealized the urban planning for Brasília, as discussed in Chapter 4) was responsible for evaluating the site and its potential for being preserved as a historical site by the National Institute of Historic and Artistic Heritage. Part of a major complex, which includes the Museu das Missões, a museum project of Costa, the ruins have been under government administration, and access is restricted to paying visitors. In other words, indigenous people, the Guarani living on the margins of the São Miguel ruins, are not considered an intrinsic part of that tourist narrative or even allowed inside their own lands.

At one point, Ortega and Ferreira, accompanied by Indian Mariano Aguirre, visit a historic monument in Caaró, Rio Grande do Sul, a Christian sanctuary that pays tribute to the Jesuit priests involved in the Guarani War

Figure 15.1: Tava São Miguel.

when the reduction was under European siege. The camera covers all three of them, interested in their facial and bodily expressions while reading the text engraved in the monument. Ortega reads the words of gratitude out loud but cannot help laughing. 'They describe in detail how the priests died. But they never write anything about the Indians,' he remarks. The figure of Sepé Tiaraju, the Indian leader who fought in the Guarani War, for instance, has only a brief mention in the text. The monument, in fact, is just one of the tactics mobilized to corroborate the convenient official narrative, a sort of *restorative nostalgia*, as Svetlana Boym (2001) would put it, more concerned with institutionalizing national identity than problematizing different perceptions of history. Roland Joffé's *The Mission* (1986), another example of the conservative status that nostalgia can acquire, is also part of the narrative in *Tava*, as the film is screened for the Guarani people to watch. Starring Jeremy Irons and Robert De Niro, the feature film fictionalizes the Jesuit-Indian interaction and was awarded a Palme d'Or for that. A British period drama, *The Mission* actually wipes out the Indian perspective, carrying a European-biased discourse that promptly collapses once *Tava* had created the conditions for the Indian perspective to be effectively heard.[6] The screening for the Guarani people implies willingness to expose the white narratology for what it is and subsequently challenge it. The formal strategy of recording Natives watching their misrepresentation on screen seems to underline two points: it problematizes the sort of audiovisual material usually taken for granted as impartial and accurate, and it suggests the urgent need for indigenous image-makers to contribute their points of view. In doing this, as Ferreira argues in the Itaú Cultural (2017) interview, the image 'functions as a mirror for us. ... We don't realize what is happening to our village or ourselves if we don't look in the mirror and reflect upon it.'

No fake ruins allowed: Guarani (hi)storytelling

The ruins of São Miguel Arcanjo constitute the central space of two other co-authored VNA documentaries: *Two Villages, One Path* and *Guarani Exile*, Coletivo Mbyá-Guarani film projects also resulting from the above-mentioned partnership between VNA and the National Institute of Historic and Artistic Heritage. Interestingly, the latter's title itself carries quite explicitly the main focus of the project: that of reclaiming indigenous land, as in Portuguese the word *desterro* relates to *terra* or *terreno*, meaning, in fact, that there is no land or terrain available for the Guarani. Co-directed by Ortega, Ferreira, Carvalho and Carelli, *Guarani Exile* features many of the same sequences shown in *Tava*. While *Tava* is more focused on Ortega and Ferreira's pilgrimage through indigenous villages to allow the indigenous perspective of Tava São Miguel to bear witness, *Guarani Exile* is more didactic, concerned with the urgency for land demarcation, explaining through Ortega's voice-over what is at stake. 'We ended up moving back and forth between the few free spaces in this territory. As well as being invisible, we became foreigners in a land we had always inhabited.' The innovation in *Guarani Exile*'s narrative is the use of archive material, especially TV reports about the Guarani struggle for land demarcation aired in the 1990s and regrettably still relevant.

The sequences in which *The Mission* is screened are also used in the final montage of *Guarani Exile* as part of its visual texture. This time, the Guarani people are shown watching the film and the viewers hear spontaneous comments from the Guarani audience: 'Look at the ruin,' one says; 'The fake ruin,' adds another, when Tava São Miguel (or its Hollywood version) appears on screen. Challenging the conclusion of the film (a Spanish-Portuguese force exterminating the Guarani completely), Ortega poses a genuine question in the voice-over: 'But if they all died, who are we?' In addition, historical photographs belonging to the National Institute of Historic and Artistic Heritage (probably dating back to the early twentieth century) show Tava São Miguel in a complete state of destruction, as its rehabilitation only commenced a few decades later. The images show white men and women amid the ruins (and the vegetation already taking over), as if they were indeed posing for the camera. In fact, these are photos also shared in *Tava*. The most relevant aspect of both the still images (historical photographs) and moving images (*The Mission*) is their use in the documentaries for the purpose of destabilizing space. After all, São Miguel is neither as Roland Joffé portrays it nor what the archive images show.

To a certain extent, this kind of film seems to exemplify what Jaimie Baron (2014) has called the *appropriation film* in her study of the archive effect. This notion helps one reflect on how a film may repurpose materials to challenge the perception of the past and, consequently, of history. That is to say, it can do this by using a temporal disparity strategy (the use of historical photographs, for instance, attests to the passage of time to prove an issue continues to be relevant) and/or by using an intentional disparity strategy (when film excerpts are incorporated to add another layer to the main narrative, excerpts not originally made or used for that purpose or in that context). 'What is at stake, then, is precisely how certain film practices can help us to locate and trace the changing ways in which we think about history and our access to it and how we may be able to transcend reified notions about our relationship to the past' (ibid.: 10). For her, 'the use of archival footage can support or be disruptive of established historical knowledge' (ibid.: 6). Considering the historical knowledge referring to São Miguel, disruption is what interests the filmmakers. The use of the above-mentioned archival images helps to infer that the São Miguel ruins should belong to the Guarani and they do not – and that is the real ruin. As Ortega says at the opening of *Guarani Exile*, 'these temples, the *tavas*, are ruins that merge into our own history'.

In *Two Villages, One Path*, the directors are all Guarani. In addition to Ortega, Jorge Morinico and Germano Beñites also joined the project. It is no coincidence then, that the very title of the film is seen in Guarani language at the opening of the film, as if reaffirming their perspective: *Mokoi Tekoá Petei Jeguatá*. The film is, in fact, Ortega's first documentary (the outcome of his first VNA workshop)⁷: one hour of material focused on two villages (Aldeia Verdadeira and Aldeia Alvorecer, in Rio Grande do Sul state) and the struggle of their peoples to survive regardless of their lack of allocated land. Of all three documentaries, *Two Villages* perhaps allows the camera more time in the villages under threat of disappearing. In the first few minutes, a wide shot gives an idea of the ongoing situation: the growth and spread of the surrounding white city towards the Aldeia Verdadeira. Their camera zooms in to emphasize the difference between the green area and the built environment. The first half of the film is mainly devoted to addressing this kind of problem. The territorial dispute is exemplified in sequences, for example, when an Indian man walks around a cleared area and speaks to the camera: 'Here the white people cleared everything, and here they are already growing eucalyptus, and they will grow more. Look, all this does is ruin the land. They plant this because they only care about money.' But it is not just that. There is also a cinematic consciousness at the core of the territorial dispute, that is, an understanding that cinema must be courted as an ally. That is why one hears at a certain moment: 'So, we have to show the white people how we live. Show the truth. Not just empty talk. Why is it that we are close to the city? Why don't we have forests, and live in these houses? So that not just the white people speak for us, but you may film the things we really need to show.'

The second half of the film brings Mariano Aguirre back on screen, not only him, but Tava São Miguel as well, as Aldeia Alvorecer is located nearby. *Two Villages* follows the journey of the Guarani people to the ruin complex where they display craftwork to the occasional (white) visitors. More than in the other two documentaries, the ruins are framed from their tourist-attraction perspective, that recalls what happened to Machu Picchu, in Peru – a multilayered discussion that Regina Harrison has delved into, aware of the fact that 'the ancient site has become a much contested space' (2009: 73). Likewise, in the São Miguel ruins, that kind of tension is implied in the film itself. Tourists accompanied by tour guides as well as students with school teachers visit the place and eventually meet the Guarani traders. As mentioned earlier, first-contact interaction between whites and Indians in that specific context was famously tackled by Clarisse Alvarenga (2017) in her research. In this specific sequence, she emphasizes Ortega's self-assured response to a white visitor who questions the Guarani situation as craftwork sellers in the area.

When interviewed by Ortega, the interviewee says that the Guarani look dirty and dependent on the tourist's willingness to tip them. Operating a handheld camera, Ortega incredulously replies while filming the visitor: 'Dirty?' The interlocutor seems a bit surprised but sticks to his opinion, claiming the Guarani charge for letting tourists take photos of them. 'Do you think the Guarani are selling their image?' Ortega asks. When the interviewee says 'yes', Ortega then explains, in a gentle yet confident way, that many white tourists come, do not buy Guarani crafts, take photos and leave – most of the time, they use these photos to make money for their own work. There is nothing left for the interviewee to say but 'maybe, that's it ...' It is worth noting that the camera places Ortega in a position of power and allows him to argue back. His approach creates an unusual situation in which the Indian is finally able to voice his viewpoint. Moments like that stand as good examples of moments 'in which indigenous people have been using the inscription of their screen memories in media to "talk back" to structures of power and state that have denied their rights, subjectivity, and citizenship for over two hundred years', as Faye Ginsburg (2002b: 51) points out.

Figure 15.2: Ariel Ortega and his camera in action.

It is precisely the line separating whites and Indians, or sellers and buyers, that I wish to highlight here. If the controversies over space are at the core of the documentary (seen through the opposition between the city and the village, or more precisely, between the Tava and what surrounds it), the sequences where white buyers approach Indian sellers equally points to that contrast. One moment in particular visually translates that kind of relationship embedded in discomfort. The glass wall of the Museu das Missões separates the white visitors inside from the Indian sellers outside – and the documentary uses that architectural element to expose the division. As the wall is made of glass, white visitors can also see what is going on outside, so they look at the Indian sellers with a certain curiosity about their products but also about the Indians themselves. In a way, it suggests a demarcation line between social groups that is almost invisible (in this sense, the glass reaffirms the idea of invisibility) but, as we know, is actually quite concrete.

When the camera shows the tour guide and school teacher providing their audience with the official narrative, there is a reverse strategy underway at the same time. The camera follows the Indians walking amid the ruins, while they

Figure 15.3: The glass demarcation: Sellers and buyers, indigenous and non-indigenous.

answer questions and explain their version of the facts. The montage works so that this parallel sequence contains a revolutionary tone, as if the Indians are challenging history *in loco*. What *Two Villages* does (similarly to *Tava* and *Guarani Exile*) is revolutionary indeed. 'All this is an accurate look from the Indian at the white colonizing gaze addressing the Indian: it is the Indians who frame the "white gaze" and reveal not only its historical dimension, but its real presence in today's world,' as Caixeta de Queiroz (2008: 116) claims. 'This is what I would call a Native or reverse anthropology by audiovisual practice' (ibid.). In order to circumvent the spatial restrictions imposed by the whites – materialized in road signs and demarcation fences, as Alvarenga (2017) points out – these documentaries necessarily understand that scrutinizing how space is defined is the only possible way to proceed. Considering *Tava's*, *Guarani Exile's* and *Two Villages'* on-screen elaborations, one can see the level of urgency required to reclaim territories, as, ironically, there is nothing but a ruined space contested here. Moreover, what those documentaries seem to suggest is that if there is anything more threatening than being in the middle of ruins, it is being on the margins of these ruins – which is certainly the case of the Guarani people in the surroundings of the remains of Tava São Miguel.

In discussing indigenous ruins and archaeological sites, Gustavo Verdesio points out that 'the nature of space is not a neutral variable but something that is qualitatively experienced', that is, 'our bodies do not always relate to their surroundings in the same way throughout history, across cultural boundaries, and, of course, through space' (2010: 340). In this sense, the ruins of São Miguel are inescapably experienced according to distinct parameters, as Indians and whites inhabit distinct worlds, to refer back to Viveiros de Castro (2004). If, for the whites, the ruins of São Miguel are a commodity, it is because colonialism 'allowed foreign, imperial eyes, to see and produce knowledge about those decaying material remains of societies from the past' (Verdesio 2010: 350). Hence, the challenge to the Indians (and postcolonial discourses, in general) is to expand 'the limitations of our regimes of visibility' (ibid.: 351). Considering the artistic and political leap from Cinema Novo to VNA, this has been an ongoing development that is intimately related to Natives acquiring more control over narratives. Drawing from Ginsburg, I argue that VNA 'turned the footage instead into an index of their cultural persistence and a basis for indigenous claims to their land and cultural rights in the present' (2002b: 51).

Figures 15.4 and 15.5: Two different versions of history in dispute through documentary montage.

When addressing indigenous territory as damaged territory, VNA subverts any possible lasting romantic connotations associated with the topic and abandons the colonized mindset that prevents one from overcoming underdevelopment and its ruins.

If the act of gathering the broken pieces implies acknowledging the ruination of a territory, it also offers the opportunity to fight back to rebuild that same territory in new terms. Carelli is aware of this. He argues that these documentaries may give the impression that 'everything is a tragedy but it is not, in the sense that they give an answer to all attacks', that is, the Indians, the Guarani-Kaiowá, the Kanoê, the Akuntsu and many other indigenous groups linked to VNA, 'they have a survival strategy, they are not passive', Carelli (2018) highlights in his interview. In making this claim, the VNA founder refuses to accept a simplistic view, which limits the Indian role to that of the victim. After all, 'for every aggression, there is an affirmation, there is a process of resistance and appropriation' (ibid.). What Carelli articulates here is the understanding that, where there is *expropriation* of territories on the one hand, there is *appropriation* of technologies on the other, a move that finally allows the remains to be restructured for the purpose of a new history.

***

In 1977, Caetano Veloso released an album entitled *Bicho* (in English, Beast). A decade after the advent of Tropicália, the album encapsulated for many the last breaths of the movement, not that it would ever come completely to an end – Tropicália outlives time. In one of the songs, Caetano sings: 'An Indian will descend from a bright, colourful star/From a star that will come at dizzying speed/And will land in the heart of the Southern Hemisphere/In America, in a clear instant/After the last indigenous nation has been exterminated/And the spirit of the birds of the clear water fountains/More advanced than the most advanced of the most advanced technologies.'[8] Beautifully written, *Um Índio* (An Indian) is not a manifesto but a prophecy. Those lyrics are both resigned and hopeful. They acknowledge the exterminations of indigenous people of past and present times but reimagine a future in which the Indian is the answer. 'The Indians are not the past, they are the future; they are the great reference for rethinking our civilization, if we want to survive. So many civilizations have come to an end throughout history. It is very arrogant to think that ours will not end either,' says Carelli to Brasil et al. (2017: 250). More than a reckoning with history, *Um Índio*, serenely but with great confidence, warns: 'And what at that moment will be revealed to the peoples/It will surprise everyone not because it is exotic/But for the fact that it could have always been hidden/When it will have been the obvious.'[9]

Conclusion: A walk amid the cinematic ruins

'Brazil's gaze is directed toward the future,' Stefan Zweig (2000: 124) once wrote. Born in Vienna, the Austrian writer lived his last days in Petrópolis, a municipality located in the forested hills just outside the city of Rio de Janeiro, after escaping Nazi Europe in 1940. Fascinated by the country, Zweig published *Brazil: A Land of the Future*, in which he praises the nation he believed was destined to lead the world in the wake of the imminent crumbling of Europe. Even though his somewhat naïve enthusiasm pervades the manuscript, Zweig does not hold back, pointing out that Brazil 'is a country of constant changes and abrupt transformations' (ibid.: 75), seemingly 'further and further behind in modern development'. However optimistic he is about Brazil, he still refers to the cycles of economic booms followed by the downfalls that have been the history of the country since the Portuguese colonization. After the sugar cane, the gold mines and the rubber phenomena, 'Brazil remains at a hopeless standstill' (ibid.: 101). He never saw the end of the hopeless standstill that was supposedly preventing Brazil from thriving. Devastated by the horrors of the Second World War, Zweig committed suicide alongside his wife in 1942, two years after his arrival and one year after the publication of the book. Their deaths were a political act, scholar Maria Augusta Vilalba Nunes[1] insists, one that 'may lead the most sensitive of us (because sensitivity is always necessary) to open their eyes and see the ruin of the world that they saw' (2016: 115).

The above-mentioned *the ruin of the world* refers to the debris of the Old World, more specifically, to the debris of the Second World War. Indeed, dreadful ruins whose historical significance has been at the core of Western literature along with the long ruin heritage of Europe. The sense of ruination in the so-called New World, however, still struggles to be considered part of the equation. This is one of the reasons why the contribution of Michael J. Lazzara and Vicky Unruh (2009) in *Telling Ruins in Latin America* remains of the utmost importance: it overtly advocates the elaboration of narratives on the ruins from which the region was put together. Hovering between 'the collapse of utopian artistic, political, and ideological projects' (ibid.: 3) and 'the search for models of change' (ibid.: 4), Latin America (and Latin American scholarship) seems to be finally aware 'that the ruin – as a merger of past, present, and future, and as a material embodiment of change – offers a fertile locale for competing cultural stories about historical events, political projects, and the constitution of communities' (ibid.: 1). It is no coincidence that historical events, political projects and the constitution of communities lie at the heart of the contemporary Brazilian cinema productions analysed in this book. The invention of Brasília as a paradoxical historical event, the failure of political projects in the urbanization of Rio de Janeiro and the reclaiming of territory by torn-apart indigenous communities make up this cartography of ruins.

In this respect, the substantial research conducted by Ismail Xavier (2012) seminally referred to the dimension of the crisis inscribed in moving images to Brazil. 'The context of rapid cultural and aesthetic transformations in the 60s marked a cinema that internalized the political crisis of the time in its formal construction, mobilizing allegorical strategies marked by the sense of history as catastrophe' (ibid.: 13), he famously states in relation to Cinema Novo, Tropicália and Cinema Marginal outputs. Two decades later, Rodrigo Lopes de Barros (2013) took up Xavier's argument reaffirming that 'one of the defining characteristics of the Third World is that it lives in a constant state of catastrophe', a state whose 'main by-products of catastrophes are their debris, wreckages, and fragments: or, the ruins' (ibid.: 1). The step further given by Barros is his approach to ruins in the context of Latin America/Brazil. For him, 'modern ruins acquire their full significance especially in the Third World. For, to the contrary of the central nations of capitalism, the Third World cannot be turned into ruins. It has already been born as such a thing' (ibid.: 13). As if attempting to demarcate a visual regime of ruins within Brazilian cinema, Barros centres his analysis on *Entranced Earth* (Terra em Transe, 1967) and *The Red Light Bandit* (O Bandido da Luz Vermelha, 1968) – two of the 1960s films examined by Xavier earlier.

The cinematic allegories that Xavier analyses expose the underdevelopment underpinning the crisis. Discussions about underdevelopment, however, are not confined to that historical moment. Although today one could use developing economy as a term, the impressions of a deficient development have been present for long. As Paulo Emílio Salles Gomes put it, 'the incredible backwardness of Brazil ... is a backdrop without which any manifestation of national life, including its finest literature and even more so, its crude cinema, becomes incomprehensible' (1996: 8). Sometimes accused of relying on a Eurocentric perspective, his critique needs to be seen as dialectical in the sense that he was actually pushing for cultural emancipation. In his combative approach, Paulo Emílio postulates that underdevelopment in Brazilian cinema 'is not a phase, a stage, but a state' (ibid.: 85) that defines it not only technically but also aesthetically – a vision that mirrors Celso Furtado's (2009) landmark judgement that the underdeveloped condition of the Brazilian economy within the capitalist regime has been dictated by the developed nations. Unlike any other filmmaker, Glauber Rocha (2017) took account of that situation through allegorical imagery in films such as *Black God, White Devil* (Deus e o Diabo na Terra do Sol, 1964), *Entranced Earth* and *The Age of the Earth* (A Idade da Terra, 1980). Moreover, Glauber faced up to the ongoing crisis by writing the 'Aesthetics of Hunger' manifesto, in which he reads hunger as the very essence of Brazilian society – and the *ugly, sad films* of Cinema Novo as a catalyst for change.

That change did not come, though. Nevertheless, the *ugly, sad films* of Cinema Novo propelled a cultural upheaval that still resonates. Stemming from Cinema Novo, Tropicália and Cinema Marginal responded to the failures of modern Brazil with originality and boldness. That time was by no means an ordinary period in Brazilian arts; rather, it was marked by the eruption of images dealing with the controversial notions of progress and (under)development that haunted the nation. As Xavier claims, 'the best Brazilian cinema films refused to accept a false notion of wholeness and took on the uncomfortable task of internalizing the crisis' (2012: 32). This highly complex task was handed over to documentarists, as Xavier points out and this monograph has attempted to explore. According to him, Eduardo Coutinho's *Man Marked to Die* (Cabra Marcado Para Morrer, 1984) symbolizes the twilight of modern cinema and the beginning of contemporary cinema in Brazil. Coutinho not only poignantly addresses the military dictatorship's great impact on 1960s and 1970s artistic output but also begins a new documentary aesthetics based on interaction and self-reflexivity that had its heyday in the productions of the 2000s and 2010s. As mentioned earlier, Xavier argues that it is precisely 'on the boundary between the documentary and the essay film that today's experience connects in a special way with the discussion in question' (ibid.: 27). He points out that contemporary documentarists frequently 'seek alternatives that engender a reunion not exactly with a reality free of theatricality, but with theatricality itself, developed from other bases' (ibid.: 10).

Albeit situated in a different historical context, Xavier believes that 'a matter of substance brings together the filmmakers whose interventions were expressed in Baroque drama, ironic pop or deconstruction', that is, Cinema Novo and Cinema Marginal directors, 'to those who expose the theaters of the world in their experiments of *new frictions with the real*' (ibid., emphasis added), that is, contemporary documentarists. In terms of truly experimenting with reality, Cezar Migliorin (2010) suggests that the most interesting contemporary Brazilian documentaries aim to challenge the conventions usually associated with nonfiction films. They interrogate not only the definition of documentary itself but also perceptions of the world. Borrowing from Giorgio Agamben's philosophical writings, Migliorin also argues that, because contemporary documentary shies away from any categorical definition, this makes it more complicated for institutional powers to suppress or belittle its claims. This is indeed the case for many of the films analysed here. Experimental documentaries like *The Age of Stone* (A Idade da Pedra, 2013) and *White Out, Black In* (Branco Sai, Preto Fica, 2014) fit into what Dellani Lima and Marcelo Ikeda (2011) define as *garage cinema*, not necessarily low-budget productions but those fostering new aesthetics, ethics and politics through moving images. Released in the context of a *post-industrial cinema* (Migliorin 2011) in Brazil, those are not market-oriented films but films relying on an alternative mode of production and exhibition circuit, as discussed.

The documentary power of such productions seems to engage with the concept of the *unviable nation* developed by Fernão Pessoa Ramos (2003). If Brazil is a country doomed to never come to terms with itself, an eternal *land of the future* as Zweig (2000) prophesied, there is a branch of contemporary Brazilian documentaries delving into Ramos's concept in order to then subvert it – and this seems to be a notable stance taken by contemporary artists. On the one hand, these narratives are built upon the failures of Brazil, indeed rendering visible its incapability to have remarkable achievements as a nation. On the other hand, these documentaries are specifically interested in gathering and reassembling the debris brought about by *historical events, political projects, and the constitution of communities* in dispute. In other words, they are films that acknowledge failures in order to retell history from another perspective and perhaps point out a different route ahead. In the context of Cinema da Retomada, Ramos's argument relates to Lúcia Nagib's claim that '1990 was cinema's real year zero' (2007: xvii), and it made room for 'the resurgence of the utopian gesture in Brazilian cinema from the mid-1990s onwards, as well as its variations and negations' (ibid.: xix). In present-day film production, I argue that the negation of the utopian gesture has become a sign of the accuracy of Ramos's view, but not exactly in its self-deprecating tone. Rather, it prompts one to wonder how to better navigate these turmoiled times and act. Considering the three unconventional groups of documentaries analysed, they enable images of ruins to come to the fore as a means of not only attesting the progress and development that never quite arrived but also questioning the controversial notions of the meanings of progress and (under)development when applied to Brazil. Was the country really left behind? What could one infer about Europe, the United States and the decline of their democratic certainties? It may be the case of the ruination of the modern project itself.

Their questioning is central to my contribution: if filmmakers are aimed at challenging those meanings through moving images, they are pretty much saying they are not interested in that modern project. And it is precisely in resorting to images of ruins that they succeed in turning those meanings suspicious on screen. They implode – and sometimes explode – an outdated idea of modernity, as if rejecting a stereotypical sense of backwardness based on a European perspective. Certainly, that is not the same as closing their eyes to precarious conditions inherited from that failed project in terms of socio-economic indicators, which still affect, for instance, the infrastructure, education and health sectors. Yet, immersed in the neoliberal age, these artists seek to imagine other futures, other worlds, rather than unreservedly embarking on the 1960s artistic rhetoric, as discussed. It is undeniable the technical progress, internationally recognized, of Brazilian cinema today, leaving the label of an underdeveloped cinema definitively behind. On the other hand, the notion of underdevelopment itself, so present in ideological discussions of past decades, seems to continue as an object to be dissected – a continuous unveiling that would only be resolved with the end of inequality and criminality within society. In this sense, the films of Ana Vaz, Adirley Queirós, Daniel Santos, Clarissa Campolina, Julia de Simone, Luiz Pretti, Ricardo Pretti, Luisa Marques, Pedro Urano, Joana Traub Csekö, Vincent Carelli, Ariel Ortega, Patrícia Ferreira, Ernesto de Carvalho, Jorge Morinico and Germano Beñites, in their diverse ways, all articulate powerful critiques in contemporary Brazil. By contrast with Cinema Novo, Tropicália and Cinema Marginal members, the names mentioned above do not belong to a cinematic movement per se. With their focus on particular backgrounds (Brasília, Rio, indigenous territories), they rather seem to share the will to make this criticism feasible while simultaneously reaffirming the power of documentary as an appropriate tool for that criticism. In parallel with an enriching dialogue with the artistic contribution from the 1960s and 1970s, as I have attempted to demonstrate, most of the films seem to draw their power from the multiple possibilities open to documentary today – or the non-definition of documentary today, as Migliorin (2010) has pointed out.

The sci-fi elements in *The Age of Stone* or the intermedial approach in *Tropical Curse* (A Maldição Tropical, 2016), for instance, reassure that being undefined might be the strength of that crop of films. To some measure, Vaz's and Marques's outputs even experiment with the essay film domain, defined by Timothy Corrigan as 'the discourse of thinking out loud' (2011: 15) while interplaying with fiction and nonfiction, documentary and experimental film. While these are not exactly first-person documentaries, 'they are … practices that undo and redo film form, visual perspectives, public geographies, temporal organizations, and notions of truth and judgment within the complexity of experience' (ibid.: 4). On the other hand, it is actually the reverse of what happens with Vídeo nas Aldeias (VNA) productions. Interestingly, the directors' strategy is to make use of their voices and firmly indicate where they are coming from. In this case, the documentaries voice their claims from a well-defined location so that they can grow stronger in the face of institutional powers. Alternatively, it could be argued that, by supporting the indigenous media, VNA is also undermining a certain documentary tradition that took no proper account of the voices of indigenous peoples.

Most importantly, what these documentaries have in common is the elaboration of narratives upon the ruins from which Brazil was composed, as if cinematically answering Lazzara and Unruh's (2009) calling. Their critique is engendered via the ruin (a city, a monument, a viaduct, a museum, a hospital, a *tapera*) because the ruin has 'radical potential' (Dillon 2011: 18). Filmmakers resort to images of ruination, destruction, abandonment and decay to elaborate on what has failed – and ask what one could do with them. In this sense, ruins have the ability to re-evaluate controversial notions of progress and (under) development, as ruins themselves are the real outcome of those notions put into practice. Furthermore, they encourage reflection on the historical world, reflection that might prompt new imagery and critical storytelling to arise and challenge the official narrative. In questioning the reading of reality, filmmakers consequently expand one's understanding of documentary by radically blurring boundaries and/or welcoming new voices to be heard.

According to Andreas Huyssen (2006), there is no place for authentic ruins in late capitalism, as the era of restoration and commodification of ruins is upon us. Nevertheless, he claims that the imaginary of ruins may be a 'powerful trigger for nostalgia' (ibid.: 7) as they still preserve 'the promise of an alternative future' (ibid.: 8). In this regard, I would argue that the films analysed here do extend to thinking about the construction of possible futures, but not necessarily by resorting to nostalgia strategies, at least, not a *restorative nostalgia*, one that thinks of itself as being both 'truth and tradition' (Boym 2001: xviii). Instead, this group of filmmakers might be interested in *reflective nostalgia*, one that 'does not follow a single plot but explores ways of inhabiting many places at once and imagining different time zones' (ibid.). Not surprisingly, this is what fascinates Lazzara and Unruh when they approach ruins in Latin America, as they believe 'ruins ... do not invite backward-looking nostalgia, but a politically and ethically motivated "reflective excavation" ... that can lead to historical revision and the creation of alternative futures' (2009: 3). To excavate. To unearth the ruins in Brazil. This might be the absolute common thread between these films and the outcome of the efforts made by these documentarist-diggers.

The understanding of ruins in the context of Latin America/Brazil developed by Lazzara and Unruh opens up a dialogue with several other definitions of ruins throughout this book. The most interconnected come from Barros's (2013) examination of Cuban and Brazilian artworks produced by the likes of Tomás Gutiérrez Alea, Glauber Rocha, Rogério Sganzerla, Néstor Almendros, Antonio José Ponte and Francisco Brennand, among others. As mentioned above, Barros's *Third World ruins* result from the never-ending catastrophes that have defined the twentieth-century modern experience in countries like Cuba and Brazil, and which those artists have attempted to depict. In a sense, his argument links to Julia Hell and Andreas Schönle's (2010) wider discussion of the ruins of modernity, ruins that materialize in the breakdown of modern utopia. As both authors suggest, modern ruins stand as what Paul Klee's *Angelus Novus* sees *growing skyward* in Walter Benjamin's (1968) unique interpretation of history as catastrophe. 'There is no document of civilization which is not at the same time a document of barbarism' (ibid.: 256). The storm that Benjamin calls progress is ruthless. Wreckage upon wreckage, as Hell and Schönle unfold its debris, the legacy of the failure of the modern project for the world.

The contemporary documentaries discussed here also engage with more precise definitions. Reflecting on the way *cinemanovistas*, *tropicalistas* and *marginais* framed the nationalist modernization of 1960s' Brazil, present-day filmmakers are rather more rooted in the globalized, neoliberal present. Consequently, their reflections result in an imaginary filled by images of ruins, as if the outcome of the rotten modernization and the savage neoliberalization was the very dereliction of contemporary life. In this regard, Idelber Avelar argues that the *neoliberal ruin* actually represents 'the destructive utopia of privatization' (2009: 192), producing the economic and political collapse of society. What neoliberalism has done to public spaces and urban planning might find a parallel in Robert Smithson's idea of *ruins in reverse*, a term that reads 'all the new construction' as 'the opposite of the "romantic ruin" because the buildings don't fall into ruin after they are built but rather rise as ruins before they are built' (1996: 72). If the new is the anticipation of decay, it means that present-day constructions are already in the process of ruination. Beatriz Jaguaribe strikes a similar note when looking at 'the decrepitude of the new' (1998: 101) that many Brazilian modernist buildings embody, suggesting not only that they might not age well but also that sometimes they are not even completed. Celeste Olalquiaga and Lisa Blackmore call those 'incomplete and decaying' buildings *living ruins*, ruins that are right there before our eyes offering 'opportunities to reassess a modern culture shaped simultaneously by material excess and quick obsolescence' (2017).

More relevant than the importance of each of these definitions is the acknowledgement that they are closely interlinked. The categories (Latin American ruins, Third World ruins, modern ruins, ruins in reverse, modernist ruins, living ruins) do not exclude, but are complementary. Above all, they cooperate in establishing a network for critical thinking about the role played by ruins in contemporary culture. In the Brazilian context, they pave the way for discussion about the overlap between ruins and controversial notions of progress and (under)development – a discussion that Cinema Novo, Tropicália and Cinema Marginal were very much interested in, and that found perhaps its best translation in Caetano Veloso's reading of the work of Claude Lévi-Strauss. 'Here everything seems/It is still under construction/And is already a ruin' (Veloso 1991) are Caetano's lyrics reiterating the impressions of the French anthropologist of the New World. For Lévi-Strauss, 'certain European cities sink gently into a moribund torpor; those of the New World live feverishly in the grip of a chronic disease; they are perpetually young, yet never healthy' (1973: 119). The sloppiness and abandonment reserved for Brazil make it clear that the ruins which have sprouted there are not merely the consequence of progress and development that never arrived; rather, they seem to be in response to 'not a phase, a stage, but a state' (Salles Gomes 1996: 85) of underdevelopment that must be overcome.

The aesthetics of ruins in Brazilian cinema quite openly refers to the *allegories of underdevelopment* brilliantly investigated by Xavier (2012) in his analysis of Cinema Novo and Cinema Marginal films. It does so because present-day ruins seem to contain in themselves the echoes of the recent past. To a certain extent, the images of ruins depicted by contemporary filmmakers are the product of a dialogue with that tradition, as I attempted to demonstrate in Parts Two, Three and Four. In this sense, the ruins of underdevelopment suggest that those allegories were accurate and meaningful in their critique of rotten modernization – the debris seen today being their outcome. On the other hand, the ruins of underdevelopment are also in tune with the neoliberal agenda that has deepened the socio-economic abyss and transformed public spaces into commodities in Brazil. It is precisely the conjunction of both historical moments that seems to have ignited these images. Paradoxically, when documentarist-diggers unearth such ruins for the camera, one realizes that these are failures that have always been present on the surface. Documentaries, thus, illuminate them for all to see at last.

Of ruin-gazers and ruinscapes

On the top of that discussion, Hell and Schönle claim that 'the ruin is predicated on a particular gaze cast upon it' and that 'the ruin could not exist without such creative appropriation' (2010: 6). In short, it is the ruin-gazer who invents the ruinscape. Considering the ruins of a failed modern project marked by the notion of underdevelopment, this makes even more sense, since it is a notion that escapes any fixed location. Ranging from the centre (Brasília) to the periphery (Ceilândia), as well as from the urban (Rio de Janeiro) to the rural (indigenous territories) areas, these are geographical localities that rely on the gaze of the documentary-maker to turn them into ruinscapes on the screen. According to Johannes von Moltke, 'slow, ostentatious camera movements, long takes, contemplative viewing' (2010: 414) are the three most prominent characteristics of a cinematic gaze cast upon ruins, but this group of documentaries goes far beyond those rules to forge new spaces, as discussed throughout this book. These new spaces, however, are always subject to the historical world, as the 'ruin is always inseparable from an experience of history and territory, more or less contemporary, but also from a complex referential and iconographic heritage', as André Habib (2008: 265) points out.

In the case of Brasília, the emergence of the federal capital as a ruinscape comes from the gaze of Vaz and Queirós in *The Age of Stone* and *White Out, Black In*, respectively. Vaz undertakes a visual elaboration inspired by the rhizomatic thinking of Gilles Deleuze and Félix Guattari (1987), breaking the chains of a dogmatic, dualist understanding of the world while embracing the freedom to articulate potential connections within reality. Intermingling documentary techniques and speculative cinema, the Brasília of Vaz is science *friction with reality*. More than a failure or an error, her CGI monument is a query posed from the quarry. Interested in the multiple answers that such an incognita might entail, Vaz constructs her Brasília as a ruin that embodies a *radical potential* (Dillon 2011), that bears the *fecund* within itself (Edensor 2005). In this sense, it should come as no surprise that Glauber Rocha's *The Age of the Earth* best resonates with Vaz's output. She is fascinated by *The Age of the Earth* precisely because, in contrast to previous films, its 'latent Marxism becomes something else, something much more carnivalesque, pagan, unruly and indefinable as it consistently tries to escape classification' (Vaz 2017b: 217). In direct dialogue with Glauber, Vaz and her camera-body provide an animist response to his classic film, wandering amid fauna and flora, interested in detailing an alternative world prior to history itself. 'I return to the *planalto central* in search for ways to shift and re-imagine what the monumental city could become beyond the preserving fetishes of its architectural legacy. To my eyes, the city had to change, to evolve, to finally become organic' (ibid.: 219). Holding hands with Clarice Lispector's speculation on Brasília and Maya Deren's avant-garde cinema, Vaz questions the traditional representation of the city by wondering if things could be redefined from the very start.

Set in the satellite city of Ceilândia, it is from that unique viewpoint that Brasília gains the controversial contours delineated by Queirós in *White Out, Black In*. Ceilândia stands out in counterpoint to Brasília. If the white, wealthy Pilot Plan rejects the debris of history, the satellite city is specifically constructed upon them. The film makes this visible through its articulation at three different levels: the strict boundaries between both cities (one even needs a passport to cross them); the intimate spaces inhabited by Marquim and Sartana (from the imprisoned *laje* to the no-wall house); and the characters' own fractured bodies (Marquim is in a wheelchair, Sartana uses a prosthetic). Like Vaz, Queirós opts for blurring the boundaries between fiction and nonfiction by adding sci-fi elements to his documentary narrative – or documentary elements to his sci-fi narrative? In *White Out, Black In*, the police violence suffered by Marquim and Sartana in 1986 is brought to the screen as a fable. They are 'cyborgs of the past' (Hora 2016: 14) planning to drop a sonic-atomic bomb on the political hub created by modernism. Queirós's *White Out, Black In* is a science *non*fiction film, an example of *borderlands science fiction* (Suppia 2015) that mixes sci-fi and documentary strategies to tell a (hi)story. To a certain degree, Queirós shares with Rogério Sganzerla's *The Red Light Bandit* the desire *to explode the Third World*. The explosion of the Third World is the explosion of Brasília. Then you have the real ruin on screen.

Similarly, Queirós's and Vaz's outputs are perceived as sci-fi documentaries, two attempts at cinematically (re)constructing the federal capital. Moreover, both films use the ruin as the catalyst for that to happen. The ruinscape here refers to the invention of Brasília and the way it has impacted on the lives of many. It is the outcome of a paradoxical premise that rarely gets revised or revisited. In *The Age of Stone*, Vaz wonders if progress itself ever arrived. Hence, her ruin is a monument that encapsulates the question in its material form: is it thriving or collapsing? In the final sequence, the CGI structure simply disappears – the camera looks for it but there is nothing there. Vaz refuses to answer. Queirós, on the other hand, takes up the task. For him, progress has never arrived. Rather, its absence has produced the legacy of the underside of progress. (Re)constructing Brasília means altering the common perception of the capital, and that could only happen with Queirós taking the lead to bring its underside to the surface. His ruin, therefore, aims to end the *status quo*. Narratively, Brasília in ruination is a new beginning for Marquim, Sartana and Queirós himself.

If Brasília epitomizes the birth of modern Brazil, Rio de Janeiro seems to capture the ups and downs of the modern fever, unlike any other Brazilian city. Framed as a (de)construction site, the Rio that appears on screen suggests a laboratory of failed projects. Prompted by the chaotic context of the 2014 FIFA World Cup and the 2016 Olympic Games, artists were compelled to encounter the city in the middle of construction (and deconstruction) work – once again. Even though not necessarily interested in the damaging consequences brought about by these sporting events, filmmakers recall previous historical occasions where construction works revealed Rio's obsession with erecting buildings and then not necessarily taking care of them – I argue that this continuous process could be seen as an obsession with *constructing ruins*.[2] Together, these images seem to work towards creating a network of images that relate to each other, evoke past events and thread an imaginary of ruins for the city.

In this sense, Lévi-Strauss's *pensée* is sharp. For him, the towns of the New World 'pass from freshness to decay without ever being simply old' because 'the passing of years brings degeneration' to those towns. For instance, when new districts are created, 'they are more like stands in a fairground or the pavilions of some international exhibition, built to last only a few months'. After a short period, 'the original layout disappears through the demolitions caused by some new building fever' (1973: 118–19). As stated in the opening of this conclusion, Zweig stands as another European intellectual whose impressions are similar to those of Lévi-Strauss. When in Rio, Zweig also noticed that 'the city has actually been turned inside out, and everything or almost everything historical has fallen victim to this impatient transformation' (2000: 159). According to Zweig, Rio, then the capital, managed to conjure up a rare duality of both timelessness and transitory things. 'Here everything develops and, to be sure, grows antiquated more rapidly' (ibid.: 163). Again, as Caetano famously sings: 'Here everything seems/It is still under construction/ And is already a ruin' (Veloso 1991).

In interviews, filmmakers echo that perception in both their speech and works. Santos (2017) highlights the warlike scenario that Rio foregrounds. Pretti (2019) believes that there is a sense of exhaustion in the way city and society are being shaped. Marques (2018) notes the city's modern syndrome of praising the new and abandoning its heritage. Urano (2017) is convinced that the ruin in Brazil is not a work of chance, but a project. Csekö (2017) claims that underdevelopment and its power games are still issues to be dealt with. A reflex of a hybrid (Canclini 2005), peripheral (Prysthon 2002) modernity, their work articulates criticism whilst elaborating on an architecture of failure using the debris of a viaduct, the decadence of a museum and the implosion of a hospital. The effort to render visible that *chronic disease* (Lévi-Strauss 1973) merges the rotten modernization and savage neoliberalism that have affected the way the city is projected, experienced and visually represented.

Also, I argue that those films draw on the critical potential of the 1960s artistic upheaval of Tropicália to nurture their own output, though to very different degrees. Apart from following on from the heated debate about the country's controversial (under)development suggested by *tropicalistas*, it is precisely the blending of media and art practices that seemed to stimulate a new generation of image-makers. This is a trend that recently gained a more in-depth analysis from Stefan Solomon (2017) by shedding light on the role of Tropicália in provoking intermedial dialogues across Brazilian film history. Revisiting Tropicália through a contemporary version of intermediality and the execution of intermedial aesthetics in the documentary mode worked towards rendering visible the above-mentioned architecture of failure. That is, the ruins inhabiting Rio. In so doing, artists sought to reclaim the radical potential of art from a neoliberal regime that works to weaken it (Rolnik 2006, 2011). This is the case with Daniel Santos's *ExPerimetral* (2016) and Clarissa Campolina, Julia de Simone, Luiz Pretti and Ricardo Pretti's *The Harbour* (O Porto, 2013), experimental short documentaries focused on the debris of the imploded Perimetral in Rio's harbour zone.

Similarly, Marques uses her art gallery background to frame the Carmen Miranda Museum as a ruinscape in an open tropicalist way. In *Tropical Curse*, the director takes on the persona of Darks Miranda, a sort of ghostly presence of the singer. Covered in white fabric with a pineapple on her head, the ghostly presence wanders around the museum, a spaceship-like building as ghostly as the performer. Marques meditates on both the museum and the singer as a means of questioning Brazilian modernity via two of its controversial symbols. The Carmen Miranda syndrome elaborated in *Tropical Curse* mirrors the modern syndrome which praises the new and abandons its heritage, as Marques (2018) claimed in her interview. It is a syndrome of sloppiness and abandonment. The visual elaboration is playful in a very tropicalist tone, as Miranda's figure was already one of Caetano's most emblematic appropriations in his *Tropicália* unofficial anthem. Music also plays an important role in the film. In the climax, Darks Miranda performs to the famous song *South American Way*. Plus, Marques claims that the phantasmagorical figure from the lyrics of *Carmen Miranda's Ghost*, played by Leslie Fish, was crucial for her to reach the mood she intended for the film.

Noteworthy at this point of the conclusion, the intermedial aesthetics present in those films can certainly be found in many other contemporary experimental documentaries. In *The Age of Stone*, for instance, sculpture and literature define the form of the film as much as the work of the camera itself. At the core of the sci-fi documentary, the monument is the creation of French sculptress Anne-Charlotte Yver in collaboration with Vaz. Furthermore, the girl, Ivonete dos Santos Moraes, says little, but when she does, she recites excerpts from the writers Clarice Lispector, Hilda Hilst and Machado de Assis. Needless to say, Clarice's writings about Brasília are rooted in the very origins of the project. In *White Out, Black In*, music and drawings are intermingled with the audiovisual narrative. For a start, the bomb that Marquim and Sartana are crafting is made of songs and sounds collected in the streets of Ceilândia. Marquim spends his days playing old vinyl in his underground radio station, as if paying homage to the black music ball where the violence he suffered took place. Sartana, on the other hand, is responsible for drawing the bomb-attack sequence, the one that will show Brasília in ruination. Another point of connection that also deserves being mentioned is the use of virtual elements in both *The Age of Stone* and *The Harbour*. The CGI-generated ruin in the first and the digital mock-up in the second point out the provocative depiction of ruins made by contemporary artists. If a ruin merges past, present and future within itself, if it may 'embody a set of temporal and historical paradoxes' (Dillon 2011: 11), a futuristic, simulated reality that suggests abandonment and/or destruction seems to play a suitable role.

Initially a photographic series, Urano and Csekö's documentary *HU Enigma* (HU, 2011) pays tribute to the diptychs developed by her in the gallery. By splitting the screen in two, the directors are able to combine different aspects of the ruination process taking place in the hospital building. Like the museum, the hospital stands as a modernist project that has both the grandeur and the failure of the modernist experience – Brasília is the epitome. Despite being a leading university hospital, *HU Enigma* creates a visual analogy between the decaying architecture and the equally decaying public health system. On screen, the body of HU seems as ill as the body of the nation – Urano and Csekö imply this in shots of peeling, muddy walls as the skin of the building. Before its implosion, the living body of HU spent many years as an actual *living ruin* (Olalquiaga and Blackmore 2017, 2018), not just because it stood incomplete and decaying but because its presence invited a reassessment of a certain modern discourse and practice. Built as if anticipating the ruination ahead, the hospital was a *ruin in reverse* (Smithson 1996), too inadequate, too unlikely to stand erect. Like the museum, and, to a certain degree, the elevated highway, these construction works were lured by the developmentalist mindset whose failings actually contradict it, as the filmmakers suggest.

Centuries prior to the invention of Brazilian cities, however, the Native territories had already been a target of a similar mindset. Cinema Novo insightfully pointed that out in daring films produced throughout the military dictatorship, as discussed in Chapter 12. In their ferocious, leftist critique of progress and (under)development, *cinemanovistas* like Joaquim Pedro de Andrade, Walter Lima Jr., Jorge Bodanzky and Orlando Senna, among others, helped to foreground a discussion interested in revealing the indigenous territory as damaged territory through allegorical Indian figures in *Macunaíma* (1969), *Brazil Year 2000* (Brasil Ano 2000, 1969) and *Iracema* (Iracema – Uma Transa Amazônica, 1974–81), respectively. In the last one, directors depict the interaction between Paulo César Pereio, a professional actor, as Tião Brasil Grande, and Edna de Cássia, a non-professional actress, as Iracema, an Indian who denies being an Indian. She represents the consequences of *peripheral modernity* (Prysthon 2002): although she is energetic and impetuous, Iracema never overcomes her marginalized condition. Her voice does not resonate at full power. Indeed, it would take more than a decade for an indigenous media to emerge in Brazil – and people like Iracema/Edna be heard. In the wake of the emergence of international indigenous media groups, the non-governmental organization (NGO) VNA was founded in 1986 in São Paulo.

The target of ruthless capitalist strategies, the damaged territory becomes a ruinscape through the gaze of VNA documentarists. *Corumbiara: They Shoot Indians, Don't They?* (Corumbiara, 2009) is built upon an all-pervading sense of loss, as the documentary tells a story of defeat. Over two decades, Vincent Carelli documented his search for evidence of the massacre of the Kanoê and Akuntsu groups in the Corumbiara territory. In analysing this ruinscape, four sequences can be mobilized to provide a detailed reading of that environment, as discussed in detail in Chapter 14: Carelli together with Marcelo Santos, his friend and collaborator, arriving in the bleak scenario for the first time in 1986; their first contact with two Kanoê Indians after finding a ripped-apart indigenous village in 1995; the sharp contrast between the Kanoê village and the safe white-man's settlement; and the final encounter with the Indian of the hole in 1998, and the impossibility of establishing any kind of trust in the face of such devastation. In exposing the ruinous state of indigenous areas, VNA reaffirms one of its main purposes: reclaiming land demarcation through documentary images in order to stop the damage continuing.

Even more symbolic in terms of documentary images are the collaborative indigenous documentaries *Tava, The House of Stone* (Tava, A Casa de Pedra, 2012), *Two Villages, One Path* (Duas Aldeias, Uma Caminhada, 2008) and *Guarani Exile* (Desterro Guarani, 2011), bringing the seventeenth-century Jesuitic ruins of São Miguel Arcanjo to attention. The history of the controversial construction of the grand stone-built *tava* triggers a reassessment of the meaning of those ruins and to whom they belong. Tava São Miguel is a ruin that merges into the history of the Guarani people. Furthermore, at the same time that it is a ruinscape in itself, it also stands as a sign of the long-standing ruination that has devastated the indigenous lands, from colonial to modern and neoliberal times. The most interesting (and symptomatic) aspect that emerges on scrutinizing the reason for these ruins is the fact that they are, indeed, real ruins. In essence, both the discursive and the territorial disputes deal with reclaiming what is no longer there – it is a dispute over a ruin, which says a lot about the place of the Indian within present-day society. Forbidden to enter the UNESCO World Heritage complex, they are not even part of the ruin; they are at the margins, at the *out-of-the-ruin*. There is no time for shallow nostalgia, though. As Carelli (2018) claimed in his interview with me, for every expropriation, there is appropriation. That is, their narratives transform loss and grief into resistance and action. Here, the *radical potential* (Dillon 2011) of the ruin has come full circle: it embodies the opportunity to redefine the world as radically as possible.

Expanding the map

The cartography of ruins engendered by this group of filmmakers is an attempt to challenge the world system and its representation. In questioning the official narrative, filmmakers have questioned the ways through which that version was put together. Documentary, this so-called capturer of the real in modern society, seems to be an appropriate means to turn one's common-sense perception of reality inside out. In countries like Brazil, the cultural logic of late capitalism implies the need to resituate, to restore the ability to counteract. The need for what Fredric Jameson (1991) has called *cognitive mapping* is the need to resist the market rhetoric that weakens any sort of counteraction. According to him, overthrowing the alienation intrinsic to the traditional city 'involves the practical reconquest of a sense of place and the construction or reconstruction of an articulated ensemble which can be retained in memory and which the individual subject can map and remap along the moments of mobile, alternative trajectories' (ibid.: 51). For Jameson, cognitive mapping will of necessity have to deal with 'this now enormously complex representational dialectic and invent radically new forms in order to do it justice' (ibid.: 54).

Through thought-provoking moving images, the ruinscapes of Brasília, Rio de Janeiro and the indigenous territories bear that complex representational dialectic and invent new ways of shedding light on the real, all in very particular ways. Rather than being a group within the same aesthetic movement, these films seem to share a similar sensibility when they gaze upon the ruins of Brazil. They ended up creating images that function as the catalyst for viewers to redefine the way they relate to the world. 'Film, like an emotional map, here becomes a geographic vessel, a receptacle of imaging that moves, a vehicle for emotions,' as Giuliana Bruno (2002: 207) poetically put it when designing her *Atlas of Emotion*. For the scholar, a film, just like a map, 'collapses time and space, mapping out diachronies and spatialities, known and unknown, for the viewer to traverse virtually' (ibid.: 275). In the case of the Third World, Jameson, although somewhat sceptical of the term *Third World* itself, reads it as 'the last surviving social space from which alternatives to corporate capitalist daily life and social relations are to be sought' (1992: 188). In this regard, 'it is obviously encouraging to find the concept of mapping validated by conscious artistic production', one that 'seems to have conceived of the vocation of art itself as that of inventing new geotopical cartographies' (ibid.: 189).

The map suggested here, however, is not self-sufficient and complete in itself. Its connections are multiple and endless, as if under the influence of a rhizomatic thinking (Deleuze and Guattari 1987). In terms of space, it ranges from the Central Plateau to the coastline, from the Pirenópolis quarry to the Quarentão nightclub, from the crumbling hospital to the ruinous *tapera*, from the Chapada dos Veadeiros mountains to the *toothless mouth* of Guanabara Bay. It time-travels from the *Entranced Earth* in 1967 to *The Age of the Earth* in 1980. On board a flying saucer, one departs from *The Red Light Bandit* in 1968 to land in the *Tropical Curse* in 2016. Trapped in 1986, cartographers wander around the promising backstage of *Brasiliários*, witness the foundation stone of VNA, contemplate Caetano's directorial debut in *O Cinema Falado* and become suddenly paralysed on hearing of the racist police shooting in the satellite city of Ceilândia. Shortcuts and detours, of course, could have taken one somewhere else: to the dismantlement of a historic hill in *The Dismantling of the Mount* (O Desmonte do Monte, Sinai Sganzerla, 2018); the absent Monroe Palace in *Chronicle of the Demolition* (Crônica da Demolição, Eduardo Ades, 2017); the literally collapsing prison system in *The*

Prisoner of the Iron Bars (O Prisioneiro da Grade de Ferro, Paulo Sacramento, 2003); the ecological disaster in *River of Mud* (Rio de Lama, Tadeu Jungle, 2016); the phantom village of Fordlândia in *Ghost Towns* (Cidades Fantasmas, Tyrell Spencer, 2017); or even the sentiments of poet Manoel de Barros recited by singer Maria Bethânia in *Ruin* (Ruína, Gabraz Sanna, 2016).

Cinema is certainly not the only realm for the ruins of Brazil. The failures of modernity can be a trigger to other artistic practices aimed at reflecting upon such debris. Throughout the research process, examples ranging from photography and literature to theatre and television were encountered. Far from making a final list, I mention some of them here as evidence of the presence of ruins in Brazil's contemporary culture – also, as suggestions for further research into the particularities of each media and what each of them could add to the debate. Amid a growing number of visual artists working on the topic, it is worth mentioning Giselle Beiguelman's two installations *Unmonument* (Monumento Nenhum) and *Luz Massacre* (Chacina da Luz), both displayed in São Paulo in 2019. The first is a collection of fragments, most certainly pieces from dilapidated past monuments. She named these pieces *ready-made forgetfulness*, questioning the link between city dwellers and the collective memory. The second urban intervention goes in the same direction: the work is made of the debris from eight neoclassical statues once located in a famous park. Three years ago, the statues were pushed over by vandals in what the artist considered an act of violence. Needless to say, Beiguelman's artistry is intrigued by the role played by historical and cultural heritage in contemporary society. Focusing on abandonment, photographer Romy Pocztaruk has been taking pictures of abandoned areas since the beginning of this decade. Apart from international projects, in *The Last Adventure* (A Última Aventura, 2011) she produced a series of photographs interested in the material and symbolic evidence of the pharaonic Trans-Amazonian Highway that was never finished. Depopulated empty spaces are foregrounded as the outcome of the project's failure and the military repression of the time.

Intermingling photography and literature, visual artist Jonathas de Andrade transformed the city of Recife of the 1970s into a modernist, post-utopian ruin in *Tropical Hangover* (Ressaca Tropical, 2016). Narrated as an intimate journal, texts and images overlap in Andrade's commentary on the passage of time and how it can affect both the urban and the personal experience. In past photographic series like *Designing the Opening of a Home, As It Could Be* (Projeto de Abertura de Uma Casa, Como Convém, 2009) Andrade had already addressed the connection between modern architecture and ruination. Photographs are also an important element in the literature of Marília Garcia. In *Parque das Ruínas* (2018), the poet contemplates two of Rio de Janeiro's museums timely named Parque das Ruínas and Chácara do Céu and meditates on the never-ending crisis and the way images relate to it. Appropriately, the book ends with two of those images: Jean-Baptiste Debret's drawing of the National Museum (1831) and a photograph of its ruined state due to the large fire that took place in 2018, as discussed in the introduction.

In theatre, director Bia Lessa's *Pi – Panorâmica Insana* captured the transience of ruins unlike any other theatrical performance in 2018. A play about the human condition in contemporary times (in close dialogue with dance and the visual arts, and citing Franz Kafka and Paul Auster), *Pi* had its debut in a very particular venue in São Paulo, the Teatro Novo (New Theatre), chosen by Lessa precisely because it was still under construction. When attending the performance, the audience was able to encounter the remains of the old building and the first step towards the new theatre – an in-between situation, just like present-day society. On mainstream TV, the plot of the miniseries *Thirteen Days Away from the Sun* (Treze Dias Longe do Sol, 2018) concerned a medical centre that collapses in the final stages of its construction. Co-produced by O2 Filmes and TV Globo, the fictional story follows a group of survivors struggling to escape while discussing the irregularities that may had led to similar tragedies. On cable TV, actor and presenter Michel Melamed filmed the third season of his talk show *Bipolar Show* (2015–17) in the ruins of Cassino da Urca, in Rio de Janeiro, where he and his guests talked about the dark times through which the country was passing with an appropriate backdrop.

Ruin-gazer documentary-makers have resorted to images of ruins as a means of shedding light on the underside of so-called progress and development. The ruin makes anti-development visible, a paradoxical representation of a discourse that intended to thrive, yet failed. In fact, its images refer to the broader condition of a country in a state of continuous collapse. In some measure, this book has attempted to combine these films as fragments that, once assembled, can provide different angles of national history. In constant, yet sometimes conflicting, dialogue with the revolutionary generation of Cinema Novo, Tropicália and Cinema Marginal, they update and recontextualize that legacy through new imagery and critical storytelling, as observed in their interviews. For Csekö, after all, much of what Glauber Rocha discussed in his films 'has not been resolved' (2017). In attempting to touch on the issues initiated by Cinema Novo, Urano, her collaborator, replaces one of the movement's main concerns: 'Cinema Novo brought a little of this modern perspective, a certain passion for the idea of the "new" etc., but this is perhaps its most problematic aspect. This love of the "new" in me has given way to the love of difference …. I am a xenophile, like my best contemporaries' (2017).

Striking a similar note, Santos argues that he and some of his contemporaries are perhaps 'making a new Cinema Novo' (2017). Calling to attention the fact that there were no black *cinemanovistas*, Santos, referring to his own work, says: 'In a way, we are making a new Cinema Novo, because we are black youngsters, and share not only an aesthetics but also life experience' (ibid.). In this sense, Vaz has also made clear that it is about time filmmakers empathize with 'female bodies and other sexualities' and take into account 'the rituals, spirituality and mythical thoughts' (2017) of other ethnic cultures that were once dismissed. Indeed, the indigenous voice has also become part of the narrative in present-day documentary production. As Ortega claims, 'if we don't do this, it will always be the non-indigenous who will go to the villages to register' (2018). Carelli, however, fears the end of an era with the new political environment in Brazil: 'It was a dream back then, now … it has turned into a nightmare' (2018), referring to an indigenous museum project that is currently at a halt. At the time of his interview, the country was already immersed in neoliberal austerity under the then president, Michel Temer (2016–18), a situation that was aggravated with the election of far-right president, Jair Bolsonaro, as he openly stated his opposition to NGOs like VNA.[3]

For Pretti, dystopia seems to be located more in the present than in the future: 'Dystopia does not only occur in the human frame, but also in the remains humans have erected, and, in all nature, whether the sea, birds or trees' (2019). Inviting the Austrian writer into the debate, Marques finally wonders: 'Was it Stefan Zweig who threw this curse at Brazil? Or did he just recognize the smell of promises without ever realizing that these promises would never be kept?' (2018). The answer might still be under construction, but Queirós seems to be building one in moving away from models and paradigms when constructing a film narrative. 'From the moment you fabulate, you also create political layers, layers of interventions, layers of possibilities, layers of territory' (2018), he suggests. The layers of territory intended by *cinemanovistas, tropicalistas, marginais* and ruin-gazer documentary-makers forge a map in which the ruin is placed in the main square, near the busiest road and opposite the most visited attraction, so that anyone can see the spectacular dimensions of its failure.

Within this context, an aesthetics of ruins in contemporary Brazilian cinema seems to be intrinsic to the destructive effects brought about by the rotten modernization and the savage neoliberalism of present-day society. In order to respond to that, contemporary production plays with the very definition of documentary by blurring the boundaries between fiction and nonfiction, or conventional and experimental filmmaking. The scope of films analysed in this book explores the idea of liminality: either by opening a fruitful dialogue with other genres (science fiction) and art practices (visual arts, performance, literature, music) or by taking account of different cosmologies (the indigenous mindset being finally incorporated). Furthermore, these productions also resonate with the criticism and creativity that took the Brazilian artistic scene of the 1960s and 1970s by storm, as if updating or recontextualizing that legacy. In exploring these multiple possibilities, these films not only question the conventions of documentary-making but also challenge the official narrative as conventionally told. In this sense, the ruins of underdevelopment – ruins engendered by the failed modern project which in Brazil has the mark of underdevelopment – offer a powerful possibility for reflection. As a branch of the ruins of modernity, they narrow down the discussion and bring particular concerns into consideration. In examining the highly complex culture of a country like Brazil, this may be our chance to begin something new.

Notes

Introduction: In search of Brazilian ruins

1 At the time of this writing (2021), renovation work had started aiming to partially reopen the National Museum to the public for the celebration of the bicentenary of Brazil's Independence in 2022. For more details, see Sanches (2021).
2 All translations from Portuguese to English are made by the author, unless stated otherwise.

Part One

1 Both in the media and in academic texts, Paulo Emílio Salles Gomes (1916–1977) is commonly referred to as Paulo Emílio. The same applies to Caetano Veloso (1942–), Clarice Lispector (1920–1977) and Glauber Rocha (1939–1981), usually referred to as Caetano, Clarice and Glauber, respectively. I will follow that tradition.

1 A realm for the ruins of Brazil

1 All translations from Spanish to English are made by the author, unless stated otherwise.
2 Macaulay's *Pleasure of Ruins* (1966) is considered one of the first authors to have discussed the aesthetics of ruins in the wake of the Second World War.
3 The term is derived from the Portuguese Comissão Econômica para a América Latina e o Caribe (Cepal).
4 Kay (1991) divides dependency theory into two major branches: reformist (that of Furtado, Sunkel, Cardoso and Faletto, and others) and Marxist or neo-Marxist (that of Ruy Mauro Marini, Theotônio dos Santos, André Gunder Frank and others). Roughly speaking, whereas the former believes in the modernization and industrialization of dependent countries, the latter seeks to break with imperialism and even capitalism itself.
5 In Spanish, the word *tugurio* refers to a small and shabby room, dwelling or establishment.

6 For more details, see Scardino (2016).
7 In the original: '*Aqui tudo parece/Que é ainda construção/E já é ruína*.'
8 All translations from French to English are made by the author, unless stated otherwise.

2 Cinema Novo: A country in crisis

1 The term *chanchadas* was coined by film critics during the 1930s to refer to light, musical comedies that were inspired by a Hollywood formula but challenged them through parody. In Rio de Janeiro, Atlântida studios (1941–62) heavily invested in the genre to promote carnival music at the time. For more details, see Shaw and Dennison (2007).
2 In São Paulo, bourgeois intellectuals founded the Vera Cruz film company (1949–54) inspired by the international studio system and aimed at producing non-parodic imitations of Hollywood models. Initially rejecting the *chanchada* style in favour of drama films, it also invested in popular comedies, namely those of comedian Mazzaropi. Although successful for a while, the studio was forced into bankruptcy due to management problems and commercial failure. For more details, see ibid.
3 Even though aesthetically diverse, the unity of the Marxist discourse within the plurality of regional cultures was a mark of the rise of Third Cinema. All films and manifestos had at least two major objectives in common: first, they were aimed at fighting against Hollywood and European classical narrative styles, so that filmmakers could nurture an authentic cinematic language and alternative modes of production and exhibition; and second, in so doing, they sought to raise awareness of the impact of imperialism and (neo)colonialism on so-called peripheral, marginalized societies (Pick 1993).
4 Depending on the publication, his surname is often spelled in two different ways, with an 'l' or double 'l'.
5 This publication comprises three essays turned into chapters centred on Paulo Emílio's investigation about cinema and underdevelopment: 'Pequeno Cinema Antigo' (Little Old Cinema), 'Panorama do Cinema Brasileiro: 1896–1966' (Brazilian Cinema Panorama: 1896–1966) and 'Cinema: Trajetória no subdesenvolvimento' (Cinema: A Trajectory within Underdevelopment), published in 1969, 1966 and 1973, respectively.
6 Editors Maite Conde and Stephanie Dennison for the first time published an anthology that brings together his most influential essays for an English-speaking audience. *Paulo Emílio Salles Gomes: On Brazil and Global Cinema* (2018)

also shows how Paulo Emílio's ideas of a national cinema were forged through dialogues with international trends throughout his career.

7 It is symptomatic that, under President Jair Bolsonaro's mandate, the Brazilian Cinematheque founded itself in a state of total neglect. For more details, see Oliveira (2020).

8 Both a filmmaker and a theorist, Cinema Novo leader critically revised the history of Brazilian cinema in *Revisão Crítica do Cinema Brasileiro* (2003), originally launched in 1963, and later looked at the contribution of his movement in *Revolução do Cinema Novo* (2004), in 1981. In 1983, *O Século do Cinema* (2006) was released posthumously. Responsible for the relaunch of the books, Xavier also edited *On Cinema* (2019), gathering many of Glauber Rocha's writings to English-speaking readers for the first time.

9 Full manifestos available from http://www.documenta14.de/en/south/891_the_aesthetics_of_hunger_and_the_aesthetics_of_dreaming.

10 Xavier (2007) specifically analyses Glauber's body of work in *Sertão Mar: Glauber Rocha e a Estética da Fome*.

11 This is a mythical phrase of Brazilian culture attributed to the messianic figure, Antonio the Counsellor, mentioned above. For *Black God, White Devil*, Glauber included the phrase as part of the lyrics of the song played in the cathartic, final sequence of the film. Since then, 'the *sertão* will turn into the sea, the sea will turn into the *sertão*' has been mobilized to refer to a utopian gesture in relation to the national underdeveloped condition. For more details, see Nagib (2007).

12 Considering their Portuguese titles, Nagib underlines that 'the term *terra* (land) connects three Rocha films which became known as the *trilogia da terra*, or "land trilogy"' (2011: 132). In each, the use of *land* acquires a different meaning: land as motherland, land as a mythical Latin American Eldorado and land as a political aspect of global resonance.

13 Alex Viany (1993) stresses that Humberto Mauro's *Shantytown of My Love* (Favela dos Meus Amores, 1934) had previously brought the *morro* (the hill, in English) to the screen as a means of associating the *favela* with a sense of Brazilianness that was being developed in that decade. Marcos Napolitano (2009), however, underlines that, although the shooting had taken place in Morro da Providência, the atmosphere was more of exoticism rather than realism in Santos's film.

14 Ramos (2013) highlights the work of filmmaker Humberto Mauro (1897–1983) portraying the Brazilian people in the documentary series *Brasilianas* (1945–56). Even though commissioned by the National Institute of Educational Cinema, Ramos points out the authorial aspect of the short documentaries as a remarkable attempt to subvert the official language in documenting the people.

15 Ramos (1987b) provides an in-depth analysis of the experimental movement in *Cinema Marginal (1968–1973): A Representação Em Seu Limite*.

3 Documentary in the wake of Cinema da Retomada

1 Controversially, Embrafilme symbolized the height of the intimacy between the State and the cinema in Brazil. On the one hand, it really protected national cinema production, distribution and exhibition from foreign intervention; on the other, because it was created during the military dictatorship (1964–85), its credibility had always been suspected. For more details, see Amancio (2000).
2 The Rouanet Law aims to encourage cultural investment and is used by firms and citizens to finance projects, including short and medium-length films and documentaries. This law allows a certain percentage of the investment not to be liable for income tax. The projects have to be approved by the State. Generally, the Audiovisual Law follows a similar pattern, although it focuses only on audiovisual projects.
3 Getting documentaries seen is still a mission, though. According to Amir Labaki (2006), albeit Miguel Faria Jr's *Vinicius* (2005) being Cinema da Retomada's best documentary performer with 270,000 admissions, the average number of tickets sold for documentaries is way below, around 20,000 per film only.
4 *Carlota Joaquina: Princess of Brazil* (Carlota Joaquina: Princesa do Brasil, 1995), a feature directed by Carla Camurati, is considered the first film of Cinema da Retomada due to its impressive one million ticket sales at the time.

4 A controversial spatiality: Myth and apartheid

1 The Pilot Plan's axial cross that defines the areas of the city plays a key role, as it refers to the sign of the Cross as linked to the foundation of human settlements. As Costa claimed, cited in Holston's book, the plan 'was born of that initial gesture that anyone would make when pointing to a given place, or taking possession of it: the drawing of two axes crossing each other at right angles, in the sign of the Cross' (1989: 70).
2 Director Jean Manzon (1915–1990) was famously known for making State-commissioned films, such as *As Primeiras Imagens de Brasília* (1956), *O Bandeirante* (1957) and *Coluna Norte* (1960).

5 *Realism under erasure* or not quite: New imagery and storytelling

1 Nagib discusses the concept of World Cinema as detached from the binary opposition between Hollywood and off-Hollywood cinemas. For more details, see Nagib, Perriam and Dudrah (2012) and Nagib (2006).
2 Vaz was born in Brasília, whereas Queirós was born in Morro Agudo de Goiás, in the Góias state surrounding the Federal District, but moved to the periphery of the capital at the age of three.
3 Many of the films discussed by Suppia (2007) became part of the film programme *Brasil Distópico* (Dystopic Brazil, 2017), at Caixa Cultural, Rio de Janeiro. The event screened films aimed at imagining alternative, dark futures for the country.
4 Suppia (2011) explores the use of documentary elements in sci-fi films in more detail.
5 Impossible not to note the involuntary prediction made by this short film in 1991, as in June 2013 many cities in Brazil, including Brasília, saw the eruption of protests over public services and World Cup costs. For more details, see Watts (2013).

6 *The Age of Stone*: The uchronic mode of a monument

1 In the Q&A after the Whitechapel Gallery screening of her films in September 2018, Vaz mentioned that she spent three months building an intimacy with Ivonete prior to the actual shooting. However, the director felt that that intimacy was sort of broken when the crew and the apparatus had to be incorporated into their relationship. That was also one the reasons for her to come back and do a second collaboration with Ivonete in *There Is Land!* (Há Terra!, 2016).
2 Zone à Urbaniser en Priorité (Priority Zones for Development).
3 Vaz studied cinema and philosophy at the Royal Melbourne Institute of Technology in Australia. Later on, she moved to France to attend Le Fresnoy Studio National des Arts Contemporains, and she became a member of Bruno Latour's School of Political Arts. When I interviewed her for this study, she was based in Lisbon, Portugal.
4 Guilherme Vaz (1948–2018) was one of Brazil's foremost composers. He played a major role in developing Brazilian concrete music and collaborated on many Cinema Novo soundtracks.
5 In October 2017, a fire destroyed nearly a quarter of the protected area of Chapada dos Veadeiros National Park, a UNESCO Heritage Site. In a sense, *The Age of Stone*'s investigation of space has become even stronger, as much of that area was deeply transformed. For more details, see BBC News (2017).

7 White Out, Black In: Exploding the Third World from a *laje* point of view

1 Quarentão was considered one of the birthplaces of black music in the Federal District. For more details, see Oliveira (2015).
2 Music plays a key role in Queirós's body of work. For instance, *Rap: O Canto da Ceilândia* focuses on the story of four rappers, and *Is the City Only One?* is a discussion centred on a controversial political jingle, as mentioned.
3 Suppia (2017) claims that Brazilian sci-fi films can be divided in two major strands: comedies (essentially parodies) and 'serious' films. Apart from *The Red Light Bandit*, he mentions Cinema Novo films, such as *Brazil Year 2000* (Brasil Ano 2000, 1969) and *Who is Beta?* (Quem É Beta?, 1972).
4 The author borrowed the concept from Lysa Rivera's "Future Histories and Cyborg Labor: Reading Borderlands Science Fiction after NAFTA" (2017).
5 In his analysis, Furtado argues that 'we see him drawing images that reproduce with some precision events that are in fact occurring but about which he has no direct knowledge' (2019: 136). The author gives as an example the fact that Sartana 'draws the actions of Dimas, and the film cuts from the drawing to a filmic shot that is perfectly matched, suggesting an almost photographic exactitude between the sketched vision and unfolding reality' (ibid.).
6 In *Science Fiction and Digital Technologies in Argentine and Brazilian Culture*, Edward King (2013) precisely aims at tracing how narratives produced since the last dictatorships have used devices and imagery drawn from postmodern science fiction to examine the shifts in power in a neoliberal context.
7 In the original: '*Bomba explode na cabeça estraçalha ladrão/Fritou logo o neurônio que apazigua a razão/Eu vou cobrar e com certeza a guerra eu vou ganhar*'.
8 Curated by Marcus Lontra and Max Perlingeiro, *Oscar Niemeyer (1907-2012): Territórios da Criação* (Territories of Creation) took place at Pinakotheke Cultural Rio de Janeiro, in 2017, and later on travelled to Brasília and São Paulo. For more details, see Pinakotheke (no date).

8 Tropicália: An intermedial counterculture

1 At the time Caetano Veloso was writing it, his grasp of both music and literature had become more prominent, as he released a studio album appropriately named *Livro* (Book), in 1997.

2   The artwork is part of the Inhotim collection, an open-air art gallery in Brumadinho, in Minas Gerais, Brazil.
3   The installation art piece was first exhibited in 2017, at SESI Tatuí, in São Paulo, Brazil.
4   The contribution of Caetano to cinema is vast. Apart from being the subject of many documentaries, he made a guest appearance singing in Pedro Almodóvar's *Talk to Her* (Hable Con Ella, 2002), soundtracked the Brazilian Oscar-nominated *O Quatrilho* (Fábio Barreto, 1995), worked as an actor in Júlio Bressane's *Tabu* (1982) and *Sermões – A História de Antônio Vieira* (1989), and so forth.
5   Before the film was made, he had already named one of his albums *Cinema Transcendental* (1979), indicating his leaning towards cinematography.
6   Hugh Gray translated the essay to English for the first time in 1967 under the title 'In Defense of Mixed Cinema', part of Bazin's *What Is Cinema? Volume 1* (1967). In their book, Nagib and Jerslev (2014) take issue with the term *mixed*, using Bazin's original term *impure* instead.
7   In 1967, actor, director and playwright José Celso Martinez Corrêa's adaptation of Oswald de Andrade's *The Candle King* was considered to be the birth of Tropicália in the theatre. Alongside Glauber's film *Entranced Earth*, and Oiticica's installation *Tropicália*, the play was also fundamental to the emergence of the movement.
8   The manifesto was first translated into English by Leslie Bary in 1991. For more details, see Andrade and Bary (1991).
9   The song appears on the album *Caetano Veloso*, released in 1968. In that same year, the iconic album *Tropicália: ou Panis et Circencis* was launched. Apart from Caetano and Gil, Tom Zé, Gal Costa, Nara Leão and Os Mutantes also participate.
10 Having already dived into the paradoxes of Brasília in Part Two of this manuscript, here I allow myself to point out that Caetano himself chose the new capital city to lie at the heart of his lyrics. Looking for an element that could structure the song and imply a sense of tension, he says:

> The idea of Brasilia made my heart race because it proved to be immediately effective in this regard. Brasília, the monument-capital, the magical dream transformed into a modern experiment – and, almost from the beginning, the centre of the abominable power of military dictators. I decided: Brasília, without being named, would be the centre of the aberrant monument-song that I would raise to our pain, to our delight and to our ridicule. (Veloso 2017: 202)

11 Entitled *Tropicália*, the text published on 4 March 1968 is available from http://tropicalia.com.br/leituras-complementares/tropicalia-3.

12 *Bólides* and *Parangolés* are also key works in his art process, the former being interactive small boxes made of wood or glass and the latter being a sort of colourful 'cape' meant to be worn or held by the public.
13 Caetano (Veloso 2017) says it was journalist Nelson Motta who first coined the term in the late 1960s. By giving Tropicália the suffix '*ismo*' ('ism', in English), he tried to identify and interpret the common characteristics in the movement as a whole, while unwittingly implying a shallow pattern to be followed.
14 It is important to mention the central role played by São Paulo in the advent of Tropicália as a movement. It was in that city that the famous TV Record music festivals took place, the album *Tropicália: ou Panis et Circencis* was recorded and Caetano first heard of Oiticica's *Tropicália* via Luiz Carlos Barreto (Veloso 2017).

9 The rubble as the legacy: A ruin for the World Cup and the Olympics

1 The *New York Times* published a report claiming the legacy of the Rio Olympics was, in fact, a series of unkept promises. For more details, see Kaiser (2017).
2 *O Globo* published an extensive, investigative work on Sérgio Cabral's corruption scandals. For more details, see Otavio and Biasetto (2016).
3 For a complete analysis of the first years of cinema in Brazil, see Araújo (1985).
4 The archaeological finds were the outcome of excavation work that took place because of the Porto Maravilha construction site. After that, the Valongo Wharf area was officially designated a World Heritage Site by UNESCO in 2017. For more details, see BBC News (2017).
5 For the complete Eduardo Paes's Official TED Conference presentation, see TED (2012).
6 For the complete Eduardo Paes's Columbia Global Debates presentation, see Columbia Global Centers (2013).
7 The project was much criticized by the local communities, international and alternative national media, and academic writing. For more details, see Viehoff and Poynter (2015) and Broudehoux (2017).
8 Film critic Victor Guimarães reads *The Harbour* as a visual translation of Chico Buarque's famous song *Futuros Amantes* (Future Lovers), in which Rio is depicted as a romantic, submerged city. For more details, see Guimarães (2014).
9 For more details, see Anavilhana (no date).

10 The Carmen Miranda ruinous spaceship in *Tropical Curse*

1 In analysing Tropicália's echoes in *Tropical Curse*, it is interesting to note that both the Parque Lage and the Museum of Modern Art intersect with Marques's career, as the former appears as one of the main locations in Glauber's *Entranced Earth* and the latter was where Hélio Oiticica's *Tropicália* was first exhibited.
2 Caetano Veloso actually wrote a song about the Flamengo Park itself. Considered one of his first tropicalist lyrics, *Paisagem Útil* (Useful Landscape) points out 'the almost science fiction effect of its [Flamengo Park] modernist traits' (Veloso 2017: 140).
3 For more details about Carmen Miranda's film career and star persona see Lisa Shaw's *Carmen Miranda* (2013), considered the first book in English on the subject.
4 Apart from this chapter being named after her, the idea of writing the book itself came after Caetano had written a 1991 article about Carmen Miranda called 'Caricature and Conqueror, Pride and Shame' and published in the *New York Times*.
5 The name 'Darks Miranda' was inspired by a video that went viral called *Hola Soy Darks (Original)*, in which a sort of gothic drag queen introduces herself as being 'darks'. The use of the surname Miranda is self-explanatory. For the full video, see Florencia Paz Parada Mejia (2016).
6 For more details about Orson Welles and his relationship with Latin America, see Benamou (2007).
7 For more details about the director's remarkable trajectory in Cinema Novo, see Burton (1986).

11 A lame-leg architecture: Half-hospital, half-ruin in *HU Enigma*

1 Awarded at the Tiradentes Festival (Brazil) and the Monterrey Festival (Mexico), it also participated in the CPH: DOX (Denmark), BAFICI (Argentina) and Toulouse (France), among others.
2 Considered Brazil's most important documentary-maker, Eduardo Coutinho (1933–2014) developed a powerful cinema centred on the role of the interview. In the wake of his successful filmography, Brazilian documentaries started to indiscriminately employ that strategy. Jean-Claude Bernardet (2003) says the

overuse of the interview turned it into a cacoethes. This reflection is part of the 2003 edition of *Cineastas e Imagens do Povo*, originally published in 1985.
3 For more details, see Bessa and Fiore (2017).
4 The documentary was first shown in Rio de Janeiro in the exhibition *Depois do Futuro* (After the Future, 2016), at Escola de Artes Visuais do Parque Lage. Curated by Daniela Labra, it reunited international artworks aimed at investigating the chaotic, imminent future ahead. For more details, see the online version of Curador Visitante (2016).
5 In her *HU* photographic series, Csekö also entitled one of the images *Através*, potentially establishing a dialogue with Meireles's work.

12 Setting the ground: Cinema Novo and indigenous representation

1 For more details, see Sommer (1991).
2 The controversial government initiative was aimed at installing an electrical telegraph system in isolated areas of Brazil, as well as 'civilizing' the indigenous groups found while territorial expansion was taking place. The creation of the Cinematography and Photography Section (1912) worked to provide imagery of that 'integration' and to document habits that would shortly be eradicated. For a comprehensive study on the Rondon Commission, see Conde (2018).
3 This does not mean Indian representation was entirely absent from Brazilian cinema. Humberto Mauro's iconic *The Discovery of Brazil* (O Descobrimento do Brasil), for instance, was released in 1937. Commissioned by the National Institute for Educational Cinema, the film is a visual translation of Portuguese Pero Vaz de Caminha's famous first letter, considered Brazil's birth certificate.
4 Interestingly, Joaquim Pedro de Andrade's last film, *The Brazilwood Man* (O Homem do Pau-Brasil, 1982), is loosely based on Oswald de Andrade's public life and critical thinking. According to José Geraldo Couto (2018), the director actually had the idea during the shooting of *Macunaíma*, when he realized the modernist writer had much in common with the protagonist of the book he was adapting to the screen.
5 In her manuscript about Joaquim Pedro de Andrade, Bentes mentions that, among the many references mobilized for the making of *Macunaíma*, he 'watched a series of films by the Rondon Commission for the National Campaign for the Protection of Indians, directed by anthropologist Heloísa Alberto Torres. He wanted to see, to analyse these images of Brazilian Indians' (1996: 77).

6 Not by coincidence, the soundtrack is *Peri e Ceci*, an old carnival march whose title refers to José de Alencar's famous characters in *The Guarani*: Peri, a Guarani Indian, and Ceci, a Euro-Brazilian woman.
7 The *feijoada* sequence filmed in Parque Lage is emblematic in that sense. A symbol of Brazilianness, here the classic Brazilian dish is allegorically made with human blood and served in a big swimming pool. It critically functions as a 'ritual through which a social class radically celebrates its predatory vocation', 'a discourse about modern barbarism' and 'capitalism in a peripheral country' (Xavier 2012: 257). For Bentes, 'it is a bloodthirsty reinterpretation of Oswaldian anthropophagy' (1996: 71).
8 Xavier, however, argues that *The Red Light Bandit* evokes the tropicalist mood in a much more creative and innovative way than *Brazil Year 2000*, as Lima Jr.'s film shies away from 'a provocative space of ambiguity' (2012: 219).
9 For more details, see Pinto (2014).
10 For more details, see Nagib (2017a).
11 *Iracema* was not the only documentary focusing on the indigenous issue at that time. Amalia Córdova (2014) mentions *Raoni* (Jean-Pierre Dutilleux and Luiz Carlos Saldanha, 1978), *Pankararu de Brejo dos Padres* (Vladimir Carvalho, 1977) and *Terra dos Índios* (Zelito Viana, 1979), among others.
12 Completed in 1974, the film was only released in 1981 due to military censorship.
13 More recently, films like Luiz Bolognesi's *Ex-Shaman* (Ex-Pajé, 2018), João Salaviza and Renée Nader Messora's *The Dead and the Others* (Chuva é Cantoria na Aldeia dos Mortos, 2018), and Maya Da-Rin's *The Fever* (A Febre, 2019) focused on indigenous issues, receiving international recognition in the Berlin, Cannes and Locarno film festivals, respectively. These and other contemporary films might generate insights for further research projects not necessarily centred on images of ruins and Vídeo nas Aldeias' documentaries.

13 The Vídeo nas Aldeias case: For an indigenous media to emerge

1 For more details, see Wortham (2002).
2 For more details, see Villarreal (2017).
3 Centro de Formación y Realización Cinematográfica (Cinematography Education Production Centre).
4 Coordinadora Audiovisual Indígena de Bolivia (Bolivian Indigenous Peoples' Audiovisual Council).

5 The project started in 1978, when Rouch provided his first documentary workshop in the newly independent Republic of Mozambique. Three years later, Atelier Varan was founded in Paris with the mission of teaching non-academic, collaborative documentary practice. Workshops still run, covering countries like Algeria, Bolivia, Morocco, Norway, South Africa and the Philippines.
6 As an anthropologist, Turner (2002) was in charge of the Kayapo Video Project with a grant from the Spencer Foundation and in cooperation with the Centre for Indigenous Advocacy in São Paulo. On that occasion, VNA made its editing studio and its video storage space available to help with the work.
7 Maori filmmaker Barry Barclay went a step further and conceptualized the notion of *Fourth Cinema* to refer to indigenous media output, inspired by, yet opposing, the Third Cinema concept developed by Solanas and Getino in 1969. Pamela Wilson and Michelle Stewart (2008) remind us that the term *Fourth World* was first used in 1974 by George Manuel and Michael Posluns to indicate a growing international interest in the indigenous worldview and activism.
8 *Corumbiara* won Best Film at the 2009 Gramado Film Festival in Brazil, while *Martyrdom* won Best Latin American Film at the 2016 Mar del Plata Film Festival in Argentina. Both films were awarded Best Documentary by the traditional São Paulo Association of Art Critics in 2012 and 2018, respectively.
9 Curated by Jochen Volz, the 2016 edition was entitled *Incerteza Viva* (Live Uncertainty). *The Natives' Brazil: An Open Archive* (O Brasil dos Índios: Um Arquivo Aberto) was built from images produced by VNA since 1986 (Carelli, Carvalho and Almeida 2016).
10 The title is a clear reference to Rouch's ethnofiction film *Moi, un Noir* (1958).
11 For more details of his body of work's impact on Brazilian cinema, see *Devires* journal special edition *Tonacci*, organized by André Brasil and Cláudia Mesquita (2012).
12 For more details, see Caetano (2008).
13 Orlando (1914–2002), Cláudio (1916–1998) and Leonardo Villas Bôas (1918–1961) were activists regarding indigenous issues in Brazil. In 1961, they succeeded in turning the Xingu indigenous territory into the legally protected Xingu Indigenous Park, in the state of Mato Grosso.
14 A Cinema Marginal author, Tonacci (1944–2016) directed *Blablablá* (1968) and *Bang Bang* (1971).

14 'Here, in this scenario of destruction ...': Territory of ruins in *Corumbiara*

1. In *Corumbiara*, although the main focus is on the Kanoê people, the documentary focuses on the Akuntsu as well, a group which appears later in the film. In fact, *akuntsu* is a word the Kanoê people use to refer to 'other Indians', not self-denominated members of the same group (Alvarenga 2017).
2. Mariana Cunha (2018) has discussed how *Martyrdom* addresses the Guarani-Kaiowá territoriality in the article 'The Right to Nature: Contested Landscapes and Indigenous Territoriality in Martírio'.
3. Viveiros de Castro (2004: 5):

   > Perspectivism supposes a constant epistemology and variable ontologies, the same representations and other objects, a single meaning and multiple referents. Therefore, the aim of perspectivist translation – translation being one of shamanism's principal tasks, as we know (Carneiro da Cunha 1998) – is not that of finding a 'synonym' (a co-referential representation) in our human conceptual language for the representations that other species of subject use to speak about one and the same thing. Rather, the aim is to avoid losing sight of the difference concealed within equivocal 'homonyms' between our language and that of other species, since we and they are never talking about the same things.

4. For more details, see Furtado (2019).
5. Alvarenga (2017) discusses *Corumbiara* in terms of its extensive movement (the temporal, narrative arc per se) and intense moments (as in the above-mentioned sequence).

15 Made of stone and ruins: Indigenous filmmaking in *Tava, The House of Stone, Two Villages, One Path* and *Guarani Exile*

1. Although not the focus of this study, during Bandeira's presentation at the VIII AIM Annual Meeting (Aveiro, Portugal, 2018), I asked him if it could be said that a truly autonomous indigenous cinema was underway in Brazil. Despite the growing number of indigenous-directed films, he believes it is too early to identify common features in those films and arbitrarily define a particular aesthetics for them.
2. For more details, see Lévi-Strauss (1966).

3 Sophia Ferreira Pinheiro (2015) focuses her research on investigating the cinema production made by indigenous women in Brazil. Looking, in particular, at VNA production, she claims that there are thirty-five indigenous male directors and only three indigenous female directors listed on its website.
4 Jesuit reductions were indigenous settlements administered by Jesuit priests in the New World, as part of their so-called civilizing and evangelizing work. Founded in 1687, São Miguel Arcanjo was considered the most prominent of the seven Jesuit reductions in Southern Brazil.
5 For more details, see Hansel (1951) and Simon (1987).
6 Sylvio Back's *República Guarani* (1981) could be a narrative counterpoint to *The Mission*. Instead of idealizing the Jesuit priests, the Brazilian documentary portrays them as colonial imperialists with the mission of superimposing a Western mindset on Native tribes.
7 In his interview, Ortega said that, after finalizing the edit of *Two Villages, One Path*, he realized that he could make more documentaries using the remaining material and shooting additional scenes. That is why *Guarani Exile* and *Tava, The House of Stone* came to be produced afterwards. 'There are many issues that can be explored as there are many questions to be asked' (2018).
8 'Um índio descerá de uma estrela colorida, brilhante/De uma estrela que virá numa velocidade estonteante/E pousará no coração do hemisfério sul/Na América, num claro instante/Depois de exterminada a última nação indígena/E o espírito dos pássaros das fontes de água límpida/Mais avançado que a mais avançada das mais avançadas das tecnologias' (Veloso 1977).
9 'E aquilo que nesse momento se revelará aos povos/Surpreenderá a todos não por ser exótico/Mas pelo fato de poder ter sempre estado oculto/Quando terá sido o óbvio' (Veloso 1977).

Conclusion: A walk amid the cinematic ruins

1 She wrote an essay analysing *Zweig* (1998), a film directed by Edgardo Cozarinsky and commissioned by French TV channel France 3. For more details, see Nunes (2016).
2 Scholar Kiu-wai Chu (2012) uses the term *constructing ruins* in his analysis of contemporary Chinese art and cinema focused on discussing modern ruins in China.
3 For more details, see Stargardter (2019).

References

Agência Pública (2016). 100. *Agência Pública*. Available from http://apublica.org/100/?lang=en [Accessed 28 January 2018].

Alvarenga, C. (2017). *Da cena do contato ao inacabamento da história: Os Últimos Isolados (1967–1999), Corumbiara (1986–2009) e Os Arara (1980-)*. Salvador: EDUFBA.

Amancio, T. (2000). *Artes e manhas da Embrafilme: cinema estatal brasileiro em sua época de ouro*, 2nd ed. Niterói: EDUFF.

Anavilhana (no date). Rastros. A Paisagem Invade. *Anavilhana*. Available from https://vimeo.com/26076544 [Accessed 18 April 2019].

Ancine (2017). Listagem de filmes brasileiros lançados 1995 a 2015. *Ancine*. Available from http://oca.ancine.gov.br/sites/default/files/cinema/pdf/2102_1.pdf [Accessed 5 August 2017].

Andermann, J., and Fernández-Bravo, A. (2013). *New Argentine and Brazilian cinema: Reality effects*. New York: Palgrave Macmillan.

Andrade, A. L., Barros, R. L. de, and Capela, C. E. S. (eds.) (2016). *Ruinologias: ensaios sobre destroços do presente*. Florianópolis: Editora UFSC.

Andrade, O. de, andBary, L. (1991). Cannibalist manifesto. *Latin American Literary Review*, 19 (38), 38–47.

Araújo, A. C. Z., Carvalho, E. I. de, and Carelli, V. (orgs.) (2011). *Vídeo nas Aldeias 25 anos: 1986–2011*. Olinda: Vídeo nas Aldeias.

Araújo, V. de P. (1985). *A bela época do cinema brasileiro*, 2nd ed. São Paulo: Editora Perspectiva.

Aufderheide, P. (2007). *Documentary film: A very short introduction*. Oxford: Oxford University Press.

Augé. M. (2003). *El tiempo en ruinas*, trans. Tomás Fernández Aúz and Beatriz Eguibar. Barcelona: Gedisa Editorial.

Avelar, I. (2009). History, neurosis, and subjectivity: Gustavo Ferreyra's rewriting of neoliberal ruins. In: Lazzara, M. J., and Unruh, V. (eds.), *Telling ruins in Latin America*. New York: Palgrave Macmillan, 183–193.

Badiou, A. (2006). *Being and event*, trans. Oliver Feltham. London: Continuum.

Balsom, E. (2013). *Exhibiting cinema in contemporary art*. Amsterdam: Amsterdam University Press.

Balsom, E., and Peleg, H. (2016). *Documentaries across disciplines*. Cambridge, MA: MIT Press.

Bandeira, P. (2017). *Documentário radical ou ficção como colaboração: invenção, disjunção e cinema compartilhado. Devir e cosmovisão em As Hipermulheres*. MPhil dissertation, Universidade Federal de Pernambuco.

Barbara, V. (2017). The end of the world? In Brazil, it's already here. *New York Times*, 5 January. Available from https://www.nytimes.com/2017/01/05/opinion/the-end-of-the-world-in-brazil-its-already-here.html?fbclid=IwAR3-Wq8jtVXAial6ElfKagcR4Xwx-WjhRh3u4gpR4MgF6kG5Xn2IRZo5GJo [Accessed 13 March 2019].

Baron, J. (2014). *The archive effect: Found footage and the audiovisual experience of history*. London: Routledge.

Barros, R. L de (2013). *The artist among ruins: Connecting catastrophes in Brazilian and Cuban cinema, painting, sculpture and literature*. Doctoral dissertation, University of Texas. Available from https://repositories.lib.utexas.edu/handle/2152/33413 [Accessed 12 July 2017].

Basualdo, C. (2005). Tropicália: Avant-garde, popular culture, and the culture industry in Brazil. In: Basualdo, C. (org.), *Tropicália: A revolution in Brazilian culture [1967–1972]*, trans. Christopher J. Dunn, Aaron Lorenz and Renata Nascimento. São Paulo: Cosac Naify, 11–28.

Bazin, A. (1967). *What Is Cinema? Vol. 1*, trans. Hugh Gray. Berkeley: University of California Press.

BBC News. (2017). Brazil's Chapada dos Veadeiros Park ravaged by fire. *BBC News*, 25 October. Available from http://www.bbc.co.uk/news/world-latin-america-41747575 [Accessed 26 November 2017].

BBC News. (2017). Rio's Valongo slave wharf becomes Unesco heritage site. *BBC News*, 10 July. Available from http://www.bbc.co.uk/news/world-latin-america-40552282 [Accessed 31 January 2018].

Benamou, C. L. (2007). *It's all true: Orson Welles's Pan-American odyssey*. Oakland: University of California Press.

Benjamin, W. (1968). *Illuminations*, trans. Harry Zohn. New York: Harcourt Brace & World.

Benjamin, W. (1977). *The origin of German tragic drama*, trans. John Osborne. London: NLB.

Benjamin, W., and Lacis, A. (1979). Naples. In: Benjamin, W., *One-way street and other writings*, trans. Edmund Jephcott and Kingsley Shorter. London: NLB, 167–176.

Bentes, I. (1996). *Joaquim Pedro de Andrade: a revolução intimista*. Rio de Janeiro: Relume-Dumará-Rio Arte.

Bentes, I. (2002). Terra de fome e sonho: o paraíso material de Glauber Rocha. *Biblioteca On-line de Ciência da Comunicação*, 1–10. Available from http://bocc.ubi.pt/pag/bentes-ivana-glauber-rocha.pdf [Accessed 6 November 2017].

Bentes, I. (2004). Câmera muy very good pra mim trabalhar. *Vídeo nas Aldeias*. Available from http://www.videonasaldeias.org.br/2009/biblioteca.php?c=11 [Accessed 11 December 2018].

Bentes, I. (2005). Multitropicalism, cinematic-sensation, and theoretical devices. In: Basualdo, C. (org.), *Tropicália: A revolution in Brazilian culture [1967–1972]*, trans. Christopher J. Dunn, Aaron Lorenz and Renata Nascimento. São Paulo: Cosac Naify, 99–128.

Berman, M. (1983). *All that is solid melts into air: The experience of modernity*. London: Verso Books.

Bernardet, J. (2003). *Cineastas e imagens do povo*. São Paulo: Companhia das Letras.

Bernardet, J. (2007). *Brasil em tempo de cinema: ensaio sobre o cinema brasileiro de 1958–1966*. São Paulo: Companhia das Letras.

Bessa, A. S., and Fiore, J. (2017). *Gordon Matta-Clark: Anarchitect*. London: Yale University Press.

Betim, F. (2015). Remoções na Vila Autódromo expõem o lado B das Olimpíadas do Rio. *El País Brasil*, 5 August. Available from http://brasil.elpais.com/brasil/2015/06/20/politica/1434753946_363539.html [Accessed 28 January 2018].

Birri, F. (2014). Cinema and underdevelopment. In: MacKenzie, S. (ed.), *Film manifestos and global cinema cultures*. Berkeley: University of California Press, 211–217.

Borja, B. (2013). *A formação da teoria do subdesenvolvimento de Celso Furtado*. Doctoral dissertation, Universidade Federal do Rio de Janeiro. Available from https://www.ie.ufrj.br/images/IE/PEPI/teses/2013/Bruno%20Nogueira%20Ferreira%20Borja.pdf [Accessed 22 June 2018].

Boym, S. (2001). *The future of nostalgia*. New York: Basic Books.

Boym, S. (2011). Ruinophilia: Appreciation of ruins. *Atlas of Transformation*. Available from http://monumenttotransformation.org/atlas-of-transformation/html/r/ruinophilia/ruinophilia-appreciation-of-ruins-svetlana-boym.html [Accessed 22 October 2018].

Brasil, A. (2016a). Rever, retorcer, reverter e retomar as imagens: comunidades de cinema e cosmopolítica. *Galáxia*, 33, 77–93. Available from http://www.scielo.br/pdf/gal/n33/1519-311X-gal-33-0077.pdf [Accessed 1 April 2019].

Brasil, A. (2016b). Retomada: teses sobre o conceito de História. *Forumdoc.bh.20anos*, 145–161. Available from https://www.academia.edu/30375725/Retomada_teses_sobre_o_conceito_de_historia_pdf [Accessed 22 May 2018].

Brasil, A. (2016c). Ver por meio do invisível: o cinema como tradução xamânica. *Revista Novos Estudos*, 35 (3), 125-146. Available from https://www.academia.edu/30373651/Ver_por_meio_do_invis%C3%ADvel_o_cinema_como_tradu%C3%A7%C3%A3o_xam%C3%A2nica [Accessed 18 May 2018].

Brasil, A., and Mesquita, C. (2012). Tonacci. *Revista Devires – Cinema e Humanidades*, 9 (2). Available from http://www.fafich.ufmg.br/devires/index.php/Devires/issue/view/9 [Accessed 10 May 2018].

Brasil, A., Cesar, A., Leandro, A., and Mesquita, C. (2017). Nomear o genocídio: uma conversa sobre Martírio, com Vincent Carelli. *Revista Eco Pós*, 20 (2), 232-257. Available from https://revistaecopos.eco.ufrj.br/eco_pos/article/view/12504/8766 [Accessed 10 May 2018].

Bresser-Pereira, L. C. (2012). Brasil, sociedade nacional-dependente. *Novos Estudos CEBRAP*, 93, 101-121. Available from http://dx.doi.org/10.1590/S0101-33002012000200008 [Accessed 20 June 2018].

Broudehoux, A. (2017). *Mega-events and urban image construction: Beijing and Rio de Janeiro*. London: Routledge.

Brown, W. (2019). *In the ruins of neoliberalism: The rise of antidemocratic politics in the West*. New York: Columbia University Press.

Bruno, G. (2002). *Atlas of emotion: Journeys in art, architecture and film*. London: Verso Books.

Bruzzi, S. (2006). *New documentary: A critical introduction*, 2nd ed. London: Routledge.

Buck-Morss, S. (1989). *The dialectics of seeing: Walter Benjamin and the Arcades Project*. London: MIT Press.

Burgierman, D. R. (2017). O fim do Brasil. *Nexo Jornal*, 3 August. Available from https://www.nexojornal.com.br/colunistas/2017/O-fim-do-Brasil?fbclid=IwAR3f1FBgAhnjcEAmy0e6InLA2l2W14BCgPlEAwDb96OPYJsal5CidU91vHo [Accessed 13 March 2019].

Burton, J. (1986). *Cinema and social change in Latin America: Conversations with Latin American filmmakers*. Austin: University of Texas Press.

Burton, J. (1990). *The social documentary in Latin America*. Pittsburgh: University of Pittsburgh Press.

Caetano, D. (2008). *Serras da Desordem*. Rio de Janeiro: Azougue Editorial.

Caixeta de Queiroz, R. (2008). Cineastas indígenas e pensamento selvagem. *Revista Devires – Cinema e Humanidades*, 5 (2), 98-125. Available from http://www.fafich.ufmg.br/devires/index.php/Devires/article/view/308 [Accessed 30 May 2018].

Calil, C. A. (2016). O caminho de São Bernardo. In: Calil, C. A. (org.), *Uma situação colonial?* São Paulo: Companhia das Letras, 497-516.

Campos, A de. (1974). *Balanço da bossa e outras bossas*, 2nd ed. São Paulo: Editora Perspectiva.

Canal E. (2014). Canal e cultura 25: Branco Sai. Preto Fica. *YouTube*. Available from https://www.youtube.com/watch?v=Z1oG-_gXhC0&t=610s [Accessed 2 November 2017].

Canclini, N. G. (2005). *Hybrid cultures: Strategies for entering and leaving modernity*, trans. Christopher L. Chiappari and Silvia L. López. Minneapolis: University of Minnesota Press.

Canejo, C. (2004). The resurgence of anthropophagy: Tropicália, Tropicalismo and Hélio Oiticica. *Third Text*, 18 (1), 61–68. Available from https://doi.org/10.1080/0952882032000182712 [Accessed 17 April 2019].

Capela, C. E. S. (2016). Euclides e a escritura em ruínas. In: Andrade, A. L., Barros, R. L. de, and Capela, C. E. S. (eds.), *Ruinologias: ensaios sobre destroços do presente*. Florianópolis: Editora UFSC, 289–336.

Carelli, V. (2004). Moi, un Indien. *Vídeo nas Aldeias*. Available from http://www.videonasaldeias.org.br/2009/biblioteca.php?c=19 [Accessed 12 September 2018].

Carelli, V. (2011). Um novo olhar, uma nova imagem. In: Araújo, A. C. Z., Carvalho, E. I. de and Carelli, V. (orgs.), *Vídeo nas Aldeias 25 anos: 1986–2011*. Olinda: Vídeo nas Aldeias, 42–51.

Carelli, V. (2018). Skype interview with author, 30 August 2018.

Carelli, V., Carvalho, A., and Tita. (2016). O Brasil dos índios: um arquivo aberto. *Vídeo nas Aldeias catalogue*. Available from https://www.socioambiental.org/sites/blog.socioambiental.org/files/nsa/arquivos/folhetovnabienal_final_web.pdf [Accessed 10 May 2018].

Carvalho, L. (2018). *Valsa brasileira: do boom ao caos econômico*. São Paulo: Todavia.

Castells, M. (2009). *The rise of the network society*, 2nd ed. Oxford: Wiley-Blackwell.

Cesar, A. (2013). Sobreviver com as imagens: o documentário, a vida e os modos de vida em risco. *Revista Devires – Cinema e Humanidades*, 10 (2), 12–23. Available from http://www.fafich.ufmg.br/devires/index.php/Devires/article/view/154 [Accessed 15 May 2018].

Chanan, M. (2007). *The politics of documentary*. London: British Film Institute.

Chu, K. (2012). Constructing ruins: New urban aesthetics in Chinese art and cinema. In: Munro, M. (ed.), *Modern art Asia, issues 1-8: Papers on modern and contemporary Asian art*. Cambridge: Enzo Arts and Publishing Limited, 191–212.

Columbia Global Centers (2013). Columbia Global Centers. *YouTube*, 7 November. Available from https://www.youtube.com/watch?v=t1qw3aLVHgA [Accessed 31 January 2018].

Conde, M. (2012). *Consuming visions: Cinema, writing, and modernity in Rio de Janeiro*. Charlottesville: University of Virginia Press.

Conde, M. (2018). *Foundational fictions: Early cinema and modernity in Brazil.* Oakland: University of California Press.

Conde, M., and Dennison, S. (eds.) (2018). *Paulo Emílio Salles Gomes: On Brazil and global cinema.* Cardiff: University of Wales Press.

Conti, M. S. (2019). Descida na decadência. *Folha de S.Paulo,* 16 February. Available from https://www1.folha.uol.com.br/colunas/mariosergioconti/2019/02/descida-na-decadencia.shtml [Accessed 13 March 2019].

Cordoba, A. (2017). Astral cities, new selves: Utopian subjectivities in Nosso Lar and Branco Sai, Preto Fica. In: Da Silva, A. M., and Cunha, M. (eds.), *Space and subjectivity in contemporary Brazilian cinema.* New York: Palgrave Macmillan, 128–142.

Córdova, A. (2014). Reenact, reimagine: Performative indigenous documentaries of Bolivia and Brazil. In: Navarro, V., and Rodríguez, J. C. (eds.), *New documentaries in Latin America.* New York: Palgrave Macmillan, 123–144.

Corrigan, T. (2011). *The essay film: From Montaigne, after Marker.* New York: Oxford University Press.

Couto, J. G. (2018). Eu vi um Brasil no cinema. *Blog IMS,* 6 September. Available from https://blogdoims.com.br/eu-vi-um-brasil-no-cinema/ [Accessed 10 October 2018].

Csekö, J. T. (2008). *Ponto de vista.* MPhil dissertation, Universidade Federal do Rio de Janeiro.

Csekö, J. T. (2017). Email interview with author, 18 December 2017.

Cunha, M. (2018). The right to nature: Contested landscapes and indigenous territoriality in Martírio. In: Cunha, M., and Da Silva, A. M. (eds.), *Human rights, social movements, and activism in contemporary Latin American cinema.* Basel: Springer International Publishing AG, 113–131.

Curador Visitante (2016). Depois do futuro. *Exhibition catalogue,* 4 March–1 May. Available from http://eavparquelage.rj.gov.br/wp-content/uploads/2016/07/CuradorVisitante-DanielaLabra.pdf [Accessed 2 February 2018].

De Jesus, E. (2017). The reterritorialization of urban space in Brazilian cinema. In: Da Silva, A. M., and Cunha, M. (eds.), *Space and subjectivity in contemporary Brazilian cinema.* New York: Palgrave Macmillan, 39–56.

Deleuze, G. (1989). *Cinema 2: The time-image,* trans. Hugh Tomlinson and Robert Galeta. Minneapolis: University of Minnesota Press.

Deleuze, G., and Guattari, F. (1987). *A thousand plateaus: Capitalism and schizophrenia,* trans. Brian Massumi. Minneapolis: University of Minnesota Press.

Di Tella, A. (2009). Ruins in the desert: Field notes by a filmmaker. In: Lazzara, M. J., and Unruh, V. (eds.), *Telling ruins in Latin America.* New York: Palgrave Macmillan, 87–94.

Dieguez, C. (2016). The wave. *Piauí*. Available from https://piaui.folha.uol.com.br/materia/the-wave/ [Accessed 13 March 2019].

Dillon, B. (2005–6). Fragments from a history of ruins. *Cabinet Magazine*. Available from http://www.cabinetmagazine.org/issues/20/dillon.php [Accessed 10 December 2018].

Dillon, B. (2011). *Ruins*. London: Whitechapel Gallery.

Duncan, A. (2003). Alternate history. In: James, E., and Mendlesohn, F. (eds.), *The Cambridge companion to science fiction*. Cambridge: Cambridge University Press, 209–218.

Dunn, C. (2001). *Brutality garden: Tropicália and the emergence of a Brazilian counterculture*. Chapel Hill: University of North Carolina Press.

Dunn, C. (2016). *Contracultura: Alternative arts and social transformation in authoritarian Brazil*. Chapel Hill: University of North Carolina Press.

Edensor, T. (2005). *Industrial ruins: Space, aesthetics and materiality*. Oxford: Berg 3PL.

Elduque, A. (2017). Cut it like a tambourine beat: Ricardo Miranda on the editing of The Age of the Earth. In: Solomon, S. (ed.), *Tropicália and beyond: Dialogues in Brazilian film history*. Berlin: Archive Books, 193–209.

Elsaesser, T. (2009). World cinema: Realism, evidence, presence. In: Nagib, L., and Mello, C. (eds.), *Realism and the audiovisual media*. Basingstoke: Palgrave Macmillan, 3–19.

Ferreira, J. (2006). Cinema: Music of light. *Rouge*, 9. Available from http://www.rouge.com.au/9/cinema_light.html [Accessed 18 April 2019].

Florencia Paz Parada Mejia (2016). Hola soy darks (original). YouTube. Available from https://www.youtube.com/watch?v=W6L2CqErL6E [Accessed 26 July 2021].

Foucault, M. (1986). Of other spaces, trans. Jay Miskowiec. *Diacritics*, 16 (1), 22–27. Available from https://www.jstor.org/stable/464648 [Accessed 8 November 2017].

Foucault, M. (1995). *Discipline and punish: The birth of the prison*, trans. Alan Sheridan. New York: Vintage Books.

França, A. (2006). Documentários brasileiros e artes visuais: das passagens e das verdades possíveis. *Revista Alceu*, 7 (13), 49–59. Available from http://revistaalceu-acervo.com.puc-rio.br/media/alceu_n13_Franca.pdf [Accessed 2 November 2018].

Freitas, A. L. R. de. (2008). A missa bárbara rezada por Glauber Rocha em A Idade da Terra: um êxtase místico anti-literário e metateatral. *Anais do XI Congresso Internacional da ABRALIC Tessituras, Interações, Convergências*, 1–7. Available from http://www.abralic.org.br/eventos/cong2008/AnaisOnline/simposios/pdf/062/ANNA_FREITAS.pdf [Accessed 6 January 2018].

Freyre, G. (1998). *Casa-grande & senzala: formação da família brasileira sob o regime da economia patriarcal*, 34th ed. Rio de Janeiro: Record.

Furtado, C. (1969). *Um projeto para o Brasil*, 5th ed. Rio de Janeiro: Editora Saga S.A.

Furtado, C. (2009). *Desenvolvimento e subdesenvolvimento*, 5th ed. Rio de Janeiro: Contraponto: Centro Internacional Celso Furtado.

Furtado, C. (2012). Que somos? In: Furtado, R. F. d'. (org.), *Ensaios sobre a cultura e o Ministério da Cultura*. Rio de Janeiro: Contraponto: Centro Internacional Celso Furtado, 29–41.

Furtado, C. (2014). *Raízes do subdesenvolvimento*, 3rd ed. Rio de Janeiro: Civilização Brasileira.

Furtado, G. P. (2019). *Documentary filmmaking in contemporary Brazil: Cinematic archives of the present*. New York: Oxford University Press.

Furtado, N. A. (2017). Hollywood sai, Ceilândia fica. *Trip*. Available from https://revistatrip.uol.com.br/trip/uma-entrevista-com-adirley-queiros-diretor-de-branco-sai-preto-fica-e-era-uma-vez-brasilia [Accessed 12 January 2018].

G1 Minas. (2019). Mortos identificados no desastre da Vale em Brumadinho sobem para 240. *G1*, 13 May. Available from https://g1.globo.com/mg/minas-gerais/noticia/2019/05/13/mortos-identificados-no-desastre-da-vale-em-brumadinho-sobem-para-240.ghtml [Accessed 13 March 2019].

G1 Rio. (2018a). Diretor-adjunto do Museu Nacional cita 'descaso' de vários governos e que incêndio destruiu tudo. *G1*, 2 September. Available from https://g1.globo.com/rj/rio-de-janeiro/noticia/2018/09/02/vice-diretor-do-museu-nacional-cita-descaso-de-varios-governos.ghtml [Accessed 12 March 2019].

G1 Rio. (2018b). Falta de água prejudicou combate ao incêndio no Museu Nacional, diz bombeiro. *G1*, 2 September. Available from https://g1.globo.com/rj/rio-de-janeiro/noticia/2018/09/02/falta-de-agua-prejudicou-combate-ao-incendio-no-museu-nacional-diz-bombeiro.ghtml [Accessed 12 March 2019].

Gallo, R. (2009). Modernist ruins: The case study of Tlatelolco. In: Lazzara, M. J., and Unruh, V. (eds.), *Telling ruins in Latin America*. New York: Palgrave Macmillan, 107–118.

Gauthier, J. (2008). 'Lest others speak for us': The neglected roots and uncertain future of Maori cinema in New Zealand. In: Wilson, P., and Stewart, M. (eds.), *Global indigenous media: Cultures, poetics, and politics*. Durham, NC: Duke University Press, 58–73.

Ginsburg, F. (1991). Indigenous media: Faustian contract or global village? *Cultural Anthropology*, 6 (1), 92–112.

Ginsburg, F. (2002a). Mediating culture: Indigenous media, ethnographic film and the production of identity. In: Wilk, R. R., and Askew, K. M. (eds.), *The anthropology of media: A reader*. Oxford: Blackwell, 210–235.

Ginsburg, F. D. (2002b). Screen memories: Resignifying the traditional in indigenous media. In: Ginsburg, F. D., Abu-Lughod, L., and Larkin, B. (eds.), *Media worlds: Anthropology on new terrain*. Berkeley: University of California Press, 39–57.

Ginsburg, F. D., Abu-Lughod, L., and Larkin, B. (eds.) (2002). *Media worlds: Anthropology on new terrain*. Berkeley: University of California Press.

Gleghorn, C. (2017). Indigenous filmmaking in Latin America. In: Delgado, M. M., Hart, S. M., and Johnson, R. (eds.), *A companion to Latin American cinema*. West Sussex: Wiley Blackwell, 167–186.

Gouvêa, L. A. de C. (1995). *Brasília: a capital da segregação e do controle social. Uma avaliação da ação governamental na área da habitação*. São Paulo: Annablume.

Guardian sport and agencies. (2017). Rio Olympic venues already falling into a state of disrepair. *The Guardian*, 10 February. Available from https://www.theguardian.com/sport/2017/feb/10/rio-olympic-venues-already-falling-into-a-state-of-disrepair [Accessed 13 March 2019].

Guimarães, C. (2014). Noite na Ceilândia. *Forumdoc.bh 2014*, 196-208. Available from https://edisciplinas.usp.br/pluginfile.php/4693551/mod_resource/content/1/Catalogo%20Forumdoc.bh.2014.pdf [Accessed 1 April 2019].

Guimarães, V. (2014). Ideias e formas, matéria e memória. *Cinética: Cinema e Crítica*, 8 February. Available from http://revistacinetica.com.br/home/o-porto-de-clarissa-campolina-julia-de-simone-luiz-pretti-e-ricardo-pretti-brasil-2013-em-transito-de-marcelo-pedroso-brasil-2013/ [Accessed 21 July 2018].

Guimarães, V. (2016). Que fazer? *Cinética: Cinema e Crítica*, 28 September. Available from http://revistacinetica.com.br/nova/que-fazer/ [Accessed 22 May 2018].

Habib, A. (2008). *Le temps décomposé: cinéma et imaginaire de la ruine*. Doctoral dissertation, Université de Montréal. Available from https://papyrus.bib.umontreal.ca/xmlui/handle/1866/6641 [Accessed 18 March 2019].

Hansel, J. (1951). *História dos Sete Povos da Missões*. Santo Ângelo, Rio Grande do Sul: Missioneira.

Harrison, R. (2009). Machu Picchu recycled. In: Lazzara, M. J., and Unruh, V. (eds.), *Telling ruins in Latin America*. New York: Palgrave Macmillan, 63–75.

Harvey, D. (1989). *The condition of postmodernity: An enquiry into the origins of cultural changes*. Oxford: Basil Blackwell.

Hell, J., and Schönle, A. (eds.) (2010). *Ruins of modernity*. Durham, NC: Duke University Press.

Henley, P. (2010). *The adventure of the real: Jean Rouch and the craft of ethnographic cinema*. Chicago: University of Chicago Press.

Herwitz, D. (2010). The monument in ruins. In: Hell, J., and Schönle, A. (eds.), *Ruins of modernity*. Durham, NC: Duke Press University, 232–249.

Holanda, S. B. de. (1995). *Raízes do Brasil*, 26th ed. São Paulo: Companhia das Letras.

Holston, J. (1989). *The modernist city: An anthropological critique of Brasília*. Chicago: University of Chicago Press.

Hora, T. (2016). Cenas do testemunho e memórias subterrâneas de Brasília. *XXV Encontro da COMPÓS*, 1–19. Available from http://www.compos.org.br/biblioteca/cenasdotestemunhoxxvcomposcomautoria_3439.pdf [Accessed 6 November 2017].

Hora, T. (2017). Anacronismo e dispositivos de ficção científica em Branco Sai, Preto Fica. *C Legenda*, 63-79. Available from http://ppgcine.cinemauff.com.br/pdf/C-LEGENDA_2017_02.pdf [Accessed 18 January 2018].

Huyssen, A. (2006). Nostalgia for ruins. *Grey Room*, 23, 6–21. Available from https://doi.org/10.1162/grey.2006.1.23.6 [Accessed 20 October 2018].

Ikeda, M. (2014). O cinema de garagem: desafios e apontamentos para uma curadoria em construção. In: Lima, D., and Ikeda, M. (orgs.), *Cinema de garagem 2014*. Rio de Janeiro: WSET Multimídia, 7–28.

Ikeda, M. (2017). Mostra de Cinema de Tiradentes 2017 – Curtas da Mostra Foca. *Curta o Curta*, 8 February. Available from http://curtaocurta.com.br/noticias/mostra_de_cinema_de_tiradentes_2017_curtas_da_mostra_foco-3966.html#.Woq2cqhl_IX [Accessed 2 February 2018].

Itaú Cultural (2015). Adirley Queirós – Encontros de Cinema (2015) – parte 1/2. *YouTube*. Available from https://www.youtube.com/watch?v=Hdr8C2MR8vo&t=196s [Accessed 2 November 2017].

Itaú Cultural (2017). Patrícia Ferreira – Encontros de Cinema (2016). *YouTube*. Available from https://www.youtube.com/watch?v=bEf931cDX7s [Accessed 6 April 2019].

Jaguaribe, B. (1998). *Fins de século – Cidade e cultura no Rio de Janeiro*. Rocco: Rio de Janeiro.

Jameson, F. (1991). *Postmodernism: Or, the cultural logic of late capitalism*. London: Verso Books.

Jameson, F. (1992). *The geopolitical aesthetic: Cinema and space in the world system*. Bloomington: Indiana University Press.

Jameson, F. (2005). *Archaeologies of the future: The desire called utopia and other science fictions*. London: Verso Books.

Johnson, R., and Stam, R. (1982). *Brazilian cinema*. Rutherford: Fairleigh Dickinson University Press; London: Associated University Presses.

Kaiser, A. J. (2017). Legacy of Rio Olympics so far is series of unkept promises. *New York Times*, 15 February. Available from https://www.nytimes.

com/2017/02/15/sports/olympics/rio-stadiums-summer-games.html [Accessed 28 January 2018].

Kay, C. (1991). Reflections on the Latin American contribution to development theory. *Development and Change*, 22, 31–68. Available from https://doi.org/10.1111/j.1467-7660.1991.tb00402.x [Accessed 20 June 2018].

Kay, C. (1993). For a renewal of development studies: Latin American theories and neoliberalism in the era of structural adjustment. *Third World Quarterly*, 14 (4), 691–702. Available from https://www.jstor.org/stable/3992946 [Accessed 21 June 2018].

Kay, C. (2009). Latin American structuralist school. In: Kitchin, R., and Thrift, N. (eds.), *International encyclopedia of human geography*. Amsterdam: Elsevier, 159–164.

King, E. (2013). *Science fiction and digital technologies in Argentine and Brazilian culture*. New York: Palgrave Macmillan.

Knight, A. (2007). When was Latin America modern? A historian's response. In: Miller, N., and Hart, S. (eds.), *When was Latin America modern?* Hampshire: Palgrave Macmillan, 91–117.

Labaki, A. (2003). It's all Brazil, trans. Roderick Steel. In: Nagib, L. (ed.), *The new Brazilian cinema*. London: I.B. Tauris, 97–104.

Labaki, A. (2006). *Introdução ao documentário brasileiro*. São Paulo: Francis.

Lacerda, R. (2018). The collaborative indigenous cinema of Video nas Aldeias and the Intangible Cultural Heritage. *MEMORIAMEDIA Review*, 3, 1–12. Available from https://memoriamedia.net/pdfarticles/ENG_MEMORIAMEDIAREVIEW_Video_nas_Aldeias.pdf [Accessed 12 March 2019].

Lagnado, L., and Lafuente, P. (2015). *Cultural anthropophagy: The 24th Bienal de São Paulo 1998*. London: Afterall Books.

Lane, J. (2009). Spatial truth and reconciliation: Peru, 2003–2004. In: Lazzara, M. J., and Unruh, V. (eds.), *Telling ruins in Latin America*. New York: Palgrave Macmillan, 135–145.

Lazzara, M. J., and Unruh, V. (eds.) (2009). *Telling ruins in Latin America*. New York: Palgrave Macmillan.

Larraín, J. (2014). Modernity and identity: Cultural change in Latin America. In: Gwynne, R. N., and Kay, C. (eds.), *Latin America transformed: Globalization and modernity*, 2nd ed. London: Routledge, 22–38.

Lévi-Strauss, C. (1966). *The savage mind*. London: Weidenfeld and Nicolson.

Lévi-Strauss, C. (1973). *Tristes tropiques*, trans. John Weightman and Doreen Weightman. London: Cape.

Lima, D., and Ikeda, M. (2011). *Cinema de garagem: um inventário afetivo do jovem cinema brasileiro do século XXI*. Fortaleza: SuburbanaCo.

Lins, C., and Mesquita, C. (2011). *Filmar o real: sobre o documentário brasileiro contemporâneo*, 2nd ed. Rio de Janeiro: Zahar.

Lispector, C. (1999a). Brasília. In: Lispector, C. *Para não esquecer*. Rio de Janeiro: Rocco, 40–44.

Lispector, C. (1999b). Brasília: esplendor. In: Lispector, C. *Para não esquecer*. Rio de Janeiro: Rocco, 44–63.

Lissovsky, M., and Sá, P. S. M. de (1996). O novo em construção: o edifício-sede do Ministério da Educação e Saúde e a disputa do espaço arquiteturável nos anos 30. In: *Colunas da educação: a construção do Ministério da Educação e Saúde (1935–1945)*. Rio de Janeiro: MINC/IPHAN; Fundação Getúlio Vargas/CPDOC.

Lopes, D. (2016). Ruínas pobres, cidades mortas. In: Andrade, A. L., Barros, R. L. de, and Capela, C. E. S. (eds.), *Ruinologias: ensaios sobre destroços do presente*. Florianópolis: Editora UFSC, 337–352.

Los Angeles Times (1955). Carmen Miranda. *Los Angeles Times*. Available from http://projects.latimes.com/hollywood/star-walk/carmen-miranda/ [Accessed 15 November 2020].

Löwy, M. (2005). *Fire alarm: Reading Walter Benjamin's 'On the concept of history'*, trans. Chris Turner. London: Verso Books.

Macaulay, R. (1966). *Pleasure of ruins*. London: Thames & Hudson.

Marques, L. (2018). Email interview with author, 26 January 2018.

Martí, S. (2016). Brasília at midnight. *Even Magazine*, 4. Available from http://evenmagazine.com/brasilia-at-midnight/ [Accessed 21 July 2018].

Martí, S. (2017). *Territórios de exceção: resistência e hedonismo em ruínas urbanas*. MPhil dissertation, Universidade de São Paulo. Available from http://www.teses.usp.br/teses/disponiveis/16/16136/tde-23062017-083413/pt-br.php [Accessed 6 February 2019].

Mello Franco, B. (2018). Na tragédia do Museu Nacional, o suicídio de um país. *O Globo*, 2 September. Available from https://blogs.oglobo.globo.com/bernardo-mello-franco/post/na-tragedia-do-museu-nacional-o-suicidio-de-um-pais.html?fbclid=IwAR17xQrPk2jtdHZkeWPFtRSzSjIyTCeMRCuNOYYIDSwsSgqZfGsjxTFLhTc [Accessed 12 March 2019].

Mesquita, C. (2011a). Um drama documentário – atualidade e história em A cidade é uma só? *Devires – Cinema e Humanidades*, 8 (2), 48–69. Available from https://issuu.com/revistadevires/docs/engajamentos1 [Accessed 16 August 2020].

Mesquita, C. (2011b). Obra em processo ou processo como obra? In: Eduardo, C., Valente, E., and Vieira, J. L. (orgs.), *Cinema brasileiro anos 2000: 10 questões*.

Available from http://www.revistacinetica.com.br/anos2000/questao9.php [Accessed 15 May 2018].

Mesquita, C. (2015). Memória contra utopia. Branco Sai Preto Fica (Adirley Queirós, 2014). *XXIV Encontro da COMPÓS*, 1–17. Available from http://www.compos.org.br/biblioteca/compos- 2015-1a0eeebb-2a95-4e2a-8c4b-c0f6999c1d34_2839.pdf [Accessed 6 November 2017].

Mesquita, C. (2018). The future's reverse: Dystopia and precarity in Adirley Queirós's cinema. In: Burucúa, C., and Sitnisky, C. (eds.), *The precarious in the cinemas of the Americas*. Cham, Switzerland: Palgrave Macmillan, 61–79.

Migliorin, C. (2010). Documentário recente brasileiro e as políticas das imagens. In: Migliorin, C. (org.), *Ensaios no real: o documentário brasileiro hoje*. Rio de Janeiro: Beco do Azougue, 9–25.

Migliorin, C. (2011). Por um cinema pós-industrial: notas para um debate. *Revista Cinética*. Available from http://www.revistacinetica.com.br/cinemaposindustrial.htm [Accessed 29 October 2018].

Milanez, F. (2013). Os inimigos de Adrian Cowell. *Forumdoc.bh.2013*, 320-325. Available from https://www.academia.edu/5347982/Inimigos_de_Adrian_Cowell [Accessed 1 April 2019].

Moltke, J. von. (2010). Ruin cinema. In: Hell, J., and Schönle, A. (eds.), *Ruins of modernity*. Durham, NC: Duke Press University, 395–417.

Naficy, H. (2001). *An accented cinema: Exilic and diasporic filmmaking*. Princeton, NJ: Princeton University Press.

Nagib, L. (2006). Towards a positive definition of world cinema. In: Dennison, S., and Lim, S. H. (eds.), *Remapping world cinema: Identity, culture and politics in film*. London: Wallflower Press, 30–37.

Nagib, L. (2007). *Brazil on screen: Cinema Novo, New Cinema and utopia*. London: I.B. Tauris.

Nagib, L. (2011). *World cinema and the ethics of realism*. London: Continuum.

Nagib, L. (2017a). Antropofagia e intermidialidade: usos da literatura colonial no cinema modernista brasileiro. *Rebeca – Revista Brasileira de Estudos de Cinema e Audiovisual*, 6 (1), 1–20. Available from https://rebeca.socine.org.br/1/article/view/479/260 [Accessed 30 April 2018].

Nagib, L. (2017b). Realist cinema as world cinema. In: Stone, R., and Cooke, P. (eds.), *The Routledge companion to world cinema*. Abingdon-on-Thames: Routledge, 310–322.

Nagib, L., and Jerslev, A. (2014). *Impure cinema: Intermedial and intercultural approaches to film*. London: I.B. Tauris.

Nagib, L., and Solomon, S. (2019). Intermediality in Brazilian cinema: the case of Tropicália - Introduction. *Screen*, 60 (1), 122–127. Available from https://doi.org/10.1093/screen/hjy064 [Accessed 21 April 2019].

Nagib, L., Perriam, C., and Dudrah, R. (2012). *Theorizing world cinema*. London: I.B. Tauris.

Napolitano, M. (2009). 'O fantasma de um clássico': recepção e reminiscências de Favela dos Meus Amores (H. Mauro, 1935). *Revista Significação*, 32, 137–157. Available from https://www.researchgate.net/publication/276254531_O_fantasma_de_um_classico_recepcao_e_reminiscencias_de_Favela_dos_Meus_Amores_H_Mauro_1935 [Accessed 30 October 2018].

Navarro, V., and Rodríguez, J. C. (2014). *New documentaries in Latin America*. New York: Palgrave Macmillan.

Neves Marques, P. (2014). *The forest and the school/Where to sit at the dinner table?* Berlin: Archive Books.

Nichols, B. (1991). *Representing reality*. Bloomington: Indiana University Press.

Nichols, B. (2001). Documentary film and the modernist avant-garde. *Critical Inquiry*, 27 (4), 580–610. Available from http://www.columbia.edu/itc/film/gaines/documentary_tradition/Nichols_Documentary%20and%20Avant-Garde.pdf [Accessed 12 March 2019].

Nichols, B. (2010). *Introduction to documentary*, 2nd ed. Bloomington: Indiana University Press.

Nunes, M. A. V. (2016). Zweig: a ruína, o arquivo e o fantasma. In: Andrade, A. L., Barros, R. L. de, and Capela, C. E. S. (eds.), *Ruinologias: ensaios sobre destroços do presente*. Florianópolis: Editora UFSC, 113–131.

Oiticica, H. (1999a). Position and program. In: Alberro, A., and Stimson, B. (eds.), *Conceptual art: A critical anthology*. Cambridge, MA: MIT Press, 8–10.

Oiticica, H. (1999b). General scheme of the New Objectivity. In: Alberro, A., and Stimson, B. (eds.), *Conceptual art: A critical anthology*. Cambridge, MA: MIT Press, 40–42.

Oiticica, H. (no date). Tropicália. *Tropicália*. Available from http://tropicalia.com.br/leituras-complementares/tropicalia-3 [Accessed 31 January 2018].

Olalquiaga, C., and Blackmore, L. (2017). Latin America's living ruins: El Helicoide de la Roca Tarpeya. *Colección Cisneros*, 6 October. Available from https://www.coleccioncisneros.org/editorial/statements/latin-americas-living-ruins-el-helicoide-de-la-roca-tarpeya [Accessed 12 February 2019].

Olalquiaga, C., and Blackmore, L. (2018). *Downward spiral: El Helicoide's descent from mall to prison*. New York: Terreform.

Oliveira, A. J. B. de. (2005). *Das ilhas à cidade – A construção da cidade universitária da Universidade do Brasil (1935-1950)*. MPhil dissertation, Universidade

Federal do Rio de Janeiro. Available from http://www.dominiopublico.gov.br/pesquisa/DetalheObraForm.do?select_action=&co_obra=133271 [Accessed 20 November 2018].

Oliveira, C. (2015). Filme Branco Sai, Preto Fica mostra história de violenta batida policial no Quarentão, berço da cultura black do DF. *R7*, 19 April. Available from https://noticias.r7.com/distrito-federal/filme-branco-sai-preto-fica-mostra-historia-de-violenta-batida-policial-no-quarentao-berco-da-cultura-black-do-df-19042015 [Accessed 2 November 2017].

Oliveira, J. (2020). Cinemateca Brasileira agoniza e se torna símbolo da falta de política cultural do Governo Bolsonaro. *El País Brasil*, 29 July. Available from https://brasil.elpais.com/cultura/2020-07-29/cinemateca-brasileira-agoniza-e-se-torna-simbolo-da-falta-de-politica-cultural-do-governo-bolsonaro.html [Accessed 16 September 2020].

Oliveira, M. M. (2015). The epistemological leap of anthropophagy after the 24th Bienal de São Paulo. In: Lagnado, L., and Lafuente, P. (eds.), *Cultural anthropophagy: The 24th Bienal de São Paulo 1998*. London: Afterall Books, 176–187.

Ortega, A. (2018). WhatsApp interview with author, 19 July 2018.

Otavio, C., and Biasetto, D. (2016). A tormenta de Cabral. *O Globo*, 17 November. Available from https://oglobo.globo.com/brasil/a-tormenta-de-cabral-20478798 [Accessed 28 January 2018].

Peixoto, N. B. (1987). *Cenários em ruínas: a realidade imaginária contemporânea*. São Paulo: Editora Brasiliense.

Peixoto, N. B. (2003). *Paisagens urbanas*, 3rd ed. São Paulo: Editora Senac São Paulo.

Pethő, Á. (2010). Intermediality in film: A historiography of methodologies. *Acta Universitatis Sapientiae: Film and Media Studies*, 2, 39–72. Available from http://www.acta.sapientia.ro/acta-film/C2/film2-3.pdf [Accessed 12 July 2018].

Pethő, Á. (2011). *Cinema and intermediality: The passion for the in-between*. Newcastle: Cambridge Scholars.

Pick, Z. M. (1993). *The new Latin American cinema: A continental project*. Austin: University of Texas Press.

Pinakotheke. (no date). Oscar Niemeyer (1907–2012): Territórios da criação. *Pinakotheke*. Available from http://www.pinakotheke.com.br/new/exposicao-imprensa.php?idExposicao=54 [Accessed 10 August 2020].

Pinheiro, S. F. (2015). A imagem como arma – As trajetórias das mulheres indígenas brasileiras na auto-representação e produção imagética contras as opressões de raça, gênero e classe. *39º Encontro Anual da ANPOCS*, 1–24. Available from https://www.anpocs.com/index.php/papers-39-encontro/spg/

spg10/9900-a-imagem-como-arma-as-cineastas-indigenas-do-video-nas-aldeias/file [Accessed 14 March 2019].

Pinto, C. E. P. de (2014). Quatrocentos anos num filme: Pindorama (Arnaldo Jabor, 1971) e a relação dos cinemanovistas com a história. *Resgate: Revista Interdisciplinar de Cultura*, 22(2), 47–54. Available from https://doi.org/10.20396/resgate.v22i28.8645778 [Accessed 18 April 2018].

Ponte, A. J. (2007). *La fiesta vigilada*. Barcelona: Anagrama.

Prado Coelho, A. (2018). Eduardo Viveiros de Castro: "Gostaria que o Museu Nacional permanecesse como ruína, memória das coisas mortas". *Público*, 4 September. Available from https://www.publico.pt/2018/09/04/culturaipsilon/entrevista/eduardo-viveiros-de-castro-gostaria-que-o-museu-nacional-permanecesse-como-ruina-memoria-das-coisas-mortas-1843021?fbclid=IwAR0vqf5tDtgihoje0tSAsMSwgsMVmIQ5FoRrDUQ9aObI1kmTPAAb5aGHJms [Accessed 13 March 2019].

Prado Júnior, C. (1961). *Formação do Brasil contemporâneo: colônia*, 6th ed. São Paulo: Editora Brasiliense.

Pretti, R. (2019). Email interview with author, 28 March 2019.

Prysthon, Â. (2002). *Cosmopolitismos periféricos: ensaios sobre modernidade, pós-modernidade e estudos culturais na América Latina*. Recife: Bagaço.

Prysthon, Â. (2015). Furiosas frivolidades: artifícios, heterotopias e temporalidades estranhas no cinema brasileiro contemporâneo. *Revista Eco Pós*, 18 (3), 1–9. Available from https://revistas.ufrj.br/index.php/eco_pos/article/viewFile/2763/2340 [Accessed 22 October 2017].

Prysthon, Â. F. (2017). Paisagens em desaparição. Cinema em Pernambuco e a relação com o espaço. *E-Compós*, 20 (1), 1–17. Available from http://www.e-compos.org.br/e-compos/article/view/1348/919 [Accessed 22 November 2018].

Queirós, A. (2018). WhatsApp interview with author, 29 September 2018.

Quijano, A. (1989). Paradoxes of modernity in Latin America. *International Journal of Politics, Culture, and Society*, 3 (2), 147–177. Available from https://www.jstor.org/stable/20006945 [Accessed 12 August 2020].

Rabinowitz, P. (1993). Wreckage upon wreckage: History, documentary and the ruins of memory. *History and Theory*, 32 (2), 119–137.

Ramos, F. (1987a). *História do cinema brasileiro*. São Paulo: Art Editora.

Ramos, F. (1987b). *Cinema Marginal (1968–1973): a representação em seu limite*. São Paulo: Editora Brasiliense.

Ramos, F. (2016). Discovering the world. *Mousse Magazine*, 52, 254–261.

Ramos, F. P. (2003). Humility, guilt and narcissism turned inside out in Brazil's film revival, trans. Roderick Steel. In: Nagib, L. (ed.), *The new Brazilian cinema*. London: I.B. Tauris, 65–84.

Ramos, F. P. (2013). *Mas afinal... o que é mesmo documentário?*, 2nd ed. São Paulo: Editora Senac São Paulo.

Rascaroli, L. (2017). *How the essay film thinks*. New York: Oxford University Press.

Renouvier, C. (1988). *Uchronie*. Paris: Fayard.

Rivera, L. (2017). Future histories and cyborg labor: Reading borderlands science fiction after NAFTA. In: Latham, R. (ed.), *Science fiction criticism: An anthology of essential writings*. London: Bloomsbury.

Rocha, G. (2003). *Revisão crítica do cinema brasileiro*. São Paulo: Cosac Naify.

Rocha, G. (2004). *Revolução do Cinema Novo*. São Paulo: Cosac Naify.

Rocha, G. (2005). Tropicalism, anthropophagy, myth, ideogram (1969). In: Basualdo, C. (org.), *Tropicália: A revolution in Brazilian culture [1967–1972]*, trans. Christopher J. Dunn, Aaron Lorenz and Renata Nascimento. São Paulo: Cosac Naify, 276–279.

Rocha, G. (2006). *O século do cinema*. São Paulo: Cosac Naify.

Rocha, G. (2017). The Aesthetics of Hunger and The Aesthetics of Dreaming by Glauber Rocha. *Documenta 14*. Available from http://www.documenta14.de/en/south/891_the_aesthetics_of_hunger_and_the_aesthetics_of_dreaming [Accessed 22 November 2018].

Rocha, G. (2019). *On cinema*, ed. Ismail Xavier, trans. Charlotte Smith, Stephanie Dennison and Cecília Mello. London: I.B. Tauris.

Rocha, G. W. de F. (2003). *A faculdade de medicina da Universidade Federal do Rio de Janeiro: da Praia Vermelha à Ilha do Fundão – O(s) sentido da(s) mudança(s)*. Doctoral dissertation, PUC-Rio. Available from https://www.maxwell.vrac.puc-rio.br/colecao.php?strSecao=resultado&nrSeq=4328@1 [Accessed 20 November 2018].

Rolnik, S. (2006). The geopolitics of pimping, trans. Brian Holmes. *European Institute for Progressive Cultural Policies*. Available from http://eipcp.net/transversal/1106/rolnik/en/#_ftnref12 [Accessed 12 April 2019].

Rolnik, S. (2011). Avoiding false problems: Politics of the fluid, hybrid, and flexible. *E-flux Journal*, 25. Available from https://www.e-flux.com/journal/25/67892/avoiding-false-problems-politics-of-the-fluid-hybrid-and-flexible/ [Accessed 12 April 2019].

Russell, C. (1999). *Experimental ethnography: The work of film in the age of video*. Durham, NC: Duke University Press.

Salazar, J. F., and Córdova, A. (2008). Imperfect cinema and the poetics of indigenous video in Latin America. In: Wilson, P., and Stewart, M. (eds.), *Global indigenous media: Cultures, poetics, and politics*. Durham, NC: Duke University Press, 39–57.

Salles Gomes, P. E. (1996). *Cinema: trajetória no subdesenvolvimento*, 2nd ed. São Paulo: Paz e Terra.

Salles Gomes, P. E. (2016a). Uma situação colonial? In: Calil, C. A. (org.), *Uma situação colonial?* São Paulo: Companhia das Letras, 47–54.

Salles Gomes, P. E. (2016b). Festejo muito pessoal. In: Calil, C. A. (org.), *Uma situação colonial?* São Paulo: Companhia das Letras, 491–496.

Salles Gomes, P. E. (2016c). Explicapresentação. In: Calil, C. A. (org.), *Uma situação colonial?* São Paulo: Companhia das Letras, 340–342.

Sampaio Júnior, P. A. (1999). *Entre a nação e a barbárie: os dilemas do capitalismo dependente*. Petrópolis: Vozes.

Sanches, M. (2021). Imagens mostram projeto de restauração do Museu Nacional, destruído por incêndio em 2018. *G1*, 20 February. Available from https://g1.globo.com/rj/rio-de-janeiro/noticia/2021/02/20/imagens-mostram-projeto-de-restauracao-do-museu-nacional-destruido-por-incendio-em-2018.ghtml [Accessed 15 March 2021].

Santos, D. (2017). Email interview with author, 27 December 2017.

Saraiva, L. (2009). Enfia essa câmera no rabo. *Revista Retrato do Brasil*, 27, 41–43.

Saunders, D. (2010). *Documentary*. London: Routledge.

Scardino, R. (2016). A fala que antecede a queda: a museificação de Havana por Antonio José Ponte. In: Andrade, A. L., Barros, R. L. de, and Capela, C. E. S. (eds.), *Ruinologias: ensaios sobre destroços do presente*. Florianópolis: Editora UFSC, 189–201.

Schefer, R. (2016). Ar, fogo, terra e água: o cinema de Ana Vaz. *A Cuarta Parede*, 1–12. Available from http://www.acuartaparede.com/wp-content/uploads/2016/10/Artigo-O-Cinema-de-Ana-Vaz-Pt.pdf [Accessed 28 October 2017].

Schiwy, F. (2009). *Indianizing film: Decolonization, the Andes, and the question of technology*. New Brunswick, NJ: Rutgers University Press.

Schumpeter, J. (1976). *Capitalism, socialism and democracy*, 5th ed. London: Allen and Unwin.

Schwarz, R. (2005). Culture and politics in Brazil, 1964–1969. In: Basualdo, C. (org.), *Tropicália: A revolution in Brazilian culture [1967-1972]*, trans. Christopher J. Dunn, Aaron Lorenz and Renata Nascimento. São Paulo: Cosac Naify, 279–308.

Sganzerla, R. (2017). Outlaw cinema. In: Solomon, S. (ed.), *Tropicália and beyond: Dialogues in Brazilian film history*. Berlin: Archive Books, 81–83.

Shaw, L. (2013). *Carmen Miranda*. New York: Palgrave Macmillan.

Shaw, L., and Dennison, S. (2007) *Brazilian national cinema*. London: Routledge.

Shohat, E., and Stam, R. (1994). *Unthinking Eurocentrism: Multiculturalism and the media*. London: Routledge.

Silveira. (2019). Incêndio que destruiu o Museu Nacional começou no ar-condicionado do auditório, diz laudo da PF. *G1*, 4 April. Available from https://

g1.globo.com/rj/rio-de-janeiro/noticia/2019/04/04/policia-federal-divulga-laudo-de-incendio-que-destruiu-o-museu-nacional-no-rio.ghtml [Accessed 12 April 2019].

Simmel, G. (1965). The ruin. In: Wolff, K. H. (ed.), *Essays on sociology, philosophy and aesthetics*. New York: Harper and Row, 259-266.

Simon, M. (1987). *Breve notícia dos Sete Povos*. Rio de Janeiro: Própria.

Skoller, J. (2005). *Shadows, specters, shards: Making history in avant-garde film*. Minneapolis: University of Minnesota Press.

Skvirsky, S. A. (2013). The postcolonial city symphony film and the 'ruins' of Suite Habana. *Social Identities: Journal for the Study of Race, Nation and Culture*, 19 (3–4), 423–439. Available from https://www.tandfonline.com/doi/abs/10.1080/13504630.2013.817650 [Accessed 17 March 2019].

Smithson, R. (1996). A tour of the monuments of Passaic, New Jersey (1967). In: Flam, J. (ed.), *Robert Smithson: the collected writings*. Berkeley: University of California Press, 68–74.

Sobchack, V. (1987). *Screening space: The American science fiction film*. New Brunswick, NJ: Rutgers University Press.

Sobchack, V. (2016). The scene of the screen: Envisioning photographic, cinematic, and electronic "presence". In: Denson, S., and Leyda, J. (eds.), *Post-cinema: Theorizing 21st-century film*. Falmer: Reframe Books, 88–128. Available from https://reframe.sussex.ac.uk/post-cinema/2-1-sobchack/ [Accessed 18 November 2017].

Solanas, F., and Getino, O. (1997). Towards a Third Cinema: Notes and experiences for the development of a cinema of liberation in the Third World. In: Martin, M. T. (ed.), *New Latin American cinema, volume one: Theory, practices, and transcontinental articulations*. Detroit: Wayne State University Press, 33–58.

Solomon, S. (2017). *Tropicália and beyond: Dialogues in Brazilian film history*. Berlin: Archive Books.

Sommer, D. (1991). *Foundational fictions: The national romances of Latin America*. Berkeley: University of California Press.

Sonntag, H. R., Contreras, M. A., and Biardeau, J. (2001). Development as modernization and modernity in Latin America. *Review (Fernand Braudel Center)*, 24 (2), 219–251. Available from http://www.jstor.com/stable/40241503 [Accessed 12 August 2020].

Stam, R. (1997). *Tropical multiculturalism: A comparative history of race in Brazilian cinema and culture*. Durham, NC: Duke University Press.

Stam, R. (2003). Cabral and the Indians: filmic representations of Brazil's 500 Years. In: Nagib, L. (ed.), *The new Brazilian cinema*. London: I.B. Tauris, 205–228.

Stam, R. (2005). *Literature through film: Realism, magic, and the art of adaptation.* Malden, MA: Blackwell.

Stam, R., and Xavier, I. (1997). Transformation of national allegory: Brazilian cinema from dictatorship to redemocratization. In: Martin, M. T. (ed.), *New Latin American cinema, volume two: Studies of national cinemas.* Detroit: Wayne State University Press, 295–322.

Stargardter, G. (2019). Bolsonaro presidential decree grants sweeping powers over NGOs in Brazil. *Reuters*, 2 January. Available from https://www.reuters.com/article/us-brazil-politics-ngos/bolsonaro-presidential-decree-grants-sweeping-powers-over-ngos-in-brazil-idUSKCN1OW1P8 [Accessed 26 March 2019].

Stavenhagen, R. (1974). The future of Latin America: Between underdevelopment and revolution. *Latin American Perspectives*, 1 (1), 124–148. Available from https://www.jstor.org/stable/2633533 [Accessed 19 June 2018].

Stoller, P. (1992). *The cinematic griot: The ethnography of Jean Rouch.* Chicago: University of Chicago Press.

Suppia, A. (2007). *Limite de alerta! Ficção científica em atmosfera rarefeita: uma introdução ao estudo da FC no cinema brasileiro e em algumas cinematografias off-Hollywood.* Doctoral dissertation, Universidade Estadual de Campinas. Available from http://repositorio.unicamp.br/jspui/handle/REPOSIP/285029 [Accessed 15 July 2018].

Suppia, A. (2011). A verdade está lá fora: sobre a retórica documentária no cinema fantástico ou de ficção científica. *Revista Fronteiras – Estudos Midiáticos*, 13 (1), 20-31. Available from https://www.academia.edu/3101001/A_verdade_est%C3%A1_l%C3%A1_fora_sobre_a_ret%C3%B3rica_document%C3%A1ria_no_cinema_fant%C3%A1stico_ou_de_fic%C3%A7%C3%A3o_cient%C3%ADfica [Accessed 15 July 2018].

Suppia, A. (2015). Acessos restritos: Branco Sai, Preto Fica (2014), de Adirley Queirós, e o cinema brasileiro de ficção científica contemporâneo. *Revista Hélice*, 2 (5), 21–27. Available from https://www.academia.edu/20022626/_Acessos_restritos_Branco_Sai_Preto_Fica2014deAdirleyQueir%C3%B3seocinemabrasileirodefic%C3%A7%C3%A3ocient%C3%ADfica_contempor%C3%A2neo_em_Revista_H%C3%A9lice_vol._2_n._5_pp._21-27 [Accessed 15 July 2018].

Sussman, E. (2016). Between the public and private: subterrania. In: Mariani, P., and Reily, K. (eds.), *Hélio Oiticica: to organize delirium.* Munich: DelMonico Books - Prestel, 131–142.

Suvin, D. (1979). *Metamorphoses of science fiction: On the poetics and history of a literary genre.* New Haven: Yale University.

Tacca, F. de. (2001). *A imagética da comissão Rondon*. Campinas, São Paulo: Papirus Editora.

Tate. (no date). Ruin Lust. *Tate*. Available from https://www.tate.org.uk/whats-on/tate-britain/exhibition/ruin-lust [Accessed 12 March 2019].

Tavolaro, S. B. F. (2005). Existe uma modernidade brasileira? Reflexões em torno de um dilema sociológico brasileiro. *Revista Brasileira de Ciências Sociais*, 20 (59), 5–22. Available from https://pdfs.semanticscholar.org/3966/24537169b2e9407684c3b28f746d2f19941b.pdf?_ga=2.194870949.943902802.1625672043-1394105958.1625521965 [Accessed 12 August 2020].

TED (2012). The 4 commandments of cities. *TED*. Available from https://www.ted.com/talks/eduardo_paes_the_4_commandments_of_cities [Accessed 31 January 2018].

The Economist. (2009). Brazil takes off. *The Economist*, 14 November. Available from https://www.economist.com/weeklyedition/2009-11-14 [Accessed 13 March 2019].

The Economist. (2013). Has Brazil blown it? *The Economist*, 28 September. Available from https://www.economist.com/weeklyedition/2013-09-28 [Accessed 13 March 2019].

The Economist. (2021). Brazil's dismal decade. *The Economist*, 5 June. Available from https://www.economist.com/weeklyedition/2021-06-05 [Accessed 19 June 2021].

Topik, S. (1987). Historical perspectives on Latin American underdevelopment. *The History Teacher*, 20 (4), 545–560. Available from https://www.jstor.org/stable/493756 [Accessed 19 June 2018].

Torlasco, D. (2013). *The heretical archive: Digital memory at the end of film*. Minneapolis: University of Minnesota Press.

Trabalho Indigenista. (no date). Quem somos. *Trabalho Indigenista*. Available from https://trabalhoindigenista.org.br/o-cti/quem-somos/ [Accessed 13 March 2019].

Turner, T. (2002). Representation, politics, and cultural imagination in indigenous video: General points and Kayapo examples. In: Ginsburg, F. D. Abu-Lughod, L., and Larkin, B. (eds.), *Media worlds: Anthropology on new terrain*. Berkeley: University of California Press, 75–89.

Urano, P. (2017). Email interview with author, 11 November 2017.

Vaz, A. (2017a). Skype interview with author, 22 August 2017.

Vaz, A. (2017b). Cosmovisions, dreaming beyond the sun. In: Solomon, S. (ed.), *Tropicália and beyond: Dialogues in Brazilian film history*. Berlin: Archive Books, 211–223.

Veloso, C. (1971). *Maria Bethânia* [song]. Available from https://open.spotify.com/album/0lq9Ise0K45Nh8mZ5OERzk [Accessed 5 February 2019].

Veloso, C. (1977). *Um índio* [song]. Available from https://open.spotify.com/album/2rXCY07TM8KFD4af2u6eaV [Accessed 27 November 2018].

Veloso, C. (1989). *O estrangeiro* [song]. Available from https://open.spotify.com/album/3RIdNxR4rPdLUnbigaRqZS [Accessed 7 February 2019].

Veloso, C. (1991). *Fora da ordem* [song]. Available from https://open.spotify.com/album/6jclg8GUlvPIiFWBhphdnw [Accessed 20 July 2018].

Veloso, C. (2017). *Verdade tropical*. São Paulo: Companhia das Letras.

Verdesio, G. (2010). Invisible at glance: Indigenous cultures of the past, ruins, archaeological sites, and our regimes of visibility. In: Hell, J., and Schönle, A. (eds.), *Ruins of modernity*. Durham, NC: Duke Press University, 339–353.

Viany, A. (1993). *Introdução ao cinema brasileiro*. Rio de Janeiro: Revan.

Vídeo nas Aldeias (no date-a). Apresentação. *Vídeo nas Aldeias*. Available from http://www.videonasaldeias.org.br/2009/vna.php?p=1 [Accessed 18 December 2017].

Vídeo nas Aldeias (no date-b). Realização. *Vídeo nas Aldeias*. Available from http://www.videonasaldeias.org.br/2009/vna.php?p=2 [Accessed 18 December 2017].

Viehoff, V., and Poynter, G. (2015). *Mega-event cities: Urban legacies of global sports events*. London: Routledge.

Villarreal, G. Z. (2017). *Indigenous media and political imaginary in contemporary Bolivia*. Lincoln: University of Nebraska Press.

Viveiros de Castro, E. (2004). Perspectival anthropology and the method of controlled equivocation. *Tipití: Journal of the Society for the Anthropology of Lowland South America*, 2 (1), 1–21. Available from http://digitalcommons.trinity.edu/tipiti/vol2/iss1/1 [Accessed 22 April 2018].

Viveiros de Castro, E. (2014). *Cannibal metaphysics: For a post-structural anthropology*, ed. and trans. Peter Skafish. Minneapolis: Univocal Publishing.

Volney, C. (1853). *Volney's ruins: or, meditation on the revolutions of empires*. New York: G. Vale.

Watts, J. (2013). Brazil protests erupt over public services and World Cup costs. *The Guardian*. Available from https://www.theguardian.com/world/2013/jun/18/brazil-protests-erupt-huge-scale [Accessed 21 November 2017].

Weyrdmusicman (2011). Carmen Miranda's Ghost 01 - Carmen Miranda's Ghost. *YouTube*. Available from https://www.youtube.com/watch?v=D5p8YhhaVlA [Accessed 2 February 2018].

Whitehead, L. (2007). When was Latin America modern? In: Miller, N., and Hart, S. (eds.), *When was Latin America modern?* Hampshire: Palgrave Macmillan, 191–206.

Wilcken, P. (2010). *Claude Lévi-Strauss: The poet in the laboratory*. London: Bloomsbury.

Wilson, P., and Stewart, M. (2008). *Global indigenous media: Cultures, poetics, and politics*. Durham, NC: Duke University Press.

Wortham, E. C. (2002). *Narratives of location: Televisual media and the production of indigenous identities in Mexico*. Doctoral dissertation, New York University. Available from https://www.worldcat.org/title/narratives-of-location-televisual-media-and-the-production-of-indigenous-identities-in-mexico/oclc/427557037 [Accessed 10 December 2018].

Xavier, I. (2001). *O cinema brasileiro moderno*, 2nd ed. São Paulo: Paz e Terra.

Xavier, I. (2007). *Sertão mar: Glauber Rocha e a Estética da Fome*. São Paulo: Cosac Naify.

Xavier, I. (2012). *Alegorias do subdesenvolvimento: Cinema Novo, Tropicalismo, Cinema Marginal*. São Paulo: Cosac Naify.

Xavier, I. (2016). A crítica não indiferente. In: Calil, C. A. (org.), *Uma situação colonial?* São Paulo: Companhia das Letras, 12–30.

Xavier, I. (2017). Red Light Bandit: Allegory and irony. In: Solomon, S. (ed.), *Tropicália and beyond: Dialogues in Brazilian film history*. Berlin: Archive Books, 85–121.

Zilio, C. (2009). Da antropofagia à Tropicália. *Arte e Ensaios: Revista do Programa de Pós-Graduação em Artes Visuais*, 18, 115–147. Available from http://www.carloszilio.com/textos/2009-da-antropofagia-a-tropicalia.pdf [Accessed 20 September 2020].

Zweig, S. (2000). *Brazil: A land of the future*, trans. Lowell A. Bangerter. Riverside, CA: Ariadne Press.

Filmography

2012 (2009). Directed by Roland Emmerich. USA: Columbia Pictures, Centropolis Entertainment, Farewell Productions and The Mark Gordon Company.
33 (2002). Directed by Kiko Goifman. Brazil: TV Cultura.
A Hungarian Passport (Um Passaporte Húngaro, 2001). Directed by Sandra Kogut. Belgium, France, Brazil: Cobra Films, Hunnia Filmstúdió, RTBF, República Pureza Filmes and Zeugma Films.
All is Brazil (Tudo é Brasil, 1997). Directed by Rogério Sganzerla. Brazil: Tupã Filmes.
Amazonas, Amazonas (1965). Directed by Glauber Rocha. Brazil: Luiz Augusto Mendes Produções Cinematográficas.
Antonio das Mortes (O Dragão da Maldade Contra o Santo Guerreiro, 1969). Directed by Glauber Rocha. Brazil, France, Germany: Mapa Filmes.
Arraial do Cabo (1959). Directed by Mário Carneiro and Paulo César Saraceni. Brazil: Saga Filmes.
Aruanda (1960). Directed by Linduarte Noronha. Brazil: Noronha e Vieira.
As Primeiras Imagens de Brasília (1956). Directed by Jean Manzon. Brazil: Atlântida Empresa Cinematográfica do Brasil S.A and Jean Mazon Films S.A.
Back to the Good Land (De Volta à Terra Boa, 2008). Directed by Vincent Carelli and Mari Corrêa. Brazil: Vídeo nas Aldeias.
Bang Bang (1971). Directed by Andrea Tonacci. Brazil: Total Filmes.
Barbosa (1988). Directed by Jorge Furtado. Brazil: Casa de Cinema de Porto Alegre, Luz Produções e NGM.
Barren Lives (Vidas Secas, 1963). Directed by Nelson Pereira dos Santos. Brazil: Luiz Carlos Barreto Produções Cinematográficas, Regina Filmes and Sino Filmes.
Berlin: Symphony of a Great City (1927). Directed by Walter Ruttmann. Germany: Les Productions Fox Europa and Deutsche Vereins-Film.
Bicycles of Nhanderu (Bicicletas de Nhanderú, 2011). Directed by Ariel Ortega and Patrícia Ferreira. Brazil: Vídeo nas Aldeias.
Blablablá (1968). Directed by Andrea Tonacci. Brazil: Total Filmes.
Black God, White Devil (Deus e o Diabo na Terra do Sol, 1964). Directed by Glauber Rocha. Brazil: Copacabana Filmes and Luiz Augusto Mendes Produções Cinematográficas.
Blade Runner (1982). Directed by Ridley Scott. USA: The Ladd Company, Shaw Brothers, Warner Bros. and Blade Runner Partnership.

Blood of the Condor (Yawar Mallku, 1969). Directed by Jorge Sanjinés. Bolivia: Ukamau Group.

Bororo Rituals and Feasts (Rituais e Festas Bororo, 1917). Directed by Luiz Thomas Reis. Brazil: Conselho Nacional de Proteção aos Índios.

Brasil S/A (2014). Directed by Marcelo Pedroso. Brazil: Símio Filmes e Vilarejo Filmes.

Brasília Segundo Feldman (1979). Directed by Vladimir Carvalho and Eugene Feldman. Brazil: CNRC.

Brasília: Contradictions of a New City (Brasília: Contradições de Uma Cidade Nova, 1967). Directed by Joaquim Pedro de Andrade. Brazil: Filmes do Serro

Brasilianas (1945-1956). Directed by Humberto Mauro. Brazil: Instituto Nacional de Cinema Educativo.

Brasiliários (1986). Directed by Sérgio Bazi and Zuleica Porto. Brazil: Candango Promoções Artísticas.

Brazil Year 2000 (Brasil Ano 2000, 1969). Directed by Walter Lima Jr. Brazil: Mapa Filmes and 2000 Film.

Bus 174 (Ônibus 174, 2002). Directed by José Padilha. Brazil: Zazen Produções.

Carlota Joaquina: Princess of Brazil (Carlota Joaquina: Princesa do Brasil, 1995). Directed by Carla Camurati. Brazil: Copacabana Filmes.

Carmen Miranda: Bananas is My Business (1995). Directed by Helena Solberg. Brazil, UK: Riofilme and Channel Four Films.

Cattle Callers (Aboio, 2005). Directed by Marília Rocha. Brazil: Anavilhana Filmes.

Central Station (Central do Brasil, 1998). Directed by Walter Salles. Brazil, France: Videofilmes, Riofilme, MACT Productions, E.S.R. Films Ltd. and Cinematográfica Superfilmes.

Chronically Unfeasible (Cronicamente Inviável, 1999). Directed by Sérgio Bianchi. Brazil: Agravo Produções Cinematográficas.

Chronicle of the Demolition (Crônica da Demolição, 2017). Directed by Eduardo Ades. Brazil: Imagem-Tempo.

City of God (Cidade de Deus, 2002). Directed by Fernando Meirelles. Brazil, France, Germany: O2 Filmes, VideoFilmes, Globo Filmes, Lumière, Wild Bunch, StudioCanal, Hank Levine Film and Lereby Productions.

Coluna Norte (1960). Directed by Jean Manzon. Brazil: Atlântida Empresa Cinematográfica do Brasil S.A. and Jean Mazon Films S.A.

Come Back, Sebastiana (Vuelve Sebastiana!, 1953). Directed by Jorge Ruiz and Augusto Roca. Bolivia: Bolivia Film.

Conversas no Maranhão (1977–83). Directed by Andrea Tonacci. Brazil: Andrea Tonacci.

Copacabana Mon Amour (1970). Directed by Rogério Sganzerla. Brazil: Belair Filmes.

Corumbiara: They Shoot Indians, Don't They? (Corumbiara, 2009). Directed by Vincent Carelli. Brazil: Vídeo nas Aldeias.

Defiant Brasília (Avenida Brasília Formosa, 2010). Directed by Gabriel Mascaro. Brazil: Plano 9 Produções Audiovisuais.

Diary of a Pregnant Woman (L'Opéra-mouffe, 1958). Directed by Agnès Varda. France: Ciné-tamaris.

Di Cavalcanti (1977). Directed by Glauber Rocha. Brazil: Embrafilme.

Drifter (Andarilho, 2006). Directed by Cao Guimarães. Brazil: Cinco em Ponto.

Elena (2012). Directed by Petra Costa. Brazil, USA: Busca Vida Films.

Elite Squad (Tropa de Elite, 2007). Directed by José Padilha. Brazil, USA, Argentina: Zazen Produções, Posto 9, Feijão Filmes, The Weinstein Company, Estúdios Mega, Quanta Centro de Produções Cinematográficas, Universal Pictures do Brasil and Costa Films.

Entranced Earth (Terra em Transe, 1967). Directed by Glauber Rocha. Brazil: Mapa Filmes.

Entre Temps (2011). Directed by Ana Vaz. Brazil, France: Le Fresnoy Studio National des Arts Contemporains.

ExPerimetral (2016). Directed by Daniel Santos. Brazil.

Ex-Shaman (Ex-Pajé, 2018). Directed by Luiz Bolognesi. Brazil: Buriti Filmes and Gullane.

Favela X Five (Cinco Vezes Favela, 1962). Directed by Marcos Farias, Miguel Borges, Cacá Diegues, Joaquim Pedro de Andrade and Leon Hirszman. Brazil: Centro Popular de Cultura da União Nacional de Estudantes and Saga Filmes.

Off the Field (Fora de Campo, 2010). Directed by Adirley Queirós and Thiago Mendonça. Brazil: Ceicine.

Found Memories (Histórias Que Só Existem Quando Lembradas, 2012). Directed by Julia Murat. Brazil, Argentina, France: Taiga Filmes, MPM Film, CEPA Audiovisual, Bonfilm, Ancine, Programa Ibermedia and CNC.

Germany Year 90 Nine Zero (Allemagne Année 90 Neuf Zéro, 1991). Directed by Jean-Luc Godard. France: FR2, Production Brainstorm, Gaumont and Périphéria.

Germany Year Zero (Germania Anno Zero, 1948). Directed by Roberto Rossellini. Italy, France, Germany: Tevere Film, SAFDI, UGC and DEFA.

Ghost Towns (Cidades Fantasmas, 2017). Directed by Tyrell Spencer. Brazil: Casa de Cinema de Porto Alegre, Galo de Briga and Globo Filmes.

Girl's Celebration (A Festa da Moça, 1987). Directed by Vincent Carelli. Brazil: Vídeo nas Aldeias.

Good Manners (As Boas Maneiras, 2017). Directed by Juliana Rojas and Marco Dutra. Brazil, France, Germany: Canal+, Centre National du Cinéma et de l'Image, Animée, Dezenove Som e Imagem, Filmes do Caixote, Globo Filmes, Good Fortune Films, Urban Factory and ZDF/Arte.

Guarani Exile (Desterro Guarani, 2011). Directed by Ariel Ortega, Patrícia Ferreira, Ernesto de Carvalho and Vincent Carelli. Brazil: Vídeo nas Aldeias.

Habana – Arte Nuevo de Hacer Ruinas (2006). Directed by Florian Borchmeyer. Germany: Glueck Auf Film, Koppfilm and Raros Media.

Here We Are, Waiting for You (Nós que Aqui Estamos por Vós Esperamos, 1999). Directed by Marcelo Masagão. Brazil: Agência Observatório.

Hills of Disorder (Serras da Desordem, 2006). Directed by Andrea Tonacci. Brazil: Extrema Produção Artística.

Homo Sapiens (2016). Directed by Nikolaus Geyrhalter. Switzerland, Germany, Austria: Nikolaus Geyrhalter Filmproduktion, ORF Film/Fernseh-Abkommen, ZDF/3sat and Filmfonds Wien.

Housemaids (Doméstica, 2012). Directed by Gabriel Mascaro. Brazil: Desvia.

How Tasty Was My Little Frenchman (Como Era Gostoso o Meu Francês, 1971). Directed by Nelson Pereira dos Santos. Brazil: Condor Filmes, Luiz Carlos Barreto Produções Cinematográficas and Regina Filmes.

HU Enigma (HU, 2011). Directed by Joana Traub Csekö and Pedro Urano. Brazil: Alice Filmes.

I've Already Become an Image (Já me Transformei em Imagem, 2008). Directed by Zezinho Yube. Brazil: Vídeo nas Aldeias.

Independence Day: Resurgence (2016). Directed by Roland Emmerich. USA: Twentieth Century Fox, TSG Entertainment, Centropolis Entertainment, Electric Entertainment, Moving Picture Company, Street Entertainment and Twisted Media.

Iracema (Iracema – Uma Transa Amazônica, 1974–81). Directed by Jorge Bodanzky and Orlando Senna. Brazil, West Germany: Stop Film and ZDF.

Is the City Only One? (A Cidade É Uma Só? 2011). Directed by Adirley Queirós. Brazil: 400 Filmes and Cinco da Norte/Ceicine.

Karioka (2014). Directed by Takumã Kuikuro. Brazil: AIKAX e Museu do Índio – FUNAI.

Kill Me Please (Mate-me, Por Favor, 2015). Directed by Anita Rocha da Silveira. Brazil, Argentina: Bananeira Filmes, Fado Filmes and Rei Cine.

Killed the Family and Went to the Movies (Matou a Família e Foi ao Cinema, 1969). Directed by Júlio Bressane. Brazil: Júlio Bressane Produções Cinematográficas.

Land of the Devil (El País del Diablo, 2008). Directed by Andrés Di Tella. Argentina: Secretaría de Cultura de la Nación.

Letter from Siberia (Lettre de Sibérie, 1957). Directed by Chris Marker. France: Argos-Films and Procinex.

London as a Village (2017). Directed by Takumã Kuikuro. UK, Brazil: People's Palace Projects and Brazil's Ministry of Culture.

Lucifer Rising (1972). Directed by Kenneth Anger. USA, UK, West Germany: Puck Film Productions.

Macunaíma (1969). Directed by Joaquim Pedro de Andrade. Brazil: Difilm, Filmes do Sêrro, Grupo Filmes and Condor Filmes.

Mad Max (1979). Directed by George Miller. Australia, USA: Kennedy Miller Productions and Mad Max Films.

Man Marked to Die (Cabra Marcado Para Morrer, 1984). Directed by Eduardo Coutinho. Brazil: Mapa Filmes.

Manassés (2009). Directed by Luisa Marques. Brazil.

Maranhão 66 (1966). Directed by Glauber Rocha. Brazil: Mapa Filmes.

Martyrdom (Martírio, 2017). Directed by Vincent Carelli, Ernesto de Carvalho and Tatiana Almeida. Brazil: Vídeo nas Aldeias.

Midnight (O Primeiro Dia, 1999). Directed by Walter Salles. Brazil, France: Haut et Court, La Sept-Arte, Riofilme and VideoFilmes.

Moi, un Noir (1958). Directed by Jean Rouch. France: Les Films de la Pléiade.

Nada Consta (2006). Directed by Santiago Dellape. Brazil: Lumiô Filmes.

Navajo Film Themselves (1966). Directed by Mike Anderson, Susie Benally, Alta Kahn, Johnny Nelson, Maxine Tsosie, Mary J. Tsosie and Al Clah. USA: Library of Congress, National Audiovisual Center and University of Pennsylvania.

Neighbouring Sounds (O Som Ao Redor, 2012). Directed by Kleber Mendonça Filho. Brazil: CinemaScópio.

News from a Private War (Notícias de uma Guerra Particular, 1999). Directed by João Moreira Salles and Kátia Lund. Brazil: VideoFilmes.

Night and Fog (Nuit et Brouillard, 1955). Directed by Alan Resnais. France: Argos Films.

O Bandeirante (1957). Directed by Jean Manzon. Brazil: Jean Mazon Films S.A.

O Cinema Falado (1986). Directed by Caetano Veloso. Brazil: Sky Light and Elipse.

O Quatrilho (1995). Directed by Fábio Barreto. Brazil: Filmes do Equador and Luiz Carlos Barreto Produções Cinematográficas.

Old-Time Veteran Countrymen (Conterrâneos Velhos de Guerra, 1990). Directed by Vladimir Carvalho. Brazil: Vertovisão.

Once There Was Brasília (Era Uma Vez Brasília, 2017). Directed by Adirley Queirós. Brazil, Portugal: Cinco da Norte e Terratreme Filmes.
Os Arara (1980). Directed by Andrea Tonacci. Brazil: Interpovos and TV Bandeirantes.
Our Indians (Yndio do Brasil, 1995). Directed by Sylvio Back. Brazil: Usina de Kyno.
Pacific (2009). Directed by Marcelo Pedroso. Brazil: Símio Filmes.
Pankararu de Brejo dos Padres (1977). Directed by Vladimir Carvalho. Brazil: Embrafilme.
Passage (Trecho, 2006). Directed by Clarissa Campolina and Helvécio Marins Jr. Brazil: Anavilhana Filmes.
Pierrot Le Fou (1965). Directed by Jean-Luc Godard. France, Italy: Films Georges de Beauregard, Rome Paris Films, SNC and Dino de Laurentiis Cinematografica.
Pindorama (1970). Directed by Arnaldo Jabor. Brazil: Columbia Pictures of Brasil, Companhia Cinematográfica Vera Cruz, Kamera Filmes and Screen Gems of Brasil.
Planas: Testimony about an Ethnocide (Planas: Testimonio de un Etnocidio, 1971). Directed by Marta Rodríguez and Jorge Silva. Colombia: Fundación Cine Documental.
Playing (Jogo de Cena, 2007). Directed by Eduardo Coutinho. Brazil: Matizar and VideoFilmes.
Prîara Jõ – After the Egg, the War (Prîara Jõ – Depois do Ovo, a Guerra, 2008). Directed by Komoi Panará. Brazil: Vídeo nas Aldeias.
Projeto Pulex (1991). Directed by Tadao Miaqui. Brazil: Núcleo de Animação RS.
Raoni (1978). Directed by Jean-Pierre Dutilleux and Luiz Carlos Saldanha. France, Belgium, Brazil: Pierre Louis Saguez Produções Cinematográficas, Société Nouvelle de Doublage SND and Valisa Films Prod.
Rap: The Song of Ceilândia (Rap: O Canto da Ceilândia, 2005). Directed by Adirley Queirós. Brazil: Universidade de Brasília.
República Guarani (1981). Directed by Sylvio Back. Brazil: Embrafilme and Sylvio Back Produções Cinematográficas.
Returning from Extinction (Fugindo da Extinção, 1999). Directed by Adrian Cowell. UK: Nomad Films/Channel 4.
Rio, 40 Degrees (Rio, 40 Graus, 1955). Directed by Nelson Pereira dos Santos. Brazil: Equipe Moacyr Fenelon.
River of Mud (Rio de Lama, 2016). Directed by Tadeu Jungle. Brazil: Academia de Filmes, Beenoculus and Maria Farinha Filmes.
Ruin (Ruína, 2016). Directed by Gabraz Sanna. Brazil: Gabriel Sanna Castello Branco
Ruins (Ruínas, 2009). Directed by Manoel Mozos. Portugal: O Som e a Fúria.

Sacris Pulso (2008). Directed by Ana Vaz. Australia, Brazil: Royal Melbourne Institute of Technology.
Sangue de Tatu (1986). Directed by Marcos Bertoni. Brazil.
Santiago (2007). Directed by João Moreira Salles. Brazil: VideoFilmes.
Scorpio Rising (1963). Directed by Kenneth Anger. USA: Puck Film Productions.
Sermões – A História de Antônio Vieira (1989). Directed by Júlio Bressane. Brazil: Embrafilme and Júlio Bressane Produções Cinematográficas.
Shantytown of My Love (Favela dos Meus Amores, 1934). Directed by Humberto Mauro. Brazil: Brasil Vita Filmes.
Should I Kill Them? (Mato Eles?, 1982). Directed by Sérgio Bianchi. Brazil: Sérgio Bianchi Produções Cinematográficas.
Stalker (1979). Directed by Andrei Tarkovsky. Soviet Union: Mosfilm.
Star Power Ready (2011). Directed by Luisa Marques. Brazil.
Still Life (2006). Directed by Jia Zhangke. China, Hong Kong: Xstream Pictures and Shanghai Film Studios.
Strike Days (Dias de Greve, 2009). Directed by Adirley Queirós. Brazil: Ceicine.
Suite Habana (2003). Directed by Fernando Pérez. Cuba: ICAIC.
T,O,U,C,H,I,N,G (1968). Directed by Paul Sharits. USA.
Tabu (1982). Directed by Júlio Bressane. Brazil: Embrafilme and Júlio Bressane Produções Cinematográficas.
Talk to Her (Hable Con Ella, 2002). Directed by Pedro Almodóvar. Spain: El Deseo, Antena 3 Televisión, Good Machine and Vía Digital.
Tava, The House of Stone (Tava, A Casa de Pedra, 2012). Directed by Ariel Ortega, Patrícia Ferreira, Ernesto de Carvalho and Vincent Carelli. Brazil: Vídeo nas Aldeias.
Terra dos Índios (1979). Directed by Zelito Viana. Brazil: Embrafilme and Mapa Filmes.
The Age of Stone (A Idade da Pedra, 2013). Directed by Ana Vaz. Brazil, France: Le Fresnoy Studio National des Arts Contemporains.
The Age of the Earth (A Idade da Terra, 1980). Directed by Glauber Rocha. Brazil: C.P.C. Cinematografica, Centro de Produção e Comunicação, Embrafilme, Filmes 3, Glauber Rocha Comunicações Artísticas and Ponto Filmes.
The Angel Was Born (O Anjo Nasceu, 1969). Directed by Júlio Bressane. Brazil: Júlio Bressane Produções Cinematográficas.
The Brazilwood Man (O Homem do Pau-Brasil, 1982). Directed by Joaquim Pedro de Andrade. Brazil: Embrafilme, Filmes do Serro and Lynx Filmes.
The Cult (A Seita, 2015). Directed by André Antônio. Brazil: Ponte Produções.

The Day After Tomorrow (2004). Directed by Roland Emmerich. USA: Twentieth Century Fox, Centropolis Entertainment, Lions Gate Films, Mark Gordon Productions and Mel's Cite du Cinema.

The Dead and the Others (Chuva é Cantoria na Aldeia dos Mortos, 2018). Directed by João Salaviza and Renée Nader Messora. Brazil, Portugal: Entrefilmes, Karõ Filmes and Material Bruto.

The Demolition of a Wall (Démolition d'un Mur, 1896). Directed by Auguste Lumière and Louis Lumière. France: Lumière.

The Discovery of Brazil (O Descobrimento do Brasil, 1937). Directed by Humberto Mauro. Brazil: Instituto Nacional de Cinema Educativo and Instituto do Cacau da Bahia.

The Dismantling of the Mount (O Desmonte do Monte, 2018). Directed by Sinai Sganzerla. Brazil: Mercúrio Produções.

The Fever (A Febre, 2019). Directed by Maya Da-Rin. Brazil, France, Germany: Tamanduá Vermelho, Enquadramento Produções, Still Moving and Komplizen.

The Guns (Os Fuzis, 1964). Directed by Ruy Guerra. Brazil, Argentina: Copacabana Filmes, Daga Filmes and Inbracine Filmes.

The Harbour (O Porto, 2013). Directed by Clarissa Campolina, Julia de Simone, Luiz Pretti and Ricardo Pretti. Brazil: Mirada Filmes, Alumbramento, Teia+Anavilhana and Toada Filmes.

The Hour of the Furnaces (La Hora de los Hornos, 1968). Directed by Fernando Solanas and Octavio Getino. Argentina: Grupo Cine Liberación and Solanas Productions.

The Hyperwomen (As Hipermulheres, 2011). Directed by Takumã Kuikuro, Carlos Fausto and Leonardo Sette. Brazil: Vídeo nas Aldeias.

The Last of the Hiding Tribes (1999). Directed by Adrian Cowell. UK: Nomad Films/Channel 4.

The Man with a Movie Camera (1929). Directed by Dziga Vertov. Soviet Union: VUFKU.

The Mission (1986). Directed by Roland Joffé. UK: Goldcrest Films.

The Motorcycle Diaries (2004). Directed by Walter Salles. Argentina, Brazil, United States, Chile, Peru, United Kingdom, Germany and France: FilmFour, Wildwood Enterprises, Tu Vas Voir Productions, BD Cine, Inca Films S.A., Sahara Films, Senator Film Produktion and Sound for Film.

The Prisoner of the Iron Bars (O Prisioneiro da Grade de Ferro, 2003). Directed by Paulo Sacramento. Brazil: Olhos de Cão Produções Cinematográficas.

The Red Light Bandit (O Bandido da Luz Vermelha, 1968). Directed by Rogério Sganzerla. Brazil: Urano Filmes.
There Is Land! (Há Terra!, 2016). Directed by Ana Vaz. France, Brazil: Spectre Productions and La Fabrique Phantom.
The Struggle Goes On (Vamos à Luta!, 2002). Directed by Divino Tserewahú. Brazil: Vídeo nas Aldeias.
Thirteen Days Away from the Sun (Treze Dias Longe do Sol, 2018). Directed by Luciano Moura. Brazil: Rede Globo.
Toda Cor Abandonada É Violenta (2014). Directed by Luisa Marques. Brazil.
Tribute to Matta-Clark (Homenagem a Matta-Clark, 2015). Directed by Joana Traub Csekö and Pedro Urano. Brazil: Pedro Urano.
Triste Trópico (1974). Directed by Arthur Omar. Brazil: Melopeia Cinematográfica.
Tropical Curse (A Maldição Tropical, 2016). Directed by Luisa Marques. Brazil.
Two Villages, One Path (Duas Aldeias, Uma Caminhada, 2008). Directed by Ariel Ortega, Jorge Morinico and Germano Beñites. Brazil: Vídeo nas Aldeias.
Two Way Street (Rua de Mão Dupla, 2004). Directed by Cao Guimarães. Brazil.
Vinicius (2005). Directed by Miguel Faria Jr. Brazil: 1001 Filmes and Globo Filmes.
White Elephant (Elefante Blanco, 2012). Directed by Pablo Trapero. Argentina, Spain, France: ARTE, Borsalino Productions, Canal+ España, Canal+, Full House, INCAA, ICAA, Maneki Films, Matanza Cine, Morena Films, Patagonik Film Group, TVE and Wild Bunch.
White Out, Black In (Branco Sai, Preto Fica, 2014). Directed by Adirley Queirós. Brazil: 400 Filmes and Cinco da Norte/Ceicine.
Who is Beta? (Quem É Beta?, 1972). Directed by Nelson Pereira dos Santos. Brazil, France: Regina Filmes and Dahlia Films.
Wings of Desire (Der Himmel über Berlin, 1987). Directed by Wim Wenders. West Germany and France: Basis-Film-Verleih GmbH and Argos Films.
Zweig (1998). Directed by Edgardo Cozarinsky. France: Les Films d'Ici and France 3.

Index

33 69
'100' 151
2012 11

abyssal identity crisis 192
Adair, John 204
aesthetics 56, 59, 72, 221, 248, 253, 266
 aesthetic experimentation 52
 aesthetic movement 262
 and Cinema Novo 44–5, 47
 and discourse 110
 of garbage 58, 59, 115–16, 117
 of hunger 49–50, 52, 59, 117, 247
 intermedial aesthetics 14, 133, 138, 140, 257, 258
 and sci-fi genre 39–40, 116
 spatial aesthetics 81
 and Tropicália 144, 145
'Aesthetics of Dreaming' 50, 52, 96
'Aesthetics of Hunger' 49, 50, 95, 247
Afghanistan, invasions of 20
African percussion 117
Agência Pública 151
Age of Stone, The 1, 13, 25, 73, 77, 83, 84, 87, 90, 93, 98–9, 128, 248, 250, 254, 256, 258, 259
 camera movement 99–100
 CGI-generated ruin 13, 92, 93, 98, 254, 256, 259
 circular panoramic view 99–100
 demystification 95
 form and content 95
 monumental structure 91–2
 monument-ruin 103
 multi-temporality of the even 95
 panoramic shot 105
 science friction documentary 102–8
 as a sci-fi documentary 102–3, 129
 silence as part of soundtrack in 105
 sound design 100–1
 space and time in 102–3

Age of the Earth, The 2, 13, 52, 77, 91, 96–8, 100, 101, 105, 109, 130, 131, 247, 255, 262
Aguirre, Mariano 234–5
Akomfrah, John 154
Akuntsu people 15, 243, 260, 278277 n.1
Aldeia Verdadeira 238
Alea, Tomás Gutiérrez 252
Alencar, José de 141, 191, 202
allegories/allegorical strategies 8–9, 10, 51, 52, 96, 119, 138, 202, 246–7, 253
 mode of 110
 power 123
 of underdevelopment 16, 41, 50, 51, 253
All is Brazil 171
Almendros, Néstor 252
Alvarenga, Clarisse 222, 223, 230, 238, 241
Amancio, Tunico 62
Amazonas, Amazonas 55
Amerindian perspectivism 223
Andrade, Ana Luiza 26, 28
Andrade, Joaquim Pedro de 43, 82, 137, 192, 194, 195, 196, 259, 276 n.4 (Ch 12)
Andrade, Jonathas de 263–4
Andrade, Mário de 192, 193
Andrade, Oswald de 58, 141, 142, 143, 193, 273 n.7
Angel of History 7, 8, 9
Angelus Novus (painting) 7, 9, 252
Angel Was Born, The 52, 58
Anger, Kenneth 163
another history 95
anthropophagy 14, 58, 96, 135, 139, 141–6, 160, 193, 196, 214
anti-art 139–40, 142, 143
anti-imperialism 43, 59
antiteleological themes 51–2, 58
Antônio, André 86
Antonio das Mortes 51, 57
appropriation film 73, 167, 237, 261

Aqui Tudo Parece Que É Ainda Construçãoe Já É Ruína, A Partir de Fora da Ordem 136
Araújo, Nancy 111–12
architectural failure(s) 14, 147–8, 257
  Brasília as 79–80, 81, 102, 109
  Carmen Miranda Museum as 164, 172–3
  Ceilândia as 113
  HU as 176, 177, 178, 180, 181, 185, 187, 259
  National Museum 4
  Rio's *favelas* as 142
architecture
  Lévi-Strauss on 31
  nature's taking over of 222
  and ruination 264
  as a sign of history and the passage of time 93
archives 3, 5, 63, 166, 236–7
  archival footage 40, 82, 101, 237
  archival photographs 121, 165, 218
  archiving as intervention 166
  and cinema, intersection of 165
  fake visual achieves 111–12
Argentina 22, 44, 218, 233
Arraial do Cabo 55–6
art and life 139
Aruanda 47–8, 55–6
assimilation
  of literary excerpts 173
  of performance art 167
  of technical precariousness into aesthetics 56
Assis, Machado de 105, 258
asymmetric symmetry 181
Atelier Varan 278 n.5
Atlântida studios 137, 268 n.1
Atlas of Emotion 262
Através 185
audience, establishing a connection with 39, 45, 58, 84, 140, 143, 207, 208, 219
Audiovisual Law 63
audiovisual production 74, 178, 208
Aufderheide, Patricia 70
Augé, Marc 20–1, 31–2, 38
authenticity 69, 70, 71, 117, 135, 202, 208, 251
authorship 45, 210–11, 231
avacalhar 110, 116, 118

avant-garde 10, 51, 57, 71, 73, 74, 88, 100, 142, 177, 255
Avelar, Idelber 14, 22, 156, 252

Back, Sylvio 214, 280 n.6
Back to the Good Land 215
bad conscience 57, 67–8, 230
Badiou, Alain 87
Balsom, Erika 71, 73, 74
Bandeira, Philipi 16, 231
Bang Bang 52, 58, 278 n.14
Barbosa 89
Barclay, Barry 278 n.7
Baron, Jaimie 237
Barra, Pablo Léon de la 173
Barren Lives 45–6, 48, 54
Barreto, Eric 171
Barreto, Luiz Carlos 45, 54, 141
Barros, Manoel de 263
Barros, Rodrigo Lopes de 8–9, 12, 16, 17, 26, 28, 40, 41, 42, 55, 59, 118, 246, 252
Basualdo, Carlos 145
Baudelaire, Charles 8
Bazi, Sérgio 94
Bazin, André 71, 86, 121
Beiguelman, Giselle 263
Be Marginal, Be a Hero 144
Beñites, Germano 15–16, 237, 250
Benjamin, Walter 7–8, 10–11, 29, 37, 51, 94, 219, 252
Bentes, Ivana 145, 193, 196, 232, 276 n.5 (Ch 12)
Berlin: Symphony of a Great City 71
Berlin Wall 3, 40, 65, 127, 146
Berman, Marshall 157
Bernardet, Jean-Claude 56, 57, 61, 67, 82, 215, 275 n.2 (Ch 11)
Bertoni, Marcos 89
Bethânia, Maria 263
Betim, Felipe 150–1
Bianchi, Sérgio 214
Biardeau, Javier 37
Bicho 243
Bicycles of Nhanderu 213
Bingham, Hiram 21
Bipolar Show 264
Birri, Fernando 44, 54
Black God, White Devil 46, 51, 52, 57, 66, 247, 269 n.11

Index

Blackmore, Lisa 176, 252–3
Blood of the Condor 212
Bodanzky, Jorge 199, 201, 228, 232, 259
Bólides 274 n.12
Bolivia 44, 65, 203–4, 210
Bolognesi, Luiz 277 n.13
Bolsonaro, Jair 4–5, 64, 66, 265
bombardments 3, 7, 14, 27, 39, 153
Borchmeyer, Florian 27
Bororo, Chico 101
Bororo Rituals and Feasts 191–2
Bota-abaixo 149, 150
Boym, Svetlana 19, 184, 235
Brasil, André 219, 232, 244
Brasil Distópico 271 n.3 (Ch 5)
Brasília 1, 13, 16
 access to 113
 as an untouchable icon 127
 architecture as segregation and social control 81
 architecture errors 102
 contentious on screen 81–4
 contradictory 81
 as a delirium 96, 98
 displacement of vulnerable population who helped to build 111
 dualities of 80
 heterotopia 128–30
 and its satellite cities, segregation between 110
 natural-artificial aspects 105
 origins of 99
 questioning the official narrative of 129
 (re)construction of 88
 and Rome, comparison between 80
 ruins of 129
 spatiality of 83
Brasília 80, 94
Brasília: Contradictions of a New City 82
Brasilianas 269 n.14
Brasiliários 94, 101, 262
Brasília Segundo Feldman 82
Brasil S/A 86
Brazil
 backwardness of 187, 247, 249
 cinema production, and underdevelopment (*see also* contemporary documentaries; *specific documentaries and films*)
 luxury in 33
 modernity/modernism of 36–7, 96, 164, 165, 167, 180
 modernization process 24–5
 new Brazil, making of 66, 80
 notion of anthropophagy in 146
 progress 29–37
 underdevelopment debate in 24
 Brazil: A Land of the Future 245
 Brazilian Cinema Foundation 62
 Brazilian Cinematheque 49
 Brazilian Documentarist Association 62
 Brazilian identity 30, 137, 142, 171
 "Brazilian" image 142
 Brazilianness 17, 30, 42, 96, 180, 192
 Brazilwood Man, The 276 n.4 (Ch 12)
 Brazil Year 2000 2, 15, 51, 197–8, 202, 260
 Brennand, Francisco 252
 Bressane, Júlio 58
 Brown, Wendy 22
 Brumadinho tailing dam 4
 Bruno, Giuliana 262
 Bruzzi, Stella 71
 Buck-Morss, Susan 8, 29
 building cuts 184–5
 building/Nation analogy 180
 building promises 151–2
 Burton, Julianne 53, 54
 Bus 174 68, 85

Caaró, Rio Grande do Sul 234–5
Cabral, Sérgio 149
CachoeiraDoc 64
Caesar, Augustus, statue of 30
Cais do Valongo (Valongo Wharf) 154, 159
Caixeta de Queiroz, Ruben 16, 231, 232–3, 241
Calil, Carlos Augusto 48
camera as an extension of the body 100
Campolina, Clarissa 14, 62, 133, 158, 160, 250, 258
Camurati, Carla 270 n.4
Canclini, Néstor García 34, 35, 36, 37
candangos 81, 82
Candle King, The 273 n.7
Canejo, Cynthia 142, 143
cannibalism 139, 141, 146, 193, 194, 195–6, 202
cannibalism/anthropophagy duality 196

'Cannibalist Manifesto' 58, 141
Capela, Carlos Eduardo Schmidt 26, 28, 33
capitalism 37–8, 156–7
  cultural capitalism 145
  cultural logic of late capitalism 261
  dependency capitalism 24
Cardoso, Fernando Henrique 65, 66
Carelli, Vincent 12, 15, 16, 74, 189, 190, 204–5, 206, 207, 210–11, 213–14, 215, 216, 217, 218, 220, 221, 222, 224, 227–7, 228–30, 233, 236, 243–4, 250, 260, 261, 265
Carlota Joaquina: Princess of Brazil 270 n.4
Carmen Miranda: Bananas is My Business 171
Carmen Miranda Museum 14, 134, 163–4, 171, 176, 258
Carmen Miranda's Ghost 168, 258
Carmen Miranda syndrome 152, 257, 258
Carneiro, Mário 55
Carvalho, Ernesto de 16, 82, 205, 233, 236, 250
Carvalho, Vladimir 81
Cássia, Edna de 199, 260
Cassino da Urca 171, 264
Castells, Manuel 156
Castro, Amílcar de 143
Castro, Fidel 27
catastrophes 4, 5, 7, 12, 17, 27, 40, 41, 51, 59, 92, 118, 124, 138, 140, 198, 200, 246, 252
Cattle Callers 62
Ceilândia 82, 83, 113, 114, 128, 254, 255, 262
Central Plateau 79, 262
Central Station 67, 85
Centre for Indigenous Advocacy 204–5
cepalista 23, 24, 25
Chácara do Céu 264
Chambers, Emma 2
chanchadas 43, 58, 268 n.1
Chapada dos Veadeiros 103, 128, 262, 271 n.5 (Ch 6)
Cheuiche, Jacques 101
Chichen Itza pyramids, Mexico 21, 38
Chile 44
Christ the Redeemer 5
Chronically Unfeasible 67

Chronicle of the Demolition 262
CineDocumenta 64
cinema and literature, relationship between 139
Cinema da Retomada 13, 18, 61, 63, 64, 85, 140–1, 249
  and global picture 65
  and present-day filmmaking 66–7
Cinema Marginal 2, 9, 12, 40, 50, 58, 59, 63, 77, 115, 116, 117, 119, 246, 247, 250, 253, 265
cinemanovistas 43, 44, 45, 46, 49, 51, 53, 55, 58, 66, 67, 100, 192, 216, 252, 259, 265, 266
Cinema Novo 2, 9, 12, 15, 40, 42, 43–4, 50, 57, 59–60, 63, 65–6, 67, 72, 77, 115, 117, 137, 176–7, 188, 189, 192, 193, 198, 201, 202, 203, 215, 228, 246, 250, 253, 259, 265
  and aesthetics 44–5
  class tension 67
  as continental project 44
  criticism of middle-class stance 57
  dissolution of 59
  inequality and roughness depiction 46
  innovative aesthetics of 45
  and Italian Neorealism 45
  marks of underdevelopment 46
  nonfictional values 55
  phases of 59
  replacement with foreign films 47
  transformation of social criticism into central political issue 49–50
  ugly, sad films of 50, 247
  violence and misery, representation of 68
  and VNA documentaries 216
cinema-process 218
Cinéma Vérité 53
Circuladô 30, 135
City of God 85
Clark, Lygia 143
Coca-Cola-Indian allegory 199–202
cognitive mapping 261
Coletivo de Cinema em Ceilândia (Ceicine) 110
Coletivo Fulni-ô de Cinema 202
Coletivo Kuikuro de Cinema 202
Coletivo Mbyá-Guarani 202, 215
Colombia 65

colonialism/colonialization 6, 21, 23, 25, 32–3, 34, 47, 48–9, 54, 65, 83, 97, 154, 186, 189, 194, 199, 202, 203, 213, 233, 234, 241, 245, 261
Come Back, Sebastiana 204
commodification 8, 14, 22, 38, 133, 134, 142, 144, 146, 187, 251
Concannon, Amy 2
Conde, Maite 150, 268 n.6 (Ch 2)
Conquista del Desierto, La 218
constitution of communities 246, 249
contact films 222, 227
contemporary documentaries 1, 2, 42, 86, 211, 246, 247–9, 252, 266; *see also* documentaries
  aesthetic experimentation 52
  aims of 71–2
  and authenticity 71
  boldness of 9
  and Cinema Novo 72, 216
  focusing on human-made landscape 147
  framing ruinous reality 6–7, 11, 54, 69, 253
  indigenous media 212
  intermedial aesthetics 258
  of progress and (under)development 74, 149
  and tradition 98
  and Tropicália 140, 141, 143, 257
  within unviable nation 66–75
  and VNA 211, 212, 213
  ways of registering reality 69
Conti, Mario Sergio 5
contradictions 137
  of living in ruins 28
  of progress and (under)development in Rio de Janeiro 147
  of ruins functioning as home for the characters 27
Contreras, Miguel 37
conventional documentaries 69, 70, 77, 83–4, 118, 121–3
Conversas no Maranhão 214
Copacabana Mon Amour 169–71
Corbusier, Le 79, 158, 173
Corcovado mountain 147
Cordoba, Antonio 127
Córdova, Amalia 212, 213, 234
Corrêa, José Celso Martinez 273 n.7

Corrêa, Mari 206, 215, 219–20
Corrigan, Timothy 73, 250
Corumbiara territory 220–1
Corumbiara: They Shoot Indians, Don't They? 1, 15, 74, 189, 213, 217–20, 228, 230, 231, 260
  common language, lack of 223–4
  damaged indigenous territory 220–1
  deforestation 200, 220, 222, 228
  ethics of political action 220
  indigenous *maloca* 194, 195, 227–8
  presence of visiting anthropologists 224–7
  Santos's house 221–2
  spatial representation in 220
  visit to an indigenous village 221–4
cosmopolitanism 193, 200
Costa, Lúcio 13, 79, 80, 180, 234, 270 n.1 (Ch 4)
Costa, Petra 69
Coutinho, Eduardo 69, 247–8, 275 n.2 (Ch 11)
Couto, José Geraldo 276 n.4 (Ch 12)
Cowell, Adrian 215
Cox, Carlos 97
creative destruction 156
critical short films 56
critical storytelling 75, 77, 88, 251, 265
critical thinking 16, 46, 93, 95, 130, 142, 215, 253
criticism and creativity 52
Csekö, Joana Traub 12, 15, 134, 152–3, 175, 176, 177, 178, 180–1, 182, 184, 185, 250, 257, 259, 265
Cuba 26–9, 40, 44, 252
Cuban Revolution (1953–9) 27, 44
Cult, The 86
cultural anthropophagy 58, 139, 142, 143, 145–6
cultural emancipation 48, 247
cultural uprising 57–8
Cunha, Euclides da 33–4

D'Almeida, Neville 58
Da-Rin, Maya 277 n.13
Day After Tomorrow, The 11
Dead and the Others, The 277 n.13
death of populism 137
Debret, Jean-Baptiste 264

decaying film stocks 40, 56
decentralization, of traditional film production 203
decontextualization 80
Defiant Brasília 41
dehistoricization 80
de Jesus, Eduardo 81, 82, 83, 86
Deleuze, Gilles 13, 93, 103, 105, 254
Dellape, Santiago 89
Delpeut, Peter 40
democracy 33, 109, 138
Demolition of a Wall, The 39
De Niro, Robert 235
Dennison, Stephanie 61, 68, 268 n.6 (Ch 2)
dependency theory 24, 25, 267 n.4
Depois do Futuro exhibition 276 n.4 (Ch 11)
Deren, Maya 100, 255
Desfile aos Heróis do Brasil 195
Designing the Opening of a Home, As It Could Be 264
Detroit 6, 37
development *see* progress and (under) development
Diary of a Pregnant Woman 73
Di Cavalcanti 55
diegetic sound 45, 59, 101, 103, 186, 224
diegetic space 59
Diegues, Carlos 43
digital 165–6
digital revolution 141
digital technology 74, 165–6
  access to 208, 216
  advantages of 63, 64
  digital mock ups 159, 160, 259
  and nonfiction production 141
Dillon, Brian 2, 20, 42, 84, 136, 184
Director, El 22
disappearing landscapes 41
discourse, and aesthetics 110
Discovery of Brazil, The 276 n.3 (Ch 12)
Dismantling of the Mount, The 262
disruption 237
Di Tella, Andrés 218–19, 230
DOCTV 64, 178
documentaries 8–10, 11, 13, 14, 15, 16, 62, 248, 250; *see also* contemporary documentaries

blurring the boundaries between fiction and nonfiction 266
categorization 72–3
as a conveyor of reality 54
digital documentaries 64
experimental documentaries 109, 140, 161
experimentalist impetus 62
experimental or hybrid documentaries 63
film festivals 64
increase in 63
and photography, intersection of 175
as political tool 65
principles 70
production interruption 61
and revolutionary cinema 53–7
and science fiction 12, 13, 16, 77, 84, 90, 102, 118, 121, 256
science friction documentary 13–14
science nonfiction documentary 14
for self-reflection and change 206
sensu stricto 69
stylistic diversity 68
TV reportage and news broadcasting 70
unveiling stories in uncertain and fluid way 70–1
and video art, proximity between 141
video format 62
voice of 250
documentarist-diggers 251, 254
Documentary School of Santa Fe 54
Drifter 62
Duarte, Luiz Fernando Dias 3
Dunn, Christopher 145
Dutra, Marco 86
dystopia 125, 265

ecological disaster 2, 200, 202, 220, 222, 228, 263
Economist, The 5
Ecuador 65
Edensor, Tim 37–8, 39, 123, 129, 182
Eisenstein, Sergei 117
Elduque, Albert 97
Elena 69
Eletrobrás 208
Elevado da Perimetral 14, 133
Elite Squad 85

Elsaesser, Thomas 86–7
Embrafilme 61, 63, 270 n.1 (Ch 3)
Emmerich, Roland 11
Enlightenment 23
Entranced Earth 8, 40–1, 42, 51, 52, 55, 117, 133, 137, 138, 147, 177, 188, 246, 247, 262
Entre As Ruínas 33–4
Entre Temps 93, 95, 101
environmental art 143
Equilíbrio de Frutas Sobre a Cabeça, Sobos Olhares de Carmen Miranda 167
equivocation 223, 224
Espinosa, Julio García 212
essay films 72–3, 248, 250
ethics 72, 248
 of political action 220–1
 of realism 86–7, 91, 112
É Tudo Verdade 64
Eurocentricism 40, 48, 86, 247
excavations 251
experimental films 89, 250
experimentation cinema 83
ExPerimetral 1, 14, 25, 153–8, 160, 187, 258
Ex-Shaman 277 n.13
extra-diegetic sound 59, 186

Fabris, Annateresa 146
Faria, Miguel, Jr. 270 n.3
Fausto, Carlos 231
favelas 31, 43, 55, 68, 85, 111, 149
Favela X Five 43
Feldman, Eugene 82
Ferreira, Jairo 139
Ferreira, Patrícia 16, 233–6, 250
Ferreyra, Gustavo 22
Fever, The 277 n.13
fiction and nonfiction 83–4, 250
 blurring boundaries between 2, 9, 44, 59, 112, 255, 266
 dialogue between 68
 overlapping 83, 121–2, 199
FIFA World Cup (2014) 4, 14, 133, 149, 152, 153, 156, 256
Filho, Kleber Mendonça 41
film preservation, neglect of 49
film's second *novum* 124
Fish, Leslie 168, 258

Five Days in Brasília 80, 94
Flamengo Park 152, 164, 165
flying saucers 102, 117–18, 120, 168, 173, 262
Folha de S.Paulo 5
Fora da Ordem 30, 36, 135
Fordlândia 263
foreignism 173
form and content 95
forumdoc.bh 64
Foucault, Michel 113, 128
Found Memories 41
four Christs 96–7, 98, 109
Fourth Cinema 278 n.7
França, Andréa 74, 141
French New Wave 45, 53, 100
Freyre, Gilberto 32, 33
frivolity 86, 88
furious frivolity 86, 116
Furtado, Celso 1, 12, 24–5, 46, 47, 247
Furtado, Gustavo Procopio 71, 74, 82, 89, 111–12, 124, 127, 191–2, 206, 227–8, 272 n.5
Furtado, Jorge 89

Gallo, Rubén 180
Gallois, Dominique 205
garage cinema 13, 72, 86, 248
Garcia, Marília 264
gender issues 164
genocide and ethnocide 217–18, 219
geography 34
German Trümmerfilm 39
Germany Year 90 Nine Zero 65
Germany Year Zero 28, 65
Getino, Octavio 9, 54, 73
Geyrhalter, Nikolaus 11
Ghost Towns 263
Gianikian, Yervant 40
Gil, Gilberto 141
Ginsburg, Faye 15, 204, 208–9, 239, 241
Giorgio Agamben 248
Girl's Celebration 205, 217
Gleghorn, Charlotte 15, 212
Godard, Jean-Luc 65, 117
Goiânia 221
Goiás 83
Goifman, Kiko 69
Gonzalez-Foerster, Dominique 173

Good Manners 86
Goulart, João 25, 43, 51
Gouvêa, Luiz Alberto de Campos 111
governmental scheme 64
graffiti 154–5
Gray, Hugh 273 n.6
Grupo Ukamau 212
Guanabara Bay 262
Guarani, The 191
Guarani Exile 1, 16, 190, 210, 236, 237, 241, 260
Guarani-Kaiowá 190, 213, 219, 243
Guarani people 16, 233–5, 236–7, 239, 241, 260–1
Guattari, Félix 13, 93, 105, 254
Guerra, Ruy 43, 46, 137
Guimarães, Cao 62
Guimarães, César 113
Guimarães, Victor 219, 274 n.8
Gullar, Ferreira 143
Guns, The 46
Gustafsson, Mats 160
Gustavo Capanema Palace 180

Habana – Arte Nuevo de Hacer Ruinas 27
Habib, André 8, 40, 56, 182, 254
Harbour, The 1, 14, 25, 133, 158–61, 187, 258, 259
Hargreaves, Inês 227
Harrison, Regina 21, 238
Harvey, David 156
Havana 26–8, 38
Hell, Julia 6, 19–20, 40, 252, 254
Hendrix, Jimi 117
Here We Are, Waiting for You 63
Herkenhoff, Paulo 146
Herwitz, Daniel 127
heterotopia 128–30
Hills of Disorder 214, 232
Hilst, Hilda 105, 256
Hirzsman, Leon 43
history as catastrophe 138
Holanda, Sérgio Buarque de 32, 33
Hollywood 58
   cultural colonialism imposed by 47
   dystopic obsession 11
Holston, James 13, 82–3, 186
Homo Sapiens 11
Hora, Tatiana 114, 124

Hospital Universitário Clementino Fraga Filho *see* HU
Hour of the Furnaces, The 73
Housemaids 69
How Tasty Was My Little Frenchman 199, 202
HU 176, 179, 181, 186–8, 259
   collapse of south wing 185
   lame-leg 182, 186, 188
HU Enigma 1, 15, 134, 152–3, 175, 177–8, 259
   camera use in 185
   concrete structure and human body, parallel between 181–2
   decayed architecture and fractured ethos 180–8
   soundscape of 185
Hungarian Passport, A 69
hunger, aesthetics of 49–50, 52, 59, 95–6, 117, 247
Huyssen, Andreas 19, 156, 251
hybridity 35, 36, 63, 211, 257
Hyperwomen, The 231–2

Ignez, Helena 169
Ikeda, Marcelo 13, 72, 167, 168, 171, 248
Ilha do Fundão 175–6, 179, 180
imperfect cinema 212
Independence Day: Resurgence 11
independent documentary-makers 63, 64, 71, 211
Indians 191
   absence of 197–8, 202, 222
   capacity to make films 209–10
   Indian of the hole 228–7, 229–30, 260
   native territories 259–60
   and whites, distinct worlds of 241
   and whites, line separating 239–41
indigenous media 189, 201, 203
indigenous peoples 64–5, 191
   filmmaking training programmes 205–7
   indigenous imaginary 193, 196
   massacre of the Kanoê and Akuntsu groups 217–18, 219
   portrayal of 192
   portrayal of indigenous lands as invaded by rotten modernization 196
   power control over the production and distribution of images 204

as trainers 207
voices of 250
indigenous territories 16, 254
    assumption as damaged territory 221–4
    dispute over land 213
    impact of modernity/modernization on 202
    indigenous ruins 15
    and Vídeo nas Aldeias (VNA) 241, 243
industrialization and emancipation, tension between 50
Industrial Revolution 23
industrial ruins 37–8, 182
Institutional Act Nº5 (AI-5) 50, 192
Instituto Marlin Azul 64
intercultural approaches to film 139
intermediality 138, 139–40, 178, 250
    and cultural anthropophagy 139
    intermedial aesthetics 14, 133, 138, 140, 257, 258
    and Tropicália 139–40
    tropicalist intermediality 163, 167–73
Inter Povos 214
intimacy barriers 206
Invasion Eradication Campaign (CEI) 111
Iracema 2, 15, 25, 191, 199–200, 202, 228, 232, 260
Iraq invasions 20
Irons, Jeremy 235
Is the City Only One? 111–12
Italian Neorealism 39, 45, 53, 55, 59, 65, 86, 100
I've Already Become an Image 213

Jabor, Arnaldo 198
Jaguaribe, Beatriz 180, 252
Jameson, Fredric 13, 87–8, 261–2
Jardim, Reynaldo 143
Jerslev, Anne 139
Jobim, Tom 141
Joffé, Roland 235, 237
Johnson, Randal 59
Jor, Jorge Ben 228
José, Paulo 194
Julien, Isaac 154

Kanoê people 15, 190, 243, 260
Karioka 232
Kay, Cristóbal 23, 25, 26, 267 n.4

Killed the Family and Went to the Movies 52, 58
Kill Me Please 86
kind of Faustian dilemma, a 208–9
King, Edward 272 n.6
Kisedjê, Kamikia 207
Klee, Paul 7, 252
Kogut, Sandra 69
Kubitschek, Juscelino 25, 79
Kuikuro, Takumã 231

Labaki, Amir 68, 140–1, 270 n.3
Labra, Daniela 276 n.4 (Ch 11)
Lacerda, Rodrigo 207, 211
Lacis, Asja 29
Lafuente, Pablo 146
Lagnado, Lisette 146
Land of the Devil 218–19
Lane, Jill 230
language barriers 206
Larraín, Jorge 34
Last Adventure, The 263
Last of the Hiding Tribes, The 215
Latin America 6, 53, 203, 246
    comprehension of time and history 34–5
    economy of 23, 26
    indigenous people of 204, 212
    modernity in 34, 35
    neoliberalism in 22
    rise of new cinema in 55
    ruins in 21, 28, 246, 251–2
    underdevelopment of 23, 44
    and United States 164
Latin American artists 44
Latin American identity 164-165
Latin American militancy 95–6
Latin American Coordinating Council for Indigenous Film and Media 203
Latin American Magical Realism 96
Lazzara, Michael J. 21, 22, 26, 245, 251–2
Ledoux, Arno 100
leftism 109–10
legislations, and documentary production 63
Lessa, Bia 264
Letter from Siberia 73
Lévi-Strauss, Claude 1, 12, 29, 30, 32, 135, 173, 232, 253, 256, 257

on fragile urbanization of Brazilian
    metropolises 31
pessimistic view of progress 30, 31, 138
on Praça da Sé 30
in Rio de Janeiro 31
on ruinous Brazil 147
on statue of Augustus Caesar 30
view on distinction between the Old and
    New Worlds 31
view on Rio 147
Lima, Dellani 13, 72, 248
Lima, Walter, Jr. 2, 197, 198, 259
Lins, Consuelo 62, 64, 73–4, 141
Lispector, Clarice 13, 80, 92, 94–5, 101,
    102, 105, 255, 258
Lissovsky, Maurício 180
living ruins 176, 180, 253, 259
London as a Village 232
Lopes, Denilson 41
Löwy, Michael 7–8
Lucas Faulhauber 151
Lucchi, Angela Ricci 40
Lucifer Rising 163
Lumière brothers 39
Lund, Kátia 68
Luz Massacre 263

Macaulay, Rose 7, 21, 267 n.2 (Ch 1)
Machu Picchu, Peru 21, 38, 238
Macunaíma (film) 2, 15, 51, 192–3, 194–7,
    196, 202, 228, 260
Macunaíma (novel) 193–4
maloca 194, 195, 227–8
Manassés 163
Man Marked to Die 247–8
Mann, Thomas 137
Manuel, George 278 n.7
Man with a Movie Camera 71
Manzon, Jean 270 n.2 (Ch 4)
Maranhão 66, 55
marginais 252, 266
Maria Bethânia 150
Mariana tailing dam 4
Marins, Helvécio, Jr. 62
Marker, Chris 73
market-oriented art consumption 142–3
Marques, Luisa 12, 14–15, 73, 134, 152,
    163, 167, 171, 173, 250, 257, 258, 265
Marques, Pedro Neves 146

Marquim do Tropa 14, 83–4, 112, 113,
    255, 258–9
Martí, Silas 151–2, 164
Martyrdom 213, 219
Marxism 95–6, 130, 156
Masagão, Marcelo 63
Mascaro, Gabriel 41, 69
Matta-Clark, Gordon 184–5
Mauro, Humberto 269 n.13, 269 n.14, 276
    n.3 (Ch 12)
Meireles, Cildo 185–6
Melamed, Michel 264
Mello, Fernando Collor de 61, 65
Mello Franco, Bernardo 3
memory 27, 123, 263
    and creation 165
    and ethnology 32
    screen memories 209, 239
    and trauma 19
Mesquita, Cláudia 62, 64, 73–4, 111, 114,
    123, 141, 218
Messora, Renée Nader 277 n.13
Mexico 6, 21, 23, 65, 203
Miaqui, Tadao 89, 125
middle class 56, 57, 67, 146, 167
Midnight 67
Migliorin, Cezar 13, 69, 70, 71, 140,
    248, 250
Milanez, Felipe 215
military coup d'état (1964) 50, 51, 96, 110,
    130, 135, 138, 189, 192
military dictatorship 51, 259
Ministry of Culture 64, 178, 207
Miranda, Carmen 164–5, 167
Miranda, Ricardo 97
mirror game/mirror effect 205
Mission, The 235, 236
modern cinema, rise of 86
modernism/modernity 34–5, 39, 80, 150,
    186, 200, 257
    architecture starting from ground
        zero 186
    in Brazil as peripheral modernity 35–6
    dismissal of national colonial past 186
    figures, destructiveness of 42
    impact on urbanism of Rio 180
    landscape and division 150
    modern cities 36
    modernist architecture 176

modernist cities 79–80
rotten modernization 253, 257, 266
Mokoi Tekoá Petei Jeguatá 237–8
Moltke, Johannes von 8, 39–40, 45, 182, 254
Monroe Palace 262
montage 171, 233, 241
monument 93, 103, 256
monumentalization 128
'Monuments of Passaic, The' 136
Moraes, Ivonete dos Santos 103, 105, 258
Moraes de Sá, Paulo Sérgio 180
Moreira, Jorge Machado 179
Morinico, Jorge 15, 237, 250
Morrison, Bill 40
Motorcycle Diaries, The 21
Motta, Nelson 274 n.13
Mozos, Manoel 11
multinational interventions 25
Murat, Julia 41
Museu das Missões 234, 240
Museum of Modern Art 275 n.1 (Ch 10)

Nada Consta 89
Nagib, Lúcia 65, 86, 87, 91, 112, 138–9, 140, 143, 249, 269 n.12
Naples 29
Napolitano, Marcos 269 n.13
national-dependent society 24
National Film Agency 63
national identity 135, 146, 164, 195, 235
National Indian Foundation 204, 218, 222
National Indigenist Institute 203
National Museum 3, 4, 5, 264, 267 n.1(Intro)
naturally artificial 101
nature 182, 184, 222
Navajo Film Themselves 204
Neighbouring Sounds 41
Neo-Concrete Movement 143
neoliberalism 22, 37, 146, 249, 252
  and development problems of the Third World 26
  effects in Latin American society 22
neoliberal ruin 14, 22, 156, 159, 252
Neruda, Pablo 21
New Brazilian Objectivity exhibition 141
new imagery 75, 77, 88, 251, 265
New Latin American Cinema 44, 54, 59

News from a Private War 68, 85
New World 31, 245, 253, 256
New York Times 5
Nexo 5
Nichols, Bill 10, 53, 69, 71, 72, 73
Niemeyer, Oscar 13, 79, 80, 130
Night and Fog 73
non-diegetic sound 45
nonfiction production 85, 191, 248; *see also* fiction and nonfiction
  and Cinema Novo/New Latin American Cinema 53
  sobriety 69–70
  structure 70
non-professional actors 105, 112–13
Noronha, Linduarte 47, 55
North American Direct Cinema 53
North American experimental productions 100
Northern England 37
Norway 207–8
Norwegian Agency for Development Cooperation 207
nossa senzala graffiti 154–5
nostalgia strategies 19, 235, 251, 261
novum 124

O Cinema Falado 137, 262
O Estrangeiro 147
Off the Field 111
Oiticica, Hélio 2, 15, 133, 139–40, 141, 142, 143, 144, 147, 177, 184, 185, 188
Olalquiaga, Celeste 176, 252–3
Old-Time Veteran Countrymen 81–2
Oliveira, Mirtes Marins de 146
Olivetti company 82
Olympic Games (2016) 4, 14, 133, 149, 152, 158, 164, 256
  (de)construction 156
  displacement of families from Vila Autódromo for 150–1
Omar, Arthur 214
Once There Was Brasília 110
Ortega, Ariel 12, 15, 16, 210, 233–5, 236–7, 238–9, 250, 265, 280 n.7
Os Arara 214
Os Sertões 33
Otelo, Grande 194
Our Indians 214

Pacific 69
Padilha, José 68
Paes, Eduardo 149, 155, 156
Paisá 28
País Brasil, El 150
País Tropical 228
Pampasand Patagonia regions, extermination of Indians in 218
Panará, Komoi 207
Pape, Lygia 143
Parangolés 274 n.12
Parque das Ruínas 264
Parque Lage 275 n.1 (Ch 10)
Partido dos Trabalhadores 110
Passage 62
Passos, Pereira 149
Pedroso, Marcelo 69, 86
Peixoto, Nelson Brissac 36, 41
Peleg, Hila 71
Penetrable PN2 140
penetrables 140, 141, 142, 143, 144, 147
Pereio, Paulo César 260
Pereira, Cláudia 94
Pereira, Margareth 186
Pérez, Fernando 27, 28
performative documentaries 73
Perimetral 153–8, 176, 258
Perimetral Elevated Highway 25
peripheral cosmopolitanism 193
peripheral modernity 35–6, 200, 260
peripheral nations 23
personal filmmaking 69
Peruvian territories 230
Pethő, Ágnes 138, 140, 178
Petrobras 64
photography/photographs 264
  and documentary, intersection of 175
  photographic series 178
Pick, Zuzana M. 43–4
Pierrot Le Fou 118
Pindorama 198, 202
Pinheiro, Sophia Ferreira 280 n.3 (Ch 15)
Pi – Panorâmica Insana 264
Pirenópolis quarry 128, 262
Planas: Testimony about an Ethnocide 212
Playing 69
Pleasure of Ruins 267 n.2 (Ch 1)
Pocztaruk, Romy 263

politique des auteurs 45
Ponte, Antonio José 26, 27, 252
poor ruins 41
populace
  criminalized populace 68
  representation of 67–8
popular culture 50
Popular Culture Centre 43
Porto, Zuleica 94
Porto Maravilha Urban Operation 156, 157, 158–9, 160
Posluns, Michael 278 n.7
post-industrial cinema 13, 71, 86, 248
post-industrial ruins 182
post-war cinematic movements 39
poverty 96
Praça da Sé 30, 176
Prado Coelho, A. 5
Prado Júnior, Caio 32, 33
Prebisch, Raúl 23
Pretti, Luiz 14, 133, 158, 250, 258
Pretti, Ricardo 12, 14, 133, 158, 159, 160, 250, 257, 258, 265
Prîara Jõ – After the Egg, the War 207
prison environments 85
Prisoner of the Iron Bars, The 68, 85, 263
prison system, collapsing 262–3
production modes 87
progress and (under)development 1–2, 6, 12, 16, 19, 22–3, 29, 46, 48, 128, 137, 187, 189, 192, 246–7, 251, 253, 256, 257
  allegories/allegorical strategies 16, 41, 50, 51, 253
  alternatives to 37
  as an autonomous historical process 24
  Cinema Novo marks of 46
  and colonialism 23, 54
  contemporary documentaries 74, 149
  contradictions 147
  and destruction 37
  and neoliberalism 26
  pessimistic views of 29–37
  problems 25–6
  and ruination, imbrication between 33
  in a Third World nation 26, 89, 96
Projeto Pulex 89, 125
Prysthon, Ângela 13, 35, 41, 42, 85, 86, 88, 116, 193, 200

Quarentão nightclub 262
Queirós, Adirley 12, 13, 14, 74, 77, 78, 82, 83–4, 87, 88, 89, 90, 109, 118–19, 123, 128, 129–30, 168, 250, 254, 255, 256, 266, 271 n.2 (Ch 5)
Quijano, Aníbal 34, 37

Rabinowitz, Paula 9, 10
radical potential 2, 4, 20, 42, 251, 255, 261
Ramos, Fernão Pessoa 13, 48, 66, 67, 71, 248, 249, 269 n.14
Ramos, Graciliano 45–6
Rap: The Song of Ceilândia 110
Rascaroli, Laura 73
ready-made forgetfulness 263
realism 13, 53–4, 71, 77, 85–6
  under erasure 13, 85–6
  mode of production and address 87
  for portraying and scrutinizing national issues 85
realist cinema 86
reality 72, 128, 129, 251
Recife 263
Red Light Bandit, The 2, 8, 13, 40–1, 42, 51, 58, 78, 115–16, 117, 118, 119, 125, 130, 131, 168, 246, 255, 262
red-light district, urban culture of 117
reflective nostalgia 19, 251
reflexive anthropology 231
Reidy, Affonso 164
Reis, Luiz Thomaz 191–2
Renouvier, Charles 93
República Guarani 280 n.6
Resnais, Alan 73
restorative nostalgia 235, 251
Returning from Extinction 215
Revelando os Brasis 64
reverse strategy 240
rhizome philosophy 93, 105, 262
Rio, 40 Degrees 55, 56
Rio, João do 150
Rio de Janeiro 1, 3, 11, 14, 15, 16, 36, 43, 133, 149, 187–8, 254, 256
  as an ongoing (de)construction site 149
  Federal University of Rio de Janeiro 15
  Lévi-Strauss in 31
  neoliberal ruin 156
  port 158–61
  sloppiness and abandonment 152
  as a war scenario 153–6
River of Mud 263
roads 228
Robadey, Roberto 3
Roca, Augusto 204
Rocha, Glauber 2, 8, 13, 15, 16, 40, 43, 45, 46, 49–50, 52, 55, 57, 66, 77, 91, 95, 96, 97–8, 99, 100, 101, 105, 109, 133, 137, 141, 147, 148, 177, 188, 247, 252, 255, 265, 269 n.11
Rocha, Marília 62
Rodríguez, Marta 212
Rojas, Juliana 86
Rolnik, Suely 14, 100, 145, 146, 147, 149, 188
Rosa, Guimarães 137
Rossellini, Roberto 65
Rouanet Law 63, 270 n.2 (Ch 3)
Rouch, Jean 206, 231
Rousseff, Dilma 4, 66, 109, 138
Ruin 263
ruination 21, 182
  of human-made landscapes 182, 184
  within the national context 32
  of neoliberalism 22
  process in the Third World environment 42
  time of, and future 84
Ruin Cinema 39
ruin-gazers 254, 264, 266
ruin lust 21
Ruin Lust exhibition 2–3, 20
ruin returns 21
ruins 19
  cinema compared with 39
  cinematic ruins 37–42, 45, 187
  constructing ruins 256
  as dynamic and in process 136
  essence of 40
  imaginary of 156
  interpretation of 38–9
  of modernity 19–20
  and national environment 29–30
  nostalgic for 19
  positioned in a celebratory fashion 38
  and prosperity 33
  questioning progress and development 19, 253
  relationship with the present 20

restoration of 251
  in reverse 136, 176, 252, 259
  reworking of 22
  romantic ruin 136
  ruinscapes 254, 256, 262 (*see also* Brasília; indigenous territories; Rio de Janeiro)
  of the world 245
Ruins 11
Ruins of Brasília 130
Ruiz, Jorge 204
Russell, Catherine 10, 11
Ruttmann, Walter 71

Sacramento, Paulo 68
Sacris Pulso 94, 95, 101
Salaviza, João 277 n.13
Salazar, Juan 212
Salles, João Moreira 68, 69
Salles, Walter 21
Salles Gomes, Paulo Emílio 1, 46–7, 48–9, 59, 66, 247
Sangue de Tatu 89
Sanjinés, Iván 203, 212
Sanjinés, Jorge 212
Santiago 69
Santos, Daniel 12, 14, 133, 153, 154, 155–6, 157, 158, 163, 175, 230, 257, 258, 265
Santos, Marcelo 217, 220, 221–2, 227, 228, 228–9, 260
Santos, Nelson Pereira dos 43, 45, 55, 137, 199
São Miguel Arcanjo 234, 236, 260
São Paulo 36, 58, 274 n.14
São Paulo Art Biennial 62
São Paulo Biennial 146, 213
São Paulo Modern Art Week 141
Saraceni, Paulo César 55
Saraiva, Leandro 220, 221
Sartana 113, 255, 258–9
Saunders, Dave 70
savage mind 232
savage neoliberalism 257, 266
Schefer, Raquel 95, 99, 100
Schiwy, Freya 15, 65, 203, 209–10, 211, 212
Schönle, Andreas 6, 19–20, 40, 252, 254
Schumpeter, Joseph 156
Schwarz, Roberto 144
science fiction 40, 86, 89, 250
  and aesthetics of ruins 39
  borderlands science fiction 121, 255
  and documentaries 77, 89, 255
  and reality 87–90
  ruins 39–40
  as a suspension of belief in realism 88
  theme of underdevelopment and the Third World 89
  as visuality of postmodernity 88
science friction
  documentaries 102–8
  with reality 254
Scorpio Rising 163
screen memories 209, 239
Secco, Edson 186
Second World War 65, 86, 245
self-reflection 73, 206
self-reflexive strategies 69, 248
self-representation 65, 214
semi-documentary 55
Senna, Orlando 199, 201, 228, 232, 259, 278 n.13
sertão 43, 45, 52, 66
Sette, Leonardo 231
Sganzerla, Rogério 2, 8, 13, 16, 40, 58, 78, 115–17, 119, 168, 252, 255
shallow nostalgia 261
Shantytown of My Love 269 n.13
shared anthropology 231
Sharits, Paul 165
Shaw, Lisa 61, 68
Shohat, Ella 89, 193, 196
Shokito 14, 83–4, 112
Should I Kill Them? 214
Silk, Sônia 169
Silva, Ernesto 80
Silva, Jorge 212
Silva, Luiz Inácio Lula da 66, 109, 207
Silveira, Anita Rocha da 86
Sílvio Renoldi 168
Simmel, Georg 182, 184, 222
Simone, Julia de 14, 133, 158, 250, 258
Skoller, Jeffrey 88
Skvirsky, Salomé Aguilera 27–8
Smithson, Robert 136, 176, 252
Soares, Lota de Macedo 164
Soares, Raul 97
Sobchack, Vivian 13, 88
social activism 70

socio-economic issues 4, 6, 21, 22, 66, 136, 253
Solanas, Fernando 9, 54, 73
Solberg, Helena 171
Solomon, Stefan 14, 97, 138, 139, 140, 147, 168–9, 257
Sonntag, Heinz 37
South American Way 258
Spanudis, Theon 143
spatial debate, and arts 152
spatial representation 44, 81, 189, 197, 220, 222
spatial/social tension in film 81
split-screen strategy 179, 181
Stalker 182, 184
Stam, Robert 59, 89, 139, 191, 192, 193, 194, 196, 200
Star Power Ready 163
state of negligence 56
Stavenhagen, Rodolfo 23
Still Life 11
Strike Days 110
structuralism 26
Struggle Goes On, The 207
subjective documentaries 69, 73
Subterrania 184
Sugar Loaf 147
Suite Habana 27–8
Suppia, Alfredo 13, 89, 118, 121, 125, 272 n.3
Surrealism 96
Suvin, Darko 124

Tacca, Fernando de 191–2
taperas 195, 196, 218, 222, 224, 228, 228, 230, 262
Tarkovsky, Andrei 182, 184
Tate Britain exhibition 2–3, 4
Tava, The House of Stone 1, 16, 189, 210, 233–5, 236, 237, 241, 260
Tava São Miguel 190, 236–7, 241, 260–1
Tavolaro, Sérgio 36–7
Teatro Novo 264
technology, role in documentary-making 25, 63
Telling Ruins in Latin America 245–6
Temer, Michel 4, 66, 110, 265
Temps Décomposé, Le: Cinéma et Imaginaire de la Ruine 40

Third Cinema 46, 212, 268 n.3
Third World 40, 89–90, 137–8, 169, 246, 262
Third World ruins 8–9, 16, 42, 252, 253
Thirteen Days Away from the Sun 264
Thousand Plateaus, A 93
Tiaraju, Sepé 235
Toda Cor Abandonada É Violenta 163
Tonacci, Andrea 58, 119, 214, 215, 232
Topik, Steven 23
Torlasco, Domietta 165–6
Torres, Tiago Campos 205
T,O,U,C,H,I,N,G 165
tourists/visitors 21, 238–9
Traces: The Landscape Fills In 160
Trans-Amazonian Highway 25, 199, 263
Transfer of Audiovisual Media to Indigenous Communities 203
transparency of film 71
Trapero, Pablo 11
travel films 40
Tribute to Matta-Clark 185
Tristes Tropiques 173
Triste Trópico 214
Tropical Curse 1, 14–15, 73, 134, 152, 163–6, 187, 250, 258, 262
  Darks Miranda 167–8
  flying saucer 167, 168–9, 173, 262
  ghost 168–73, 258
  intermediality 167–73
Tropical Hangover 263
Tropicália 2, 9, 12, 14, 57–9, 63, 133, 136–40, 160–1, 165–6, 168, 176, 188, 193, 196, 243, 246, 247, 250, 253, 257–8, 265, 273 n.7
  as artistic practice and form of critical thinking 142
  and consumerism 142
  and Tropicalismo, distinction between 145
  turning into a commodity 144–5
Tropicália 141, 142, 143–4, 167
Tropicália, Penetrable PN2 "Purity Is a Myth" and PN3 "Imagetic" 141
Tropicália and Beyond: Dialogues in Brazilian Film History 97, 138, 169
Tropicalism 161
Tropicalismo 57–8, 145
tropicalist anthropophagy 145

tropicalistas 252, 257, 266
tropicalist intermediality 12, 16, 134, 163, 167–73
Tropical Truth: A Story of Music and Revolution in Brazil 135, 141–2, 167
Truffaut, François 45
Tserewahú, Divino 207
Tudo É Sempre Construção, e Também Ruínas 136
tugurización 26–7
Turner, Terence 209, 278 n.6
Two Villages, One Path 1, 16, 189, 210, 236, 237–41, 260
Two Way Street 62

Ubirajara 191
uchronia 93–4, 103, 105
Um Índio 243–4
underdeveloped cinema 249–50
underdevelopment *see* progress and (under)development
United Nations, Economic Commission for Latin America and the Caribbean (ECLAC) 23
United States, economic embargo 27
Unmonument 263
Unruh, Vicky 21, 22, 26, 245, 251–2
unviable nation 13, 18, 66–75, 85, 248
Urano, Pedro 12, 15, 134, 152, 178–9, 180–1, 182, 184, 185, 186–7, 250, 257, 259
urban environment 36
urbanization 32
urban planning 81–2, 151–2
utopia 180
utopian gesture, negation of 249

Valadão, Virgínia 205
Vale 208
Varda, Agnès 73
Vargas, Getúlio 25, 175–6, 179
Vasconcelos, Naná 99
Vaz, Ana 12, 13–14, 73, 77, 78, 83, 87, 88, 89, 90, 93, 95–6, 98–9, 100, 128, 129, 250, 254–5, 256, 265, 271 n.1 (Ch 6), 271 n.2 (Ch 5), 271 n.3 (Ch 6)
Vaz, Guilherme 94, 271 n.4 (Ch 6)
Veloso, Caetano 1, 2, 29–30, 36, 58, 133, 135, 137, 138, 139, 142, 147, 150, 164, 167, 188, 193, 243, 253, 257, 262, 272 n.1 (Ch 8), 273 n.4, 273 n.10, 274 n.13, 275 n.2 (Ch 10)
Vera Cruz 43, 137, 268 n.2
Verdesio, Gustavo 241
Vertov, Dziga 71
Viany, Alex 269 n.13
video artists 62
Vídeo nas Aldeias (VNA) 12, 15, 64, 65, 190, 201–2, 203, 204, 205, 231, 250, 260, 265
    as an integral process 211
    collaborative documentaries 15, 211, 212, 231–2, 233
    filmmaking workshops for indigenous peoples 208
    funding for the workshops 207
    high productivity 190
    indigenous territory 241, 243
    and National Institute of Historic and Artistic Heritage 236
    online platform 208
    political role in fighting for indigenous rights 190
    projects 189, 217
Vídeo nas Aldeias (VNA) productions
    and Cinema Novo 215
    as a cinema of co-authorship 15, 231, 233
Vieira, Rucker 48
Vila Autódromo, displacement of families from 150–1
Vilalba Nunes, Maria Augusta 245
Villa-Lobos 195
Villas Bôas brothers 278 n.13
Vinicius 270 n.3
visual arts 62–3, 137, 163
visualization 15, 177
Viveiros de Castro, Eduardo 5–6, 223, 227, 241, 279 n.3 (Ch 14)
Volney, Comte de 7
Volz, Jochen 278 n.9

war and period dramas 40
War of Canudos 33
War of the Worlds, The 117
Weissman, Franz 143
Welles, Orson 117, 171
Wells, H. G. 117

White Elephant 11
White Out, Black In 1, 13, 14, 25, 74, 77, 78, 83–4, 87, 90, 109, 111, 119, 130, 168, 248, 254, 255, 258
   aggression towards Brasília in 112
   as a contradictory film 130
   cyborgs 114, 115–20, 255
   design of characters' houses 113–14
   dystopia 125, 127
   laje point of view 113–14
   precarious sci-fi aesthetics of 116
   regime of historicity 123
   Sartana's drawings 124–8
   science nonfiction documentary 120–8
   as sci-fi documentary 129
   sonic-atomic bomb plot 113, 120, 124, 127, 128, 130, 255, 258–9
   spaceship-container 121, 122, 124, 132
   spatial-temporal vagueness 123–4
workshop model 205–7
World Cinema 86
World Trade Center, collapse of 20–1
Worth, Sol 204

Xavier, Ismail 1, 9, 12, 16, 41, 48, 50, 51, 52–3, 57, 58, 59, 72, 98, 100, 109, 117, 120, 138, 168, 192, 194, 195, 197, 198, 246, 247, 248, 253, 277 n.8
Xenakis, Iannis 154, 158

Yver, Anne-Charlotte 92, 258

Zhangke, Jia 11
Zignnatto, Andrey 136
ZUP buildings, demolition of 93
Zweig, Stefan 245, 248, 257

www.ingramcontent.com/pod-product-compliance
Lightning Source LLC
Chambersburg PA
CBHW052144300426
44115CB00011B/1516